DORA CARRING
ANNE CHISI

Dora Carrington was born in 1893 in Hereford.
At seventeen she enrolled at the Slade School of
Fine Art, part of an extraordinary generation of
painters including Mark Gertler and Paul and
John Nash. She painted her friends, her house,
her animals, her furniture and designed jackets
for books published by Virginia and Leonard
Woolf's Hogarth Press. She was the long-time
companion of writer Lytton Strachey, though
in 1921 she married Ralph Partridge, who
joined her and Lytton in a largely harmonious
ménage à trois. In 1932, after the death of
Strachey from cancer, she committed suicide,
aged thirty-eight.

Anne Chisholm is a biographer and critic who
has also worked in journalism and publishing.
She has written biographies of Nancy Cunard,
which won the Silver PEN Prize for non-fiction,
Lord Beaverbrook (with Michael Davie) which
was runner-up for the Hawthornden Prize, and,
most recently, of the diarist and Bloomsbury
insider Frances Partridge, which was shortlisted
for the Marsh Biography Award. She is a former
chair and now vice president of the Royal Society
of Literature.

DORA CARRINGTON

Carrington's Letters

EDITED BY
Anne Chisholm

VINTAGE

2 4 6 8 10 9 7 5 3 1

Vintage
20 Vauxhall Bridge Road,
London SW1V 2SA

Vintage Classics is part of the Penguin Random House
group of companies whose addresses can be found at
global.penguinrandomhouse.com.

First published in Great Britain in 2017 by Chatto & Windus
First published by Vintage in 2019

www.vintage-books.co.uk

A CIP catalogue record for this book is available from the British Library

ISBN 9781845951887

Printed and bound in Great Britain by Clays Ltd, Elcograf S.p.A.

Penguin Random House is committed to a sustainable future
for our business, our readers and our planet. This book is
made from Forest Stewardship Council® certified paper.

For Alison, Paloma and Tabitha

CONTENTS

ILLUSTRATIONS

Letters and drawings

See Note on Sources for information about archives, collections and libraries.

Plate sections

Unless otherwise mentioned, all paintings and drawings are by Carrington.

Section 1:
1: Self-portrait, aged seventeen, 1910 (© National Portrait Gallery, London)
2: Drawings of her two brothers, Noel and Teddy Carrington, c. 1915 and 1912 (© Cecil Higgins collection; courtesy of Bloomsbury Workshop)
3: Christine Kuhlenthal, 1919 (© National Portrait Gallery, London); the Cropheads: Carrington, Barbara Hiles (later Bagenal) and Dorothy Brett; Slade School picnic, 1912. Front row from the left: Carrington, Barbara Hiles, Richard Nevinson and Mark Gertler (both © Tate Images)
4: *Carrington* by Mark Gertler, c. 1912 (© Bridgeman Images); *Mark Gertler*, 1912 (© National Portrait Gallery, London)

Section 2:
1: *Tidmarsh Mill*, 1918 (© Private Collection); at Garsington, 1920: Michael Llewellyn Davies, Ottoline Morrell's daughter Julian, Carrington and Ralph Partridge (© National Portrait Gallery, London)
2: *Lytton Strachey reading*, 1916 (© Bridgeman Images)
3: Ralph Partridge in 1919 and 1920 (both © Private Collections); Ralph, 1920 (© National Portrait Gallery, London)
4: Carrington and Gerald Brenan, August 1921 (© Tate Images); *Portrait of Gerald Brenan*, 1921 (© National Gallery, London)

Section 3:
1: *Portrait of Annie Stiles*, Carrington's cook-housekeeper at Tidmarsh, 1921 (courtesy of Bloomsbury Workshop)
2: Painted tiles, mid-1920s (courtesy of Bloomsbury Workshop); painted cabinet, also mid-1920s (© Portsmouth City Museum and Art Gallery)
3: *Tulips in a Staffordshire jug*, 1924 (© Bridgeman Images); *Cactus*, c. 1924; *Larrau in the Snow*, 1922 (both courtesy of Bloomsbury Workshop)
4: *Mrs Box*, the farmer's wife and Carrington's landlady at Welcombe, near Bude in Devon, c.1919 (© Bridgeman Images)

Section 4:

1: Henrietta Bingham, 1924 (© Chatsworth); Henrietta with Stephen Tomlin, at Ham Spray, 1924 (© Private Collection)

2: *Portrait of Julia Strachey*, 1928 (© Tate Images); *c.* 1928 (courtesy of Bloomsbury Workshop)

3: *Portrait of Stephen Tomlin* by John Banting, 1925 (© Private Collection); Bernard (Beakus) Penrose, at Ham Spray, 1929 (© Getty Images)

4: The trompe l'oeil window at Biddesden, painted for Bryan and Diana Guinness, 1931 (© Private Collection)

ACKNOWLEDGEMENTS

This edition of Carrington's letters was suggested to me by the literary executor of her estate, my former agent and friend Gill Coleridge. My thanks are firstly due to her. Michael Holroyd was the godfather of the project and, as always, has been generous with encouragement and advice.

For much help with research and for many enjoyable and enlightening conversations, I thank in particular Susan Fox, whose knowledge and expertise has been invaluable. I am also very grateful to Roger Louis of the British Studies Center at the University of Texas, whose invitation to speak there enabled me to undertake essential work in the Ransom Center's collections, with the assistance of its helpful staff. Patricia McGuire, the Archivist at King's College, Cambridge, was invariably responsive and efficient. For help with organising, filing and transcribing material that seemed at times overwhelming I thank: Gillian Adam, Henrietta Freeman-Atwood, Eleanor Jenyns, Jessica Maybury, Molly Rosenberg and Eilis Smyth.

For exemplary patience and confidence in the project I must thank Zoe Waldie, who succeeded Gill Coleridge as my agent, and Juliet Brooke, my editor, whose perceptive suggestions have clarified and enhanced the text at every stage. I am also grateful to Madeleine Hartley for her work on the illustrations, Matt Broughton for the cover and Vicki Robinson for the index.

The following people gave me information, hospitality and help in many different ways, and I am grateful to them all: Ariane Bankes, Emily Bingham, Xandra Bingley, Ann Blaber, Tony Bradshaw, Carlyn and Colin Chisholm, Susannah Clapp, Mary Clemmey, Virginia Duigan, Maggie and Jamie Fergusson, Henrietta Garnett, Gretchen Gerzina, Adelheid and Grey Gowrie, Rosaleen Guinness, Selina Hastings, the late Antony Hobson, Rebecca John, Trudy McGuinness, Fay Maschler, Christopher Ondaatje, Wendy Perry, Jans Ondaatje Rolls, Karl Sabbagh, Sally Sampson, Caroline Sandwich and Polly Toynbee.

Finally I want to thank Caroline Moorehead, who helped me cut and shape this text.

The book is dedicated to three women in my family who could not be more different from Carrington but who all share her originality and capacity for love: Alison, Paloma and Tabitha Stoecker.

EDITOR'S NOTE

Any posthumous portrait of an individual, whether by an editor or a biographer, depends on the material available, which can never be complete. Around two thousand of the letters written by Dora Carrington between 1911 and 1932 have survived; many more have not, including all those to her family apart from her brother Noel, to her husband Ralph Partridge, to two significant lovers, Henrietta Bingham and Bernard (Beakus) Penrose, and all but a handful to her close and life-long female friends, Barbara Bagenal and Alix Strachey. The three most complete surviving letter series are the 155 or so written to Mark Gertler, over 500 written to Lytton Strachey and 434 to Gerald Brenan, which therefore form the core of any selection.

Although there is inevitably considerable overlap between my choices and David Garnett's published in 1970, I made my initial choices without reference to his and have included as much as possible that is different and new. Letters unavailable to or unused by him include a number to John Nash, Christine Kuhlenthal, Noel Carrington, Peter Lucas, Poppet John and Roger Senhouse.

My aim has been to provide a clear, lively and readable account of Carrington's doings and feelings in her own words, to unclutter the text and to allow her to tell her own story without too much editorial interjection but with context and guidance.

I decided from the outset that her idiosyncratic spelling and punctuation would distract and annoy the reader, so I have corrected her constant errors (which suggest mild dyslexia: 'minute' was always 'minuet', for example), inserted missing words and cleaned up her peculiar punctuation. She was in the habit of using frequent ampersands and sprinkling her pages with ellipses almost at random; I have removed most of these.

It was impossible to reproduce all the charming drawings she included in letters, and to alert the reader to a missing drawing seemed pointless. She often made visual puns out of names – so Waley was often a fish, and Henry Lamb usually a sheep and the Partridges small round birds; she added draw-ings to letters when she wanted to amuse, as when writing to Lytton Strachey,

though not when she was deep in a tricky emotional relationship, as with
Mark Gertler or Gerald Brenan.

All cuts in letters are marked with ellipses between square brackets. When
an address or a date is missing, and they often are, I have tried to make an
educated guess of my own or followed David Garnett's edition.

INTRODUCTION

It is eighty-five years since the death by suicide of Dora Carrington, artist and companion of Lytton Strachey. She was thirty-eight, and left behind her a small number of unfashionable paintings and a sad story of a great but unfulfilled love. Luckily, she also left behind her a great number of letters, which captivated, amused and moved the recipients at the time and which, re-read today, bring her out of the shadows and show her as she really was: one of the most original and emotionally courageous women of her time in her pursuit of love, art and the art of living.

My own discovery of Carrington's story began some ten years ago when I was writing the biography of Frances Partridge, who took up with Carrington's husband, Ralph. Carrington was the lynchpin of one of Bloomsbury's two celebrated ménages à trois: at Charleston in Sussex Vanessa Bell lived with her husband Clive but loved Duncan Grant, while at Ham Spray in Berkshire Carrington lived with Ralph but loved Lytton Strachey. Both husbands were heterosexual; the two other men were both almost exclusively gay. As I investigated the emotional ramifications of the Ham Spray situation, although my focus was on Frances, I kept finding my attention being drawn to Carrington, not least when I read her letters, which were irresistibly open, fresh and moving. I came to realise that she was not, as has been the narrative for so long, one of the minor characters of Bloomsbury, but one of the most interesting and surprising.

Bloomsbury remains interesting to us today not just because we admire the work of its artists and writers, but because of the way they lived their lives. They disregarded social rules, acknowledging and accepting homosexuality and bisexuality and regarding sexual freedom and friendship as just as important for human happiness as marriage and parenthood. Carrington, who grew up uncomfortable with being female, who was attractive to men but increasingly attracted by women, who never wanted children and who deeply loved a homosexual man, was at the heart of these experiments in living pioneered by Bloomsbury. Virginia Woolf acknowledged this when she wrote in 1925 that 'Lytton's way of life, in so far as it is unconventional, is so by the desire and determination of Carrington.'

Although this unconventionality came naturally to Carrington, it would be a mistake to think it was easy for her. As her letters constantly show, she found her own nature difficult to understand and accept; her efforts to do so are strikingly relevant today, when gender boundaries are being explored and questioned. And the perennial struggle facing female artists – of how to balance their creative and their personal lives – remains as hard to solve now as it was then, as Carrington reveals in her letters.

As companion to a more famous man, Carrington, like many women before and since, lived in his shadow. Unmarried and from a modest middle-class background, her position in the social and sexual hierarchy after she openly began to share Lytton Strachey's life in 1917 was always ambiguous – both central and insecure. She herself compounded this impression by building her life around his needs and wants, always putting him first. Doing so perhaps answered a fundamental need of her own. Even before she met him she wrote to a female friend: 'It must be contentment to so arrange your life that only one person matters.'

The effects of this partly self-imposed secondary status have become her legacy. From time to time Carrington has been reconsidered: in the late 1960s Michael Holroyd's biography of Lytton Strachey brought her to the fore, and led to the publication in 1970 of the first selection of Carrington's letters by David Garnett, himself a part of Bloomsbury and an early admirer of hers. The letters were praised for their vitality and charm, but Garnett's presentation emphasised her position as what he called 'an appendage' to Bloomsbury in general and Lytton Strachey in particular. He was mildly patronising about her art, her intellectual limitations and her social standing. According to him, the society hostesses who invited the great writer to their soirees and weekends would no more have included Carrington 'than his housekeeper or his cook'.

Although she never stopped working at her painting, she became, after her promising start at the Slade, increasingly reluctant to submit her work for exhibition and sold very few paintings in her lifetime. Her artistic reputation suffered; she did not have a solo show until a small exhibition was mounted in 1970 to coincide with Garnett's edition of her letters. Then in 1989 the American academic Gretchen Gerzina turned her doctoral thesis on Carrington as a painter, into a well-researched full biography. The book discussed her as a serious artist for the first time, someone whose work deserved as much consideration as her personal life. But because her art was not in tune stylistically with the better-known Bloomsbury painters Roger Fry, Duncan Grant and Vanessa Bell, who were heavily influenced by the French post-Impressionists, notably Cézanne and Matisse, she continued to be underrated by scholars and curators. Even though she was described by Sir John Rothenstein, Director of the Tate Gallery from 1938 to 1964, as 'the most neglected serious painter of her time' she was only represented by one small painting, a portrait of E. M. Forster, in Tate Britain's major exhibition The Art of Bloomsbury in 2000. The curator of that exhibition, Richard Shone, considered her 'aesthetic temperament was fundamentally different' from Fry, Grant and Bell and that her work was closer in style to that of her Slade contemporaries the Nash brothers, Mark Gertler and Stanley Spencer. He also wrote that he would gladly exchange all Carrington's paintings for just one of her letters.

The only comprehensive exhibition of her work, at the Barbican in London in 1995, coincided with the release of the feature film *Carrington*, based on Michael Holroyd's biography of Strachey and written and directed by Christopher Hampton. This show included most of her major paintings as well as examples of her work as a decorative artist such as bookplates, book covers and tiles, it also showed some short home movies filmed at Ham Spray evoking her surroundings and way of life, swimming in the river and riding her pony on the lawn. The year before Jane Hill had published the one substantial illustrated monograph on her work. All this raised her profile, and drew attention to her, but the film, though intelligent and moving, was in some ways misleading, even diminishing. The story it told was of Carrington's devoted and ultimately tragic love for Lytton, and was structured entirely around her unsuccessful sexual relationships with three other men. Her success in running the household at Ham Spray, her many platonic but intense friendships with both sexes and her passionate physical love for one woman in particular were simply ignored. The film has helped to consolidate an oversimplified and inaccurate image which a fresh look at her letters will help to correct.

In the many photographs that Bloomsbury took of itself (the camera was one of its favourite toys) Carrington usually appears uncomfortable with being the focus of attention. Often, she drops her head or turns away from the camera. Nevertheless, for those around her she was always a vital, attractive presence, with a style and demeanour all her own. She would appear shy and diffident, with her light, breathless voice and pigeon-toed posture like a little girl's, her thick blonde bob shielding her face and hanging over her keen blue eyes; but she was never insignificant. She struck several writers powerfully enough to find her way into their novels. She can be recognised, not always flatteringly, in books by Aldous Huxley, Gilbert Cannan, Wyndham Lewis and D. H. Lawrence, and the encounters prompting these fictional representations are to be found in her letters. For all her apparent diffidence, Carrington attracted and kept attention. Her friend Julia

Strachey, Lytton's niece, wrote of her as 'so glowing with sympathetic magnetism and droll ideas for them all that there wasn't a person of her vast acquaintance who did not get the impression that she was their very best friend. There wasn't a lover, or a servant or a cat that did not preen him or herself on being the most favoured of the lot.'

Naturally secretive, hating to feel she was under scrutiny or anyone's control, she needed to create private, intimate connections with those she cared about and, in the days when letters could arrive several times a day or even within the very same day, her correspondence enabled her to maintain these friendships. Bloomsbury valued emotional and intellectual intimacy highly and relished gossip and jokes; letter-writing was a crucial component of an intricate web of constant communication. 'The humane art, which owes its origin to the love of friends', was how Virginia Woolf, a great and brilliant correspondent herself, described it.

Carrington found that letter writing came naturally to her, unlike painting, which was always a hard struggle. Indeed, much of her creative energy went into her letters, which were frequently small works of art in themselves, with her delicate curly writing decorating the pages and sprinkled with many drawings, some tiny, some taking up much of a page. She drew portraits and caricatures of herself and Lytton and other friends and lovers, interiors of rooms and views of wild landscapes, and above all the flowers and birds she loved, as well as many cats, sometimes curled on the lap of a naked girl, and once or twice a small phallus in the margin to amuse Lytton. The fact that her spelling and punctuation were wildly inaccurate, with dots for commas, ampersands and random squiggles, only added to the effect. Virginia Woolf described them as 'tearing like a mayfly up and down the pages' and 'completely like anything else in the habitable globe'. For Michael Holroyd, the great appeal of Carrington's letters lies in their timeless emotional power: 'Love, loneliness, beauty, elation and harrowing despair – these are what she wrote about with such freshness and immediacy that, fifty years later, the ink seems only just to have dried.'

In making this new selection of Carrington's letters, my aim has been to provide a fresh portrait of her in her own words and to show her as I believe she was: a woman at the centre, not on the margins, of her world. A gifted and serious artist, she was above all as someone who quietly, with some difficulty but also much delight, built a life for herself, her lovers and her friends, outside the conventions of the time.

PART ONE

Growing Up: 1893–1915

No letters from Dora de Houghton Carrington's childhood have come to light; the earliest to have survived were written when she was in her late teens. She always looked back on her childhood with distaste, describing it as 'awful', although her brother Noel, the only sibling to whom she remained at all close, called it 'uneventful and certainly not unhappy'.

She put some of her memories and feelings about her childhood into a letter written to a lover in 1924 when she was thirty-one. She began by explaining that her mother's family were socially inferior: 'Her father was a sanitary inspector or something like that [...] my mother's mother said "ain't" which I remember shocked me as a child [...]' Her maternal uncles 'frankly weren't gentlemen'. This sense of a class division in her own family lingered, and helped to alienate her from her socially anxious mother. She was born on 29 March 1893 in a house called Ivy Lodge in Hereford, the fourth of five children, with two older brothers, Sam and Teddy, an older sister, Charlotte, and a younger brother, Noel. Her father, Samuel, was sixty-one when she was born. He had retired from a long career with the East Indian Railways and married Charlotte Houghton, a family governess twenty years his junior, in 1888. Dora grew up adoring her large, powerful-looking father, whose travels and adventures in India she found thrilling and romantic, and at odds with her mother, whose religiosity and obsession with respectability she came to despise.

One of her earliest memories was of locking Noel out of the house and telling her parents he was lost. 'I remember my intense pleasure at thinking I alone knew he was running round the outside of the garden trying to get in.'

Like most children, she went through a stage of being fascinated by her and her brother's excretions, but her memories of watching them performed seem especially detailed and vivid. She was punished after cutting a hole in her dress 'just there': 'I was then beaten on my naked bottom by a nurse with pale yellow frizzy hair rather like Queen Alexandra. I turned my head round as I lay on her knee and saw my bottom. I was mortified to see it. I thought very large, and pink.' She wet her knickers a lot, and remembered having diarrhoea but being too embarrassed to ask to leave the room, 'so I was constantly being punished, and was disliked by the nurses.'

She also recalled, before she was six, 'having a character implanted on me. I was made to feel "good". I had mixed feelings. I liked being praised. But I also disliked being made to be "good" when secretly I wished to do other things'. She was also not happy with her appearance. 'I was called Dumpty because I was very fat and always falling down.'

The adult Carrington remembered herself as having been a child well aware of the social hierarchy, easily embarrassed by her body, who liked having secrets. All these traits, as she no doubt realised, were with her for life. Any pressure on her to behave in a certain way led to trouble, and often to lies and deceit.

Dora Carrington arrived at the Slade in the autumn of 1910 when it was in its heyday. Founded in 1871, and housed in dignified grey neoclassical buildings alongside University College in Gower Street, it combined a reputation for artistic excellence (former students included Walter Sickert and Augustus John) with social acceptability, particularly for the daughters of upper- and middle-class families where drawing and painting were traditional female accomplishments. There were three women students to each man; the emphasis was on draughtsmanship and the classical tradition, but at the same time it was considered less formal and stuffy than the Royal Academy.

It wasn't long before she had made new friends, cut off her long golden hair and dropped the first name she had always disliked. Both were gestures of rebellion for art students of her generation, and from 1911 on she was always just Carrington. Her social horizons broadened: at the hostel off Gordon Square where she first lived, she met two other new Slade girls who became close and lasting friends, pretty dark-haired Barbara Hiles, the daughter of a businessman living in Paris, and the plain, slightly deaf and eccentric Dorothy Brett, daughter of the royal family's trusted courtier Viscount Esher. They too chopped their hair off and dropped their first names, and were soon nicknamed the Cropheads. Carrington was not conventionally pretty, despite her thick blonde bob, cherry-blossom complexion and intensely blue eyes; but having grown up with three brothers she was not shy of young men, and was soon being pursued by several fellow students. She enjoyed their company, their admiration and especially their shared excitement about art, but was not interested in romance; she seems to have had an innate fear of sex, exacerbated by her upbringing. She and Noel both recalled how any acknowledgement of physical relations between the sexes was anathema to their mother, and Carrington grew up detesting the monthly reminder that she was female. She later admitted that she had always found the prospect of sex and childbirth disgusting and terrifying.

At the Slade, she soon fell into a pattern of behaviour: men were drawn to her, she responded eagerly to their admiration and friendship, but as soon as they wanted more, she pulled away. Tensions and complications inevitably ensued.

Three of her most talented male contemporaries fell in love with her: John Nash, Richard Nevinson and Mark Gertler. Paul Nash, the elder of the two Nash brothers, arrived at the same time as she did, in 1910, and spotted her at work in the Antique Room, drawing from casts of classical sculpture. She seemed to him 'clever and good-looking to an unusual degree'. Nevinson and Gertler were already there, having arrived in 1909 and 1908 respectively, and were good friends; now Nash introduced her to his brother John, who was seriously smitten by her. Her disregard for convention and passion for art, as well as her slightly androgynous appearance and dress (she and Brett, when they could get away with it, liked to wear men's corduroy breeches), drew these young men to her; when she proved shy and elusive they pursued her even more. Nevinson called her 'a gorgeously egotistical, impulsive, unsettled youth'. It was at the Slade that Carrington's lifelong tendency to fall into love triangles, playing rivals off against each other, first began. Both the Nash brothers were able to find their way out of love and back to friendship based on shared artistic interests, and both, before long, had married other girls; but it was very different with Nevinson and Gertler.

None of her letters to Nevinson have survived, nor any to Gertler at this point; but her friendship with the Nash brothers, and her life during and just after the Slade can be glimpsed through the letters she wrote to John Nash between 1912 and 1915.

1912

To John Nash

1 Rothesay Gardens, Bedford
Saturday [n.d.]

Dear Jack,

You are going to to Florence! And you announce it calmly in a word. And again you tell with a coolness only found in *Strand* magazines, that M– has bought your Gypsies! Try & have a little enthusiasm about it. I know after selling so many pictures it must be hard. But surely one doesn't go to Florence every afternoon. Is Paul going too? And can you speak Italian?

[...] I did a painting of my youngest brother, side view, which met with some approval in the family circle. But a great discussion still continues as to whether his nose is too long or his upper lip too short.

In a rash moment I was taken to a dance in my tiny native town the other night, by my brother. It was sad. For the village lads had quite forgotten me, & taken unto themselves new lasses. They gaze askance at my shorn locks – little did they realize who it was who was in their midst. No, sad it is to relate but I was <u>not</u> appreciated [...]

Paul sent me a good book by Borrow.[1] Which delighted me very much. I am just going to write to him so your letter must be curtailed somewhat. Today I return to London, which has made me very happy! I have done no work these hols of any worth, as the family do not encourage my efforts, & won't let me use the study to paint in. I have a loud dress with a ballet frill round it, orange on purple, a little daring perhaps. But bright & cheerful. Paul, I hear, has run amuck in a near check suit. I hear of it with grief.

Well, I hope I shall see you soon. But I've got a great deal of work to do when I get back the first two weeks – But you must write & say when you will come & see us. I am in much haste.

Carrington

The next letter was written from Brett's father's estate, the Roman Camp at Callendar in Perthshire, Scotland. Two other Slade friends, Ruth Humphries (later Selby-Bigge) and Constance (Cooie) Lane, were also there.

1 George Borrow, 1803–81, traveller and writer on Gypsies (*Lavengro*, 1851, and *The Romany Rye*, 1857).

To John Nash

The Roman Camp
2 August 1913

Dear Jack,

I am sorry to have been so long answering your letters.

On Monday night I travelled up here. What a journey! Everything cold & noisy, & do you know of the hardness of a carriage seat, and the fear of a cockchafer on the ceiling, & trains that run in the night & shriek to each other in passing. A slothful clergyman & his sister disturbed my frenzied slumbers at Crewe & cuddled up in blankets & cushions spent a voluptuous night [...] worn out I arrived at Callander at 6.30 on Tuesday morning. Gosh! But ... the excitement of these big hills and forests and lochs. Humphries is here too. The house is pink outside with slate pointed towers, & the garden has many flowers of purple red & purple blue. More flowers, & more beautiful than if you thought hard you could imagine. We go out every day drawing on these big mountains, and one day Humphries & me swam in a big loch. The sun shining hot & all round towering mountains, & the water very deep and clear, and nobody else to be seen. The whole world was ours. Everyday is hot here. It is never even cool. From the top of the mountain one can get a most gorgeous view, of big lakes & these mountains sliding down to them, & a little river wending through coloured fields, pale green with new wheat & yellow with hay, and more distant mountains. But how hard to draw.

And when we return at 8 we have astounding dinners. Are you above grub? I hate ascetic people who pretend not to be interested. The strawberry & fruit ices are beyond all comparisons. Venison & 'pasties of the doe'. Brett's father is a nut, in his highland kilts and aristocratic demeanour [...] We ran barefooted with big leaps across the fields through sleeping cows, till we climbed the slope to a cornfield. The moon was new, & shimmering, & the elms big clumps against the emerald purple grey sky, all the fields were dark green grey. Do you ever go out when everything is over at night? The corn field was greeny purple, & poppies making dark black red stains, and you grabbed at them, for they seemed only stains on the waving mane of wheat, and Lane's nightdress shone a wonderful colour in the midst of the field, and behind a big dark wood [...]

The strain of the perfect lady is rather much, as it is now almost a month since I was natural. But all day we can break out & shout and run on the hills [...]

On Tuesday I am going away, right down to Hove, Sussex, with my family. Noel, the little brother, will be with me, and Pendennis his friend, who has a good head to draw. But it will seem smooth and slippery after this land. But a sea to swim in, so I shall be happy.

I am yours sincerely,
Carrington

1913

During the summer of 1913 Carrington and Cooie Lane worked on a cycle of frescoes commissioned by Lord Brownlow for his library at his nineteenth-century Gothic house, Ashridge, in the Chilterns. They stayed nearby in the Lanes' cottage at Nettleden.

To John Nash

Tuesday [n.d.]

[...] Your pictures were good [...] One day I shall ask politely a big landscape of fields & trees & figures from you to put up on my walls, and try & coerce Paul too. Alas! I am neither rich nor famous! would that I were dead for my design is indeed lamentable, and it fills me chock up with despair [...]

At present we have not done much as all the time we have been working hard at our cartoons, drawing & painting them. Cooie Lane's is best. She is doing sheep shearing. She sings whilst we work, lustily with much force old ballades & folk songs & Handel. The plastering is a joy to do [...] But you have no idea how frescoeing wearies the brain.

 I am yours,
 Carrington

1914

To John Nash

Clearwell, Portland Avenue, Exmouth
4 April 1914, 11:00 in bed

Dear Jack,

[...] And now, good morning! I arrived here at 11 o clock on Monday night. On Tuesday I expored with Teddy & Noel who are splendid brothers. Teddy is at Cambridge, & Noel at Oxford. The country here surpasses all belief. The cliffs are huge, & towering & Indian Red in colour, & long reaches of smooth sand, & a cobalt sky, & a blazing hot sun. Which makes one's face shine like a bronze from the shore looking over the cliffs you see the landscape trees & ploughed fields all wooded like a Francesca[1] landscape. Flowers grow here in abundance, and the garden is full of violets, white & purple & polyanthus, & primroses, daffs in great quantities & many others. On the cliffs yellow gorse & celandines grow. Going to the New Forest, until I return to London. Aren't you glad I am coming back. It has made me enormously happy [...] What pictures are you working at now? I did so like your Adoration. I think it will be very good. What work is friend Paul doing? I hope you are well. I saw the boat race last Saturday, it was rather amusing.

Although the surviving correspondence of Carrington and her Slade painter friends that summer gives no hint of approaching disaster, their lives, like millions of others, would be changed for ever by the outbreak of war in Europe on 4 August 1914. Carrington was preoccupied by a scheme, never realised, to collaborate with John and Paul Nash on the decoration of a church near Uxbridge with a fresco of Jacob's meeting with Rebecca. She was, and remained, diffident about her work. Meanwhile John was trying to take their relationship further, but she was determined just to stay friends.

Before long, Carrington's three brothers, Sam, Teddy and Noel, had joined up. Noel was wounded within a few weeks and brought home to recover. Mark Gertler, who had a weak chest, was eventually exempted as unfit; but Paul and John Nash and Richard Nevinson were all to serve at the front as war artists. The work they produced remains among the most powerful depictions we have of the horror and

---

1 Piero della Francesca (c.1415–92), one of Carrington's favourite painters.

J

going to the New forest, until I return to
London. arn't you glad I am coming back.
It has made me enormusly happy.
Will you write to me about the church
- & decide a subject soon, so I can start
thinking about it.
Have you read R.L. Stevensons "wing box", it is good.
what pictures are you working at now?
I did so like your adoration. I think it
will be very good.
What work is friend Paul doing?
I hope you are well. I saw the boat Race
last Saturday it was rather amusing

university
man   me   rom   Humphs   bad
                                                 storage   crys
                                                                Lees
                                                                & Lees   others

from the top of a
roof at Hammersmith

devastation of the First World War. Carrington's letters contain very little about the war, which she appears at first to have supported, and nothing, apart from one brief impersonal reference, about her friends' paintings from the front. She turned away from it as best she could, into her painting and her personal life.

To John Nash

Clearwell, Portland Avenue, Exmouth
Friday [summer 1914]

My Dear Jack,

Thank you for your long letter ... & the rebuffs or reproof dealt out to the slothful, & ungodly. I am sorry I didn't measure it right. But I only have an inferior old school ruler, so perhaps that is why. Nothing could upset my design! I will add to it breadth as you suggest. Thanks you also for your advice. I know Jacob was badly drawn, but I only had my brother for about 3 mins, to look at, & his face I was aware, was a failure [...]

But no matter. I will also give him more suitable rayment & obviously bathing drawers. I am returning to London next Monday & will get a model & draw them better, as I simply find it impossible to draw anything with any regard to the truth, from memory. So if I let you have a fair copy by say, next Monday week, will that do? and a touch of colour about it [...]

Thank you. I am quite happy – I only get sad intervals over the war, as I am sorry to admit it but I forget it often. Yesterday morning at 6.30 I went for a fine swim in the sea by myself as my youngest brother has gone back to London, to enlist. Tell Paul I am sorry he did not get through his medical, & give him & Barbara [Hiles] my love [...] I cannot say with positiveness that I can frescoe in October, as so much depends on the war primarily, & other things. I've got to earn my living if I live in London, so if that fails I shall have to return home, and my people are leaving here to go to Hampshire in the middle of October. But to the best of my knowledge I could frescoe then.

But I hope you are well, & able to do some work. I have done practically nothing this summer. For most of the day I seem to spend picking apples & storing them, & picking beans, & making large pots full of blackberry jam. The blackberries here are the best in any land, the like of which have not been seen before. I want to see your work badly. So I hope you have done some. But who will buy? [...] I expect I shall see you after you return from Cheltenham in London, then we could, with more satisfaction than is gained by writing, discuss the frescoe project. I tried to draw a field of Indian corn yesterday. For I have never seen such a wonderful sight before. But it was almost impossible to draw. Have you ever seen a field of it? Today it is raining hard. Did Paul do some very good work in the north? This is a stupid letter, I am sorry. But somehow it is difficult to write just now. My eldest brother was wounded only not badly I think. I hope he will get well enough to fight again soon.

Thank you for being so kind about my bad design. When I get more settled in my brain I will do something better, at least I trust so.

Now I will stop & remain

Carrington

Even at night I see apples in my dreams & all day long I pick & eat them & realize the many resources of an apple, ie apple charlotte, apple stewed, A baked, A boiled, A turnover, A pudding, A fritters, A with cream & without, & in the streets they sell A's for 2 lbs a penny! What shall she do with them?

To John Nash

c/o Mrs H. Game, 3 Primrose Hill Studios,
Fitzroy Road, London NW
[n.d.]

Dear Jack,

Now I have two letters to answer, & much to discuss & talk over. I hesitate to write, as there is so much to say ...

Letter the first

The winter is bad, so my book tells me, to frescoe in owing to the fact that the wet & cold affect the plaster. But the fault to whom does it lie? Nobody but my erring self, so I can't complain. But you asked me, so I tell you to the best of my knowledge, a hot summer or spring is the most favourable season wherein to paint in the frescoe.

I saw Sam, my brother, when he was in the hospital & listened to the gory & sanguinary accounts of the battles. It sounds so like Goya, who is a fine man withal at depicting battles & bullfights. Yes, I agree with you Cheltenham is of all English towns the most stagnant & over grown with seedy colonels & their wives – would that the Germans would erase it, & a few other of our cities, entirely to the ground, & lessen its inhabitants in their numbers.

I have been in London a little while now & am working hard on a beastly scholarship job, as we are poorer than ever now through this old war.

Letter the second

Yes farmyard scenes are the best, & the country. I know that definitely now & dislike this city London, with its ugly faces & hard pavements. I am neither well nor happy here, as I have a bad cold, & miss the summer, & my work is no good! I hope you have done some.

You must come to tea with Bunty[1] when I go, & take your drawings to show me. Durer at the British Museum is sustaining, & keeps one from getting too depressed amongst these people who talk so constantly of the war. Well I shall be glad to see you again also. But do not be too angry if I fail over my design. Now I remain in haste,

Carrington

By early 1915 Carrington had left the Slade and was living with her parents in a handsome old house in Hurstbourne Tarrant, a village near Andover in Hampshire, where she turned an outhouse into a studio and went for long walks exploring the nearby downs. Her pleasure in and need for country life grew stronger, and she began to dream of a place of her own with a congenial companion.

John Nash had recently taken up with Christine Kuhlenthal,[2] another Slade friend and his future wife. This appears to have intensified Carrington's feelings, not for him but for her. Her female friends were increasingly important to her, and she never liked to lose friends, male or female, to marriage, which she regarded with increasing distaste.

1 Margaret Odeh (1887–1960), known as Bunty, was part Arab, born in Jerusalem, had an Oxford history degree and was a keen suffragist. She married Paul Nash in 1914.
2 Christine Kuhlenthal (1895–1976) had a German-born father which caused her some difficulty during the war.

1915

To Christine Kuhlenthal

Ibthorpe House, Hurstborne Tarrant, nr Andover, Hampshire
14 February 1915

Dear Christine,

I thank you for two letters. Which according to my habit & custom I will answer in turn [...]

I loved your description of Garsington, it told me so much. But I am not jealous! Lady Ottoline[1] has often kissed me, I am sure really she likes me better than Barbara also. Yes dear Christine I will write you a poem. But the inspiration has not yet arrived. Generally it comes in the bath. Awful, since I have no paper or pencil at hand & thus lose whole stanzas of valuable rhyming matter. But soon I will write you one & illustrate it [...] Yes, yes I will come and live in a cottage, only do let us keep it a secret. Let us pretend we might not go. Like a 'liaison' in a book, we will stay a week in a cottage. I have thought already of heaps of things we will do [...] would you be frightened to sleep in an empty ruined cottage in a wonderful bleak mountainous valley near here? Do come & live with me there a week in the summer. I discovered it by accident the other day Wednesday when I was on a walk about 9 miles from here. It was all in ruins except for two rooms; & it was quite alone on the side of a big bare hill. Christine, be brave & live with me there. Nobody would ever see us, or discover us. You must come. Even if the remaining roof falls in on us, we shall at least die together! and do not thousands of men die every day?

How pleased I was with your second letter. I was so happy you really liked my poetry ... and also glad you do not like Barbara as much as me. She is friendly & kind. But don't you wish she had just one vice. If only she wasn't quite so smiling & cheerful. I also ward her off with my hand. I don't know why. It is just because she is so easy & never unhappy. I feel she doesn't play fair. It is not human to be continually bright & cheery.

But when I come up to London you must come & dance with me. I like best to dance out of doors, then one doesn't run into the walls and easel. Our garden will be great, lovely yew hedges very thick, & then green mossy grass. Just behind my studio I am making a wild garden, all grass & wild

---

1 Lady Ottoline Cavendish Bentinck (1873–1938) was the half-sister of the Duke of Portland. She married Philip Morrell (1870–1943) in 1902; he became a Liberal M.P. in 1906. They lived in Bloomsbury and, after 1915, at Garsington, a Tudor manor house in Oxfordshire.

plants, under the tall fir trees. On Friday it was like a summer's day. A lovely golden sunshine shone all day, so I walked to Inkpen Hill, 8 miles away, where the country is as wonderful as you could wish for, and where I can sit in the deserted garden of the old empty house. I did tell you about it, did I not? a house which I dream of all day & I live in constant terror lest someone should take it before I can live there,. You will I am sure love it as much as I do.

In a field in the sunshine I saw such a pretty sight, two hares fighting. It was really the tragedy of an over ardent suitor & the reluctant lady hare, but it was a fine sight to see them wrestling on hind legs, twisting & turning somersaults, up again, & tearing in pursuit, & so on. They came quite close to me, & never saw me. It was indeed an earnest battle & all in the lovely sunshine. I am indeed so happy that I feel it cannot last long. Brett can say as much as she likes that the country makes one stodgy, but she is wrong. It is a thousand times more stimulating here. Does one ever see two hares fight in London? and the house at Old Combe[1], with its wonderful garden? [...] Sam, my brother, is just writting a poem on the Slade. He is so happy because it rhymes. I have told him to send it to Brett to read to you. Do you like having her back at Slade again? she tells me she goes two days a week. Of course Barbara has usurped my place entirely. Even Gertler likes her better than me I'm sure, as she doesn't have sulky or hilarious moods. I am reading *Wuthering Heights* again. How excellent it is [...]

I wouldn't go back to Slade for anything. Oh this freedom is wonderful! & nobody who cares whether I work or not or if I do whether it is good or bad. All over the garden plants are coming up, little green leaves. What will they turn out to be? – and tiny black lambs are being born in the fields, surrounded by hurdles. I wish I could make a hedge, & a hurdle. They look so satisfactory.

I wear great thick woolly stockings, heather mixture. Does this repulse you? [...]

Write to me again soon won't you, & tell me what you do.

I sold my New English[2] picture. Oh I was so happy. What a good thing money is to be sure! I shall give you a big party in Brett's studio when I come up.

Goodbye now.

Love from,

Carrington

---

1 Combe House, near Hurstbourne Tarrant, had been discovered empty and half-ruined by Carrington, who fantasised about living there.

2 The New English Art Club, founded in 1886, was more inclined than the Royal Academy to show work by young artists.

This is a stupid letter. But I cannot help it. Perhaps it is because I am growing stupider myself. Really I wanted to tell you what I was doing & also that I am glad we are friends.

Lady Ottoline Morrell, the flamboyant, emotional, generous befriender of artists and writers, had already taken up with Dorothy Brett and Mark Gertler and asked them to her London gatherings before 1915, when she moved to Garsington Manor near Oxford. They introduced her to Carrington, and before long she became keenly interested in the puzzling relationship between Carrington and Gertler.

Meanwhile, through Gertler and his friend the writer Gilbert Cannan, Carrington had also met the young David Garnett (who claimed to have been at once 'powerfully attracted') and the already well-known and controversial novelist D. H. Lawrence and his German-born wife Frieda.

To Mark Gertler

Ibthorpe House, Hurstbourne Tarrant, nr Andover, Hants
Sunday, April 1915

Dear Gertler,

Thank you so <u>very</u> much for *Jude the Obscure*[1] it is good of you to give it to me. [...]

What fun you all seem to be having in London. Did you all go that night to Lady Ottoline's in fancy dress? or didn't it come off? I felt for you. For if the atmosphere had been intense & learned it would have been truly tiresome. Brett, who by the way is fifty times a better correspondent than you!, sent me a little plan of your studio & told me all about it. It sounds splendid. I do hope you will take it. No No, the part about the Lawrences didn't bore me. It was only I wanted to hear <u>more</u> about yourself & your work, instead of which you told me of the Lawrences! But I like his book *Sons & Lovers*[2] so much that I want to know him. Mrs Lawrence[3] I admit tries me sorely [...]

Since I last wrote I have been starting some work. I am just going to do a still life, in green, yellow, & orange, of apples, & some little orange pumpkins. Last night I did a drawing of my father. He's rather a good head to draw. But he was suffering so much time at the time, that in the end I had to stop. In

1 *Jude the Obscure* by Thomas Hardy, published 1895.
2 *Sons and Lovers* by D. H. Lawrence, published in 1913.
3 Frieda Weekley (1879–1956), born von Richthofen, married D. H. Lawrence (1885–1930) in 1914. Her German origins caused them trouble during the war; their relationship was famously tempestuous.

the cold weather his leg gets so stiff & hurts him terribly. My brother takes me rides sometimes on his motorcycle. It's so exciting rushing through the air, with the cold wind hissing in one's eyes & ears. The country round here is wonderful. Two days ago the snow came, & fell. It was a fine sight, all the hills & valley, became white, & the little bushes stood out in little spotted patterns all over the hills. And the river rushing on, looking quite green in contrast to the white snow. I am going to grow all sorts of wonderful flowers in my garden this summer. I have just been choosing the seeds. I hope you are keeping well, & taking care of yourself. It will be splendid to live so near the Heath won't it. Think of it in the spring. You might be happy now.

Directly you tell me you are in your studio I will send you some leaves, to put in your vases. Yesterday morning I went rabbiting, to try & catch a rabbit for Brett. But we couldn't catch one. It was too cold & they all stayed in their holes, & refused to come out. Next week I will try again. I am going to learn to make some puddings & good dishes to cook for you when I come back, as I am sure in time we will get tired of eggs on plates. Have you ever worked out the idea of Cain, a small man fleeing across a desolate country? Do go on with it sometime. Do you see much of Strachey?

Brett is so wonderful, I simply marvel more & more at her unlimited endurance of other people, & her kindness. I have just finished reading the old Ranee's book on Sarawak.[1] It was so interesting. She repeats some wonderful old legends that the Malays used to tell her. They were so inspiring to read.

Early this morning as I lay awake upstairs about 5 o'clock I heard a big crash, & fumbled my way downstairs in the dark & found my father had fallen out of bed on the floor. (I know you laugh, but please don't.) It was so terrible to see this big helpless form lying there, & I had to help my brother lift him on the bed again. His brain is so clear & active, it is painful to see his limbs like lumps of carved stone, which his brain cannot make move. He bears it all so patiently & never complains [...]

> With best wishes
> I remain
> Carrington

Her casual question to Gertler about Lytton Strachey is her first reference to him. Strachey, still a minor writer not yet renowned ouside his circle of devoted friends, had been attracted to Gertler for some time, and although there was nothing romantic or sexual between them they met often. By now, the question of Carrington's refusal

---

1 The Ranee was Margaret Brooke (1849–1936), who in 1869 had married Charles, the second White Rajah of Sarawak, Borneo, ruled by the Brookes since 1839. Her book, *My Life in Sarawak*, came out in 1913. Brett's younger sister Sylvia married the Ranee's eldest son, also Charles, in 1911. He became the last White Rajah in 1917.

to sleep with Gertler was becoming common knowledge in their circle. She found his physical demands and emotional pressure, poured out in anguished letters, almost unbearable. In the following letter, Carrington cut out and pasted the passages written in capitals from Gertler's latest letter at the top of her reply.

To Mark Gertler

Hurstborne Tarrant
16 April 1915

NEXT LETTER. WHEN YOU WRITE, WHENEVER YOU DO *DON'T* MENTION OUR SEX TROUBLE ETC ETC ETC: *AT ALL* I AM HEARTILY SICK OF IT – JUST WRITE AND TELL ME ABOUT YOURSELF THE COUNTRY AS USUAL. AND IF EVER I WRITE ABOUT IT TO YOU, *PLEASE* TAKE NO NOTICE.

OUR FRIENDSHIP IS NO WORSE OR BETTER THAN ANY OTHER FRIENDSHIP. AT ANY RATE WE ARE INTERESTED IN EACH OTHER – ENOUGH. WHY SHOULD WE FUSS?

I WANT *SIMPLY* YOUR *FRIENDSHIP* AND *COMPANY* MORE THAN ANYTHING IN THE WORLD.

You wrote these last lines only a week ago, and now you tell me you were *'hysterical and insincere'*. When you talked to me about it at Gilbert's and said you loved my friendship were you hysterical and insincere? Yes I know that your real love is 'beautiful and not low'. Do not think I ever doubted that.

Only I *cannot* love you as you want me to. You must know one could not do, what you ask, sexual intercourse, unless one does love a man's body. I have never felt any desire for that in my life: I wrote only four months ago and told you all this, you said you never wanted me to take any notice of you when you wrote again; if it was not that you just asked me to speak frankly and plainly I should not be writing. I do love you, but not in the way you want. Once, you made love to me in your studio, you remember, many years ago now. One thing I can never forget, it made me inside feel ashamed, unclean. Can I help it? I wish to God I could. Do not think I rejoice in being sexless, and am happy over this. It gives me pain also. Whenever you feel you want my friendship and company, it will *always* be here. You know that. This is all I can say.

REMEMBER THAT I WOULD SACRIFICE ALL FOR YOU, MY VERY LIFE IF YOU ASKED IT OF ME.

You write this – yet you cannot sacrifice something *less than your life* for me. I do not ask it of you. But it would make me happy if you could. Do not be angry with me for having written as I have. And please do not write back. There can be nothing more to say. Unless you can make this one sacrifice for me. I will do everything I can to be worthy of it.

This exchange coincided with Carrington being a reluctant bridesmaid at the wedding of her sister Charlotte. The correspondence with Gertler and her refusal to have sex with him continued.

To Mark Gertler

Hurstbourne Tarrant
Wednesday evening [May 1915]

I am writing again as I promised I would. It has been a lovely day, a beautiful hot sun, and cobalt blue sky with passing clouds. I have been hard at work on my picture of saint John the Baptist. It was good having a model this morning, as I got on much better with it. Mancini's[1] figure is quite good to draw. But his face fills me with depression. Curious how no models have good heads to draw. He comes again tomorrow and Friday.

I am so glad all this wedding is over, you have no idea how terrible a real English wedding is. Two people, with very ordinary minds want each other physically, at least the man does, the woman only wants to be married and have his possessions and position. To obtain all this they go through a service, which is comprised of worthy sentiments uttered by the old apostles and Christ! Many relatives come and friends all out of curiosity to see this presumably religious rite; afterwards they all adjourn to the house, and eat like animals and talk, and view each other's clothes and secretly criticise everyone and then return home. All this costs a great deal of money: a bouquet of flowers which the bride carries into the church for 15 mins, and afterwards leaves in the house behind her, which dies the next day as none of the flowers have stalks, costs £2. It seems curious. The dress she wears for about 1 hr costs about £10. And yet this is a so called 'quiet' middle class wedding. But it astounds one, the ridiculous farce, the sham festivity. If only they all got merry and drunk, and danced: or if only they were all moved and religious it wouldn't matter. But to be nothing real. Thank god it cannot happen again now. I was almost glad it rained. I felt my sky and country here anyrate were not 'pretending' to shine and be happy.

1 Mancini was a regular model at the Slade.

It makes it much worse for me now, coming up to London. I long, and long for you to talk to. Everything they say jars so terribly. They are so commonplace and material. This morning I just longed to run away from them all, and escape to London. You can never know what it is to have a Mother and a family, and surroundings like those people in *The Way of all Flesh*.[1] Like 'Ann Veronica's' parents.[2] The only thing to do is to make up your mind not to be irritated by it all, but to love the country, the trees and the good hot sun. Soon I will pick you some flowers but there aren't any out just now. I had a long letter from both my brothers which made me happy. I have a beautiful little bantam cock and hen now of my own; a farmer gave them to me. They look like a lovely Chinese silk painting.

I hope you are keeping well. I am glad you are so happy working at your picture now. You will write again soon, will you not please! I am glad you like Strachey so much. Does he talk more when you get him alone? Thank you especially for the photograph of your cottage. I do like it very much. I expect you will have Brett back soon. She is with that terrible Zena[3] in Paris. How can she endure being with people like that. But she said she was going to see the Puvis de Chavannes which I would like to see. It's just like being in a bird cage here, one can see everything which one would love to enjoy and yet one cannot. My father is in another cage also, which my mother put him in, and he is too old to even chirp or sing. I am sorry to give you such an outburst of self-pity but I didn't quite realize until I saw you again how much I miss not being with you more. The little green stream still flows swiftly through the meadows.

My love to you,
Carrington

To Christine Kuhlenthal

Hurstbourne Tarrant
Wednesday [spring/summer 1915]

Dear Christine,

I was so sorry also I couldn't come. Especially as the moon was particularly bright that night and the day seemed so hot [...] I am still depressed. I cannot really make out why. Mostly because I am longing for something

1 *The Way of All Flesh* by Samuel Butler, published in 1903, depicted a son's revolt against a repressive father.

2 *Ann Veronica* by H. G. Wells, published in 1909, was a *succès de scandale*. The eponymous heroine rebelled against her bourgeois background, became a suffragette and had a child outside marriage.

3 Zena Dare, star of pantomime and musical comedy, had married Brett's brother Maurice in 1911.

which I cannot have, accentuated by the joy of spring everywhere. I hoped
that this country could cheer me, but I feel so much further away now, &
even more unhappy. This evening mother said 'How the evenings are drawing
out' & I was thinking so far away, and then I realised how stupid it is to
long for other things when one always comes back to one's home, & the
long dreary evenings ... I feel I want to escape myself to the world. Really,
tell everyone what I feel & what I am. Do you realize that perhaps 3 people
love you for what you are and the rest, if they even think of why they do,
love quite an imaginary character, a fake idea which you give them?

Is getting irritable & nervy a malady which all young females suffer from?
But I hate these people so much sometimes, especially the middle aged ones.
Just because they say stupid remarks & are narrow minded that I want to
scream.

All this isn't because I want to love a man, as Havelock[1] would probably
tell me. I never felt less disposed. I just feel always melancholy, & haunted
by the idea that I am hypocritical.

But enough. Why burden you with all this ... In the end who does one
like? That is what one has to find out. I suppose.

I bought a beautiful dog in London, at the Battersea dog home. He would
have made me happier here. But I had to leave him with a friend whilst I
went to the Nashs & they lost him in London. I am sure the best thing
would be to have to work so hard all day that one hasn't time to think of
all these dismal thoughts. That is the worst of painting, one cannot sit down
& do it like one makes shoes, & feeds cattle, with a blank brain [...]

The garden looks really very lovely. But I hate it almost because mother
thinks it lovely too. Fortunately she doesn't really know why she does. But
what is the good of all this when one is alone. Christine I apologise for all
this. But I felt I must overpour somewhere. Write to me soon. Here is a
photo of me in my bridesmaid dress, now you know all about it! the check
is green & red, the coat & hat tête de nègre as they in Selfridges catalogues.

Well goodbye. What would I not give to come & live in your £5 cottage.
A little riches would procure much freedom for one. Do not sympathise
with me I pray you. I shall survive it unless I lose my appetite then I will
communicate with you for it would be serious.

My love dear fawn

Carrington

---

1 Henry Havelock Ellis (1859–1939), doctor and social reformer, studied and wrote about sexuality.

To Christine Kuhlenthal

Hurstbourne Tarrant
May 1915

I owe you for two letters now. So I will write before my debt increases
[...] Oh such excitement this week! On Wednesday 2,000 soldiers arrived
on manoeuvers from Salisbury Plain, & were billeted in our village! We
had four officers dumped on us. Only one was interesting. He was Irish
the son of a linen manufactor in Ulster, with a plain red face, & greenish
moustache & hair like stubble after the wheat is cut, only greenish brown
stubble. But – he played the piano marvellously. Everything I asked him
to play, good Bach & Beethoven, Chopin, & the Hungarian Dances by
Brahms & the Appassionata Sonata, which nearly made me weep because
I loved Brett's studio & Gertler thumping away on the Pianola so much,
and it seems much a long time ago, and I know it will never be again.
He played all one evening & the next day. Mother got so cheerful – 'at
last I am going to get Dora married' – & she encouraged the young man
& hoped he would come over again. & would I take him round the garden.
She didn't know that it was Brett's studio, the windmill at the Cannans,
and so many other things which made me happy. Why should she know?
They all went away on Friday evening. In the dust, over the little bridge,
the evening sun shining on their hot red faces, the big wagons, & gun
carriages lumbering along. The soldiers cheering & singing. They have
all gone further to another village & forgotten all this, and we are all
stationary behind. It seemed so strange to have sleeping on my little
landing upstairs two men, in the attic opposite my female bedroom. Men
who had never seen me, or me them before, whereas people who I have
known for so long & love so much I am not allowed to ask here to stay
[...] It must be contentment to so arrange your life that only one person
matters [...] I keep on waiting for something & letting the year slip by.
Yet I do not know what I wait for. I suppose it's the war. It is such a
surprise to suddenly see a rose out on the side of the house, & realize it
is nearly June. Do you feel like this? often I wish I could wake up & be
more alive [...]
    Carrington

To Mark Gertler

37 Carlisle Road, Hove, Sussex
Saturday morning [n.d.]

Dear Mark,

Thank you for your letter. I am sorry they did not accept your 'still life' at the New English. But then you cannot expect men whose whole aim in life you disagree with to like your work. Do not be depressed about it ... Did you see in the paper that Eddie[1] has been made Asquith's private secretary!!![2] Yesterday I went a wonderful ride over the downs. Lovely grand big shapes! I did enjoy it. Brett is good – without her encouragement, I would often despair – I hate this cold weather & my feet are all chill-blaney, which hurt awfully. But really, Mark, it doesn't count because they don't appreciate your work. As long as you are happy over it, & know it to be as good as you can do, & really sincere. Why it doesn't matter a bit what they think. I bet Cezanne's landscapes weren't appreciated like they are, or pretend to be, by so many people when he first showed them. I saw some pictures down here the other day, a Sloane exhibition. Sickerts, & all the N.E.A.C.[3] pictures which didn't sell![4] [...] As you say nicely matched mauves & greens. So artistic so as not to hurt the eye, or wake people up, like a drapers shop 'soft' coloured materials. And such bad drawings. Everything rotten. Did you have a good time with Gilbert in London?

I am reading *Roderick Random* by Smollett.[5] It is so good.

It will be good to see you again, & be happy! You were happy this summer weren't you. Down at the cottage? Let's go again when I come back to London. How glad I shall be to see the spring again, & the hot days [...] Dear, don't be unhappy because it makes me unhappy also, & remember I do care so much for you, & your work. And after all in this insincere world is something if only a few people appreciate one truly. Be happy, little onion.

Love from Carrington

---

1 Sir Edward Marsh (1872–1953), civil servant, sometime private secretary to Winston Churchill, patron of the arts and friend of Rupert Brooke.

2 H. H. Asquith (1852–1928), Liberal statesman and prime minister from 1908 to 1916.

3 New English Art Club.

4 The Sloane was a gallery in Brighton. Walter Sickert (1860–1942) was a leader and founder artist of the Camden Town Group.

5 *Roderick Random* by Tobias Smollett, a picaresque novel published in 1748.

By the end of 1915, Carrington had met Lytton Strachey. She described the encounter to her two closest friends.

To Christine Kuhlenthal

87 Carlisle Road, Hove
Monday, December 1915

My Dear Christine
   [...] Well last week the Clive Bells¹ asked me to stay with them near Lewes, just about 8 miles from Brighton where we are, so I went. It was indeed a romantic house² buried deep down in the highest & most wild downs I have ever seen. Duncan Grant³ was there, who is much the nicest of them & Strachey⁴ with his yellow face & beard, ugh! I used to walk along the ridge of the downs every morning early when the sun was just rising, and the wind on the top was more fierce & powerful than anything you could imagine. It roared in my ears, and I had to lie flat down on the wet grass in order to look at the land below & the sea beyond Newhaven which shone all silver. We lived in the kitchen & cooked & ate there. All the time I felt one of them would suddenly turn into mother & say 'what, breakfast at 10:30! Do use the proper butter knife!' But no. Everything was behind time. Everyone devoid of table manners, & the vaguest cooking ensued. Duncan earnestly putting remnants of milk pudding into the stock pot! They were astounded because I knew what part of the leek to cook! What poseurs they are really.
   I may come up next weekend, if I hear of a job before then. But I will tell Brett & then we can have a party. But these escapes are matters of a moment. Nothing can ever really be decided before hand [...]
   Noel goes to London today to have his arm treated. I shall miss him. You would love the country here. I found a good cottage in the downs where they take people for £- a week. Shall we go one day next summer? This I mean in all earnestness. My love to you.
   Carrington

---

1 Clive Bell (1881–1964), art critic, had been married to Vanessa Stephen (1879–1961), Virginia Woolf's sister, since 1907.
2 Asheham House, rented by Leonard and Virginia Woolf as a country retreat.
3 Duncan Grant (1885–1978), painter, cousin and former lover of Lytton Strachey.
4 Lytton Strachey (1880–1932), writer and critic.

To Mark Gertler

87 Carlisle Road, Hove
Friday, December 1915

Dear Mark,

[...] I have just come back from spending three days on the Lewes downs with the Clive Bells, Duncan, Mrs Hutchinson[1] and Lytton Strachey. God knows why they asked me!! It was much happier than I expected. The house was right in the middle of huge wild downs, four miles from Lewes, and surrounded by a high hill on both sides with trees. We lived in the kitchen for meals as there weren't any servants, so I helped Vanessa cook. Lytton is rather curious. I got cold, and feel rather ill today. They had rum punch in the evenings which was good. Yesterday we went a fine walk over tremendous high downs. I walked with Lytton. I like Duncan, even if you don't! What traitors all these people are! They ridicule Ottoline! even Mary H[utchinson] laughs at the Cannans[2] with them. It surprises me. I think it's beastly of them to enjoy Ottoline's kindnesses and then laugh at her.

I am sorry that you have been ill and worried lately. I am still amazed at them chucking your still life. I can see no reason for it. Except a personal dislike for you, because you do not pander, and pay them homage.

I got up every morning when I was with them very early at 8 o'ck and went for long walks by myself over the downs. It was grand. The huge sun rising upon the edge of the down. So near and so powerful that one felt like a small moth compelled to draw near to it, blinking in its brilliant light. I have never been so near the sun before and then when one did reach the summit the wind was terrific, it shouted in one's very ears, and pushed and pushed till one was perforced to lie down on the wet morning grass, and then what a sight greeted the eye: way over to Lewes in the north with huge distant downs, and then Newhaven and the shining sea in the south, and far below behind the deep deep basin, the little house surrounded by the trees and all the time the mighty rushing wind, and glaring sun. They never got up till about ten o'ck, so when I returned they were still in bed. I am going

---

1 Mary Hutchinson, a cousin and close friend of Lytton Strachey's, was married to the barrister St John Hutchinson and a long-term mistress of Clive Bell.

2 Gilbert Cannan (1884–1955) was an actor turned writer who married Mary Barrie, formerly the wife of the play wright J. M. Barrie, in 1910.

to get some job soon in London. And then I will come up and stay [...]
Goodbye now for a little while. I will send you the end of Gilbert's
book[1] soon.

My love to you.

Carrington

To Mark Gertler

87 Carlisle Road, Hove
Monday, December 1915

Dear Mark,

Thank you for your letter. But you really are annoyed without cause! For
the Bells were only 8 miles from here, so naturally it wasn't very difficult
to get over to them. Whereas London costs nearly 10/- to get up to. But I
hope to come quite soon now. Possibly next week. Now will you be happy?
But you make me unhappy, surely it was *you* who left me after this summer
for nearly three months without a word [...] and then you reproach me for
not seeing you now for a few weeks! I do not love you physically, that you
know, but I care for you far more than I do for anyone else.

I have written about a job, and hope to hear this week. Probably it will
mean working all day. But we can see each other in the evenings and at the
weekends. But it will be good to earn my own living at last! Your letters of
course excited me terribly. I am still always excited about motor cars and
duchesses!!! So you are famous, and *also* infamous to judge by the critics! I
hope you will sell your pictures. That is most important when one has to
do with these idle rich. We leave here on Friday I think, at least I hope so.
Yes, I'll go with you to Gilbert's[2] but it will be nearly Xmas by then. But I
really will try and come.

What a damned mess I make of my life and the thing I want most to do,
I never seem to bring off. My work disappoints me terribly. I feel so good,
so powerful before I start and then when it's finished, I realise each time, it
is nothing but a failure. If only I had any money I should not be obliged to
stick at home like this. And to earn money every day, and paint what one
wants to, seems almost impossible.

1 Gilbert Cannan's novel, *Mendel*, published in 1916, is a barely disguised if overheated portrait of Mark
  Gertler, his poor Jewish background, his struggles with his art and his tormented relationship with
  Carrington. The book, which she detested, is dedicated to D.C.
2 The Cannans had a house by a windmill at Cholesbury, Bucks, where Gertler and Carrington would
  sometimes go alone.

Yesterday I walked over to Rottingdean over the downs with Noel. It was lovely country. I am afraid I shall never really get intimate with him; he is so governed by conventions, and accepts the 'public school' opinions. It's a pity, perhaps he will get out of it in time. You would like him, but it wouldn't be any use now because he's so patriotic, that I am sure you would hate him, and he you! It's a good thing Eddie doesn't know him, for he's almost as beautiful as Rupert Brooke.[1] I wonder who all the Baronesses are who you are meeting? It wasn't Baroness D'Erlanger was it? How pleased your people must be with you at last! Have the Lawrences ever gone to Florida?[2] Well when I really do come up, I will tell you, and we'll have a party in Brett's studio. I hope you are well, and taking care of yourself. Do not think of me bitterly; rather be glad that you are of value to me because I am often so weak, and need you. Goodbye, and soon I will see you now.

Carrington

Do send me your newspaper cuttings to read about your pictures next letter.

The next letter suggests that Carrington had told Gertler that Lytton, despite being homosexual, had tried to kiss her as they walked on the downs.

To Mark Gertler

Hurstbourne Tarrant
Wednesday, December 1915

Dear Mark,

[...] I am sorry I told you about Lytton, I did not mean to. Only I would rather you knew about it from me. Please don't ever mention it again, as I am annoyed enough as it is because I let the fact make me so miserable. As a man so contemptible as that ought not ever to make one miserable or happy. And so I shall try and forget it. I am going on Saturday to Ottoline's with Brett so I don't expect I shall see you until I return on Monday. I had a weary time hunting for a job. It's fearfully hard to get anything. And they always keep me waiting 2 hours before they will interview me [...] I did

---

1 Rupert Brooke (1887–1915), whose patriotism, death in Greece and poetry moved the nation, had been a lover of James Strachey at Cambridge.
2 Lawrence had launched a plan to set up an artists' commune, Rananim, perhaps in Florida.

enjoy our evening so much at Brett's. I hope you are better now – I am
sorry you have been so ill lately.

Carrington

*As the last three letters show, Carrington was not especially impressed by Bloomsbury
manners or morals when she first encountered them, and nor was she taken with
Lytton Strachey. After his unwelcome attempt to kiss her, she learned (apparently
from Barbara Hiles, also at Asheham that weekend) he was homosexual, which
appears to have shocked and infuriated her. What she did not tell Gertler was that,
determined to punish Lytton, she planned to cut off his beard and crept into his
room while he slept; but, as she told Barbara later,[1] he opened his eyes as she bent
over him with the scissors, looked at her and she fell in love. From then on, a mutual
affection and attraction began to grow, wholehearted on her part, more guarded on
his. Meanwhile she kept the increasingly jealous and suspicious Mark Gertler on a
string. She would not sleep with him, but she did not want to lose him; his devotion,
and his belief in her as an artist, was necessary to her, but his strong sexuality
frightened and repelled her. The more he badgered her, the more devious and elusive
she became.*

1 See Michael Holroyd's account of the incident in *Lytton Strachey,* published in 1995.

PART TWO

Building Love: 1916–1923

The next stage of Carrington's life saw her building her world around Lytton Strachey. Her love for him drove her determination to make a home in the country for them both. Over the next eight years, she saw this aim realised, although not without difficulty and some sacrifice. Her interest in art and her own ambitions as a painter remained strong, but her output was small as she struggled to combine painting with her emotional and domestic life. It did not help that her painting was not in tune with, or much appreciated by, the leading artists in the Bloomsbury world, Duncan Grant and Vanessa Bell, or the two critical arbiters, Clive Bell and Roger Fry. Carrington admired the French painters presented to London by Fry in exhibitions in 1910 and 1912, especially Cézanne and Matisse, but she was more deeply attracted to the art of fifteenth-century Renaissance artists and her own style was always in the English, naturalistic tradition. Apart from Gertler, she lost touch with her Slade contemporaries; perhaps because, under Lytton's influence, she became strongly pacifist as the war ground on, and her most distinguished contemporaries – the Nash brothers and Stanley Spencer – all went to war and recorded their experience memorably in their art. The war paintings of the Nash brothers, Nevinson and Stanley Spencer are not discussed in her letters.

During 1916, Lytton and Carrington's relationship deepened; but both were shy about it, Lytton because he knew his circle would be astonished that he was at all interested in a girl, even a cropheaded bohemian one, and Carrington because she did not want to lose Mark Gertler's devotion. She became increasingly secretive.

They were, as they both knew, an unlikely couple. During the summer Lytton told at least one friend, David Garnett, that he thought he was in love. Several of his other old friends, Ottoline Morrell and Virginia Woolf in particular, were not pleased when they perceived that Lytton's attachment to Carrington was more than a passing experiment. For his part, as his many letters to her show, he was never just the passive recipient of her devotion. He wrote often and at length, never openly emotional but always responsive, intimate and affectionate. She undoubtedly touched, charmed and amused him, and there were obvious advantages for him in having a devoted young woman to arrange and manage his domestic life, and by her presence to protect him from the suspicions of curious or disapproving onlookers who might suspect him of illegal passions.

At the beginning, it was essential that their move to the country was as discreet as possible, to avoid gossip and scandal. To both sets of parents, it was presented as a group enterprise, a retreat for some friends, which to an extent was true. Both of them needed to escape family scrutiny of their unconventional loves and friendships; Lytton wanted a place in the country where he could write, and Carrington wanted a studio where she could paint. By the end of 1917 the Mill House at Tidmarsh, outside Pangbourne, found, furnished and decorated by Carrington, was becoming such a place.

It appears that she accepted from early on in their relationship that, despite some early excitements, sex between them, what Lytton called 'the physical', was not going to be successful or lasting. At first she found this painful, but it is striking how quickly, after her initial distaste, she accepted his essentially homosexual nature and even encouraged it, both by play-acting herself and by drawing pretty boys and handsome men to his attention. Within Bloomsbury, gender and sexuality were recognised as fluid and various, and that a predominantly heterosexual man or woman could sometimes be erotically drawn to someone of the same sex was taken for granted. In this atmosphere, Carrington's own feelings for women gradually came to the surface.

Moreover, her own long-standing fears and ambivalences about her own sexuality meant that Lytton's nature had great advantages. Unlike Mark Gertler, whose position in her life was inevitably eroded by her new attachment, Lytton had no interest in possessing or dominating her, sexually or otherwise, and he was never jealous. On the contrary – when in 1918, her brother Noel brought to the house a handsome fellow officer, Reginald Sherring Partridge, then known to friends and family as Rex, she came to realise that she could strengthen her position in Lytton's life by attracting a man whom he found attractive.

None of the letters between Carrington and Partridge have survived, so there is no direct evidence of a relationship which was also, in its way, unlikely. He was the product of a conventional middle-class Anglo-Indian family, an adored only son and brother, a tall, strapping, blue-eyed young officer and brave soldier with predictable opinions about the war. When they first met he was about to return to the Italian front. He was not in the least bohemian or much drawn to art or literature, but had a good brain; high-spirited, sporting and well-educated, he had gone from Westminster school to Christ Church, Oxford, to read law before joining up. He was, in a way, the embodiment of the Victorian and Edwardian values that Lytton had set out to subvert in *Eminent Victorians*, published and acclaimed that same summer. Before long, Carrington and Lytton were to liberate and transform him.

He remained, however, conventional enough to become determined to make Carrington his wife, and despite her extreme reluctance she finally acquiesced in May of 1921. His hold over her was largely dependent on his hold over Lytton, who was for several years in love with him. Carrington knew that he was essential to their 'triangular trinity of happiness'. Fundamentally, though, she resented him for forcing her to marry him, and retaliated within weeks by starting a romance with his great friend Gerald Brenan, an aspiring writer of intense literary ambition and a natural bohemian with whom she was soon exchanging very long and very emotional letters about love, life and art. When Rex Partridge – now renamed Ralph by Lytton – discovered what was going on in 1922, Lytton had to exercise all his wiles to hold the Tidmarsh ménage together. Carrington was more honest about the centrality of Lytton in her life and her problems with sex and commitment in her correspondence with Gerald than with anyone else.

By 1923, despite weathering these emotional storms, the early happiness of Tidmarsh was starting to fade. The damp of the Thames valley did not suit Lytton's health; he was spending more time away in the wake of his literary success. Ralph was openly carrying on affairs in London, one of which was becoming serious. And Carrington herself had encountered a young woman who before long was to extend her understanding of her own nature. As both Lytton and Ralph now had some capital, it was decided that they would look for a house to buy. By 1924, the Tidmarsh years were over. The Ham Spray years were about to begin.

1916

To Mark Gertler

[n.d. February/March 1916?]

I am miserable Mark to think my selfishness in being happy this last week[1] has made you wretched now. But I am sure it is impossible for us to party always. I shall only try later, if you still wish, to spend more of my life with you. But I think it would be unfair if I promised to live with you, because I do not think I ever could. Do not tell Brett please this time. Yes, it is my work which comes between us. But I cannot put that out of my life because it is too much myself now. If I had not my love for painting I should be a different person. I understand. But I think a few months spent together in a year is worth it – but you do not think so – later perhaps we might spend longer together. I really am certain I could never live with you sexually day after day. [...] I at any rate could not work at all if I lived with you every day. It is because you want me sexually that you are miserable. Do not deceive yourself. Otherwise you would not be so miserable seeing that only my corporeal body has left you.

Oh why did we ever leave those woods that Friday night. You understood me then for the first time. Well I leave it to you. I wish to God I was not made as I am.

Carrington

To Mark Gertler

Garsington
31 May 1916

Dearest Mark,

Your letter came this morning & filled me with the uttermost sorrow because I know how miserable you have been. It makes such a big gap & makes me realize how little you believe in me. Do you not see an island in the middle of a big lake, many islands of adventures which one

---

1 Carrington had been down to Cholesbury with Gertler and allowed him inconclusive embraces in the woods.

must swim across to? But one will <u>always</u> return to the mainland. You are that mainland to me. I will leave you sometimes perhaps. But always I shall come back and when the best state of our friendship is arrived at, you will love my adventures as you do your own. Mental & physical adventures perhaps. Perhaps none. This world is so big & full of surprises, but the great thing is, a simple faith in you & a greater love for you than mankind. Do you never feel the excitement of this big world & ships & many people?

To return to your letter – Gilbert [Cannan] is not worthy of discussion as he was not an adventure. Honestly you must know how little he even affects me, simply because he is too like myself. I find no excitement in his company for he tells me nothing new or seldom and it is really a disapoint-ment. I went & saw him that morning for breakfast, simply out of friend-liness. When I came into his room he seized my hand, with his outward form of enthusiasm, & gave me a hearty kiss. But this I swear to you <u>as he does to Sammy.</u>[1] That I know annoys you – but it seems to me you must take the habits of a man along with him [...]

Do you not see a colossal difference between the way I kiss you & you me & anything else? I am not defending myself & I hate as much as you do the casual kiss to a stranger meaning nothing. But some people grasp your hand to show pleasure. Others kiss, others silence. They are all modes of expression. Accept them as such [...]

I care so little for anything except making you happy that I will promise not to kiss anyone, since it causes you pain. But do you not see that you cast a cloud of doubt on our trust in each other, by thinking for one moment that anything else or anyone could interrupt it?

[...] You must cease being miserable at once & believe me. What do I care for anyone else? & you know it.

I am not affecting anything, when I say that I had entirely forgotten the whole incident so little impression it made on me. No more than a kiss from my brother [...]

I will not fail you. Do not fear. But I am human also. You have had phases & moods. I also am mortal & am like unto you. I may have phases also. You must <u>never</u> be surprised or distressed. Because you know I shall come through & we are in the whole part together.

Carrington

1 The Cannans' dog.

To Lady Ottoline

16 Yeoman's Row, Brompton Road
1 June 1916

Dear Lady Ottoline,

You know how much I have enjoyed myself, so it is useless for me to try, & write you an eloquent letter of thanks, or express my extreme misery at having to leave you [...]

It was exciting reading the paper yesterday about what Snowden said in Parliament.¹ Brett is going swimming with me tomorrow morning.

I am so full of affection for you this morning that I cannot write properly. Give my love to the Bearded Bard. I hope he is regaining spirits & still continues with his light nourishment.

I felt like writing you a marvellous letter like sunshine on the water. But C'est Impossible. Alas I have no 'partner' to congratulate you & myself over. Still Pug. Pug. Pug.

And again Pug. Pug. Pug.²

Yours most affectionately

Carrington

During the summer of 1916 Brett took up semi-permanent residence at Garsington, which Ottoline and her husband, the pacifist MP Philip Morrell, were turning into a refuge for friends who, like them, were opposed to the war.

Carrington was soon sharing their views; she too became a regular visitor, and it was there that she and Lytton were much together and subject to the inquisitve gaze of their circle, who found the new alliance very strange, especially as Mark Gertler was evidently still in hot pursuit. Carrington's letters to Lytton show their adoption of private jokes and nicknames; they liked to pretend he was her venerable grandfather or aged uncle (athough he was only thirteen years older) while she was his naughty niece or granddaughter or simply baby. Sometimes she called herself Doric, an acceptable version of Dora. Soon he was calling her Mopsa after the simple shepherdess in As You Like It, *while he became the Fakir or Count Lytoff. She was always his eager pupil, thrilled that he was ready to instruct her in French and English literature. She liked to address him in her grammatically eccentric French.*

1 Philip Snowden, later 1st Viscount (1864–1937), elected Labout MP for Blackburn 1905, opposed conscription into the forces during the war.
2 Ottoline was devoted to her many pugs.

To Lytton Strachey

16 Yeoman's Row, Brompton Road
Sunday evening, June 1916

Mon chère grand-père Lytton,

[...] Have you recovered from your greyest gloom yet? Indeed I sympathise with you. It seems long ages since we were at Garsington, everything seemed bare, and so chilly here and then I hate more and more having to go to the mouldy museum everyday. My greatest pleasure is a motor bike which I am going to learn, and then all England is within my grasp. Will you meet me at Newbury and then away to the Inkpen Hills, and Combe? [...] Barbara came to supper on Friday with me. I am miserable over my work just now. All grey stones compared to what I want to paint. What do you do all day now? I still am writing this letter with a censor inside. I trust you so little sometimes. Are you still starved? I shall send you like a poor soldier biscuits and bully-beef?

No, I cannot write you anything, and I thought I had so much to say ... But send me the Rimbaud poem.

My studio is incredibly dirty and I sit knee-deep in crockery, and old letters, and everywhere drooping flowers, with pools of deep-red petals and on the mantel shelf long spines with vertebras hanging brown and musty by little threads. These were once lupins.

The buses and tubes disappoint me, only aged hags, and men with yellow teeth sit and chuckle, and the soldiers have pink raw faces with boils.

Will you write a tale about the grove on the little hills at Wittenham?[1] Surely, you cannot but do so. The deaf lady [Brett] sends you her greetings. Write a long letter again soon. I send you a small brown paper parcel and remain

Votre grosse bébé Carrington

1   The Wittenham Clumps, above Dorchester in Oxfordshire, where Carrington and Lytton walked together from Garsington.

To Lytton Strachey

16 Yeoman's Row, Brompton Road
Tuesday morning, 13 June 1916

Chère grand-père,

It was indeed ungrateful of me not to write before, and thank you for the amazing poem.[1]

But so many things happened at once, and I got frantically depressed, and so it was no use trying to write. You will believe me I know when I tell you, that the poem made me ill with excitement. I cannot understand how all these people go on so calmly. And when it becomes too much, and one tells them, how little are they astounded. I will ask you, because I care so much that I do not mind even if it is a nuisance to you. But you *must* send the poems about the dove-cot and the Brown sky and the ladies with the silver finger-nails searching for bugs, almost immediately. Are you coming with Lady Ottoline this week to London? We have just been down to Wittering[2] for Whitsun. It was an exciting place, but the company, repeat it not, was dull. I had a wonderful walk from Chichester late at night there, with only a half sucked acid-drop of a moon for company. I like Mary H so much. The conversation was merely lewd without being amusing, and a dreadful domestic couple made everything dismal for me. Do not you hate united pairs. But is not the shore with the long flat stretches of mud, and sea grass beautiful and a wild black horse which ran madly on the grass. I came back in a motor car with Shearman[3] and Mark. Yellow wine, and pate de Foie Gras on the top of High hills near Arundel for lunch. Do you know I can ride the motor bicycle now all around Regent's Park before breakfast tearing quicker and quicker leaving gaping faces of city clerks behind on either side [...]

Last Thursday, the arch-bugger Lou Lou Harcourt[4] came to supper with us at Brett's studio, a terrible long creature tightly buttoned in a frock coat all the way up, and then a face bulging out all pink, and very tight above his collar. Really a nightmare of a face.

Of course my grievance is purely personal for he dared to say to Mark outside afterwards that I was a nice 'plump little thing'. But you are laughing. I will spoil his tight pink face for him one day. He made up to Mark with great

---

1 He had sent her Rimbaud's 'Le Bateau ivre', written in 1871 when the poet was sixteen.
2 St John and Mary Hutchinson's seaside house, Eleanor, at Wittering near Chichester.
3 Sir Montague Shearman (1857–1930), known as Monty, was a prominent judge with a keen interest in contemporary art and a friend and patron of Mark Gertler.
4 Loulou was the widely used nickname of Sir Lewis Harcourt, Liberal MP and Cabinet minister from 1905 to 1915. Married to an American heiress and a father, he was nevertherless an active paedophile. A friend of Brett's father Lord Esher, he had traumatised her with his sexual advances when she was fifteen. He killed himself in 1921 after an assault on an Eton schoolboy caused a public scandal.

rapidity outside. His conversation was as bombastic as Philip's![1] Now this letter cannot be published at breakfast. Are you writing your Clump story? do not be so carelessly lazy. What sort of gossip do you want? But Faith [Henderson][2] will have told you everything at the week-end. She came to tea with me last Friday and had a curious conversation. Brett told me afterwards it was with a purpose. I do hate having conversations with good motives behind them. Are you still crouching over the fire reading life upon life of Rimbaud?

[...] Tomorrow Ottoline comes to dinner with us at Brett's studio – a wonderful picture is in the making – which you will like also I think ... and next week I shall see Combe again. But you would never get as far as Newbury alone. Some motor bus on the way would devour you. I shall wait and only strands of your red beard would be blown up to me from the valley of Newbury. And to wait with only a red beard for company under the gibbet on Inkpen Hill – too much. This is no letter. But you know how much I loved Rimbaud.

Votre bébé Carrington

To Lytton Strachey

Hurstbourne Tarrant
Monday evening, 19 June 1916

Promise you will *not* show my letter to a Wisset breakfast[3] or I will *never never* write to you again quickly. Promise.

Chère grand-père Lytton, I can hardly believe it is true. For it has just happened. It seemed like some vile nightmare. You must realize it; and yet you never can because you never went there.

I went out to tea with a neighbour. Canny Scotch farmers. When suddenly the old lady, curse her yellow face and grey hair, told me with much malicious glee (for she had long past known of my great love) that Combe House had been taken by some woman and was now under repair. You can imagine what this meant. Taken! By whom? what repairs? At last I managed to escape and rushed away on my bicycle to The House. What repairs! But it had to be. The grass was all cut in the garden. The orchard pruned, walls mended, and neat. Little violas with pert yellow faces and geraniums sniggered round the foot of the house in newly made beds. Think! Violas, in such a garden!

I found the master builder in an undignified position behind the wall, round the corner. He retreated before me, abashed, doing up many buttons.

1 Philip Morrell was inclined to be ponderous.
2 Faith Bagenal (1889–1979) was the sister-in-law of Carrington's great friend Barbara Hiles. In 1915 she had married Hubert Henderson (1890–1952), an economist and rising Liberal politician.
3 Wissett Lodge was a Suffolk farmhouse rented by Duncan Grant so that he and his lover David Garnett could work as fruit farmers instead of joining up. Lytton, and all Bloomsbury, had the unnerving habit of sharing letters over breakfast.

The painters in the house smiled. But I persuaded him to forgive me, and went over the house with him. Lytton it was more amazing that I had ever seen it before and one room upstairs had black-lead wall painted all over with a pattern of white flowers by hand! They discovered this under an old wall paper. Traces of red walls with yellow patterns were found in all the other rooms, but distempered over! The dining room was entirely panelled with Jacobean oak. Thank God the woman does not seem to be so bad. But the spirit has been driven out by distemper, and white paint everywhere. It will never be what it was. A huge chunk of me is cut away, so many dreams. It all seems impossible. What right had they to come and steal it? Oh, Lytton why is one so small against these creatures. No more.

Lady Ottoline had dinner with us all last Wednesday and after went to the Palladium where we heard the incomparable song: 'I'm Burlington Bertie of Bow'. She was very lively with a tall purple ostrich feather, no doubt purloined from Loulou's estate [...] But what of Philip the King and the Pugs? also now I know from Brett *what was said* when I sat enthralled beside you on the lawn. And when we came back glowing with inspired eyes from The Clumps! Wissett sounds a long way off. It will need much persuasion to make me walk so far I fear. Besides you are not very kind, are you? You laugh much and often ...

Farewell. Dans un misère gris je reste votre bébé[1]

Carrington

A plan was being hatched for Carrington to join Lytton on a walking holiday in Wales with Barbara Hiles and her suitor Nick Bagenal. Needless to say this required deceiving Mark Gertler. Meanwhile at Garsington her refusal to surrender her virginity, which Gertler had made known, became a topic of keen interest.

To Lytton Strachey

Shandygaff Hall [Garsington Manor], Oxford
Sunday afternoon, 30 July 1916

Reverend Sir,

It is all very complicated! Jack Hutch has just written to me, a long letter *insisting* that I go on the 15th to Eleanor! Mark's affection has increased in my absence.

---

1 'In a grey gloom I remain your baby'.

And I want so much to go to this land of mountains and (since this disgusting cult of truth has begun) so much to be with you again [...]

Ottoline insists on trying her best to get my state of virginity reduced, and made me practically share a bedroom with Norton!![1] And Poor Brett got sent out four times in one morning with Bertie [Bertrand Russell] for long walks across remote fields by her Ladyship!! So you betrayed me to Maynard [Keynes]! But he is much more truthful than you only really cryptic. I read John Donne all day now. A lovely poem about Fair ships in harbours. But what will ever be written as wonderful as Rimbaud's 'librarians'. Her ladyship has now taken on your duties as educator to the young, and read us the Irish and English poets during the long evenings. Even Philip plays the missionary and recites Shelley through his hairy nostrils. This is a poor letter but I lie exhausted, in the sun after swimming in that cess-pool of slime.[2]

Monday morning in bed, 5 o'ck
I spent a wretched time here since I wrote this letter to you. I was dismal enough about Mark and then suddenly without any warning Philip after dinner asked me to walk round the pond with him and started without any preface, to say, how disappointed he had been to hear I was virgin! How wrong I was in my attitude to Mark and then proceeded to give me a lecture for quarter of an hour! Winding up by a gloomy story of his brother who committed suicide. Ottoline then seized me on my return to the house and talked for one hour and a half in the asparagrass [sic] bed, on the subject, far into the dark night. Only she was human and did see something of what I meant. And also suddenly forgot herself, and told me truthfully about herself and Bertie. But this attack on the virgins is like the worst Verdun on-slaughter and really I do not see why it matters so much to them all. Mark suddenly announced that he is leaving today (yesterday), and complicated feelings immediately come up inside me.

Brett sold her big picture of Black Widows to Lady Hamilton. So she is happy. I leave here about Friday probably. Il y en a qui m'enseignent à vivre – et d'autres qui m'enseignent à mourir – Maintes et maintes fois.[3] I look at the hills. On these hot days they once again seem very near.

I am glad you are working hard, and eating vigorously. Ici il fait de plus en plus chaud chaque jour! Goodbye. Votre bébé très triste.[4]

---

1 Harry Norton was a brilliant young Cambridge mathematician, a lifelong friend of Lytton Strachey's and a lover of Lytton's brother, James.
2 Much naked bathing took place in the long rectangular pool in the lower garden. On one such occasion Ottoline, a keen photographer, took pictures of Carrington posing on one of the classical statues at the pool's edge, as shown on the cover of this book.
3 'There are those who teach me to live – and others who teach me to die – many a time.'
4 'Here it is hotter and hotter each day ... your very sad baby.'

To Lytton Strachey

London
Saturday, 8 o'ck, 5 August 1916

Write me another letter soon please.

At last I have left! It seems strange to be out of that mass of intrigue. You have no idea how *incredibly* complicated just before I left. But isn't it wonderful about going to Wittering *and* Wales! Ottoline in one of the many farewell interviews that I had with her yesterday morning, asked me if I was really a fraud. All very embarrassing.

Wittering, 7:30

It is Sunday now, and I write sitting up in bed in the big barn with shrieking birds all round, and a wonderful picture of green grey mud, and little grey blue distances outside [...]

It is wonderful here. We walked from Bosham, and had lunch, in yellow cornfields with Jack and Mary and then sailed down the river, in a big ship with a bulging white sail, and pale yellow mast. It was exciting, riding up and down, with smacks on the green waves [...] Then we had tea at Eleanor, and swam in the warm sea. Even Mark came in, looking very absurd, in a bathing dress! I liked Aldous Huxley[1] at Garsington. We used to sleep on the roof together, as it became so unbearably hot in those attics. Strange adventures with birds, and peacocks, and hordes of bees. Shooting stars, other things [...]

I felt almost light headed with joy gazing over miles of empty flat land yesterday! we lit candles up the ilex tree one night. Great black shadows on the reptile branches. I was worn almost thin trying to capture my letters before Ottoline saw who they were from. Your first note which only arrived on Friday nearly brought about the fall or decline of Doric, especially as her Ladyship was in high wrath because you had written curtly demanding some books, and told her no scandal! She makes me steeped in debt by giving me *all* her letters to read. And then has long jabberfications about people deceiving her and being reserved! But I did enjoy it very much in between all these confusions. I did a Goya-esque portrait of our Lady of mystery which gave me some pleasure. But as I made her look like a pole-cat it had to be suppressed from the public eye.

[...]

Goodbye chère grandpère
Votre grosse bébé Carrington

---

1 Aldous Huxley (1894–1963), whose first novel, *Crome Yellow*, published in 1921, was a satirical portrait of goings-on at Garsington with a disobliging and very recognisable portrait of Carrington as a tiresome virgin.

To Mark Gertler

c/o Mrs Hiles, Llanbedre, Taly-cafn S.O., N. Wales
Monday, August 1916

I arrived here on Saturday evening. After a terrible, one of the most terrible, journeys I have ever undergone. Crowds of horrible sticky sweating people.

I am most happy here. Just Lytton, Barbara and Nicholas. We go out most of the day for long walks, and bathe in a wonderful pool with water-falls. The mountains are quite high, and one gets Cézanne landscapes of mountains with dull green trees, and ugly white cottages with Slate roofs. Lytton has brought John Donne so I read him in the garden. He seems to me one of the most marvellous poets! How vividly he felt everything. He once had a Great Love for a little girl of 15 years and wrote the most violent outbursts of passion every anniversary of her death. But such comparisons. It is very long or I would copy it out for you. Barbara's cottage is very small, all white outside with a small garden filled with flowers. And all round these huge mountains and a big river in a flat valley below. I hope you are enjoying yourself at Cholesbury. What are you painting now? Give Gilbert and Mary my love. What happened to Gilbert at his tribunal in the end?[1] The Weather is wet here, and quite cold. Horrible after the heat of the south! and those hot sands [...]

Donne is so wonderful you must have a book. I will give you one myself. Also Shakespeare's sonnets I am reading. I have not heard from you since Wittering do you realize that? Willain. The people all speak Welsh here and but little English. I miss you. The intimacy we got at lately makes other relationships with people strangely vacant, and dull. Are you writing any more Philosophy? Again I laugh at Gilbert's remark on the top of the bus. How annoying it is to be able to write so little of what I want to you. But it always seems rather false directly I put it down. But you must believe much more now by what I have felt with you.

Yours with love
friend Carrington

---

1 Cannan, like all pacifists, had to go before a tribunal to be exempted from military service.

To Mark Gertler

N. Wales
August 1916

Dear Mark,

Thank you for your letter. I was glad to hear from you. Write me your poem about Spring in the park or I may never see it. Write it on the last page of your next letter. I cannot write to you about my inner self because it is all confused & very agonizing to pull out. If you cast your mind back to the period before you painted your 'fruit gatherers' could you have told me then about your future desires? No – you never could have. Besides may I say so frankly – you asked from two reasons. Neither of which were real interest. Be frank with yourself you will find it was so.

One was a kind of curiosity to know what I do not tell you and the other a mixture of knowing I would like you to be interested in my work as I am in yours. Am I not right? You will never have a passion for another person's point of view & desires as your own is so great. Don't be vexed, & rush at me with protests. It is only truthful and why not let us both be thus.

Of course you like Lytton & praised him before I did. Because I did not even know him in those days, when you did. But I felt at Mary's & do feel that you do not appreciate Lytton very much. Probably as you say because that other objection comes so much always before you.[1] I have altered my views about that and think one always has to put up with something, pain or discomfort to get anything from any human beings. Some trait in their character will always jar. But when one realises it is there, a part of them & a small part – it is worth while overlooking it for anything bigger and more valuable [...]

To Maynard Keynes

The George Hotel, Glastonbury, Somerset
29 August 1916

Dear Maynard,

We are staying here. A very Christian atmosphere prevails, which Lytton is enjoying incredibly. Also a miller's lad. I doubt if Lytton will ever return. He wanders day after day with a guidebook on architecture in his lean hand gazing at ancient ruins.

---

1 It seems Gertler was not at ease with Lytton's homosexuality, while Carrington increasingly was.

[*The rest of the letter is missing. On the opposite page in Lytton Strachey's handwriting is:*]

> When I'm winding up the toy
> Of a pretty little boy,
> – Thank you, I can manage pretty well;
> But how to set about
> To make a pussy pout
> – *That* is more than I can tell.

Carrington and Lytton shared a bed together during their walking tour after they left the Welsh cottage. What exactly happened between them sexually is far from clear, and the verse above is hardly conclusive; but it was to Lytton, both his and her biographers agree, that she surrendered her much discussed virginity. There can be no doubt, as later letters show, that she found him physically attractive; for a time, the feeling seems to have been mutual. On their return, she wrote him loving, intimate letters, while trying, not altogether successfully, both to reassure and to fend off Gertler.

To Lytton Strachey

Hurstbourne Tarrant
Friday evening [1 September 1916]

Dear Uncle Lytton,

I feel burdened with so much affection and gratitude towards you tonight that I will pen you a letter whilst the inclination is heavy upon me. What a journey! That train was *more than one hour* late at Templecombe so I did not get here until six o'ck. But I had a happy time however exploring the village in the hot sun [...]

Home. No discoveries! As I expected, the most utter boredom and peevishness [...] BUT – an aged doctor of 92 years who died at Bath, left me a legacy of £20! My Father just told me as I was bolting down some kedgeree. For I was ravenous. So it does not matter how extravagant we have been! The downs round Salisbury are lovely. It was wonderful to see them again. You are lying on your couch now, with its crochet background reading Gardiner [...] I did enjoy myself so much with you, you do not know how happy I have been, everywhere, each day so crowded with wonders. Thank you indeed. It is melancholy here, their heavy dullness, and this dimly lit room burdened with dreary furniture.

Il faut que vous boutonniez vos boutons des mouches (toutes les) chaque nuit! n'oubliez-pas mon ami![1] Go to bed at 10:30 and take your Gregory pills. Write to me sometimes, and tell me of your travels, perhaps Rimbaud. Thank you so much for giving me Dr Donne, dear Lytton. I have been so happy, incred i a b l y [going up a musical scale] happy! Quelque fois je voudrais être un garcon de moulin![2]

Votre niece Carrington

To Mark Gertler

Hurstbourne Tarrant
3 September 1916

Dear Mark,

I was sad to have made you anxious about me. Thank you so much for both your letters. I am glad you read Marvel & Donne, & liked the latter so much. I cannot read Marvel's 'Coy Mistress' because I have not got any poetry books here with the Early English poet in them. Could you possibly get me a Marvel? I should like one so much.

[...] What have you been doing in London? Who have you seen? In two weeks I may be back again. I am always sorry afterwards that I write in the way I do, as it makes controversies. Whereas it is really interesting to get at what we both think. I wish also that I knew you better. But it is very difficult. Everyone is so complex [...]

I am excited over everything lately. The fullness of life. So many people alive who one doesn't know, so many wonders past which one finds everyday, & then the things to come. Oh the wonder of it all! [...]

To Lytton Strachey

Shandygaff Hall!!
Wednesday morning, 6 September 1916

Well you may be surprised at my being here chère Grandpère! quite suddenly yesterday morning I bicycled over – as I had to see Brett (who is still here) about the London house. An Excellent arrangement is now made. Maynard

---

1 'You must do up your fly buttons, all of them, every night. Do not forget, my friend!'
2 'Sometimes I would like to be a miller's boy!'

and Sheppard[1] are to live in Clive's house and we take 3 Gower Street for nine months. Katherine [Mansfield] and [Middleton] Murry[2] will live in the bottom floor, Brett on the second, and I in the attics. But my rent will only be nine pounds a year!!! So what affluence I shall have for Hotel life!!! I shall like living with Katherine I am sure. Murry has a job at the W.O. [War Office]. It was strange arriving here again [...] Numerous questions at once from Clive about you, and Wales. I refrained from all enthusiasm – which you will hardly believe, and created no mysteries. Ottoline dislikes me! Rather plainly. Had a long talk with Katherine in bed this morning, she and Murry have been here for weeks.

A concert is in preparation for this evening. Great confusion. Like Clapham Junction, chairs and tables being shunted about everywhere. The performers and Pipsie at the Pianola! What an evening last night. Philip reading Boswell's life of Johnson with his own remarks freely strewn in between the passages. 'That's good, excellent', 'all this part is very dull I'll leave it out'. Clive cackling in the comfortable chair, your chair, pugs snoring, Ottoline yawning, Maria, Mademoiselle[3] and even Katherine knitting woollen counterpanes. Brett with her telephone. What a scene! I thought of you, and longed to transport it all to you, lying on your sofa with its garden, but all conversation absolutely failed. I suddenly realized I did not want to talk to her in the least. It is extraordinary being here again. They all seemed enchanted. I cannot explain it. I think I shall not wait for the concert tonight, but bicycle home after lunch. I feel so desperately lonely. Your letters gave me much pleasure [...]

By this time, Lytton and Carrington had started to talk of finding a country retreat together, to be shared with other friends for financial reasons and also for discretion. She and Barbara began to look around. Suspicions and rumours about the unlikely romance were building up.

To Lytton Strachey

Hurstbourne Tarrant
Friday morning, 8 September 1916

[...] Tomorrow I am going to look at a house near Hungerford for you. I boldly went into all the estate agents in Newbury yesterday, and enquired

1 John Sheppard was an early love of Lytton's at Cambridge.
2 Katherine Mansfield (1888–1923), born in New Zealand, had been living in London since 1908; her first collection of stories, *In a German Pension*, was published in 1911. In the same year she met her future husband, John Middleton Murry (1889–1957), editor and writer.
3 Two attractive young women, Maria Nys, from Belgium, and Juliette Baillot, known as Mademoiselle because she was French and governess to the Morrells' daughter, Julian, lived at Garsington during the war. Later both married Huxleys: Maria to Aldous and Juliette to his brother Julian.

about houses. This house is only £32 with a huge orchard four miles from Hungerford. But more anon when I have seen it. Clive is writing to you. He will share if it's near Newbury, so that he can come over from Oxford. Will you like this? Brett has taken your Garsington house. ('Her great leap.' 'The great plunge.' They are merely trying to excite our curiosity with those letters!) If you were here, and could see these downs. So lovely, you would tremble with excitement at the prospect of your little cottage. I have maps of every square inch of the country now! And correspondence with every auctioneer in Newbury, Marlborough, and Reading! There is an amazing house to let in the middle of Savernake Forest. But £70 a year! Lytton, *all* the books arrived yesterday! I was so thrilled at having John Donne again last night. Thank you very much. And for *Tom Jones* also.

Katherine is writing to you a description of the concert so I will refrain. It was full of comic incidents, and humour abounded. We wished you had been there.

Never have I seen the garden look so wonderful. A moon shining on the pond, covered with warm slime, bubbling, and fermenting underneath and great black shadows cast from the trees over it all. And inside, music and these strange villagers with their babies, and young men in hard white collars and thick serge suits. Clive sitting lost in thought on the steps. Maria in her yellow trowsers, lying, covered in a black cloak in the passage, distractedly in love with Ottoline. We acted a play. Katherine sang some songs and danced ragtimes. We talked late into the night together after it was all over in bed.

What fun we will have in Gower Street. She will play all the games I love best. Pretending to be other people and dressing up and parties! What weather. I am so full of energy that I cannot concentrate on this letter. I long to rush off and be on the downs.

Here are some photographs. I loved your long letters about your walk, and Westbury. There is great indignation at Garsington because I refrained from any excitement about our journey and merely gave a short description of the landscape! To hell with them! If one is ecstatic they accuse one of being superior and uplifted. If one is silent, and tempered, of being cryptic and exclusive! What news from Barbara about her pursuit of the cottage? [...]

My love to you
Carrington

To David Garnett

Hurstbourne Tarrant
Saturday [postmarked 14 September 1916]

Dear Bunny,

I am sorry to have taken such a long time in answering your letter.

Will you when we come to London come to dinner with me? I made a muddle about sending your letter to some wrong address and sat waiting for you to come to tea with a clean table cloth and new buns, and no Bunny [...]

Such an evening at Garsington. The d'Aranyis[1] gave a concert to all the village people. In the hall a gathering of nearly a hundred aged mothers with babies and children in red flannel dresses and white pinafores, all the labourers in those thick grey serge suits and white washed collars. It was a strange assembly to see standing round the table in that shiny red panelled room eating rock cakes!

May I come and see you in the winter with Barbara if you still stay at Wissett? We (Brett, the Murrys and I) are going to live in Maynard's house in Gower Street, the end of this month. I shall be rather glad to live in a civilized house again; the mice, and general dirt of that studio of mine in Yeoman's Row rather suffocated one. I have fine days here wandering over these downs. They are terrifyingly big, but it's rather lonely after living with such excellent company for so long. How did your poem end about the Bubble? I think I shall go back to London next week to do some work for Roger [Fry] restoring Mantegna frescoes at Hampton Court[2] and move in to Gower Street afterwards.

My love to Duncan and Vanessa and you,
Carrington

To Mark Gertler

Hurstbourne Tarrant
September 1916

Thank you indeed for the Marvel Marvell books! How glad I am to have them and your letter. It seemed so long since I had heard from you.

---

1 Jelly and Adila d'Aranyi were sisters and renowned violinists, born in Hungary but living in London since 1913.

2 Roger Fry (1886–1934), leading painter and critic of his day and close friend of the Bells and the Woolfs, was restoring the *Triumph of Caesar*, the great frescoes at Hampton Court painted by the late-fifteenth-century artist Andrea Mantegna and brought to Britain from Mantua by Charles I in 1629.

I love that poem 'To his Coy Mistress'. It is difficult to stand up against such poetic persuasion! Donne & Marvell together may bring about my fall. Who knows [...] Last Thursday evening I bicycled over to Garsington to see Brett about the house business & Katherine was there. I shared a room with her. So talked to her more than anyone else late at night in bed & early in the morning. I like her very much. It is a good thought to think upon that I shall live with them & Brett in Gower Street. For we are all going to share 3 Gower Street, as doubtless you already know. How glad I am Iris is back! She must indeed look lovely. Give her my love. What parties we shall have in Gower Street in the evenings. Katherine was full of plans. She was splendid at a concert there was at Garsington, and sang coon songs, & acted a play. It was a curious night, all very strange. I am out of favour now! completely! I do not know why – But her ladyship loves & fondles me no more! and Brett was rather severe. I got rather lonely & depressed there. Except for Katherine I should not have enjoyed it much. But she surprised me. I did not believe she would love the sort of things I do so much. Pretending to be other people & playing games [...] Maria was there. Looking rather lovely in a voluptuous way. She became morbidly depressed the evening of the concert over Ottoline, and walked about pale, with heavy eyes in the moonlight. I felt a strange desire to torment & tease her, & let her have one of her crises. As it was she felt a strange heroine with no one to notice her. I don't believe Ottoline ever noticed her mournful attitudes on the floor once!! I went out into the garden with her [...] Katherine & I wore trousers. It was wonderful being alone in the garden. Hearing the music inside, & lighted windows, and feeling like two young boys – very eager. The moon shining on the pond. Fermenting, & covered with warm slime.

How I hate being a girl. I must tell you for I have felt it so much lately. More than usual. And that night I forgot for almost half an hour in the garden, and felt other pleasures strange, & so exciting, a feeling of all the world being below me to choose from, not tied with female encumbrances, & hanging flesh.

Do you mind me saying this. What nights now! and I am alone. Closed in by these walls & hateful things – my mother and dark furniture. What would I not give to roam alone over these high downs, with the huge moon above me [...]

Clive was at Garsington and Professor Brown.[1] It seemed almost like a lunatic asylum at tea. Everybody equally enchanted. Brett is doing a huge painting of Ottoline. But not finished so I give no opinions. Barbara said she had tea with you. She has changed don't you think so, for the better.

1 Frederick Brown (1851–1941) was a painter and teacher who was Slade Professor of Art from 1893 to 1918. He was for a time romantically involved with Brett.

She was not affected any more when I stayed with her. Write to me again. If I find many more poems by Donne urging me to forsake my virginity I may fall by next spring when the sun is hot once more. I think he is a man of such rare wisdom that I take his words very seriously. Far more so, than Philip & Ottoline [...] But I ought not to write this to you as my moods vary like a sky of clouds! But my love. Carrington

May I have a Bond Street photograph?[1]

To Vanessa Bell

3 Gower Street, London
Saturday [n.d.]

Dear Vanessa,

I must write & tell you that we went and saw Charleston on Thursday. Never, never have I seen quite such a wonderful place! We sat round the pond and marvelled at it all, the house and the orchard, and the great downs behind.

This is to tell you that if you want a strong lad, or girl to cut down the overgrowth in the garden, till the vegetable beds, paint the house inside, prune the trees, plant seeds or any other occupation – Barbara & I are willing (or move your furniture for you), we would work very hard for you, & sleep in a loft in some hay over the kitchen up some back stairs –

I will admit to you frankly that I am distractly [*sic*] enamoured with a boy on Tracey's farm who milks the cows! N.B. do not tell Duncan of him & no account the vile wretch Lytton.

A charming old hag came, & asked us to tell you that her daughter wanted a situation, & that she would speak to you of her when you came down – what excellent things there will be to paint in that garden with the pond & buildings.

We are telling nobody about the glories of Charleston. So you will not mind us having seen it will you?

Our search for a house for Lytton was rather a failure. As after seeing Asheham, & Charleston, it was difficult to be satisfied with the curious erections the Lewes agents sent us to inspect.

I am taking some relics of Duncan's round to Gordon Square this evening. And two old chairs of mine. I thought you perhaps like them for the garden.

May I come & see you when you come back to London this time if you are not too busy?

1 Gertler had been professionally photographed.

Did you notice the very exquisite fireplaces in the upstairs rooms? Bunny said you never told them a bit of all its wonders! And that you called the pond rectangular – did you see it had a punt on it?

Bunny has already seized most of the pantries, and all the possible positions where one would like to lie under the trees for his bees!

My love to Duncan.

Yrs affectionately

Carrington

David Garnett, Barbara and Carrington had been over to inspect Charleston, a farmhouse near Lewes in Sussex, ahead of the Bells' move there, having spent the night before at Asheham, without the Woolfs' permission. They had eaten some apples, borrowed a book, found sheets, made up one bed and all slept in it together. The Woolfs were not pleased.

The next letter probably marks the moment when Carrington finally went to bed with Gertler. Her decision coincided with the publication of Gilbert Cannan's novel Mendel, with its overheated portrayal of a girl who drives her intense Jewish lover nearly mad by refusing to sleep with him. Sex with Gertler turned out to be a sad disappointment to them both. She found contraception humiliating and difficult and his demands excessive. Such difficulties did not arise with Lytton.

To Mark Gertler

3 Gower Street
1 November 1916

Dear Mark,

I am sorry not to see your sculpture before next week. But I am glad you have got it back to work on. I am afraid I hurt you the other night. Do not think about it anymore. It will probably be alright of itself. Let us not talk of it more. As it's getting almost preposterous in size and importance. Which isn't true really. It doesn't count for as much as all that even to you [...]

How angry I am over Gilbert's book! Everywhere this confounded gossip & servant-like curiosity. It's ugly & so damned vulgar. People cannot be vulgar over a work of art, so it is Gilbert's fault for writing as he did.

I am going to paint two portraits soon. One today & one tomorrow. I am losing hope rather of Teddy.[1] It's beginning to depress me terribly sometimes [...]

I hope you are happy. You <u>must</u> be. It's absurd really the way we both go on. It's my main reason for having done with it, & coming to you. Simply because it's ridiculous to talk so much about it, when it doesn't count for anything [...]

Good bye,
Carrington

To Mark Gertler

3 Gower Street
[n.d.]

[...] I scribble pictures of myself in the looking glass in my drawing book. What a dull show today! If you come tomorrow evening do not ask me about that and please do not make love to me. Leave it all until we go to the country as it distresses me sometimes rather. It's wonderful being alone up so high by myself. I wish sometimes I could bolt the door and live in here for days and days and not get disturbed by all the outside world of people [...] Goodnight Carrington

---

1 Her brother Teddy, after first serving in the navy, had transferred to the Wiltshire Regiment where his older brother Sam and younger brother Noel had been serving since 1914. He had been reported missing since the Battle of the Somme in the summer.

I wonder what you are talking to
Miss Berry about now. In
front y the fire , with that light
on your faces
Well I must return to my
candlesticks. & leave off
wondering about all these
things. & you .
        Goodnight .
Zoch unless you have a wife
                    Carrington

To Mark Gertler

3 Gower Street
Saturday, December 1916

Dear Mark,

[...] I read Marlowe again last night and knew what one thing meant more than I did last week! It certainly is a necessity if one wants to understand the best poets. No she's not going on to say that is *why* she takes sugar in her coffee now. But taking sugar incidentally does make one appreciate those poets more fully. But I only like sugar some times, not every week and every day in my coffee. I think you would like it so much and take it so often in your coffee that you wouldn't taste anything in time, and miss the taste of the coffee. But darling I shall look after that alright and only allow you three lumps a month. You've had more than three for this month. So no more till next year, you sugar eater you!

Goodbye then till Tuesday evening
Yr periwinkle
Crinkle Crinkle

To Mark Gertler

Hurstbourne Tarrant
Saturday, December 1916

Dear Mark,

[...] Today it is snowing white, and a piercing wind. But I love the hugeness of it. The great space between one and the hills opposite, after the houses in Gower Street which press against my very nose, on every side. The irregular shapes of the sky and hills are a joy after the square shapes of London houses and square slits of sky. I am sorry if I have annoyed you lately about that business and making such a fuss. It is only my inability to really get interested I am afraid and really I did try that thing. Only it was much too big, and wouldn't go inside no matter what way I used it! But I won't be so childish any longer [...]

Are you working again yet? I am so excited about my painting now. I want to do nothing else all day long. Today I shall go for a long walk over the Downs. But it is cold. Almost too cold out to be really happy [...]

1917

As she did not tell Gertler, it was during the autumn and winter of 1916/17 that Carrington completed one of her best paintings, her delicate, loving portrait of Lytton, head and shoulders in profile, propped on cushions on a sofa under a red rug, his spectacles on his nose, his beard softly auburn, a book in his pale slender hands. On New Year's Day 1917 she wrote in her diary:

I wonder what you will think of it when you see it. I sit here, almost every night it sometimes seems, looking at your picture, now tonight it looks wonderfully good and I am happy. But then I dread showing it. I should like to go on always painting you every week, wasting the afternoon loitering, and never showing you what I paint. It's marvellous having it all to oneself. No agony of the soul. Is it vanity? No, because I don't care for what they say. I hate only the indecency of showing them what I have loved [...]

I would love to explore your mind behind your finely skinned forehead. You seem so wise and very coldly old. Yet in spite of this what a peace to be with you, and how happy I was today.

There is no record of what Lytton thought of the portrait.

During the winter of 1916 to 1917 Carrington was writing regularly to her brother Noel, with his regiment in France. Her letters were affectionate and teasing, frequently contained grumbles about their parents and occasionally pleas for a loan. She was often short of money.

To Noel Carrington

3 Gower Street
[n.d.]

Dearest Noel,
   I am up a gum tree as the debts close in about me and next week on the 14th we have to move from here and I have no where withal.
   Dear brother hearken unto my prayer
prayer
Least [*sic*] I be
utterly
consumed

3 Gower Street
W.C.1.

Dearest Noel

I am up a

a gum
tree

I swear faithfully I am making earnest attempts now to earn the bright sovereigns & give up my profligate life. Oh Saint Lewis hearken upon my supplications.

The next amount of Bills is £8.10. But I swear the golden day will come when all will be returned to you.

Miserably your sister Dora

To Noel Carrington

3 Gower Street
Tuesday [n.d.]

Dearest Noel,

[...] Thank you so much for the cheque it was indeed useful as Brett has decamped to Garsington, & all is left to me & my purse.

Well you require a brief summary of my affairs de Coeur, & my doings in this city [...] I went to tea with the Johns' yesterday, Sunday I mean, with old Lytton, & the great man showed me some awfully good drawings, & gave me one! When you come home I will take you to tea with him, you would like his work I think. Lytton has been reading me *Julius Caesar* in the evenings lately, which we have now finished. I did like it. We are now going to do *Antony & Cleopatra*. I started a painting of the little man Saxon-Turner² who came with us to Sussex, Barbara's devoted swain. He is one of the most classical mortals who ever stept on god's earth, & reads Lucretius. & the ancients. You would like him I think. For his learning is great & yet unostentatious withal. Roger Fry has started a club in Fitzroy Square called the Omega Club³, of which I was elected a member. It has no advantages except a meeting once a week in his big rooms, & the pleasure of taking 2 friends [...] The first meeting was on Saturday evening.

But such controversies ensued. One Clive Bell by name making many complications by asking idiotic questions, & losing his temper on being snubbed. But it was fairly interesting as people like Maynard Keynes of the Treasury give one the Government Gossip & it's pleasant seeing people again sometimes.

1 Augustus John (1878–1961), painter, had been married to his first wife, Ida, by whom he had five children, until her death in 1907. He was by ths time living with Dorelia, by whom he had two further children; she was a friend of Ida's and his mistress since 1904.
2 Saxon Sydney-Turner (1880–1962), another friend of Lytton's from Cambridge, a classicist who worked in the Treasury all his life. In love with Barbara Hiles, he remained devoted to her after her marriage to Nick Bagenal.
3 The Omega Workshop was set up by Roger Fry, Duncan Grant and Vanessa Bell in 1913 in Fitzroy Square, London, to dissolve the division between the fine and decorative arts and enable artists to design and sell their own work, including furniture, textiles and pottery. As well as woodcuts for the Hogarth Press, Carrington designed tiles and public house signs through The Omega Workshop.

I've been put on some charity at Chelsea Palace, on the Executive
Committee with all the nuts. Yesterday I had to go to Lady Ian Hamilton's
to a meeting. Heavens! They are fumblers & muddle headed idiots. So I
soon up & spoke with my usual intelligence & greatly impressed them with
my vast understanding!

I send you a programme [...] There is going to be a 'John' Beauty Chorus,
Bloomsbury chorus & caricatures of all the old Chelsea people, Whistler
etc. Carlyle, & then again, all the moderns, Lady Ottoline, etc. & all the
great actors leaping about. Barbara & I are going to walk the Plank just for
fun – & not sing! What have you been reading lately?

I will try & send you some more papers soon.

Mother sent me snowdrops from Hurstbourne today, which made me
rather long to fly away down there. Write to me again soon. I've been rather
wretched lately. I find it hard not to get miserable over Teddy. As I am now
certain he cannot be alive [...]

Goodbye little brother

Much love & my blessing, Dora

Along with some forty other artistically inclined and well-connected young women,
including Brett and Barbara, Carrington was in the Beauty Chorus (for which she
had designed gypsyish costumes made by the Omega Workshops) for the finale of
the show at the Chelsea Palace Theatre on 20 March 1917, singing:

> John! John!
> How he's got on!
> He owes it, he knows it, to me!
> Brass earings I wear
> And I don't do my hair
> And my feet are as bare as can be;
> When I walk down the street
> All the people I meet
> They stare at the things I have on!
> When Battersea-Parking
> You'll hear folks remarking:
> There goes an Augustus John!

To Noel Carrington

c/o [illegible] Home Farm, Welcombe, Bude, Cornwall
[n.d. spring 1917?]

Dearest Noel,

I've not heard from you this week. But I daresay unlike me you are hard at work. So I therefore write you a letter, to while away your business hours & cast a ray of pleasure into the dreary darkness of the G. H. Q. Rouen ...

I do wish these idiots like Winston Churchill wouldn't make these speeches against peace, when people are just at some decent negotiations with Germany.

Kerensky[1] seems to have been a dirty villain after all. What a corrupt business all that Russian officialism is. Even the pseudo democratics are really as bad as Roman Caesars working for their own ends & caring nothing for the butchery of hundreds in the mean time. It's a bit ironical saying we must have reprisals in order to give the Germans in Germany a taste of war, & what it means. When for two years we have starved them so successfully that it's appalling the state of poverty & hunger of the lower classes, & their lack of food, and as if the logic of giving people back what they give you had any effect. We give the German soldiers back underground explosions, gas fumes, hand grenades & every horror that they give us & yet it has not altered their state of mind. What idiots these political people are. If one really believes it is brutal to kill non combatants, & women, well then we ought to try & guard our towns efficiently & let alone the populace of Germany. But I doubt if you agree. I've no general news as it's so remote down here. I'm getting on with my painting every day. Shall I try & send you some cream? Please write to me again soon. I shall go back to HBT [Hurstbourne Tarrant] on my way to London I expect. I hope you keep well & haven't got any chills. The waves yesterday were terrific yesterday with the wind, a grand sight. My progress with the History of Gibbon progresses slowly.

This letter to her brother shows that for all her usual detachment from the war and politics, Carrington's views by this time were clear, deeply felt and in tune with Lytton Strachey's. He loathed the war from the start, believed the right course was to work for peace and applied for exemption from military service for himself on health grounds. He was granted temporary exemption in April 1916. After some early confusion and hesitation, Bloomsbury became almost entirely pacifist as the war went on.

1 Alexander Kerensky (1881–1970) was a leading member of the Socialist opposition to the tsarist regime in Russia and was to play a leading part in the Revolution of February 1917. Briefly prime minister before Lenin and the Bolsheviks took over in October 1917, he supported Russia's involvement in the war.

To Noel Carrington

3 Gower Street
Sunday afternoon tout seul! [n.d.]

Dearest Noel,

[...] Last Monday Augustus John gave a party. We all went. It was great fun. And I enjoyed myself very much. Dancing vigorously. Last Wed. Mrs Gough [?] gave another party. And it was even better. Alix Sargant Florence[1] (who I've painted a portrait of) lent me a topping Cossack dress and I was Belle of the Ball! Had great fun with Augustus John who fell completely to my charms. Also the great Horace Cole,[2] of London fame. Besides lesser members of the army! I wish the dress belonged to me. I think I shall make myself one, si possible.

Last Wed. Lytton's little nephew and niece came up to London. So I had them to lunch here, and then we went to Maskelyne and Cook's Mystery show. It was rather good. Some fearfully comic conjuring, and some wily young officers went up out of the audience to try and explore his horrid mystery – But with all their wiliness they were 'done'.

Do write to me soon again please. I should like an engraving of Moliere if you see one, or Madame du Chatelet in particular, Voltaire's friend. Please. I will write again soon.

Yrs affect. Doric

1 Alix Sargant-Florence (1892–1973) was the daughter of an American musician and a British painter, who studied briefly at the Slade before going to Cambridge.
2 Horace de Vere Cole (1881–1936) was a rich Irish eccentric famous for practical jokes, notably the Dreadnought Hoax of 1910 when he fooled a naval captain into entertaining a group of his friends (including Virginia Woolf) dressed up as Abyssinians. His second wife, Mavis, later had a son by Augustus John.

Alix Sargant-Florence had been a lover of David Garnett and was now pursuing Lytton Strachey's brother, James. After the Gower Street ménage broke up, she and Carrington shared a flat for a time in Soho and became very close friends. Meanwhile Gertler was becoming more and more suspicious and unhappy about the relationship between Carrington and Lytton; she realised she ought to bring their tormented love affair to an end. As she recorded in her diary on 13 April, they met at his Hampstead studio and had a painfully difficult talk.

I became more and more wretched and wept [...] I suddenly looked back at the long life we had had between us of mixed emotions but always warm, because of his intense love, and now I had to leave it all and go away [...] His loneliness was awful [...] He didn't talk much, hardly at all about Lytton; only '– Will you live with him?' 'No.' 'But he may love you.' 'No, he will not.' That I thought made it easier a little. He begged to be still friends and see me. But we both knew it could not be so and it was separation [...] How very much I cared for him suddenly came upon me. The unreality, and coldness, of Lytton.

Later that evening, she talked to Lytton and recorded their exchange.

I thought I had better tell Mark as it was so difficult going on.
Tell him what?
That it couldn't go on. So I just wrote and said it.
What did you say in your letter?
I thought you knew.
What do you mean?
I said that I was in love with you. I hope you don't mind very much.
But aren't you being rather Romantic and are you certain?
There's nothing Romantic about it.
What did Mark say?
He was terribly upset.
Did he seem angry with me?
No. He didn't mention you.
But it's too incongruous. I'm so old and diseased. I wish I was more able.
That doesn't matter.
What do you mean? What do you think we had better do about the physical?
Oh I don't mind about that.
That's rather bad. You should. I thought you did care. What about those
    boys, when you were young?
Oh that was just being young. Nothing.
But do you mind me being rather physically attracted?
I don't think you are really.

Why? Because of your sex?

Yes partly. I don't blame you. I knew it long ago and went into it
    deliberately ...

[...]

Then he sat on the floor with me and clasped my hands in his and let
me kiss his mouth, all enmeshed in the brittle beard and my inside was
as heavy as lead as I knew how miserable it was going to be.

You will not mind spoiling me? Just this once tonight?

Why are you so chaste?

And then I knew that he would soon go.

The misery at parting and my hatred of myself for caring so much. And
at his callousness. He was so wise and just. Then he left and I went down
later and talked long into the night with Alix. But there was no consolation. Still it was good to be able to talk of it.

*Despite deciding to part for ever, she met Gertler the next day and told him of
her talk with Lytton. Gertler told her he never wanted to see her again, adding,
'To think that after all these years you would love a man like Strachey twice your
age and emaciated and old.'*

*Carrington went back to Gower Street and Alix, feeling 'as if my nose had been
cut away'. She wrote to Gertler asking him not to tell all their friends. Their affair,
and their letters, limped on.*

To Noel Carrington

60 Frith Street, Soho W.
[n.d. spring 1917?]

My Dearest Noel,

[...] We moved here a week ago. And a very comfortable little home it
is. Only rather noisy but an excellent housekeeper looks after us, & cooks.
I have a bed sitting room, & a bathroom ajoining it.

Alix occupies a big sitting room & a kitchen, & small bed room on her
floor. But I can use the upstairs rooms also. The walls are rather decently
handled only a vile green paint over everything. But it's decent being so near
the restaurants. & not having to bother about tramping miles to find a snack
to eat. Like old Gower Street.

I am quite well & trust you are the same. I spent last weekend at
Garsington where I had not been since Xmas. The Lady Ottoline was quite
decent & rather kindly. Madmoiselle who no doubt you have forgotten
was still there, a rosebud of virtue. The Ex P.M. [Asquith] & MacKenna

with their wives came over on Sunday so I talked to the Ex P.M. & instructed him into the mysteries of what constituted a good painting.[1]

Mrs Mac was very pretty & young. But old MacKenna looked a rascal I thought and the Ex P.M. like a leery old grocer. I could write much on my indignation at such men controlling our country. But I will refrain [...]

Paul Nash is having a show of pictures which he drew at the front & sold quite a number the first day. Roger Fry gave me an order for a wood block for a book which I shall do this weekend. And next week I am going to paint a portrait of a Russian Poet, a Huzzar who I met last week.

Your affec sister Doric

During the late spring of 1917 Lytton moved in with Carrington in Frith Street for a brief period while Alix was away. She wrote about this time with him to Barbara Hiles, but these letters have been impossible to trace; Michael Holroyd copied some very brief extracts from them during his research for his biography of Strachey. These notes are included in Holroyd's archive in the British Library.

To Barbara Hiles

60 Frith Street
[n.d. May/June?]

Lytton has been living with me this last week here since Wednesday. He went on Saturday evening to Durbins.[2] So I am still so happy that I thought I would write to you. Just to inform you that I've never been so happy in my life before [...] It was fun persuading Mrs Reekes, my housekeeper, that Lytton was my uncle. But I think the general uproar that went on in the early morning in his room rather upset her belief in me!

To Barbara Hiles

60 Frith Street
[n.d. May/June?]

You must not think I am unhappy. For I am often very happy only it is just that I cannot bear sometimes not seeing him even for a day.

1 Asquith had been ousted as prime minister in favour of Lloyd George in 1916. Married to the formidable Margot, he was famously susceptible to young women. Reginald MacKenna was Home Secretary and Chancellor of the Exchequer under Asquith.
2 Roger Fry's house in Surrey.

[...] If it is fine I am going for a jaunt next week to Cambridge with him. Barbara I am so excited [...]

To Noel Carrington

6 King's Parade, Cambridge
Saturday [summer 1917]

[...] Lytton came here on Wed, to stay with a fellow at Trinity, & asked me to come & stay also if I liked, which as I did like, I came. So he met me at the station & then proceeded with a second's delay to pilot me over this city & all the colleges. I fear I am wavering a little in my affections to that past love of mine Oxford. Oh ever inconstant woman [...] All Thurs I saw colleges. On Friday had a lovely picnic in Norton's rooms & then explored more colleges with Lytton, & Fitz William Museum. In the afternoon walked to Granchester to see the Rectory where Rupert Brooke used to live, & had tea in a lovely old orchard by the little River. Walked back by way of Newnham and went & saw Lytton's sister¹ who is a Don there. Some contrast after the Cambridge College with their heavy oak ceilings, & general dinginess. The new buildings of Newnham with lovely little rosebuds of maidens in muslin frocks skipping about, & prattling. A few bottle-nosed bespectacled, blotched females of the suffragette style. But most of them very endearing creatures. Lytton's sister was just giving one of the Rosebuds a lecture when we burst in! Then we had a grand spread at the Red Lion.

I must say the officers training corps here, en passant, as they flood all the eating places, are the most vulgar, ill-bred, pimps that you ever saw. Also most of them about 38, very stout, & obviously ex-butchers! Then we walked in the gardens belonging to Trinity & read in his rooms [...] I am having lunch tomorrow at Christs & in the afternoon teaing with the Female Dons of Newnham who incidently terrify me much more than any male Dons!

I have enjoyed being here. Crikie what an idiot one was all these years never to do what one wanted to do just because of mother! How easy it is to come & stay away. When I get back I am going to work solidly. I admit I've been rioting rather much of late. So save your wind & don't read me a moral lecture [...] Dear, I wish you had been here. These

---

1 Pernel Strachey (1876–1951) taught French at Newnham, where she became principal in 1927.

creatures are very nice, but sometimes very old & crabbed. Especially
when I want to go a long row on the river! What are you reading? My
love to you dear.

Yr affect sister Dora

To Lytton Strachey

60 Frith Street
Friday, 10 August 1917

Dearest Lytton,

[...] How blessed it was to see you again yesterday. I woke up this
morning and found it difficult to believe. I *was* grieved about the spectacles and now I feel it will always happen until in the end you will forbid
all advances! Hours were spent in front of the glass last night strapping
the locks back, and trying to persuade myself that two cheeks like turnips
on the top of a hoe bore some resemblance to a very well nourished
youth of sixteen. It's an alarming spectacle seeing one's self side view. I
hardly ever have before. But, dear, promise you'll come even with a female

Page for a companion. I think those cursed military authorities make the other rather more difficult, as the life of a village policeman is so dreary, that the sight of a fat cheeked Boy and German Bearded spy would throw him into a spasm of alertness and bring up all this stupidity surging into his gullet.

I hope you were not wrecked after yesterday's exertions [...]

James [Strachey] stayed, and conversed into the late night. He is your only serious rival you must know!

But the probability of us both being arrested the first night, you, for the *offence* that I am not a disguised female, and me for the offence that I *am*! But one might find out first whether it is a criminal offence!

My love to you and write today please.

Yr loving Carrington

Carrington and Lytton were planning another walk together, perhaps with her dressed as a boy, a game they both enjoyed. Meanwhile she had been asked by the Woolfs to design some woodcuts for their new venture, the Hogarth Press, which they set up in 1917 in the dining room of their house in Richmond.

To Virginia Woolf

60 Frith Street
Wednesday, August 1917

Dear Virginia,

This is really an answer to Leonard's letter, only addressed to you because I want to ask you if I might come a day or two, just before the 23rd to stay with you, or in the cottage with Willie, or the hay rick, if your house is overcrowded? as I am going to stay with the Charleston People on the 23rd. But it does not matter really. Thank Leonard for his instructions re the Lettering. I will try some soon. The man Lawrence who cuts my wood will get the size exact. Alix has just been in here on her way to you today – I have been painting hard all this week in Chelsea and not seen anything of the world. Except on Bank holiday when I went on the Heath, and rushed up and down in swing boats and round on the whirly-gigs.

Next week my brother is getting leave, so I am going on a walking expedition with him. We are rather vague as to what part of England to explore. I am in favour of the Berkshire Downs. Barbara is just back from Charleston. I am going to cut you some paper cover designs on linoleum, which is easy to cut, and cheap. Don't you miss your printing very much?[1] There is a press just opposite us in Frith Street. I love watching the men and small boy apprentices setting up the type, and printing off with marvellously rapidity on the sheets of paper. I hope you are well. Please remember me to Leonard.

Yrs affect,
Carrington

To Lytton Strachey

Hurstbourne Tarrant
Thursday, 6 o'ck [18 October 1917]

And you are sitting in your room, toasting your feet in front of an empty grate, surrounded by your legions of paper knights and horsemen. Oh it's wretched having lost you and not to have you tonight to talk to. Dearest Lytton I can never thank you enough for these weeks. I did not realize how happy I had been until this evening. It's strangely beautiful here with the drooping beech trees and apples lying in the wet grass – But more melancholy and autumnal than a graveyard. If you were only here, and so many wishes. You have spoilt me far too long and now I feel as if suddenly I had walked into a greenhouse in the winter. For in the paper I saw the first thing on the red clothed table when I came in, Teddy's death. It was a year ago and now they announce it officially. It's rather worse being here with all his books and things about, and where I saw him last and the remoteness of my parents. Forgive me for writing but I wanted you so badly. One is not even left alone to cry. Dearest Lytton I love you so much.

Carrington

Cast down by the official announcement of her brother's death, Carrington was also unnerved by a letter from Mark Gertler: 'I am afraid that your passion for LS estranges me more and more from you. I can't stomach it at all. It's poisoning my feelings and belief in you.' She instantly set about reeling him in, while continuing the search for a house to share with Lytton in the country. Under the impression it was a joint venture with Barbara, her mother drew her attention to some promising particulars.

---

1 The Woolfs were away on holiday.

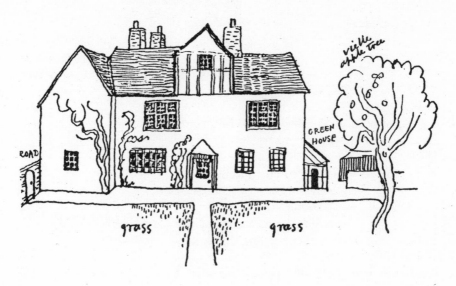

To Lytton Strachey

> Hurstbourne Tarrant, 1 mile from Pangbourne
> Friday morning [19 October 1917]

      The Mill House, Tidmarsh
Old fashioned House.
grounds over 1 acre small orchard
Hall, 3 recpt rooms, kitchen etc.
Electric Light. 6 bedrooms, boxroom.
Bath H & C
Rent £52 3 years lease.
Nr. Church & P.O. London 65 mins.

Mother gave it to me with an order to view which she had received. I've just telephoned the agents and it's still to let, so will go over tomorrow and see it. Sounds too good to be alright! Will look at Peasemore and Stanmore en route ...

    Please write soon.

    Mopsa

To Lytton Strachey

Tea shop, Newbury
Friday, 3 o'ck [Saturday, 20 October 1917]

Dear,

I've just been to all three houses. But Tidmarsh Mill it is to be. It's very romantic and lovely.

> Vast Big rooms, 3 in number,
> 2 Very big bedrooms and 4 others,
> Bathroom; water closet;
> very good garden and a shady grass lawn
> with river running through it.

The house is very old with gables and some lattice windows. It is joining on to the Mill. A charming miller showed me over it. Very well built in good condition. The miller said one could get people, old hags from village. More apple trees, fruit trees, vegetables. 2 miles from Theale Station 1 mile Pangbourne [...] Oliver[1] etc must go and see Tidmarsh on Tuesday. Electric light in every room. I'm wildly excited. Hooray!

Will write again in detail.

Carrington

Backview Of Mill
from orchard garden

---

1 Lytton's brother Oliver Strachey had worked as a civil servant in India but was now a leading cryptographer working in Military Intelligence.

To Mark Gertler

60 Frith Street
Thursday [October 1917]

I was glad to hear from you. Last night I had dinner with Monty and had a long talk with him. And he told me about your pictures, and how that you were happier. Lawrence and Koteliansky[1] came in also later. Good old Kot! How charming he is. Lawrence was in a great state at being expelled from Cornwall, and obviously could think and talk of nothing else and had a great contempt for Monty and the world in general. Afterwards I went back to Gordon Square where I am staying as Frith Street is too awful and Alix was in occupation in my room. But she didn't like being there alone because of the raids[2] so came to Gordon Square also. At 11.30 a raid started, and went on till 2.30. We sat downstairs with the maids. Alix's heart is so bad, I was rather nervous about her. She was obviously very ill, and frightened. Maynard lay in bed upstairs, and went to sleep and never moved! An extraordinary man!

[...] London's a beastly place after the country, crowded with hideous people, prostitutes, and debased soldiers, and so grey and gloomy, and then the beauty of the night torn to pieces by these guns and bombs. I long to rush away! And envy you your retreat, and good Brett by your side. Ruth [Selby-Bigge, formerly Humphries][3] is in London, but so occupied I can't get her although I telephone 6 times a day! Thus is one treated by one's ancient loves! Poor Monty was very sad without you, and glad to have me to talk to I think about you. What a nice person he is. I can't write you a long letter about myself for I've such a bad head and feel so sleepy, and in a few minutes I've got to go, and teach that little brute of a Joan Laking.[4] But dear I'm so glad to know you are friendly. Of course I am!

Love Carrington

---

1 S. S. Koteliansky (1880–1955) was a Russian Jewish translator who moved to London in 1911 where he became friends with the Woolfs, D. H. Lawrence, Katherine Mansfield and Mark Gertler.
2 In 1917, the Zeppelin airships that had been bombing Britain since 1915 were joined by planes and the raids intensified. London was bombed in October.
3 A close friend from the Slade.
4 A girl of seventeen who was trying to learn to paint. Carrington took on such work with reluctance.

To Mark Gertler

Hurstbourne Tarrant
Sunday afternoon [November 1917]

Dearest Mark,

[...] No, I'm not going away with Lytton! But my people are leaving Hampshire, and are going to live in a town, Cheltenham. So I've got to go home for a little while, when they move to help them and take away my goods and furniture.

Then I'll be back again in London all the winter I expect. It will be good to see you tomorrow. I am going to do Jack Hutchinson a wood block now. Ruth is impossible to see. Is not it maddening, a whole week and she can't find a minute to come to me! UGH! as the book says. The devil take her relations and Government work which she does in her folly.

Carrington

To Lytton Strachey

60 Frith Street
Friday, 1 o'ck [9 November 1917]

Dearest Lytton,

They tell me you are to be in bed all today. Oh wretched day! most vile day! Now everything is ruined. The gay clouds in the blue sky which I thought we would be under on the Heath this afternoon. May they turn to rain and keep me company in the gloom.

Never again are you going to behave like this! After November you will start a regular life at Tidmarsh, supported by glasses of milk, and vigorous walks [...]

If you are not well enough you won't travel tomorrow and get worse will you? And *your* SANATOGEN if you please at once.

I've caught your COLD you wretch. But the diseases are so manifold that attack this poor human frame, that this latest acquisition almost passes unnoticed. Just had lunch with Oliver at his club. Very ormolu. Beautiful curry. Surrounded by generals and Viceroys of India on the walls. Took him to Omega and London Group afterwards.

Faith has promised us two BEDS for TidderMarsh, and we are going to buy up all the Omega club crockery and chairs and Oliver has signed the lease!!!!!

Do get sprightly SOON and appear before me clad in your gay new clothes with your beard, waving like an aspen in the Breeze.

Your Pollypuss Mopsa

waving like
an aspen in the
Beeze
Your PoLLYPUSS MOPSA

To Lytton Strachey

Monty's room
November 1917

Lytton Dear,

I hope you are better now. I have just had dinner with Mark. He is so charming and gay. Full of news of Shandygaff [Garsington] – What a day! Alix with the winds of Charleston. Then teaching that petit bete – Brett to tea at Frith Street shrieking at the tops of our voices, a thousand accusations!!! But she too is delightful. Then I went in to Tilney Street for a brief while. And found Ottoline talking to a professional pearl-stringer. The gossip!!! 'But surely the duchess of Ripon had black pearls?' 'But Lady Meux she had the finest pearls I ever strung ... she said as how she'd leave me her money. But she didn't. Her maid had forty thousand pounds ... Her name was the same as mine. Barnes ... She came off the streets before she married Lord Meux!!!' Ottoline absorbed in the pearly stories of all these old hags, and their past histories. – But she looked very wonderful. Ottoline in various huge hats which she tried on to show me.

I told her about Tidmarsh vaguely – But put my foot in it slightly over a trivial matter as usual! [...]
Dear dear old yahoo I wish I could have you here now xxxxxxx
Love from your Mopsa

To Lytton Strachey

Hurstbourne Tarrant
Sunday morning [18 November 1917]

[...] This country is looking divine now. I saw a Heron standing by a lonely pond, as I came along the road, and the Downs stood up terrificallly high enveloped in mists in the distance. I've been wandering about the house and garden on a grand looting expedition all the morning. I think by Wednesday a fair collection of salvage ought to be amassed!

My mother is of course frightfully stingy when it comes to the point of giving me anything useful. And she sold to a dealer the only two things I really cared for. A very old Japanese china candlestick 14 cent. and a 18 cent. English silk embroidered picture of a bird.

I found in a stable some water-cans and jugs which will be useful. And I've got free permission to devastate the garden and green house of trees and plants – But it's rather sad leaving this place. The view from the window now that the trees are bare, is lovely. One can see right up the valley and the ridge of the hill opposite stands up hard and sharp like the backbone of a whale [...] I see by the smoke from the thatched chimney that the old man is making malt in the brewhouse just outside the back gate, so I shall go, and toast over his furnace, and gossip about the village with him [...]

Everything is just the same, even to the conversations of my parents. Even the apples lie on the grass only they are decayed, dark brown, like garrulous old men, and only a few virgin green maidens lie at their sides. The paths are thick with leaves. A few gnats in the air. Not a sign of a bird or a sound from the hills – I perceive this letter is verging towards the senti-mental. New paragraph.

How is your system? If I had the courage I would ask my mother for a number of bed pans and a commode which lie in the box room upstairs. But perhaps it would hardly be tactful. It is exciting about your Book of Lives. Will the Preface be finished by the time I come back?[1] May I have you next Sat. and Sunday? Please start taking your sanatogen instantly. I will send the grey muffler tomorrow and please get well soon. How I wish I could

---

1 *Eminent Victorians* was to be published the following year.

Heading for the Slade: self-portrait,
aged seventeen, 1910

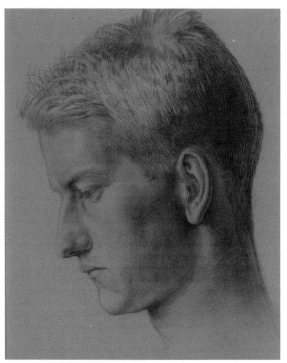

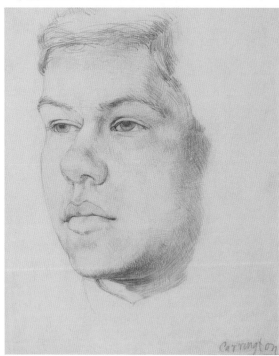

Carrington

Her younger brother and ally, Noel,
1912, and her much loved sailor
brother, Teddy, in 1915, the year
before he was killed

Girl in a blue dress: Carrington by
Mark Gertler, 1912

Mark Gertler, her passionate admirer,
by Carrington, *c.* 1912

Her close friend from
the Slade, Christine
Kuhlenthal, 1919

The 'Cropheads': Carrington,
Barbara Hiles (later Bagenal)
and Dorothy Brett, 1912

The Slade School
Picnic, 1912. Front row
from the left: Carrington,
Barbara Hiles, Richard
Nevinson and Mark Gertler

transport you here now and this second, to take you with me for a walk over the hill. Dearest Lytton. You ought to be a little happy, as I love you so entirely.

Your Mopsa xxxxxxx

PS Monday morning
The looting expedition progresses with unexpected success. An oak coffer and small gate legged table has been added to the collection, and a camp-bed! I have dug up a great many bulbs and roots to put in the garden. Did you see Brett's big picture! Please tell me what you thought of it. I shall go over on Thursday to Tiddermarsh and try and interview the old hag, and Percy or Patrick as you will.

More Love Mopsa

To Mark Gertler

Hurstbourne Tarrant
Wednesday, 19 November 1917

Dearest Mark,

Thank you for your letter it came this morning & made me die nine little deaths from various causes! I was sorry about Saturday. There was nothing mysterious about my depression. I had hardly slept all night. I had angered Alix for the first time since I saw her and was depressed over myself as a human being. But I was even sorrier to like you & your work so much & hardly be able to do anything but sit like a poached egg on your blue chair [...]

About James. Well, Well. We all have a mood of aloofness. He evidently more often than most of us! He's not bad at heart, that I guarantee from personal knowledge this summer, and as Alix loves him he can't be as bad as all that, & since she does you must forgive. I often when I'm thoroughly depressed, comfort myself that if you love me I can't be quite hopeless! I am so tired after packing up my belongings & sending them off all today. But I went for a drive along some beautiful country this afternoon. Vast woods, & the downs were salmon pink with the sunset reflections, & the sky ink blue behind! I have never seen such a sight. My mother is more aggravating than ever – the sordidness of her life & the lives of all these people who live in these neat little houses with closed windows. I'm off tomorrow morning at 7 o'ck on my bicycle, to go over to the Mill House, I told you of, near Reading that Oliver S has taken. It's lovely to think of a whole day away from my mother. I wish you could have been here sometime

with me. Later you must come & I'll show you this landscape which I love
almost passionately [...]

The little white dog here is going to have puppies in a few days. How I
loathe the spectacle of fecundity! It's so absurd.

Will you write to me, a long letter about yourself? this isn't a very good
one. It's but a bait to catch a fish from you [...] They still snore ... How
dreadful old age must be, to be so bored, or weary, that one can sleep away
an afternoon. I've been so grateful for your companionship since you came
back. It's made a difference, and I care very much for you. Love.

Yrs affec.

Carrington

To Lytton Strachey

Hurstbourne Tarrant
Tuesday afternoon [20 November 1917]

Quelle Joie! At last it is all packed. Without the heavy looting having been
discovered. But the escapes have been as narrow as the way to Heaven.
Everything is packed with apples and artichokes and potatoes, instead of
straw and paper! This method will probably insure all the china being
smashed. But anyway the food supply is guaranteed for some months!!

I have been given as a present a big wheel-back chair. But you hate those
articles I remember. I have also a huge sack of plants, and bulbs for the
garden and some carnations in pots for the greenery-house. Pots of jam,
and a big bottle of cherry brandy! Are you getting a little cheerful now old
Yahoo at the prospect of Tidmarsh complete with potatoes on the hob by
Christmas? ... I will write again on Thursday evening after I have seen Patrick
Stone and the old hag.

Please write to me soon. It seems a desperately long time since I last saw
you. The collection of baggage even includes malt extract for you – and
mosquito lotion for when you sit with Patrick conversing over Egyptian
Flour Mills under the Yew Tree next summer – also a Gurkha dagger to
keep hostile forces at bay. It's dreadfully exciting really after these years of
conversation, moving at last! Probably I shall find on Thursday the Mill was
a mirage and the evil faced carrier will be sitting there in the road on my
boxes eating the apples and drinking the malt extract. I hope you are keeping
well.

Dear, I send you my Love

Yr Mopsa

By the end of 1917 Carrington had managed the acqusition of the Mill House, started to decorate and furnish it and found local domestic help. The Tidmarsh venture was underwritten by Maynard Keynes, Harry Norton and Saxon Sydney-Turner as well as Oliver Strachey, all of whom were entitled to use the house by arrangement. But for Carrington, it meant a home for her and Lytton at last.

To Maynard Keynes

c/o Oliver Strachey, Chilling, Hants
Friday [end of 1917]

Dear Maynard,

You wretch you never wrote me a letter, or even a postcard from New York, and you promised faithfully – I hear strange stories of your goings on, the strangest. Middies [midshipmen], admirals, gambling, whales, New York Millionaires. And again middies upon middies.

[...] what a life here! smoking fires so that the rooms are dense with grey fogs & smut & Raging winds outside. Aeroplanes, sea planes and Oliver & Lytton talking politics furiously & listening to a torrent of conversation all the evening from Madame Berenson¹ who is here also. By the way we've just found a most superb Mill House at Pangbourne or a mile away from that place – where we are going to live ... and the Miller himself ... the vilest of flour could not obliterate his beauty [...] I am glad you are back.

Love Carrington

---

1 In 1911, Oliver Strachey married for the second time. His new wife Rachel (Ray) Costelloe was an ardent suffragist and her mother, Mary, was married to the art historian and dealer Bernard Berenson.

1918

After spending Christmas 1917 at the Mill with Carrington and friends, Lytton retreated to London. It is as well that she did not know he was writing complaining letters to Virginia Woolf about the cold, and even wondering, Woolf's diary records, if he had made a mistake in setting up house with her. 'That woman will dog me... She won't let me write, I daresay.'

Carrington began 1918 alone in the Mill House, while the rats in the roof, said by Lytton to sound like buzzards in wellington boots, kept her awake at night.

To Lytton Strachey

The Mill House
Sunday evening, 6 o'ck [20 January 1918]

Not a sign of a human being! Alix is pretty well damned now. To have enough energy to go to Lord's Wood with Bunny & not enough imagination or curiosity to come here. She's a dull green toad [...]

I sleep worse and worse. It must be a disease. I got up this morning at 7 o'clock and gardened from sheer boredom of lying in bed. Another electric light globe shattered. Can you abstract a few from some ODD rooms in Belsize? as it's getting a little tedious having to carry a globe in one's pocket to fit on each time one enters a room. I've rigged up my studio in that tank room. It will make a very good place to work as there are so many shelves to spread the litter out on. And the lighting is good [...] I've thought of a brilliant idea to subdue the Buzzards. Purchase a ferret or a mongoose, and put it at night under the floors and in the attics, et voila! EXIT la bottine de monsieur Wellington! I suppose you will promptly put forward some absurd objection [...] Next Sat. we shall meet no doubt in Paddington and tramp the long long platform of Reading side by side [...]

My love dearest Lytton,
Carrington xxxxxxxxxxxx

To Lytton Strachey

The Mill House
Monday evening, 6.30 [21 January 1918]

[...] A mongoose must be purchased – since Mrs Burton a farmer resident here has one, Leggett[1] just told me, to catch the Buzzards. You will have a raid tonight for a certainty. Poor moon, to be shunned now even by the POET. Dear, may I tell you how much I love you tonight? So much that if you were here I should hug your thinness into nothing. Did you ever want to strangle the thing you love, so it would be over once & for all? No more crescendos – no more horrid earthy dullness, calm & well regulated, which nobody knows better than you how to bring into force!

But I know, for when Mark wanted each day to be wildly chaotic I hated it because it had no connection with one's life & was so devastating.

Today gardening I thought how good it was that I knew you, what luck. How easily it might never have occurred.

Dearest Lytton.
My love to you
Carrington xxxxx

To Lytton Strachey

Friday morning [15 February 1918]

Dearest Lytton

[...] I am so sorry about that scene. It was rather my fault for not being more careful. I hope only you were not in any way upset by it. Maynard will go down Sat about 5 o'ck train. I do not know quite what I shall do. But I'll phone you after breakfast tomorrow and say which train definitely.

Carrington

'That scene' took place late on the evening of 14 February, when Mark, having finally realised that Carrington was indeed 'living with' Lytton in both senses, sexual and domestic, got drunk and hit him as he left a party in west London with Carrington and Keynes. Other friends came to the rescue and pulled Mark away; Lytton described the incident as 'extremely painful' and felt sorry for 'poor Mark'. They soon made up over dinner at the Eiffel Tower restaurant in Percy Street, but Carrington remained embarrassed and annoyed. She did not, however, let Mark go.

1 Mrs Legg, employed as cook-housekeeper.

To Mark Gertler

The Mill House
February 1918

Dear Mark,

I was glad to hear from you this morning. I confess I was dreadfully upset by that incident. Not so much about it. But because I felt so responsible – that it resulted through a neglect of my duties to you and lack of foresight on my part. I am rather worried about you altogether. What's to be done? Frankly, I wish you had some better friend to keep you from getting dissipated and wasting your time in the evenings. Monty's really not much good is he. I hate to hear of you at the cafes. It's just because I know you are worth more and that more intelligent people like you and would be friends with you. I am sure it's all too short this life to waste time in a boring way – & confess now you must be bored with those café people night after night. Perhaps I am wrong but I hear from so many people of your careless evening life. Will you try, Mark, to get on with the other sort of people and not drink anymore. Ruth is in Chelsea again now. Please go & see her soon. I am not preaching, it did however upset me to see you drunk at Mary's party & I felt it was so much my fault for leaving you for so long and making you unhappy. Do you know the Anreps[1] in Hampstead. I went there the other evening and they seemed friendly & simple. I care very much that you love me still and if you knew how delighted I was to hear from you the other morning and again today – are you quite well from your cold.

Could not you go & stay at Garsington with Brett for a little while. It is so beautiful in the country now that all the flowers are beginning to come out & the leaves [...] Nick, Barbara's husband, has made me a little stove for my studio so I can now work up there in the cold weather – which in fact is the state of climate this morning. Lytton told me you had met at the Eiffel Tour. He was full of sympathy with you from the first moment. But as you say it can be forgotten now. The more important thing to me is that you should be happier, so that you cannot feel so wretched about it even if you get a little drunk, ever again – will you please promise me to value yourself higher & not waste your time. And if you knew how fond immediately people like Maynard are of you! Maynard is down here this weekend. Barbara & Nick go back tomorrow. Please write & tell me about your painting. I am doing some landscapes from my attic window of the river

---

1 Boris Anrep (1883–1969), mosacist, was born in St Petersburg and moved to London in 1911. A friend of Augustus John, he married Dorelia's friend Helen Maitland in 1918. She later left him to live with Roger Fry.

below, & trees reflection & also one of the mill itself & the millstream. Tell me also when you next write more about your friend Suggia the celloist. Remember I care always very much for you. Just as much as I used to. It is in no way changed – and if you knew how much I felt your pains & griefs it would lessen them for you. I shall look forward to seeing your work again next time I come to London. I find it fearfully hard to write to you even now after all these years of writing, but you will understand I do not want to interfere with your life only to tell you what I have been thinking and to assure you that you are not isolated or very distant from me.

Love from yr
Carrington

To Mark Gertler

The Mill House
[28 February 1918]

I will come, if you want to see me, when I am back in London. But I hardly see the use of corresponding when you are so antagonistic towards me. When I said I wanted to tell you more about myself, I did not mean to make that crude statement, which I knew you already knew, but it is clear I cannot really help you, and after all it is a little discouraging and exhausting to have feelings for a person, and to know one day they care for you and the next day to receive a entirely contradictory letter saying there is no connection between the two persons. When you make up your mind for any decent length of time that I can be of use to you, I will gladly. But otherwise I would rather leave it. Evidently from your last letter *we think so very differently about relative values of everything now*. Yet it is impossible for me not to care every time I see you. Very much. This letter is not bitter; only I feel rather tired, and perhaps disappointed about it. But don't write any more. I would rather not start it again. And you also feel that, I know, permanently inside.

My best wishes for your work.
D.C.

There is no answer to this letter.

To Mark Gertler

The Mill House
Friday morning [early March 1918]

Dearest Mark,

I have just heard about you being called up. I am dreadfully sorry and so worried. Please, will you write and tell me as soon as you know anything definite. I should be glad if you could spare time to write by return and tell me exactly what happened, and what line you are going to adopt, and what the chances are? It is frightful. But I have such confidence in Fortune protecting you as she has in the past, that I refuse to believe the worst will happen and you will get put in the army. Do not get too unhappy. Remember things have always turned out better than you expected in previous calamities. I will come up to London if you would like me to do so. Dear, I fear I was unkind in my last letter perhaps, and rebuked you and perhaps it came at the same time as this bad news. If so please forgive me.

I shall be so worried until I hear news of your state. Please write as soon as you can and let it be at length, with every detail. For the moment let us forget all that has just past. The sorrows of today being yours are mine also.

My affectionate love,
Carrington

If there is anything I can do to make you happy do not fail to ask me.

In due course Gertler was exempted. In March, to Carrington's joy, Lytton was also finally exempted from military service on health grounds. She wanted nothing more than to spend the summer at Tidmarsh with him, but he remained somewhat elusive and inclined to go to parties in London without her, especially after the triumphant publication of Eminent Victorians *in June.*

To Lytton Strachey

The Mill House
9.30, Monday evening [10 June 1918]

I am sorry to add to your troubles, by badgering you with letters. But HOW else can a young lady living in the country by herself – neglected by her swain, worn out by the fatigues of the day – and tired of her own company – pass the evening? [...] Beds weeded in front of the windows. Vast bed in the orchard planted with cabbages & a print-dress nearly made!

Mary's party has just begun for it's nearly 10 o'ck. I can see all [...] The din of voices then a tall gentleman. He might almost be French, very clean, in a dark plum suit steals in – like a good boy. Very friendly – Mary at once glides up to him like a worm through the fat mass ... Everyone looks at him now.

Everyone except the hostile camp – & there always is one – talks of his book ... But no one is quite so enthusiastic as the Bugeyed Mopsa, looking at him from the arm chair of Tidmarsh [...] I wonder what you feel like inside when everyone praises your book ... & you find yourself famous? Certainly you become powerful and much lies within your bony fingers... what will you grasp? – 'we shall see' – as Macaulay says – was it Macaulay? No ... Gibbon surely... I am glad at any rate the public does not share my feelings about your appearance and character! Since you are bored with praise of your creations I will tell you that I think you are the most eminent, graceful person, the most worthy, learned & withal, charming character. And I shall always love you in your entirety.

You know, Dear Lytton, it's been rather amazing living with you for so long. Now that I am alone I can sit down & think or ponder upon it. Visions steal up – of those hot days when you wore your Fakir clothes – in the orchard – weeding on your child's chair. The one afternoon when I saw you in the bath. When I lay on your bed on Thursday & saw your eyelashes, and your face so very near, and smelt your hair, and broke the cracking beard in my fingers [...]

To Lytton Strachey

Garsington
Morning, Wednesday, 8 o'ck, in bed

Dearest Lytton,

Shandy Hall again! How familiar it all seems. Can it be a year since I was here – I left Tidmarsh at half past twelve yesterday & reached here soon after three o'ck. It was delightful renewing acquaintance with Wallingford and Dorchester.[1]

[...] DOES Tidmarsh exist? Yes. I am wondering that now. Another divine morning only broken by the screams of those uncouth birds.

1 Two handsome small towns close to Garsington.

I say! It's pretty hopeless pretending our garden grows flowers – or anything for that matter – after this vision! Those pansies and the lavender walks and the snapdragons on the wall. I see it's a matter for consideration. Some measures will have to be taken before another summer [...]

Ottoline is very friendly and the garden & smells filled me with much joy yesterday. BUT I shall certainly post off on Thursday after breakfast and it would be blessed to find that most eminent of all Victorians to greet me in the evening, with tales of the Far East and his adventures. We may drive over to the Wharf today to look at some book old ASQUITH has full of woodcuts which Ottoline says are very rare. Have you seen the sculpture of Brzeska[1] at the Leicester Galleries? From a book Brett had some of them looked very good [...]

On the lawn, 11 o'clock

Tres chér, what a good man you are to write again. It was all so entertaining I loved your description of Elizabeth [Asquith]. Do you think you are now about to travel down that large avenue, which Pozzo [Keynes] has chosen, leading to – I don't know quite what – hand in hand with Asquiths & LuLu.

Well – have a consider. Maynard receives severe criticism and whether there is a crown of glory awaiting him in that far distant grove of trees [...] The Lady O really rather overwhelms me with her kindness. It all seems so smooth compared to those rather hectic last visits. She has her little griev-ances of course which rumble on unceasingly between all conversations, Lady Connie,[2] Brett's' stupidity, Lawrence. But I am happy here and the visions of the pond & the garden with its flowers makes one very amiable to say nothing of receiving a letter from the beloved in the morning!

It's surprising how enormous this place seems after our little mill – the vistas & the mansion itself.

I forgot how primitive we were until I saw this shining silver last night, the ormolu furniture, musk smells & brocades.

Her Ladyship entreats to be asked to the Mill – I leave it to you partner.

If you dare write back & say you allowed that bitch Lulu to kiss you, I shall not touch your infected, lice-ridden, stink besotted self for a month and a day...

How splendid about the *Telegraph*. What a feast of reviews you will have to spread before me when you come back! Has any paper except the *Vigilant*[3]

---

1 Henri Gaudier-Brzeska (1891–1915), French sculptor living in London who died in the trenches in France.
2 Lady Constance Malleson (1895–1975), actress and new mistress to Bertrand Russell, Ottoline's former lover.
3 A right-wing publication.

dared to neglect your book! When you return there is that portrait to be
finished – I think it's pretty certain to be hung on the line of celebrities in
next year's R.A., a woodcut of the pug perhaps pressed against the horse-
faced Lady of Shandy Hall. What do you think?

Dearest Lytton, I love you so much. How glad I am about the book.

Yr Carrington xxxxxxxxxxxxxx

*In July, Carrington joined Noel, his Oxford friend Rex Partridge,[1] both home on
leave, and the unnamed sister of a friend of Partridge's on a trip to Scotland.
Always reluctant to leave Lytton, she wrote him long descriptive letters while they
were apart.*

To Lytton Strachey

In train to Kingussie
8.30 [4 July 1918]

Well, what a lot can happen in a day! I met Noel at 12 o'ck. We then shopped,
and talked in St James Park till 1.30. Went to the Automobile Club for lunch.
The young man Partridge had just come back from Italy, the one I was
telling you about the other evening, so he and another young Oxford man
who was A.D.C. [aide-de-camp] to Robertson[2] – had lunch with us. The
A.D.C. was very attractive but obviously rather alarmed by my appearance
and manners! A pity, he was so charming with a beautiful head. After tea
he left us, so we went down the Strand and sat in the Embankment Gardens
and talked. I found Partridge shared all the best views of democracy and
social reform, wine and cheer and good operas. He adores the Italians and
wants after the war to sail in a schooner to the Mediterranean Islands and
Italy, and trade in wine without taking much money and to dress like a
brigand. I am so elated and happy. It is so good to find someone who one
can rush on and on with, quickly. He sang Italian songs to us on the plat-
forms and was in such gay spirits – and used his hands gesticulating. But
the important thing was he seemed so enthusiastic over reconstruction after
the war and free thinking. Fortunately he is to be in England 3 months. So
I hope I shall see him again. Not very attractive to look at. Immensely big.
But full of wit and reckless. And he was in London last night and we never

1 Reginald Sherring Partridge, (1894–1960) known at this time as Rex and later as Ralph, at Lytton's
behest. He was to remain Ralph for the rest of his life.
2 Field Marshal Sir William Robertson (1860–1933), a former footman who rose through the ranks to
become Chief of the Imperial General Staff from 1916 to 1918.

knew and so one must never give up hope that there are none left. He is
sending me a book by Anatole France[1] to read – *Angels* – I cannot remember
the name.

We are travelling 1st class by ourselves in a splendid carriage! Noel is
reading your book. He is very nice. But one felt so much the difference
between Partridge, a bond of dreams and worldly things. He adores eating
and drinking and said as we sat on high chairs in the buffet at Euston: 'I
always feel sorry for women that they don't know what it is to appreciate
food. In Italy we had such amazing dishes and the wines!!' Noel just told
me the father of a College friend of his was vicar at the Vicarage where
Keble was. Southrop the name. He had been there. And you are sitting with
John and Ruth [Selby-Bigge] in front of a not too bright fire, rather bored?
I wonder, I have no idea how you will get on.

And next weekend at Tidmarsh what of that? Write to me soon. I'll send
a PC with address tomorrow. How I loved our few days in London and the
operas. Dear, thank you so much. I wish you had stayed today and met the
young man. He deplored the English women and their stodgy characters.
The Italians he said walked so well and dressed all in unity, which was
indeed a true observation as we watched those drabs slouching and stumping
past us on the Embankment. The train rushes too fast to write properly.
We are nearing Crewe now. And have fastened the door with a strap inside
so the mob cannot enter. Noel travels in full military attire ornamented
with red tapes and braids so I hope the Grants or Glasses will be pleased
with us!

I hope you'll control Legg and get her to look after you properly. Noel
just said he thought the sarcasm in your book so gentlemanly that Mary
might not see it and miss the point. So I told him the story of Claudius
Clear.[2] But I am really wondering if we will go in the ship with this young
man to those islands. He is going to learn the mandolin to play on the
ship, he said. Or whether, like all visions ... Dear, if it is at all feasible, I
will certainly try to induce you to come to the peaks and crags.

I am so excited now about going to Kingussie and your country. What a
difference it does make, it being your place. I loved you so much last night.
Please take great care of yourself for me, until I come home.

Yr Carrington xxx

---

1 Anatole France (1844–1924), French novelist and leading man of letters. The novel she's referring to is
   probably France's 1914 novel *La Révolte des anges*.
2 Claudius Clear was the pseudonym of a clergyman, the Rev. Dr Robertson Nicoll, who wrote about
   Eminent Victorians in the *British Weekly* without realising when Lytton Strachey was being ironic.

To Lytton Strachey

> On the shores of Loch Laggan
> Saturday [6 July 1918]

[...] This is indeed rather a wonderful place. The hotel seems so far devoid of the horrid Glasgowers. We have just had a lovely swim in the lake. The woman is indeed fatter than I. What a superb creature is a youth nude. The shores are yellow sand with great grey boulders & slopes with birch trees behind. I cooked a grand meal of eggs & bacon, coffee in a Tinkers Jennie. The sun was scorching hot lying bare on the sand. But it's all rather wasted without your company. The others have gone off now so I've walked round the lake & now sit high on some crags gazing at a Byronic View which perhaps the pen will trace.

[...] Matter indeed for the pen of Wordsworth with the great black clouds hanging over the lofts of indigo mountains. But the eyes still blink at the whole scene – after England it's curiously unreal and grandiose. I think perhaps the lake makes it look rather artificial. You've made me, dear, a pretty intolerant creature. I suppose two (in pencil as I've upset the ink in my pen) years ago I should have enjoyed the company of these two – but their conversation seems so pointless and there seems to be no activities – or did I detect something attempting to rise under his bathing garment. But I fear that merry acrobat will get little pleasure this holiday! ... If it is feasible you will come won't you? But I'll write later about that – oh dearest how much I love you, one feels how big a thing it is now one is alone removed up here – nothing matters except for your presence & to have you [to] talk with when I read that Greek anthology. I longed to find a youth to give you that peculiar ecstasy – to make you happy in return for all you give me.

The porridge is good in these parts. But no green peas, broad beans or raspberries – and oh hell no red beard [...]

My love to you oh very dear one

Yr

Carrington

xxxx

xxxx

To Ottoline Morrell

The Mill House
Sunday [summer 1918]

[...] We had such a very wonderful holiday in Scotland. It seems now like some vision, like those scenes Wordsworth's poetry conjures up before one eyes reading in the evenings. It has no correlation to this flat tame country. Skye was entirely magical. One felt anything might happen up there on those deserted mountains – witches & wildcats in the caves. Some of the peasants were astonishing. But it was all too quick, one longed to linger over their firesides and talk on & on. Noel was adamant however & rushed me on to a new inn every night. Except for the last four days which we spent in an empty cottage at Rothiemurchus [...]

Wretched every time I think of you, remembering your cracked head. You'll have heard any news about Tidmarsh from the 'wolves' and Brett is coming I hope tomorrow. Lytton will be away till Thursday so I shall be glad of her company. I had four riotous days in London after Scotland. Noel didn't go back till Thursday so I had to go out with him & his young Oxford friends razzel-dazzeling [*sic*]. I took him & one of them to the Sitwells one evening. They seemed to enjoy it very much. But Noel was so full of spirits that he seemed to like everyone & everything! Then on Friday we went to Coq D'Or. Lytton with the Duchess of course below in a box! It's great entertainment for all of us – his accounts of the Lords & Ladies. I saw Phyllis Boyd[1] in London, she knows them all so well [...] What stories!! But they are too appalling to commit to paper & such is paper – torn from my old virgin lesson books!! But I'll relate them all when we meet again – Phyllis is truly the most lovely creature I know – only she always vanishes into space the day after one has found her.

I will certainly come over on the old machine next month.

Alix, James, Oliver and a young lady are here this weekend. I've been busy gardening all day so haven't seen much of them. The former sit now as I write – over the chess board with solemn faces. They take nearly ten minutes over each move. But it's a wonderful picture in the lamplight. These little wooden men controlling these huge monsters [...]

I do hope you really will be well again soon.

My love to you affectionately

Carrington

---

1 Phyllis Boyd (1894–1943) was another well-connected Slade girl whose romantic looks and escapades enthralled Carrington.

To Noel Carrington

The Mill House
[Summer 1918]

Dearest Noel,

Thank you for your last letter. Well on Saturday evening Partridge came to this haunt of guile and wickedness. Unfortunately I missed his letter and as he had not turned up by the afternoon trains I gave him up for lost, and the day being fine went for a walk with Lytton who read Shakespeare sonnets to me in a delectable dell, sheltered by tall beech trees. Truly I must say there is nothing but Milton in our English verse in my humble opinion, devoid of value no doubt as it may be to you, to touch in exquisite beauty and form those sonnets.

On our return we found Partridge lying on our lawn with Oliver Strachey. I gathered separately from both of them that a heated argument had raged on that everlasting topic wars and peace negotiations. Partridge said yesterday on the river that he thought Oliver was a crank because he was opposed to war on ground of the carnage. Then R.P. made the extraordinary statement that the carnage didn't matter – he didn't think it was at all important men dying and really wouldn't mind being killed himself and eugenically it was good for the world not to be over populated. So I must admit I had to set-to and argued over this with him. Do you hold those views? I can't believe that he does really. Then I said it was appalling to think of men like Milton, Shakespeare and Darwin and that a few being killed didn't matter in the long run [...]

We went on the river all yesterday reaching Moulsford for lunch and a very good lunch at that which dulled the wits and rendered all further conversation banal and amiable. Reached Wallingford for tea and rowed back, reaching Pangbourne by about 8. He had to catch a train at Reading at 9.30 so only had time for wine and dinner and dashed off in the motor. I hope he enjoyed it. I thought he was in a curious way much more prejudiced and much less open minded that you. Lytton even thought that and said you are much more interested in things and easier to talk to than R.P.. He isn't very interested in books or poetry or painting which makes it a bit difficult.

It's my fault really. I am so anxious to find everything I want in a person and rush off ahead and believe they are what they are not really and then get disappointed. Still I think he's interesting – only not so much intellect and enquiring in human nature as you have. He merely thought those Sitwells affected and dismissed them, he was surprised because Lytton had written that book, as he said he didn't look as if he should have which was a rather superficial judgment I thought, because a man is weak to imagine he hasn't a brain and energy for creation. Then he didn't see very much in the book except that the style was 'rather good' – then he was prejudiced against Lytton slightly for his beard and his appearance and confessed it. I wonder what Brenan his friend is like.[1] He belongs much more to those Augustus John people – I was surprised a little really at our R.P. being his friend and not being more tolerant. He spoke very scathingly of that man you knew at the House who knew so much about French literature, because he was so 'effete'; – well, well. You see what a great deal I want in a young man and you know dear brother how I carry out my maxims in my tolerance of the Philistines. Yes I laugh even at myself but I think the fundamental views on life are seriously the only important things in people. And I must say I can't get over R.P. thinking people wantonly being killed in war not appalling. It did rather upset me [...]

A scotch view follows in a few days for you.

D.C.

Partridge was beginning to fall for Carrington, but in the summer of 1918 was still a serving officer due to return to the Italian front and full of conventional opinions. Neither then nor later was he a natural Bloomsbury insider, which along with his strong masculine character and physique perhaps explains some of his attraction for both Carrington and, increasingly, Lytton.

To Virginia Woolf

Tatchley, Prestbury, nr Cheltenham, Glos.
21 August 1918

My Dear Virginia,

I did enjoy that weekend with you very much, so that I must try and write a letter now to thank you and Leonard for having me. I tackled Lytton about the [Henry] James letters. You were quite wrong. He was strongly in favour of them being brought to light and refuted any idea of intrigues on his part. There was a vast gathering at Gordon Square in the evening: Clive and Mary, and all the others. Sheppard came in very decrepit and broken about 10 o'ck, and gave a ghastly account of his medical Board at Cambridge. He's been classified Grade 1. But it was impossible to gather whether the danger of Khaki really is as he made out it was. I saw Lytton off as the cock

---

1 Gerald Brenan (1894–1987) and Ralph became friends during the war in France.

crew nine at Kings X. H.B. Irving¹ got in the same train, with an actor manager. Lytton was certain they also were destined for the party at Headlong Hall!! Jack Hutchinson who wrote to Mary from some other castle in Northumberland said that Heinemann,² and many other Jews and dagoes were staying at Lindisfarne, and that all the food that one could get there was bad crab, and foul lobster. So what has become of our Marquis of Tidmarsh amidst such spiritual and corporeal horrors? I dread to think.

I have been so excited ever since I saw those artists at Charleston, and their work. I would not have missed that one day for any attractions you literary people could offer me!

It's extraordinary to be back here with my people again and the old mahogany furniture of my earliest youth. So respectable, and so highly polished. My mother's long conversation about dividends, and relations has gone on without a pause since I first entered the house yesterday afternoon. But I've a great deal of work to do, and there are Cotswolds Hills just across the lane to explore. So I expect I shall hold out for a week. We are going to Wooler [in Northumberland] first. I'll write you a long letter from there. And when we come back in September I'll come down, and dig the garden for Leonard like an old mole.

Virginia, I did enjoy staying with you so much. Please give Leonard my love.

Yrs Carrington

To David Garnett

The Mill House
Tuesday evening [2 October 1918]

Dear Bunny,

You wrote such an amusing letter from the Globe, Exeter, that I am sorry not to have answered it before. But when we returned from Gordon Square here, Mrs Legg announced brightly that she was going away the next day for a week's holiday. As if I hadn't enough already of looking after the old gentleman in London! So nearly all my time has been taken up preparing food for human consumption and cleaning rooms which I with much greater speed make dirty again [...]

---

1 H. B. Irving (1870–1919) was the actor son of the great actor manager Sir Henry Irving (1838–1905).
2 William Heinemann (1863–1920) founded the eponymous publishing house in 1890. His authors included R. L. Stevenson, Rudyard Kipling and H. G. Wells.

Last weekend Madame Bussy[1] came. I like her. She is so sympathetic and very entertaining. Mrs Legg is worse than a traitor as she promised to be back last Thursday and now it's nearly Wednesday and there is no sign of her. Lytton went up to London this morning to attend his various affaires. So I am all alone today and have quickly become a slut. I am writing to you in the kitchen with a black cat purring on the table. And I've just eaten a huge supper of coffee and marrow jam tartlets. Now how do you enjoy yourself?

Please write me a letter about the Boxes[2] and the country. How happy I was there last summer. The doe [rabbit] is going to have a family next week. We have started eating the cockerels as they consumed such vast quantities of food. I shall have 7 hens this winter. Last Friday I went up to London and Mr Partridge took me to the Ballet and we saw *The Good Humoured Ladies*. It was good. I had seen it before with Alix but right from the very back of the upper regions and Mr P. had seats in the front of the stalls. It was too exciting seeing all their faces so close – and every gesture. Brenan had been in London with him last week. Mr P. asked me if I had read *Despised and Rejected* and also made a louche joke about Lytton and Buggery.[3] But I don't think all the same there's anything between him and Brenan. By the way, the man who wrote *Despised and Rejected* is being prosecuted by the censor of morals!!! I just had a long letter from Alix this morning – seemed very happy. This is a dull letter but I feel like you do after a hard day's work at Charleston, as stupid as a cow and quite as boring. Please give Jenny and Rebecca Ann and Mrs B[ox] my love and a more intimate variety of the same to you.

Yrs affec Carrington

To Virginia Woolf

The Mill House
Tuesday [October 1918]

Dear Virginia,

Lytton (like some King whose name I forget, but I learnt a long poem about him when I was a child) went to bed and never smiled again until

1 Dorothy Bussy (1865–1960), née Strachey, was one of Lytton's five sisters and had married the French painter Simon Bussy in 1905. She became a translator and writer, notably of the novel of schoolgirl passion *Olivia* (1949).

2 The Box family lived at Welcombe Farm where Carrington and other friends often stayed. She painted Mrs Box's portrait in 1919.

3 *Despised and Rejected* was a novel by Rose Allatini published in 1918 under the pseudonym A. T. Fitzroy. It was banned on account of its sympathetic treatment of pacifism and homosexuality.

your letter came. Then he laughed outright very loud five times. And the second time he read it, ten minutes later, he laughed seven times.

So will you write again? If only you knew his state of complete despair, as only a Strachey can despair, and utter misery, your pen would not remain idle. His hand is a little better today. But much too swollen to write with yet. Where did Goldie[1] have his shingles? My conversation is now entirely on that subject. Unfortunately to Lytton's chagrin, only innkeepers, char-women and chemists' assistants seem liable to the foul disease. So your news of Goldie's suffering raised his spirits a little. For horrid thought; he believed it was a complaint of the lower classes. He is going to Glottenham to stay with Mary next Monday. D.V. your words did indeed came true, for this morning hardly had the loathsome shingles quitted its hold on his frame, when a bilious attack seized the stomach and now he cannot even eat his meals which up to now had been his one form of recreation and amusement. And you say the mange will follow? Well. I only hope it will attack him when he is at Mary's, not here. But to come to business. How can I do woodblocks when for the past month, ever since in fact we left Northumberland, I've been a ministering angel, hewer of wood and drawer of water? Honestly Virginia since I came here I've only been able to finish a picture which I sent Monty Shearman. Yes my ewe lambs are now in the market place and so one small woodblock. So you mustn't bully me. I go to Cheltenham next Monday for a week. And I'll work very hard down there. By the end of this month I will try and send you some. Roger I hear is cutting wood all over the carpets in Gordon Square. What fun life in London seems, parties, Ottoline, and feathers flying. Here it is overflowing jordans, milk puddings, poultries and then, overflowing jordans again next morning.

My love to Leonard and please write to Lytton again. If you had heard the torrent of affection and admiration which flowed over your letter, well, you would write again.

Yrs affect Carrington

To Lytton Strachey

Tatchley, Prestbury
Thursday night, 10 o'ck [31 October 1918]

Not that there is anything to write about to night dearest, – But that I am thinking of you, and wondering how you passed your day and seeing the old hand as I last saw it, and speculating if any more wrinkles can now be

2 Goldsworthy Lowes Dickinson (1862–1932), Cambridge classical scholar and philosopher who met Lytton and all Bloomsbury through his great friend Roger Fry.

seen on those two fingers. I don't think I shall ever forget the vision of that hand! And when I write to your life as an old lady, I shall draw for the preface a shingled hand [...]

I can't help feeling it's wretched to touch the money that he [her brother Teddy] saved probably through being a soldier in the war. You know it was just two years ago this October. At the very place where they are shooting now. I hate coming home because everywhere in the house I see his things and in my rooms all his school books, the queer boxes, and his carved things he made, old chemistry jars, boats, and in the drawers his note books, drawings of engines, and frigates. You remember in that poem the room with the quick silver. It was all so like him. He wasn't a bit intellectual, only so charming. Really like one of those south country people, or a sailor. But mostly I think I loved him for his exquisite beauty and strength. I cannot forget one of the last days he was at Hurstbourne. In the afternoon I found him lying fast asleep on the sofa, curled up. His dark brown face, and broad neck, the thick black shiny hair and the modelling on his face, like some chiselled bronze head.

You don't mind me talking now. But it's been so heavy inside lately. Those leaves lying on the lawn at Tidmarsh, and the cold smell made me remember Hurstbourne so vividly. And here, with all his things, I cannot forget hardly for a moment in this house.

When we passed Box Hill an incident came back. How up a certain white quarry he slipped down backwards down the loose clay and hurt his side. We ran on, and left him behind and afterwards he came running up very red and crying. And then long after when he rowed at school, he told me how the ribs were bent, and still hurt. You comforted me once when we came back from tea at Dorelia's. So I write now. You would have loved him if you had seen him. It is blessed to know you. Such a comfort. Take great care of yourself and if you want me to take you to London and do anything, you will write?

My love, goodnight.

Carrington

To Lytton Strachey

Tatchley
Monday afternoon [4 November 1918]

Isn't it good news about Austria!! Oh we shall have peace before the end of next week! You must be well by then. For think of the wine cups and the pavement-tapping, boy-accosting days of London. Very dear Lytton how are you this morning? What lovely creatures lay on your shingly beach last night?

I drew a picture all last night of figures in the Roman Bath[1] at Tidmarsh. For an oil painting I intend to do when I get back. Had a hot bath & crept lonely to bed. My very dear one. I do hope you are better [...] This letter's only cause is to convey my love to you and give you many hugs and kisses. You do believe in peace this morning don't you? Or will you deny its existence even years after it's declared. It would be just like you – you old crag of a Tory. Give Clive & Mary my love. And there will be Italy next spring! Oh gollywops! Goodbye and 1 thousand kisses. (GLS. 'Thank God the creature is at Cheltenham & not here' – 'alright, you monster.') – I wonder how many I have given you since – you first kissed me. That was an indiscretion on your part wasn't it ...

Your most charming Mopsa

To Lytton Strachey

Tatchley
Thursday night, 9.30 [7 November 1918]

Pray worthy Poet do not laugh at this somewhat curious scarf

PRAY worthy Poet do not laugh
at this somewhat curious scarf

... For with Loving hands I made it, and even if it's not successful as a sling, it will, to use my favourite phrase, 'come in' for something else. I couldn't write this morning, there was so much packing to do. And this afternoon I accompanied my mother to a concert. Mark Hambourg, at the piano. There was one good piece by Bach, but for the rest, Il ne me plaisait pas. Chopin, and numerous

1 A small bathing pool at the Mill.

minor exercises to show off his great skill at playing trills. But next to my mother sat the most exquisite creature that my eyes have yet lighted upon. He had the loveliness of a Boticcelli angel. I should think he was sixteen, slightly of the lower classes, with masses of black hair, and a very narrow fragile face – with dark brown eyes and a short curling upper lip, altogether more romantic and Italian than one could conceive possible. What he was doing in that congregation, God knows. For it might otherwise have been a Kensington High Church assembly. There were a few odd characters like Saxon, enthralled by every note. But for the most part they were the dullest most provincial, ill mannered people I've ever seen [...] This hasn't been a good looting visit. Only one small silver cream jug, and some vegetables, and eggs for Alix!

But the fur coat this morning was the greatest comfort. For it's icy cold in these regions now. I've not had a word from Legg re that empty envelope which arrived and about the ration book which did not come. Rather a nuisance. I only hope you've got yours alright.

Dearest I shall be glad when you can write again. Perhaps the wine cups and Geoffrey's[1] arms will make me forget a little how much I miss you and your letters. You can't deny you aren't excited about Peace now. I say, you must come up to London and make merry, shingles or no shingles, next week. Dear Lytton I send you all my love tonight and remain

Votre jamais charmant maîtresse[2]

Mopsa

To Lytton Strachey

45 Downshire Hill, Hampstead
Monday morning, 9 o'ck [11 November 1918]

What an angel you are! I was never so glad of a letter before! You need never write again (not to be taken literally) for I shall remain happy for weeks because you tell me you are better and, oh Lytton, it is too good to believe that the old hand can write again. It's just as good as Peace, only I wish I could hug you hard this morning because I love you so much. And Jack [Hutchinson] can, that's the peculiar thing about life. Well there's Sunday to describe. I had lunch with A. Waley[3] again, at the Isolabella and oh joy a brimming cup of Zambalaoni! [*sic* – zabaglione]. He was rather amusing,

---

1 Geoffrey Nelson was a young painter to whom Lytton was briefly attracted.

2 Perhaps she meant 'toujours' (always)?

3 Arthur Waley (1889–1966), another Cambridge friend of Lytton's who joined the British Museum Oriental Prints and Manuscripts Department in 1913 and became the leading translator of Chinese and Japanese poetry.

and talked a great deal; also read me some Piers Ploughman which I like immensely. After, in Shaftesbury's Avenue, we saw Dorelia looking amazingly beautiful. She asked after 'Strachey' which she says in a curious voice which sounds as if it must be Strakey but just avoids it at the last moment. She leaves London next Tuesday for Dorset. Boris [Anrep] is going to decorate their walls in Chelsea with a fresco of the first women taking their seats in the Houses of Parliament! Waley tells me he [Boris] has a theory now that all art should have a great underlying motive, and at present the greatest symbolic movement to him is the freedom of women! [...] Then tea at Gordon Square. Only Harry [Norton] visible when I arrived. He appeared in excellent spirits, and asked with great feeling after your condition. Then, my dear, who should come in, but Bluff Major Bell [Clive Bell's brother] just home on leave from France, thinking to find Clive at Gordon Square. You couldn't imagine the scene. It was too extraordinary. He evidently had no idea of what Harry was like and roared with laughter like a bull at every remark Harry made! 'Well I can't say I think much of this armistice now we have them on the run. I think we might as well finish the job and enter Berlin.' 'Of course I wouldn't trust Boche. But I suppose they'll take care he isn't allowed to have the chance of turning,' and many more appalling statements. Harry was a perfect gentleman, and never even looked at his watch.

Then Sheppard entered and the Major roared even louder. I thought it would never end. Finally Alix appeared, very stiff, and immensely solemn. That was too much. I think it flashed across him, we must be the young ladies of these curious friends of Clive. Anyway with a great bellow he left the room! – But it was exceedingly strange. Then until 7 o'ck we discussed: what else can one discuss in Gordon Square, Maynard and his table manners! And a forthcoming party to celebrate Peace. Harry had a great scheme for the party of a charade of Pozzo's life – all at the table – beginning with Mrs Keynes trying to teach him not to dip his bread in the soup. But Sheppard's more gentlemanly instincts suppressed the motion.

Fortunately Harry broke it up by taking us all off to the Café Royal for a great dinner, and beakers of wine. Geoffrey bored me dreadfully with more Irish stories. Alix rapidly became very drunk and Sheppard took the conversation into his own hands by relating all of his love affaires since he was four years old. Then Harry talked bawdy – and rather upset little Wolfe. Gilbert Cannan and little Gwen[1] who sat at the next table became correspondingly gloomier, as our spirits rose. And there was cherry brandy and sloe gin to finish up with! Back to Gordon Square – Alix so drunk she had to leave the company and was violently sick outside. I left her lying on

1 Gwen Wilson was Gilbert Cannan's mistress. He left his wife in 1918 and thereafter lived in a ménage à trois with her husband, Henry Mond.

Sheppard's bed groaning with mortifications and anguish. Geoffrey to my horror I find lives exactly opposite this house in Downshire Hill with his aunt, Mrs Vessey. He's alright, but oh Lytton such a bore. Bunny is Virginia in brilliance compared to him!

Harry asks me to tell you that next Thursday evening there will be crackers and squibs at Gordon Square and if you are well enough your company would greatly add to the pleasure of all concerned! Perhaps Mary will come up with Clive. I doubt it being a good party. But I always think after talking a whole Sunday afternoon about a party and the guests, one can't believe it will [be] anything but a funeral feast. I am very well and so happy Lytton this morning because you are better. Such a dull letter from the Partridge this morning. It says Brenan is going to be married soon. Geoffrey tells me that Cole is now settled in Ireland with his bride and has become a respectable landed gentleman.

I love you so much Lytton. Only sometimes it's hellish to have you so far away.

All my love,
Carrington

To Lytton Strachey

[no address – Cheltenham?]
[n.d.]

This morning is fine and all the gale & rain of last night has vanished as suddenly as it came. And the great Cotswolds rear up bathed in showers of yellow sunshine. The poet groans at such horrible similies.

A breakfast which would have pleased you.

Porridge, eggs & apple jam.

'Lloyd George spent the day pacing up & down the magnificent Terrace of Versailles discussing affaires with Lord Reading' – what a vision!

I expect any paper but *The Times* has the announcement of an armistice with Germany announced.

The sun is amazing. You won't change your mind & come here & join my Father in a double bath chair?

I suppose Peace will be nothing like what one imagines it will be. Everybody singing [...] and embraces on the village greens with all the musicians in the world playing on their instruments ... and you writing a poem to celebrate the rejoicings in the *Daily News*. I think at least the old order of things ought to collapse. And a July Summer should break upon the world and all the trees burst out onto new leaves. But they won't. Nature is all dull as stewed cabbage with far less imagination. To hell with your shingles! Oh such a morning as this it was indeed proper that I should have received a letter and sonnet from my dearest Lytton.

Love your Mopsa

To Noel Carrington

1917 Club
Tuesday [12? November] 1918

Dearest Noel,

Well there were some excitements in London yesterday. I could have wished you had been with us all. When the guns were fired at 11 o'clock I thought it was a good joke on the part of some junkers to come over and bomb us while the cats here were at play. But it soon turned out to be Peace with a big P. Instantly everyone in the city dashed out of offices & boarded the buses. It was interesting seeing how the different stratas of people looked travelling from Hampstead. Seeing first the slum girls & cockney people dancing. Pathetic scenes of an elderly plumber nailing up a single small flag over the door. Then the scenes became wilder as one reached Camden Town & more & more frantic as one approached Trafalgar Square. Office boys & girls, officers, majors, races all heaped on taxis, and army vans driving round & round the place waving flags. In the Strand the uproar was appalling. I was to meet Monty Shearman in Adelphi for lunch & it was almost impossible I would get there! He then took me off to the Café Royal to meet some other rejoicing friends of his. Some young men I might regret to say – very far gone with the liquor of the North. – Ashmead Bartlett[1] your friend at Christ Church was of the company! We then had our lunch at the Eiffel Tower restaurant. But everyone was too scatterbrained to give the customers food – which slightly reduced the spirits of the company. Finally I left them & went to the 1917 club where – as one would expect – the promoters of Peace sat deep in their Trade Union papers & discussing Reconstruction after the war! Not all of them – but many.

Then at 6 o'ck I struggled back to Hampstead in the underground. I have never seen it so jammed with people, honestly they were pressed face against face! I had the underground conductor for my partner. Dinner with Alix at 45 Downshire. Then off to Monty Shearman's room where a great party was in full swing. Everyone was there. The halt, the sick, & the lame.

1 Ellis Ashmead Bartlett (1881–1931) was an outstanding war correspondent who reported critically on the battle of Gallipoli in 1915.

Even old Lytton from his deathbed in Sussex rushed up & joined in the merriment. I disclosed to Ashmead that I was your sister – his face blanched visibly & he groped for his hat & stick – It was a great party. I danced without stopping for 3 hrs. [Augustus] John was there. Nick [Bagenal]. All the Cambridge dons. The Café Royal outcasts. The Russian Ballet dancers. The wife of the Belgian Vandervelde. Clive Bell from Garsington. Alix. The Sitwells. Gertler and many fair ladies & officers the names of whom I cannot tell – for I did not know them. I enjoyed it very much. Nick stayed the night with us at Downshire Hill. He lives at Rye now by himself in a little cottage learning the art of farming. Barbara is getting well alright and the offspring is to be called Judith Jane! A familiar young lady she will be if she lives up to such a name. It's very nice being back in London with all this merriment again. I am glad I just escaped from Cheltenham in time, imagine spending such rejoicings with mother moralizing & the provincials trying to be roistrous. Thank you dearie for your sermon. I do heartily agree with what you say and lament the laziness of my ways [...] I am very well. But as yesterday's gay crowd probably bred a thousand more microbes I doubt if anyone will live long [...] I had a very long & depressed letter from Rex in Italy yesterday. Letters of depression – I know I sin also – ought to be forbidden or held by the writers a week & then read before being posted [...]

Oh dear one it's good about Peace. One might almost start negotiations about that cottage! All my love in high spirits

Your loving D.C.

XXX for Peace

To Lytton Strachey

45 Downshire Hill, Hampstead
Thursday morning, 9 o'ck [14 November 1918]

Lytton, it was good to see you again on Monday and I am so happy because you are really better. But I felt in a bad mood, the last two days, I think really because you vanished so suddenly, so I waited till I had ceased to be peevish. You are too good a friend to me, to inflict with tedious letters about a hysterical mind. I read a letter to you in the underground last night and actually had to laugh at myself for being such an ass!

On Tuesday night we went to Gordon Square. Clive has already I expect written a long account of it to Mary. It was one of the most exciting evenings I have ever spent. I suppose if one had been a man, with Cambridge behind, it wouldn't have astounded one quite so much. The only conclusion however arrived upon by everyone was that French letters must be more advertised to reduce the population, and that all the black races must be castrated. But it was astonishing apart from the arguments to see the characters of all those people, their faces, their attitudes. Yesterday I went to tea with Mark, to see his work, and met there a Miss Ruch, a pupil of Bertie and [George] Moore. Mark was very charming and interesting. I liked a new painting of his of a Harlequinade and some pen and ink drawings. He had some singular stories about Roger and himself and Bertie.

Then the evening I spent here with Alix. Today I paint Mrs Bridgeman. With a golden crown on her head as Queen Elizabeth! – Oh I know what I did on Tuesday, which I forgot, had lunch with Aldous and then went to tea with Osbert [Sitwell] He had bought two African figures in wood which excited me very much.

His appearance was too wonderful! Lying on two chairs, surrounded by silk shawls and cushions, writing poetry on a large sheet of paper. His collar turned up straight against his cheeks, like Byron, with a black tie wound round [...] He gave a very good account of his father appearing suddenly to see him and the way he ordered the servants to pretend he was just living in lodgings in the house. He then crept into his bed, and interviewed his father, who was so charmed with the rest of house that he almost took the first floor for himself. Osbert now lives in terror of his appearing again. Aldous told me that he took the Sitwells to see Mr Mills of Chelsea, who instantly, when alone, tried to rape them, separately! Also that the Prince of Wales has now taken Mr Mills's house as a pied de terre!

Now I must stop as I have got to go and see Barbara in her nursing home.[1] Oliver gives a party next Monday. Perhaps you'll rise from the dead for it. My love to you dear Lytton.

Yr very loving Carrington

To Lytton Strachey

45 Downshire Hill, Hampstead
Friday morning [15 November 1918]

Dearest Lytton,

I see yesterday's letter isn't posted yet. But never mind. How are you? – I saw Barbara yesterday morning, she looked surprisingly well and a Japanese grub in the cot beside her. What is the female body made of? For she told me it took nearly 24 hours coming out with acute pain all the time. In the

---

1 Barbara was recovering from the birth of her daughter Judith.

end they had to pull with pincers. The next morning she woke up and had coffee, and eggs for breakfast, and now feels quite well! [...] I saw some good Cretan Figures in the Museum and, oh Lytton, Antinous![2] What a Catamite to possess!

[...] And oh Lytton I do love you so very much. I can't say this idle life of distractions makes it easier not to miss you. Yr Mopsa

To Lytton Strachey

45 Downshire Hill, Hampstead
Tuesday night, 8 o'ck [19 November 1918]

[...] Yesterday, since you never wrote, I had every hope that I should pass away before the clock struck twelve. But God who seeth all things, one too many peutêtre? saw the boney fingers of my well beloved scratching feebly with a goose's feather, and spared my life until tonight, when behold dear Alix brought me a letter from you. Oh dearest it has made me so happy that I have sat up for the first time today, and have forgotten the horrors of this loathsome

2 Antinous (III–130) was the young lover of the Roman Emperor Hadrian.

disease. Mrs Bridgman has just brought me in my bowl of bread and milk, made very differently I confess to your Tidmarsh brew! And now, oh dear dear one, I am happy. I confess today I felt wickedly towards you and cursed God for not letting me die.[1] You hate me writing neither one way or the other. So I will be serious when I mean to be serious, and tell you that your letter only just came in time. All day I have been reading *Sense and Sensibility* and when Marianne received no letter from Willoughby I could have cried in sympathy for her. You will see by this letter that I still have a temperature and am not yet normal. Oh God! I've just upset the whole of the inkpot over my sheep skin coat, the sheets and blankets. I see any reunion with Alix is fatal! For the other night she and James upset an inkpot over Faith's best Persian mat and James used my new bath sponge to mop it up with. Last night Alix who is slightly ill, also taking her temperature in the bath room, started brushing her hair with the thermometer in her mouth, hit it with the brush, broke the tube and swallowed a considerable amount of the mercury!

[...] On Saturday night I alarmed them considerably by starting a conversation on Freud, and complexes of children. Howard[2] admitted he was very interested in the theories of Freud but knew if he once started reading those sort of books it would become an obsession with him. His wife said 'you remember Howard it very nearly did once'. He said: 'Yes and I felt I should be seeing all sorts of queer things in my friends.' C[arrington]: 'It's astonishing the number of perverts one does discover.' Howard with absolute horror: 'Oh I'd never go as far as saying that,' and instantly turned the conversation.

So on Sunday night we talked of Bolshevism and in the end I got onto my pet theme of the prevention of prostitution, and suggested that if decent intelligent females lived with young men, prostitutes would considerably diminish. I saw Howard and his wife getting more and more uneasy, till at length he said, 'Personally I cannot understand the feelings of a young man who can "go" with any woman. I should have thought it essential to feel love towards a woman to get over the repugnance and disgust of the act!!' The obvious reply of referring him to other methods with another sex I left unsaid – as he seemed so upset. The next morning they said at breakfast that neither of them had slept all night as they had talked so much! I would have given a good deal to hear that conversation! But really, Lytton, can you believe such a young man could exist? And his intentions are, to teach Philosophy after the war, at Oxford to undergraduates! There was a great deal more conversation of great import, and bearing on their states of mind. But I will tell you of it later. I was glad to see however when the small boys were given a lump of dough by the cook to play with, they insisted on

1 Carrington perhaps had a mild case of the 1918 flu that decimated post-war Europe.
2 Howard Hannay, a fellow lodger in Hampstead.

making very prolonged no I don't know the plural COCKS. But I spared the already perturbed parents to any illusion to the fact. I went to bed when I got back yesterday morning, as it was so bleak and cold outside and all today I stayed in bed. You were mistaken about Alix, for she is the best of nurses. Most reassuring. And has never yet asked me how I feel! I regretted missing my lunch with Phyllis and Edgar.[1] But everything can reoccur in this life.

Maynard takes me to dine at Kettners on Thursday, and the new ballet afterwards! I shall go to Tidmarsh to recover next weekend, and stay there I expect indefinitely unless London offers any inducement to return. But these plagues hardly make existence worth living here. Dear Lytton I am so glad you are so happy and well cared for. Do you know, I wonder, how much I care? So much, that to know that you are getting better and happy, makes it possible for me to bear your absence [...]

Give Mary my love please. Don't forget. Oh the horror of this winter. My hands have become icicles, it is as if I were lying on the pier at Brighton. Yet every window, and crack is sealed! Dearest. I love you oh so much tonight.

Your ever devoted Carrington

As this last letter shows, Freud's ideas about sexuality and the unconscious were beginning to be discussed in polite circles. The first article on his work intended for the general reader was published by Leonard Woolf in The Nation *in 1914. James Strachey had been following him seriously since 1912, and was to go to Vienna to be analysed by Freud himself in 1920 before returning to London, becoming an psychoanalyst himself and undertaking to translate Freud's writings for the Hogarth Press. Even so, both Carrington and Lytton were wary of Freudianism, not least because his followers then tended to regard homosexuality as a curable disorder.*

To Mark Gertler

The Mill House
Tuesday [December 1918]

Dearest Mark,

So active & energetic do I feel this morning that I'll not allow your letter more than ten minutes. It's cold & very clear. The sky is blue and the sun shines. Its like the ballet with an orchestra ... one must dance to the tune they play. Lately it has rained every day & has been almost completely dark. You don't realize the difference a morning like this makes as London is always damp and dark! This last week I got two little village boys with

---

1 Presumably Phyllis Boyd and an admirer.

beautiful solid faces to come & sit for me in the evening – I pay them 6pence a night! But it made me realize how good your drawing is. And the jew girl head you did. What an achievement it was. My results weren't much better than what I did at the Slade 4 years ago! Next Saturday I shall do a painting of them. They are such nice creatures. Then in the mornings I sat in the Big Mill & drew the machinery. It was a wonderful feeling being up there surrounded by bulging sacks of flour & the great wheels grinding round & round & the whole room, which is indefinitely long shaking & creaking – and then the smiling miller carrying, like some Michelangelo figure the heavy sacks on his broad shoulders. And a cat with speckled kittens lay asleep in a bag of wheat. It was so unreal, like the scene in one of those French books – by Daudet[1] – one translates sometimes and never finishes – and then to know next door to that old mill house all those complicated relationships lived! I liked the incongruity of it. The drawing wasn't as interesting as my feelings I regret to say!

[...] I hope you will enjoy your Xmas at Garsington. Won't you send me a little picture please. A pen & ink drawing to celebrate our good friendship.

Now I really can't write anymore as it will be fine enough to sit outside & paint in a few minutes. Tell me what you read? In the evening Lytton has been reading *King Lear* to me. The completion of it made me dreadfully sad last night. But what a stupendous work of art it is!

I do take such pride in our art as it is. When I hear what good things people like Roger & Borenius[2] say about your work I swell out with pride! But also you know you are so progressed as a character. And that's very nearly as difficult as to have improved in painting. I found it altogether delightful being with you this last time. And that's more than we ever managed before – at least for 4 days on end. Yes, next year we'll stay in the country together. It will be enjoyable.

Best wishes

Yr Carrington

To Mark Gertler

The Mill House

8 December 1918

Dearest Mark,

Thank you so much for your letter. It's very odd how natural it seemed to see a letter in your writing again, and after a whole year! This weekend David

---

1 Alphonse Daudet (1849–1897), French writer best known for *Lettres de mon moulin* (*Letters from my Mill*), published in 1869.
2 Tancred Borenius (1885–1948) was a Finnish art historian and academic and a friend and colleague of Roger Fry's.

Garnett came. I know you dislike him, well, well. Anyway he was very kind to me, and sat for a painting, and one evening in contortionist positions without his clothes, so I am full of gratitude as it means I can now get on with some compositions. He also cut up a lot of wood and was an obedient slave in the house. How exciting it is to draw nudes. Really I wish one could have a person to sit every day, as the excitement of drawing always upsets me rather. NO not the excitement of beholding a rather over fat young man! [...] I am glad Roger liked your work so much. He is one of the best people I think. As he really cares so much for good work. And is aloof from criticising people for their personal weaknesses and characters. I've been reading a *History of the Popes* by Macaulay[1] which I liked very much. But most of this week has been spent getting my studio ready and setting the old house straight. I grudge every ½ hour spent on such things. But my nature is so dreadfully untidy that unless I start 'straight', in a week I should not be able to move because of the mess. And with painting that would be impossible as you know. I like looking back on my visit to London because I saw you. What I always feel is we are meant to persevere through this somewhat awkward time because later things will be better for us. Yes when we are very old with grey hair we will live in a little cottage, probably Miss Walker's at Cholesbury, and you will hold my withered old hands in yours. Well, well [...]

Yrs affectionate

Carrington

In late December 1918, Carrington's father Samuel died at the age of eighty-two. For ten years, since suffering a stroke, he had been helpless and often in pain.

To Lytton Strachey

Tatchley
Sunday [December 1918]

Dearest, you were so good to me all of yesterday. I must thank you at once – Well it was absolutely different from anything I had imagined. But the daughter of Lear has come down for breakfast, so I must stop for a moment: well that's over. Last night to judge from every appearance nothing might have happened. The conversation at dinner was too horrible. My sister sat there in a black evening dress, with her pale fat face as hard as a block of steel. When my mother said: 'We had to go to Davis the local undertaker; it will be just plain wood, not oak, with a cross on top of the coffin. There

---

1 Thomas Babington Macaulay (1800–59), the great Whig historian, published an essay on Ranke's *History of the Popes* in 1840.

is such a shortage of wood you see,' the sister replied: 'Naturally at a time like this with a great shortage of materials, wood is required by the Government for purposes of greater National Importance.' And so it went on from coffins, to wills and deeds of settlements. My sister's toneless voice discussing strokes, and other cases of death through paralysis she had known. Her character is such that my mother is completely dominated by it and I saw her becoming less and less human. I didn't want them to weep, but at least they might not have taken such a cold hellish interest over his relics. I couldn't help remembering all the time that a dead body lay in the next room, across the passage, instead of that human being in the bath chair in front of the fire. You are right: there's nothing so crushing and wretched as hard human beings without feelings. They were simply like two pieces of furniture conversing. The piano, and the marble mantelpiece could not have felt less. They say the funeral will not be until Thursday so I suppose I shall have to stay till then. If I was a little braver I would run out of this house.

I don't believe they can have felt physical affection for a person.

It used to be so different when I came home, and went into the dining room. He used to hug me and almost cry because he was so glad to see me. They sat eating cold turkey, and made some polite address, and then discussed my clothes and what I must buy. The little cook with her wizened face feels more grief.

Dear one, I felt some more love grow to you today. I hope you'll look after yourself properly and do ask someone if you find it lonely. I shall come back Thurs. evening if I can. But I'll write again, and let you know for certain.

Do you know they sent a wire to me on Saturday which never reached Tidmarsh. How little one knows what the last state will be. As a little boy running in these lanes of Prestbury, my father little guessed he would die amongst those women folk, in such captivity in the same village. Dearest, your friendship means so much that I must just thank you. Because today more than most days I feel the importance of knowing you, my very dearest friend.

Your Carrington

1919

Tatchley
Wednesday morning [1 January 1919]

Dearest Lytton,

It was good to get two letters from you this morning and so full of Tidmarsh and that little painted room of many colours. I don't believe if I lived alone at the Mill, small boys would cut up logs of wood for me. No, it requires a beard and long white fingers to be served like that in this world. But you must have been far more tired that I was, by the time you reached home. Let's make a vow here, and forever, never to go to Reading again.

May I write you a really grim letter. It's pure selfishness because I can't bear it going round and round in my brain.

It seemed like Sunday all yesterday for the blinds were all drawn. In the morning I had to go to town with my mother, and be fitted by the incomparably grand young Ladies at some female shop. They couldn't see that it's not very interesting choosing stockings and black coats. My mother seemed entirely engrossed and talked continuously about the 'correctness' of certain things. I couldn't see what on earth all this had to do with my father being dead. All lunch the conversation was on clothes. My sister is unparalleled in her stoniness. I bought a pair of black boy's boots when I was left alone, which enraged my sister and mother when they saw them. My spirits by the afternoon had become so depressed that at last I couldn't bear it any longer. I hated them for being so indecently interested in his death and my mother went on talking about peculiarities to my sister who was so bored that she merely said 'Yars' 'Yars'. The rooms are so arranged that to go to the lavatory one has to pass my father's bedroom, which rooms are both at the end of a long passage on the ground floor.

I went in to see him for all day I keep wondering how he lay. It was so different from anything I had imagined. I thought he would have been on his bed, as he used to lie in the mornings. But there was a long narrow coffin covered by a white sheet and the bed stood there by itself so big and empty.

When I lifted a napkin, oh Lytton, there was not his face, but a face very small, and pale yellow. So dim and icy cold. Then I knew how very much I loved him and now how lost it all was. That cragged hoary old man with his bright eyes, and huge helpless body but so big always, now lay in this narrow box in white linen and it was a ghost compared to that man, that lay there. And then a vision of all those people whose faces I have loved came. Teddy too, must have gone all pale like that.

I could not believe the change would be so horrible. I hated something for making his face so smooth. Yes it was saint like, like the marble bishops in the cathedrals. Oh Lytton why didn't I love him more when he could feel. I might have fought for him; he was too helpless himself. I knew what he cared for; how my mother tormented him, and how he suffered, and yet I did so little. I read yesterday Tolstoy's *Ivan Ilyich*. My father hadn't even Geriasim to comfort him. I miss him so dreadfully this time, here. He was so like me, that I felt he always understood and was on my side. Now I am all alone with these two. I know my mother cared and is unhappy. But I can't forgive her for taming him as she did, and for regarding all of his independence and wildness as 'peculiarities' and just making out he was a sentimental good husband. Then can she really care, when she talks as she does, knowing that pale ghost lies in that other room. I hate my sister seeing me. It's so beastly not even to be allowed to cry without my mother calling for me to go with her to some infernal shop. And when my mother leaves the room, my sister speaks in such a way that my blood rushes hot into my head.

But I am glad that he has escaped from it all. I like to think of him wandering vaguely in India in that bright light, really loved by people and perfectly happy. But instead I see him captive in all these houses, in the cold grey winters always being worried by domestic details, scolded like a child, restricted, wretched. And I knew, and never told him. Ten years must have been a long time for him.

Dearest, I am glad that there is you for me to love. I knew you care: you did not have to tell me so. I shall beg my mother to let me leave on Thursday. You'll forgive me for writing so. But it makes it better to know I can talk to you.

Oh, I wish I could forget that ghostly face and in this little bedroom, on every side I see Teddy's things. His books, and photographs. Your letters comforted me so much this morning. Dearest Lytton, you've meant more to me these past few days than ever before.

Yr loving Carrington

PS My mother has just been in the room and wants me stay on with her, I gather indefinitely. When I said I really couldn't she accused me of being selfish, and said she couldn't bear being left alone. I wish you were here to advise me, I can't believe I can do any good, as I feel too wretched to cheer her up, which is what she says she wants. I thought I could come back, and stay. Or is it really selfish of me to go away because I can't bear this?

To Mark Gertler

The Mill House
3 January 1919

Dearest Mark,

I just got your long letter this evening as I have been away at home this last week. For my father died last Saturday and I had to go back home for the funeral. Oh Mark I did suffer horribly. It was ghastly to see a little yellow ghost with a saint like marble face lying in a narrow coffin instead of that splendid old man in his wheelchair by the fire. And then that hard china faced sister & my mother with her sentimental attitude was almost more hurting.

How dreadful it is to see a human being alive and hard & callous without feelings.

It was like one long nightmare from morning & through the night. At last I couldn't bear it any longer and as I couldn't possibly cheer my mother in my frame of mind, so rushed away this morning. It's upset me rather. So many new ideas & emotions rushed through me every hour & day. Now I feel so tired & empty headed. How I hate death. He was so big and simple and more good than most people. That goodness which Blake had. Which one is compelled to reverence. Even if one does disbelieve in their religion & primitive beliefs in Heaven & Hell.

[...] Only for one thing am I sorry. That I who understood & knew what he cared for, never fought for him against my mother & her conventions & did not make his life happier. That I do regret.

I have only seen lately one Cezanne & that is the one which Maynard Keynes has[1] which I must say I like immensely [...]

Alix took me up to London for a day after Xmas to see a new ballet & before it began I slipped into the National Gallery & saw the Ingres. But what excited me most was the little El Greco & the Bellini of Mehmet. I thought the large portrait by Ingres very astounding. – But somehow less inspired compared to that El Greco – no, inspired with a feeling which interested me less is a more true statement.

I love that picture you gave me so much. Thank you again.

I shall work hard now. That was one of the horrors of being at home. It was quite impossible to do any work so all day I was at the mercy of my own gloomy moods & the whims of my mother which meant going into

---

1 Keynes bought the Cézanne, a still life of apples, in Paris in 1918. He took it to Charleston and as he had too much to carry left it briefly behind a hedge. It is now in the Fitzwilliam Museum in Cambridge.

a dreary fashionable town & buying black clothes. I get to dislike that female mind which delights in conventions & appearances more & more.

The joy this afternoon to be back in my breeches & old grey jersey sitting over a fire – with no conversation. I did love that new ballet, *Tales for Children*. The conception of the mad girl in the bed is excellent & the outspread cloak with females underneath.[1] My love to you dear creature.

Yr Carrington

To Mark Gertler

The Mill House
Friday [January 1919]

Dear Mark,

Thank you for your long letter. Tonight I feel infinitely lonely, and rather depressed. Partly because I am alone and then I suddenly realized a few moments ago what a beastly ungenerous nature I had created inside my frame. Yet, you realize all my letters to you are like woodcuts, limited in their technique, and that certain elements, as colour, will never be shown. My brother has been spending the last two days here with me. Yesterday a friend of his [Rex Partridge] came down to stay – I had been reading Berty's[2] new book on the reform of the state, and foolishly fell into the belief that it was all very possible. That except for a few bloated capitalists, and politicians everyone really wanted to see such a life of freedom, and happiness. And when this young man and my brother started talking together after dinner, I woke up into realizing how hopeless, and distant such ideals are; that the educated people make the blockade which prevents revolutions, and progress. This young man thought himself very advanced and yet was so self satisfied, and narrow-minded, as to simply dismiss with a few cynical phrases any variety of mankind who he didn't agree with. A certain callousness, and lack of reverence for life, and death appalled me. They neither of them felt any passion or interest in things like we do. They discussed their futures and weighed the advantages and disadvantages of certain professions. But there was no desire to do any creative work of their own. What a gulf this fixes between one and such people. My brother is so charming that it hurt to hear him become intolerant, and complicatedly conventional. Today was so beautiful, that I forgot, when I woke up and saw a golden moon

1 Perhaps a performance by Sergei Diaghilev's company the Ballets Russes, then taking Bloomsbury by storm.
2 Bertrand Russell had published *Proposed Roads to Freedom: Socialism, Anarchism and Syndicalism* in 1918.

disappearing like a guilty orange cat from the larder, down below the trees, and barns and the sun shone out.

And Noel was so gay and happy, after all the disappointments and problems of life of last night. We borrowed a little pony trap from the blacksmith, and drove to some enchanted woods where Monkey Puzzle trees and great dark yews, and conifers grow and had lunch in a little inn. And then drove home in the afternoon. Now they have gone. And I feel depressed because I feel I may have hurt them, and spoilt their pleasure by being standoffish and superior. Noel looked so beautiful out in the garden that I really felt after all if he had such a good nature, his views and prejudices didn't much matter. This is contrary to anything Berty [Bertrand Russell] would say. But I confess at that moment I felt it!!! I suspect this intolerance of young boisterous men is really old age on my part!

To Lytton Strachey

Tatchley
Wednesday [22 January 1919]

Dearest one,

Well here I am, and you are pavement-tapping, boy-accosting on the streets of London. I don't foresee much of interest happening to me here. So I am contenting myself with organizing a grand trunk to trunk Loot indoors. You groan. No I promise I won't bring back a single Benares brass bowl, or one carved bracket. Haydn's dictionary, a rattle to keep the birds from our cherries, some chintz to cover a chair, and an eiderdown quilt, also some new pyjamas which I suppose I shall have to give up to Le grand signor! My parent was of course perfectly well, having recovered the day of my arrival. What a waste of time all this business is. You see I am bad tempered already. You will write and tell me your plans? I gather she won't go away till next week. So if you want the house for any lofty, or base purposes I can easily stay here till Monday. But if you would like my company to assist at cutting the cottage pie, I will come back on Saturday. I saw George's name looming large in the *Telegraph* front sheet this morning! Even at the risk of driving you mad with my incessant repetition, I whisper very softly, not to disturb your siesta, that you have made me so very happy lately, and I have loved the evenings, and you become more precious to me every day.

Such a nightmare last night, with Aldous in bed [a dream]. Everything went wrong, I couldn't lock the door; all the bolts were crooked. At last, I chained it with a watch chain and two nails. Then I had a new pair of thick pyjamas on and he got so cross because I wouldn't take them off and they were all scratchy. Everything got in a mess, and he got so angry, and kept on trying to find me in bed by peering with his eyeglass, and I thought all the time how I could account to my mother for the mess on my pyjamas!

[...] All my love
from your
Mopsa

From Carrington's diary

[14 February 1919]

Talking about Lytton, if one did try and write what happened to him every day, what a grim failure it would be. All his adventures and experiences are mental, and only enjoyed by himself. Outwardly it's like the life of one of the hens. Meals dividing up the day, books read in the morning, siesta, walk to Pangbourne, more books. A French lesson with me, perhaps dinner. Reading aloud. Bed and hot water bottles, and every day the same apparently. But inside, what a variety, and what fantastic doings. And great schemes I suspect. Sometimes internal ragings which never come out. And plans for a future which I could never guess. I wonder how much his appearance captivates me. One learns very little of his inside. Some things one knew from the beginning. That his conversation is always fascinating, and instructive. He is kind and sympathetic, intolerant, prejudiced to a degree sometimes. Obstinate and with a grandness and aloofness I've never met before. But everything very sudden, like a bird flashes across the sky on a walk. I mean his angers, and laughter. Painted too vilely today. I give up the nude bathers with disgust and turn to something new tomorrow. A long walk, and talk about the Georges before tea.

[18 February 1919]

Today mother sent me Teddy's sailor clothes. How awful it is to realize how little I knew, or appreciated him – Yet one's senses become hardened by space or time. A year ago would I have not cried? And now I just felt dully miserable. Bones in some cloggy wet clay now, which used to fill those trowsers so tightly. How I loved him at Hurstbourne when he came on leave carrying his sack on his back. And in London at the Garnetts' flat when Nellie the servant showed him into my bedroom and he sat on the bed, so brown with his black shining eyes and hair. No there will never be such a face again. His beauty was so immense and solid. Why need he have died?

One feels he was a soldier. And never cared for life. He had seen so little of his life. And even if he had never would have cared for this. I selfishly wanted him. Little Roy, that child, reminds me of him, his grunts, and fat cheeks and smiles. And a little packet of sailor clothes in my bedroom is all that he has left to me. Cruel hateful war. That such loveliness should have been destroyed. There is no one to tell. They are old, and after all how can they feel when they never saw him. Yet Lytton has taught me how to feel as I do tonight.

In March 1919 Carrington set off again with her brother and his friend Rex Partridge, this time to Spain, accompanied by Rex's sister Dorothy. Her letters to both Gertler and Lytton stress how dull conventional young men were; in fact, both she and Lytton were increasingly attracted by Rex, who had returned to Oxford to pick up his interrupted studies.

To Mark Gertler

> 1917 Club, 4 Gerrard Street, London W.1
> write to c/o Thomas Cook, Madrid, Spain
> [March 1919]

Dearest Mark,

Thank you so much for your letter – Yes it was unfortunate that I couldn't come to Garsington. But this Spanish business made everything so rushed that I hadn't time to stay with Ottoline. But it was just good to see you for that little while. I enjoyed the dance. The young men were so lovely. But God how dreary, ordinary and stupid! They would make good bedding plants but not for use in the daytime. As they thought I was 16, and a nice young lady I didn't have even any consolation in any direction! We sail tomorrow morning early. It sounds extraordinary. I can hardly believe it. I wish I had other company. I don't take much to the young man, and his sister is still worse. Noel is alright, but completely influenced by the young man. Still if I see some El Grecos and Goyas I shall be quite contented, and really one always enjoys these holidays in spite of people I find. I hope you'll feel better after Brighton, and be able to get back to your work. I hope Brett's scheme of your living with her at night, may make things rather happier for you. I've got a confounded swollen neck which doesn't make me feel very cheerful today. But the doctor said it wasn't serious, only I am so vain, that I hate being hideous. I cover it with scarfs and that nearly stifles one. It also is rather painful. I expect Spain will set one up in health again. You'll write to

me? And I'll send you post cards, and a letter. It will be exciting coming
back again. I'll come and see you directly I get back to London. Be kind to
Brett.

My love to you dear friend.

Yr Carrington

*Carrington sent long descriptive letters and drawings to Lytton almost every day
from Spain. She found Dorothy Partridge, who was suspicious of her bohemian
ways, tiresome and, as always, pined for Lytton's company.*

To Lytton Strachey

Madrid
[15 April 1919]

My Dearest Lytton,

I got your letters this morning. I was overjoyed to hear from you. And
to know you were with Alix and James, and so happy. How we'll talk when
we get back: – Lyme Regis, Castro del Rey, Regis Lyme, Rey de Castro and
ad infinitum. This morning I spent in the Prado. How can one say what one
feels when all the air has been pressed out of one's lungs through the sheer
exhaustion of marvelling.

The portraits of Goya perhaps delighted me as much as anything.
Especially the reposing lady draped. I forget her name. El Greco is quite,
quite different from what you would imagine. The pictures are so large, and
the colour incredibly beautiful. [...] Several which were quite new to me.
Then I saw some wonderful Titians. And other Italians. But one can't look
at them when one knows there are Goyas to feast upon.

Downstairs there were great rooms filled with decorations by Goya and
pen and ink, and red chalk drawings, sketches for the etchings and some
new ones. Many very bawdy. But marvellously drawn. He had such wit,
compared to most painters. But it nearly killed one with fatigue. Especially
as I never slept at all last night in that 3rd class wooden seated train from
Sevilla. There are disputes going on with Thomas Cook about a passage
back, which may be difficult to arrange. Noel unfortunately is obliged to be
back on the 25th, I would give much to linger a little longer in this country.
What a statement to make to you. But oh Lytton, Lytton, Lytton, I am so
happy here, and the sun is so good and hot.

Your letter and the Prado have made this day one complete day of pleasure
for me. I feel it is like some dream. Once one wakes up and comes back to

England, it will never come again. Tomorrow I hope to go to the Prado all
the morning by myself, and on Thursday to Toledo for the day. On Friday
we shall have to leave for BilBayo: spelt wrong Bil Bao. When shall I see
you, Where shall I see you, again?

Madrid is very stuffy after those mountain towns and the people almost
as hideous as the wanderers of Tottenham Court Road. Yes, would you
believe it?

I send you all my love and xxxxxxxxxxx Oh I wish you could only be here
to make it quite perfect.

Your Carrington

To Mark Gertler

The Mill House
Saturday [April 1919]

Dearest Mark,

I came back here this morning early, so I shall not see you until next
week. Directly I know which day I shall come up to London, I will send
you a post card, so that I can be sure of seeing you. What a boost Clive
gave you in the Athenaeum! Not that it matters much, but it's always a
pleasure added to having done something good, if people who really understand about painting like Roger appreciate one's work so highly. We'll have
a regular El Greco afternoon when I come back. I will be able to tell you
the colours of all those picture, and also the Goyas. I hadn't any money,
or I would have bought you some reproductions in Madrid. It's nice to be
back here in the country, and see all the flowers in the garden. I found
London rather appalling those two days. Living quite vaguely, and wild for
more than a month makes the narrow street life, and hideousness of civi-
lization, jar on one rather acutely. I hope you enjoyed your visit to
Garsington. One comes back so full of enthusiasm about Spain, and those
pictures, and longing to, in some way, convey the pleasures one has had to
other people, only to find no one wants to hear a damn word on Spain! I
have seen sights one hardly dreamt of and people so beautiful that one
quivered to look at them, and then those El Grecos at Madrid and Toledo,
yet one has to keep it all inside. I feel so strong just now – and savage. But
I see it will wear off in this cold climate before many days. I am again sorry
to have been so stupid as not to have seen you in London. My love to you.
Do keep well.

Yr Carrington

To Lytton Strachey

The Mill House
Sunday, 11 May 1919

[...] Noel never came as some doctor Austin from Rouen who saved his arm from coming off, appeared at Oxford for the weekend to see him. The Bird Partridge however flew over to tell me. I joined him to my minor Battalion of slaves in the garden and made him plant beans & peas without a break till lunch! Whilst the small boys watered the garden & cut the grass, I rode an imaginary steed round the footpaths cracking my whip and giving orders.

All the afternoon the Partridge planted parsnips in the garden whilst the minors pumped. I've got a headache tonight so I can't write a proper letter. I think it's the fug of the valley & general heat. Not that I am in heat ... how could one be with a chest of drawers? All the same I would rather like a really exquisite lover to come to me on Sunday when I am alone here!

Legg came in & made me a treacle tart & washed up today. She is so charming that I nearly weep every time I see her to think she cannot stay here with us always. What did you think of La Crozier? Too refined is all I fear.[1] The tulips & wallflowers are so lovely in the garden. And the broad beans stand like lines of green Huzzars in their rows. Tell me in your letter, what happened at the weekend? I hated leaving you. Your conversation was so entertaining & have I ever told you before. I love it so much [...] But I think I'll stay here all this next week, & come up the Monday after. I read Donne today. He is an amazing poet.

My love
Your mopsa xxxx

To Lytton Strachey

1917 Club
Wednesday [21 May 1919]

Dearest,

[...] What fun the party sounded last night! Remember it all to tell me next week, I loved seeing you so much on Monday night. Do you know how very much I care for you? And it's a better sort of affection than it used to be, because now I am not so impatient to be always with you. Because I know always you are here.

---

1 A potential cook-housekeeper.

[...] You won't go and get ill, will you. I am only afraid you'll get too tired rushing about. I'll write from Pangbourne. I am so happy at going back. The beauty of that garden fills me more and more, and tomorrow I start my painting – and you say you'll start your writing. Well – we shall see? Dear. Dear. Why are all the inhabitants of this place like frogs and lizards from the underworld. One might write a Greek play especially for this club with a great chorus of monsters and insects!

Promise me a letter tomorrow. Lytton I must tell you what a difference just knowing you makes. But it will be good to have you next week ... and if the High Ladies of the Court grant me my wish. Hugger me, and Bugger me and cover me with kisses.

Yr Carrington

With the Mill House as their shared base, Carrington felt more secure with Lytton, despite his comings and goings; but there was about to be a new development. After they returned from Spain, Rex Partridge became a frequent visitor to the Mill. Before long, beguiled and liberated by Lytton and Carrington's company, his conventional opinions and behaviour began to alter. While it is doubtful that he and Lytton ever had a full sexual relationhip, there was certainly some sexual play between them that summer, while he also became Carrington's lover.

To Lytton Strachey

The Mill House
Sunday evening, 1 June 1919

Dearest Lytton

I did so love seeing you on Friday. It made me frightfully happy. I wonder how you are enjoying tonight. Brenan never came. He wrote & said it was too far to come even for the day. Which disappointed me a little this morning. The young man P came on Saturday after lunch and spent his afternoon in the BATH & reading volumes from our sex library on the lawn.

The slothful & despondent Jewess came again![1] I regret to say Major P did not display your courtesy. But after eating the strawberries & cream she brought, returned to the most remote corner of the lawn & read his books in silence. I admit she was more depressing and depressed even than on Friday! There was a dreadful moment when Mrs Mason came & asked me if she was to lay for three for supper. I simply felt I couldn't bear it so shook

1 Margaret Waley, Arthur Waley's mother.

my head & said 'two' – practically in the hearing of the Waley. But the creature simply went off smiling sadly. Without as much as look of reproach. I think she is one of the most revolting females I've ever seen.

Mrs Mason turns out to be a very good cook & presents us with enormous meals & teas with scones & beautiful thin & gentle cress sandwiches!!! Her only complaint is that she hasn't enough work to do! The tribe of wild children increases daily. But no doubt the treacherous bath will soon reduce their numbers. Noel says that essay on Shakespeare is exactly the sort of thing that they would appreciate and would next Monday week suit you. That's the next Monday after the Cambridge Bank Holiday Monday. Also would you mind if Raleigh[1] came to your reading? As he is an honorary member of the club – & is sometimes asked. But that would be as you like. I say that is a wondrous book! I never enjoyed – for a long time – reading any book so much. One certainly at moments found it very hard to believe a child had written it. I also so envied the life of Ethel! I shall read it once every month and every time I have a pain in my stomach [...]

Noel came over very early this morning to breakfast. He had to go to some lectures yesterday & couldn't get away. He has spent all today reading vast tomes on the French Revolution. And I've been drawing R.P. naked in the long grass in the orchard. I confess I got rather a flux over his thighs & legs. So much so that I didn't do very good drawings.

In the *Daily News* I saw Maynard had completely broken down & was back in England. Perhaps the corruptness of those friends was so bad he deliberately abandoned the sinking ship.[2]

Well, no more galavanting now for me.

I shall, like Martha or was it Mary, always be found sitting on the doorstep waiting for the Lord.

It was too infuriating to have missed you that day by going to Oxford.

Dearest Lytton how much I loved every moment with you on Friday. How completely & entirely.

Yr Carrington

PS Do go & ask Geoffrey Humpback [Heinemann] about Daisy Ashford.[3] He probably knows a good many interesting facts concerning her. I can't believe she's grown up into an average normal female and again I often think it's all a great fraud.

---

1 Walter Raleigh (1861–1922) was a fellow of Merton College and chair of English Literature at Oxford.

2 Keynes was suffering from exhaustion due to his work as the Treasury representative at the Paris Peace Conference.

3 Daisy Ashford's novel *The Young Visiters* had just been published. She had indeed written it at the age of nine.

To Lytton Strachey

The Mill House
Monday, 9 June 1919

Dearest,

I wonder if you will be able to get back tomorrow. Perhaps I will have a letter from you soon. Well, we have just returned this morning from Garsington. What a mixture of pleasures and torments. I went over alone on Saturday evening, had dinner with Noel & Partridge & then went to this meeting. The Trades Union agitator was too appalling. It's pretty grim if such men as these are going to control our futures. His stupidity nearly made one shriek aloud and when he recited in the grand melodramatic manner a poem by Kipling I thought a hasty retreat to spare one from worse horrors would be necessary. The young men who spoke afterwards however retained me.

The creature I rather loved last time, whose name is Ross, was there again. Looking extraordinarily attractive. Noel like a brute wouldn't introduce him to me. No that's not true because it probably didn't occur to him.

I slept at Temperance Hotel & early the next morning rode out to the trout farm with N and P & swam in the river.

Had an enormous breakfast outside the inn in the sun. I wish you could stay there next Monday but I'm afraid you'd not be able to get out there after the essaying as it's some two miles outside Oxford. But it's such a perfect inn & the country immediately surrounding it, so lovely.

Then far across the flat fields & the river one saw the little spires & spikes of Oxford very clear & grey. Like a miniature. We found a gramophone & danced outside on the grass & swam again & danced again until 12 o'ck. Then I helped P get lunch in his rooms and whipped up a great egg flip sherry cocktail for Alix's benefit who had promised to come. Unfortunately she got into the wrong train at Didcot & travelled to Swindon! Why she is alive in this world surprises me sometimes.

So the three of us had to fall on the cocktails & salmon & give up Alix. Then Noel went back to his studies and I continued my investigations. At four we remet & called for Delaware & bicycled out to Garsington.

Four motorcars outside gave one misgivings! But the spectacle on the lawn confirmed them a thousand times. La Princess Bibesco,[1] a Danish monster, a Mrs Holden, two young ladies from Summerville [*sic* – the then

---

1 Elizabeth Asquith (1897–1945), daughter of the former prime minister, had just married the Romanian diplomat Prince Antoine Bibesco (1878–1951), a friend of Marcel Proust's. She was twenty-one and he was forty.

women's college, Somerville], Toronto,[1] Goldie & Charlie Sanger,[2] Mr Mills, & his late Dorothy Warren, the lovely Peter & his friend Mr Cook, Alix (who had eventually reached Oxford & motored out), Her Ladyship & old crumbling Philip. Our arrival had the effect fortunately of making the Princess party & the Warrens depart. Of course it was impossible to get any tea to drink or eat. So whilst Ottoline was saying goodbye I took control & ordered fresh relays in her name, from Minnie. Goldie, Charlie & my cortege were soon hard at work discussing Trade Unions & the League of Nations. Ottoline returned to her seat at the table exhausted & in very ill humour of which I had to bear the brunt. Then the young men swam in the pond & all except Toronto went back to Oxford. Goldie was completely bowled over by the Major's blue eyes & pestered me with questions about him!!! Ottoline now raves about his appearance & even Alix ... ? I remain adamant & admit – to you – that his thighs are elegant, his private parts enorme, his deltoids as white as ivory – but his face. The face of a Norwegian dentist. The evening was in a different way really as horrible as the meeting on Saturday.

Philip played the pianola for 2 hours without stopping. Except for an appalling conversation most of the time whilst he played, about the merits & demerits of Mozart & Beethoven! Goldie & Charlie are frightfully nice. I don't quite know which one charmed me most. Ottoline was obviously rongé [ravaged] with a disease & simply hated everybody. Toronto seemed rather depressed & looked spotty & ill. This morning Noel & P were talking in the pond, so Ottoline detained the P to breakfast. When I left with Alix, Goldie like an old black spider was winding him up with his smiles into his web. He maintained they were so intelligent compared to the Cambridge creatures [...] Ottoline snuffed about your refusing to stay that weekend with her & tried to find out what you were doing. I, with truth, denied all knowledge of your movements. There were more catawaulings against Clive, and fury because Djaggers [Diaghilev] hadn't turned up with Massine & Picasso etc. to lunch yesterday as they promised.[3]

Oh Lytton I love you almost to hurting point.

Yr Mopsa

With xxxxxxx

---

1 Frank Prewett (1893–1962) was a handsome Canadian poet known as Toronto who was brought to Garsington by Siegfried Sassoon.
2 Charlie Sanger was another of Lytton's Cambridge friends.
3 Ottoline Morrell was a great enthusiast for the Ballets Russes, run by Diaghilev and starring Massine. Picasso had come over from Paris, where he had made the aquaintance of Clive Bell, to design sets.

To Lytton Strachey

The Mill House
Wednesday [18 June 1919]

Dearest Lytton,
... I wish you hadn't to be away in this marvellous weather. I find it hard to believe that it's as hot, or lovely anywhere as in this garden. I prayed earnestly for your welfare last night. I hope it wasn't as bad as you antici- pated. I feel the meeting with Shaw[1] may slightly sugar the quinine. Partridge came over today after breakfast on his bicycle. He has just gone away. He of course didn't give me any account of your essay club. Partly perhaps because I didn't ask him. He said you were a great success. But confessed regret that you didn't like him personally. Will you write me a detailed account of it? [...]

I fear I shall not see you perhaps on Sunday, as Noel wants me to go to a ball with him in the evening which means staying in Oxford for the night. I'll come back Sunday morning as the cock crows eight. N.B. James proposed himself for the week end with his second wife. As he will have told you.[2]

Drawing the bud Partridge in my studio was not without its bass accom- paniment this afternoon. It was slightly Russian, like a short story. He is so naïve and young. I felt like some mature hag boosted up with a complete knowledge of mankind!! All the while Mrs Mason sang below, and churned her plates, the Mill creaked round and at intervals the water came crashing into the tank from the pump below [...]

But gordie, gordie, when he talks about Oxford and the doings of these young men, UGH! I see it means a large bed in that cottage at Marsland if one is to put up with him for a fortnight. And painting all day long so that one doesn't have to talk [...]

Lytton, every time you come back I love you more. Something new which escaped me before, in you completely surprises me. Do you know when I think of missing a day with you it gives me proper pain inside. I can't help saying this at a risk of boring you.

Goodbye, Carrington

---

1 Presumably George Bernard Shaw (1856–1950), playwright.
2 James Strachey, who was living with Alix, later his wife, was also romantically involved with Noel Olivier.

To Lytton Strachey

Christ Church, Oxford
Thursday, 26 June 1919

Dearest,

I am sorry not to have written to you before but there has not been time. Truly. Still you know it wasn't negligence. One thinks of course life will or ought to be altered by coming bravely to this harbour of young men. But I assure you one leaves much the same as one came!

[...] The first dance on Tuesday was at Merton College in the Hall there. It is rather a lovely building inside. I was interested to see a portrait of Bishop Creighton[1] gazing down sternly at the frivolous couples below. Then one wandered in the gardens which run right along adjoining those Botanical gardens.

But somehow I became rather furious – these young men do, you know, take their pleasures so pompously. They mix their eggs up with yours & hold your hand & then stroll around the gardens or sit on iron chairs discussing rowing & the pleasures of Oxford life & worse still generalising without an end on life. But their respectability appals one. It was after this dance that we went to the big hotel to the other college Ball and danced till five thirty. R. P. really dances so perfectly that I became almost attached to him by the end of he evening. Then it is rather a relief to find a young man who does enjoy more than uncaressing leg pressures [...]

I got back to Oxford at four, & went to sleep in a punt until 7 o'ck. Then another dance, this time at the town Hall given by Trinity Hall.

R. P. couldn't go as he was too exhausted with one thing and another and is really training for Henley. So I was at the mercy of all the stray young men of Noel's acquaintance. I met the man who Noel goes out with in September to Bombay. I take the blackest view of him as a companion to work with. His views on the suppression of the natives and the censoring of literature affected me. I should think N. L. C. [Noel] in spite of his moderation would grieve the Clarendon[2] rather if that young man is typical of their officials [...]

I slept till 9.30 this morning and am now just having breakfast with R. P. He told me a good deal which will amuse you about Goldie that weekend at Garsington! And Mark [...]

I asked N. L. C. last night at the dance if he would mind me sharing a bed in Cornwall with his companion.

1 Bishop Creighton (1843–1901), a revered churchman and historian, had studied at Merton.
2 Noel was joining the Clarendon Press, part of the Oxford University Press.

*For all her protestations about the dullness of her brother's Oxford friends, and
her offhand references to Rex Partridge (also known as the Major, or Majorio,
and before long, at Lytton's request, Ralph), Carrington seems to have enjoyed
herself a good deal at the Oxford summer balls. And her 'investigations' with
Partridge were certainly sexual – one letter included a small drawing of an erect
penis. She was beginning to realise that Lytton, far from disliking him, was
becoming infatuated with Partridge and that she could amuse and delight him,
always her aim, by reporting what was going on between them. Gertler, as usual,
was kept in the dark.*

To Mark Gertler

The Mill House
Tuesday [n.d. July 1919?]

Dear Mark,

Thank you so much for a good letter. It wasn't in least selfish & its crudity
was its point. You never write dull letters and I should be bored if you wrote
polite letters asking me questions about myself [...]

[...] I am alone here just at present. I must say I always rather enjoy it,
as one gets the whole day to oneself with no distractions, although it was
very enjoyable having Alix here this last month. Last Sunday I did a little
nude painting of that friend of Noel's, who you saw at Garsington [Partridge].
It's always so exciting to have the nude to paint again. That's the main
disadvantage of the country, although I find most people, even Alix, are very
ready to sit. I have hopes this picture will be better than most of mine. If
only I can finish it in the way I want to. Three I abandoned because I couldn't
carry on with them. But I've done a good many drawings [...] Fancy you
working from 10–7. I find it seldom one can work so long.

Next week I have to go to Cornwall with Noel for 2 weeks. He goes to
Bombay in September to work in a Printing Firm. So I promised to spend
a holiday with him before he goes.

It's the same place I went to 2 years ago. So I shall I hope be able to do
some landscapes. Generally one is so distracted finding out what the county
is like that one wastes time. I shall look forward to seeing your work when
I come back in the Autumn to London [...] I like that book by Daisy Ashford
better than any book I've ever read. It was sheer pleasure to read. Someone
I know met her at a party the other night. They said she confessed she never
wrote anything after she was 14, But that the *Visiters* was entirely her own
work and she had written a great many more at the same age! Isn't it incredible? I believe a mind like that should simply never create again & grow up

into from all accounts a perfectly ordinary intelligent young woman! I am so glad you loved it also. How good it was to hear from you again!

Yrs D. C.

None of Carrington's nude paintings of Ralph have survived, but some of her drawings of unidentified male nudes look very like him. These drawings show an appreciation of the male body, although her appetite for sex with Ralph, as he later told a friend, was never great.

The holiday in Cornwall with him and Noel was a mixed success.

To Lytton Strachey

West Mill Cottage, Welcombe, Bude
Monday [14 July 1919]

Dearest,

Twenty times a day I wish you were here! [...]

On Saturday we went to shop and bought food. That took most of the morning, walking up and down innumerable valleys. One's memory fails one horribly remembering these depths. Such a lunch at the Bush Inn, Morwenstow, for 1/3, cream, saffron buns, and black-a-berrie jam. Then I went after tea to see the Boxes. On the path down the hill Mrs Box appeared driving the cows; she held up both her arms and waved them, with a stick in one hand. And then ran towards me! It was delightful to see her again. She is still full of vigour and every day she fetches the cows from the marshes by the cottage and takes them back to the farm! And she is 72!

Then we called on Jenny and Rebecca Ann. They of course thought the Major the most lovely young man they'd ever seen and inwardly thought what a nice pair we made!

The evening was spent quarrelling vigorously over the war and C. O.s [conscientious objectors] till I became so tired and angry that I gave it up. The night was pleasant but oh dearie, I see God has devised matters so that there can be no pleasures without sorrows in this damned life. I hope for the best. But there is no doubt a teapot and a tube of macaroni aren't very efficient syringes, and that Lysol mixed in equal quantities with water produces great pain. Quoth the Raven Never More. The entire story is too humiliating and Rabelasian to be written to such an indiscreet old gentleman as you are. So you must wait until we are again hob-nobbing over our winter blaze.

Noel came late on Sunday afternoon. It was such a perfect day. We went
and swam in the sea and lay in the hot sun on the rocks. He read me the
beginning of Cézanne which I enjoyed enormously. Noel seems very happy
and gay. I gathered from his account of a dinner that the Wolves had been
playing with him unmercifully. I could hear Virginia plying and probing him
with questions. Even he seemed a little perturbed by her curiosity! The
Major remains exactly the same. I'm afraid there's no chance of his ever
becoming less dull. His extreme kindness however makes him fairly easy to
get on with. This afternoon we took a long walk over Hartland way and
missed our tea. Called in on Box who had roasted us a cold fowl and a huge
bag of scones and reached the cottage at eight o'ck [...]

I wish I had been at the poetry reading of the great poet G. L. S. [Giles
Lytton Strachey] which took place one evening. And now I wish that when
I come back I'd find a new poem to read by him. I've Wordsworth here and
Blake and three new wood blocks, so I ought to be happy. We live like
Princes with masses of good food and cream every day. And tomorrow we
have eel-pie! All the same, all the same, it doesn't prevent one wishing that
a certain young gentleman (as Mrs Box called you today) was here with your
    Mopsa xxxxx

*Before leaving for Cornwall, Ralph had picked a box of raspberries for Lytton, who
promptly wrote to Carrington: 'They were indeed heavenly. I suppose he would be
shocked if I suggested you should give him a kiss from me. The world is rather
tiresome I must say – everything at sixes and sevens – ladies in love with buggers,
and buggers in love with womanisers, and the price of coal going up too. Where
will it all end?'*

To Virginia Woolf

                                            The Mill House
                                            Tuesday [n.d.]

My Dear Virginia,
    I am only too delighted at the prospect of my humble woodcuts embel-
lishing your Literary masterpiece, & going out into the world again.[1]
    But I feel they are poor feathers to adorn your hat. In fact so great is my
shame that I may do you another this morning to replace that inferior one

1 Carrington had done four woodcuts to illustrate *Two Stories* by Virginia and Leonard Woolf, the first
   book published by the Hogarth Press in 1917.

of the fireplace. I'll certainly spend my shillings coming to have tea with you, and the pounds in coming down to Lewes to your new house & taking away some horrible relic of my past which you seem to have unearthed. I'll give you a new drawing in exchange for it. There! That's a promise – and a present …

I enjoy living here with Alix, whose character is entirely reformed you'll be glad to hear. She works all day under the apple tree writing page after page – surrounded by vast Tomes & rhyming dictionaries!! If you guessed twenty times you'd never discover the name of the gentleman who has ousted James, & the King Sloth [David Garnett], from her heart [...] the ruralness of this life couldn't be surpassed. The orchard is full of hay, may flies, & children, mosquitoes bite our bare legs, & the droppings of the Bullfinch have just fallen on Alix's raven locks. Still in spite of everything Lytton says about his Duchesses, & High life in London, I don't believe it's nearly as good as this.

My love to Leonard, & you

Yrs affectionately

Carrington

To Lytton Strachey

Railway Hotel, Oxford

Friday [29 August 1919]

Dearest,

[...] I seized the opportunity of rushing off on Wednesday morning with Majorio to Cirencester. Brenan met us. I am still baffled by his character. At moments one thinks he's only an energetic talkative Bunny. He seems so vague mentally, and talks about himself and his plans about as persistently. But then unlike Bunny he is much more obstinate, and not in the least influenced by people evidently. He goes to Spain next month with over a ton of books. He had just spent £50 on books in London, and with £150 in his pocket, which he has saved and intends to live by himself in a cottage in the south. His father is a typical crusty retired major, the Irish and Indian combination, who refused to allow him a penny unless he settles down to a respectable occupation. But Brenan himself is so curiously self-centred and detached it's hard to find out very much about him. He liked your book tremendously and said he would like to come to Tidmarsh before he left England.

Do you know you simply must come with me for a walk from Cirencester to Stroud through Lord Bathurst's Park. Never have I seen such Avenues, such terrific trees and little arbours where Pope wrote and some temples of stone in groves of cypresses. Then after one emerges from this enormous forest and Park one comes into amazing valleys, with wooded sides. We went over a wonderful 12 cent. Cotswold House called Daneways which is used as a sort of show house, to exhibit the furniture and iron work made by one Gimson. The house itself had lovely ceilings, and was a feat of architecture and beauty. We walked on to a village called Bisley and spent the night in an excellent little house, very cheap only 10/- for the three of us, with a big supper and breakfast. Brenan insisted on us getting up at six o'ck in order to walk to Chedworth. But as it was pouring gallons, we only got a half mile before we were forced to take refuge in a minute shed with a cart in it, into which we clambered. There we sat till half past eleven! The rain and mist never stopped once! We returned to Bisley and chartered a high stepping dogcart. Brenan went back across the valleys to his home and we drove into Stroud. After lunch of course it came out gloriously hot. On Stroud station I recognized, simply by their features, Brenan's father and young brother. The brother is much more interesting to look at, more sensitive. He goes to Oxford next term. I got on splendidly with the crusty major of course because I praised his Cotswold country which he seemed to think he was personally responsible for. Then we trained to Oxford as the Majorio had to get his clothes for Spain. In the High I saw Noel on a bicycle, who had ridden over from the east on the vague chance of meeting us. We had a great supper and then retreated to our hotel. The major left at 2 o'ck this morning for Liverpool, and to Spain this afternoon. I really am sorry for him. He seems so unhappy and lost.[1] N.L.C. and I will go back to Tidmarsh today [...] We walked over at 9.30 to dear Garsington. As I wanted to see Brett about the furniture. There they were:– all the troupe with their Queen in their midst. Toronto was back again, looking strangely lovely on a great sienna horse. He and Noel went off riding together before lunch. I sat in the red room with Mark, Brett, Julian, and the Frog[2] more or less in complete silence for almost one hour [...] Ethel Sandys [Sands][3] turned up after lunch. So Noel and I beat a retreat to Oxford. Mark and Ottoline walked half the way with us along the road. Mark related to Noel, I suppose one of the few people who haven't heard it, the entire history of his life. Which, strangely, delighted Noel, who was very impressed by him. Ottoline regaled me with grim stories of Katherine and Murry and our other mutual friends [...]

1 Ralph was going on holiday to northern Spain, unsure of Carrington's feelings towards him.
2 Julian Morrell and her governess Juliette Baillot.
3 Ethel Sands (1873–1962) was a well-off and well-connected artist born in America who lived and entertained lavishly in London, Oxfordshire and France with her lifelong partner, Nan Hudson, also a painter. They ran a hospital in France during the war, and Sands became a British citizen in 1916.

I loved your letter. I send you a kiss and all my love. No. I didn't like Forster's novel very much. It seemed all the time as if it hadn't quite come off.[1]

Hugs to the Bugger-wug
from xxxx Mopsa

After hearing stories of him for some time, Carrington had finally met Ralph's wartime friend Gerald Brenan. She found his decision to leave his conventional background behind to live alone in Spain and become a writer romantic and intriguing. He did indeed visit Tidmarsh in July before leaving for Spain, and was himself intrigued. Looking back many years later he recalled Carrington's intense blue eyes and 'sweet, honeyed smiles' as she welcomed him. Before long, they had started to correspond, and were soon exchanging increasingly long and intimate letters, and she was spinning a plan to visit him. Meanwhile her devotion to Lytton was as strong as ever, though the Freudian symbolism in the next letter may have escaped her.

To Lytton Strachey

The Mill House
(Waiting for lunch, Tuesday, 1.30) 9 September 1919

Dearest,

I miss you so much. What a brute you are to go away almost in the same wind that brought you, and today is so divine, so lovely that I had a Roman Bath in the sauna & then walked under the plum trees in the cool grass. But all rather wasted because you aren't here! Harry came at 12.30 running with his low kneed legs up the path to me, and asked me to come on the River Thames. I resisted, & said I wouldn't. 'Very well then – I'll go alone' in a stiff grumpy voice – so of course I had to give in & say that I would go after tea. But why do people on perfect afternoons like this want to go up that vulgar piece of water & squash in locks & vie with other absurd people in marring the landscape [...]

I wish by your attitude you didn't make it almost impossible to tell you how much I care for you. Possibly it's a good thing. I suspect you of being wiser than most men.

---

1 E. M. Forster (1879–1970), novelist, had known Lytton since Cambridge. His most recent book, *Howards End*, had been published in 1910, but in 1915 he had sent Lytton the manuscript of *Maurice*, in which he attempted to write truthfully about homosexual love. Lytton approved of the intention but felt the book was not a success; it remained unpublished until 1971. Perhaps Carrington is referring to it here.

Do you remember those plaintive pen wipers made of red & blue felt with jagged edges, with 'use me' embroidered in green on the cover. That's what I would like you to remember, that I am always your pen wiper

Mopsa xxx

To Gerald Brenan

20 Springfield Road, London N.W.
21 November 1919

[...] I can't discuss Philosophy any more than R.P. can. So you must have a selection of my days at random after all. First let me say how much I would like to come and make jam for you. Really I think there is quite a chance of persuading Lytton to come out to Spain in March if only he finishes his new book[1] and the faithful R.P. as 'courier' and possible other companions. Then I might drift down, as they would certainly live in towns, and see you for a little.

You must know I was horribly untruthful to you in London. But it causes one curious pain raking up truths nakedly. Also I didn't know you well enough. But in Spain why should everything not be told? You are rather like me you know, I am sorry to say it. But you lied slightly about la Egyptienne; your assumed indifference. It wasn't an exact revelation. Still I did enjoy those days in London with you. By the way R.P. tells me you put on your accounts £1.8 to my name. Really I am sorry. I will bring you some salt butter, and a pot of marmalade when I come out. I've lived almost entirely at Tidmarsh since I returned from St Malo[2]. I enjoyed that in a way. The country was so exquisite. And the house we lived in amazingly beautiful.

I've only been over to Oxford twice. But the young man [Partridge] comes over most weekends to Tidmarsh. He is studying English Literature now, which of course he finds exciting. I think it's a very good thing for him that he's given up that law. He may get a job as a traveller in foreign books for the Clarendon Press. I like him more than I did. It's difficult not to when anyone is so excessively kind and digs my potato patch and sits for my pictures [...] tell me about the people you know. And your truthful, and untruthful adventures.

You ought to get Virginia Woolf's new novel *Night and Day*. It's very interesting [...] Still tell me when I can do anything for you. And for god's sake don't go and be reckless, and get ill, or you'll be able to eat no jam.

---

1 Strachey was writing a biography of Queen Victoria.
2 Carrington had been to stay with the Waleys.

Lytton asked me to send you his love, last time when I told him I was
going to write [...]
  I send my love
  Yr Carrington

To Lytton Strachey

20 Springfield Road, London N.W.
Thursday, 11 December 1919

Dearest Old Egotistical HumBug,
  So you've caught the humility disease? I don't believe it. You're as vain-
glorious as ever, and just pretend not to be laughing at the young males
who kneel at the foot of the mountain of iniquity. Your letter delighted me
so much [...] I had lunch at Canuto's in Baker Street avec nos roi [Partridge].
He was very charming, but you know all that. I expect he has written to
you [...] He wanted to take me to a dance, but his mother positively forbids
him to bring me to their flat! She doesn't realize how really safe I am, for I
positively don't want to marry her cherished lamb. But it's really a relief as
I hate being involved with families, and being led into vast deceits. Back to
this benighted hole to tell my mother I was going out to dinner with Brett.
Really it's incredible the way she treats me. Conversation: D.C. 'I am going
out to dinner with Brett.' M.C. 'Well that is disappointing, And I was having
a joint of lamb, now I shan't eat it. You've spoilt my dinner. And I was so
looking forward to having an evening with you, and there was to have been
a sweet omelette for dinner too. Well you must be back early. Have you got
your purse alright, do you want some pennies for a bus? I've just had a letter
from the agents at Andover.' etc. [...]
  Lytton, you give me such a happy life. One day I really hope I shall be
an artist, and then you'll see my affection. We went to a concert at Queen's
Hall last night, and heard Beethoven No. 5 which I knew well, so enjoyed.
Then we walked vaguely through the streets looking at the faces of the
whores and jam tartlets in Regent Street. Peered in le Café Royal, but the
general spectacle of bloated kippers and their Queens with [Augustus] John
like a diseased Fish King in the middle with a white cod faced Chili[1] at his
side made me fly. Finally we went into a glittering Lyons in Shaftesbury
Avenue, and sipped chocolate. Then back to my mother and your letter. I

---

1 Alvaro 'Chili' Guevara (1894–1951) was Chilean, hence his nickname. He had studied at the Slade
  1913–16, and became a fashionable portrait painter attractive to both sexes.

have risen at 7.30 this morning to write to you! Otherwise it's impossible to be alone, and without conversations about house agents!

Dearest. I send you my love. Sil vous plaits prends mes lettres dans un coin, as I don't like that young man reading all my letters to you!

Goodbye, and take care of yourself.

Yrs Carrington

To Noel Carrington

20 Springfield Road, London N.W.
12 December 1919

Dearest Noel

I was, R.P. was, we was, getting quite concerned because I, R.P., we hadn't heard from you for so long. But this morning mother got 2 letters from you. Therefore do I now write, to wile away a dreary evening. Brett asked me to her studio but mother like a dog in a manger, prefers although I don't speak to her to have me sitting in the room. She has kept me in the last two evenings sitting here in gloomy solitude. Really it is rather irritating when there are so many people I would like to see. Brett & Gertler & the Gordon Square people & Alix. And as I have spent the last four days painting a tin trunk all day. It's a bit stiff to have to spend all the evenings couped up here. I am going tomorrow morning. Really it's more than I can stand. And her curiosity & stupidity nearly drive me mad.

I won't bore you with her entirely wild doings. Also I won't take any interest in it. For the minute one does she throws all the responsibility on one, & then if anything goes wrong as of course it will one gets all the blame. But really I do feel mad tonight as I had promised Brett to go out with her, and mother made such a fuss that I had to abandon it, and last night was just the same. R.P. took me to a dance at Queens Hall however, fun, 4.30 to 6.30, which I enjoyed very much. They were 'nutty' dances. Your friend was a clumsy cow in comparison. And the damsels leapt into the air & kicked up their heels like young colts, and very elegant legs in sooth. You get a tea & consecutive dancing for 5/- for 2 hrs. I hope we shall go again.

Next week Waley's people give us a dance at the great Waley Hyde Park House, also a Slade Fancy Dress dance on the 19th ought to be fun. I shall go with Cooie Lane, & her brother & R.P. I wish oh so badly, that you would be here too. Alix has unfortunately had an operation on her nose so won't be able to come with us. I went to see her today in the nursing home.

She looked rather ill. I went up to see Gertler this afternoon before I went to Alix. He has done some frightfully good paintings lately. Much better even than those you saw in the summer. He asked after you, & sent you his love. He is so sincere. I am always more impressed by him than anyone when I talk about painting to him.

Tomorrow night I sleep chez Waley – unknown to mother – who thinks I go to Pangbourne tomorrow – & go to *Parsifal* an Opera by Wagner at Covent Garden with James S. & Lytton S. who is coming up for it.

R. P. went down to Tidmarsh this afternoon to keep Lytton company in my absence. Lytton gets on so much better with him now, in fact they are great friends and have long discussions on Einstein's theory whilst I darn the socks – I will try & get you Maynard's book tomorrow to send you. I see in the papers that it is just out.[1]

I shall go back to Tidmarsh on Sunday, & stay there until Thursday when I shall come up to London for the Whale fish dance, & the Slade dance, & then go back to Tidmarsh for the Xmas festivities. R. P. goes down to Barbara on Monday next till Thursday to help her paint. Do you know Mrs P asked him not to bring me to the flat because she said 'Carrington wasn't polite to me in the summer at Oxford. So I've told Dorothy I would rather if she didn't come here.' And that's all the thanks one gets from saving a young man, the apple of his mother's eye from the clutches of Harlots & the snares of matrimony!

What would she say if I had accepted her dear Sonnie? I think she had better perhaps be informed of my great goodness, for it behoves her not to talk of politeness, when she gibed at me at Oxford because I preferred your company to that of hers & the brood of misses. R. P. gives an awful account of his home life discussions. Dorothy trying to be advanced, Mrs P trying to be Christian & Jessie dozing over her knitting [...]

[...] and what's your news? Brenan wrote me a very long letter with the wildest doings in S. Spain. He has now taken a house in Andalusia. N. E. of Malaga – further along on Sedella[2] range. Perhaps – perhaps we might see him in April – as Lytton if Victoria gets finished thinks of wandering out to either Italy or Spain with our R. P. as courier. Now no more as I must go to bed. My love dear & take care of yourself & don't get ill.

Yr D. C.

---

1 Keynes's important and prescient new book was *The Economic Consequences of the Peace*, in which he questioned the wisdom of the Allies' punitive imposition of reparations on Germany at the Versailles Peace Conference.

2 Gerald's house was in fact at Yegen, in the Alpujarras range.

To Gerald Brenan

The Mill House
15 December 1919

Dear Muchacho,

I was delighted to get your long letter. It was so full of variety, as long as a month, with all its varying days. Lytton enjoyed it too, and now the wretch R.P. has taken it off with him. So you have the choice of a vague answer, or waiting at least a week before I get hold of it and write you a proper reply. This much I remember. R.P. says it's no good sending you skis as they will get broken and also stolen en route and they are at least 6 foot high. So he recommends you making some yourself out there!! Typical of this prudent man. He even enjoined me not to send you a plum pudding because he says it will get stolen also! But I'll defy him and we shall see. If it vanishes somebody is the happier. If it's never sent, nothing good can possibly come of it [...]

Lytton favours Italy for the spring, and Sicily, but I will if you are still in Spain do my best to get him to change his mind, and to come your way with R.P. and I.

Oh a great deal has happened in this Mill since you last set foot in it! What fun to write a letter which would incriminate everyone, and be a lasting testimony to these strange times and the nakedness of a female's mind. But I can't. Simply because the world isn't made up of such simple people as we are. Later perhaps I'll be able to write ALL to you. I find everything so interesting. But this isn't fair so I won't go on. I've become much fonder of R.P. He has become so much more charming and has given up his slightly moral character which used to tire me. So we never quarrel now, and have become a perfect pair of pigeons in our affections. I certainly will never love him but I am extremely fond of him – I believe if one wasn't reserved, and hadn't a sense of 'what is possible' one could be very fond of certainly two or three people at a time. To know a human being intimately, to feel their affection, to have their confidences is so absorbing that it's clearly absurd to think one only has the inclination for one variety. The very contrast of a double relation is fascinating. But the days are too short. And then one has work to do. So one has to abandon some people and the difficulty of choosing is great. Don't you find it so? Honestly when I get to London, and meet old loves, and friends I can hardly bear the feeling of being away from them. Yet when I am here again, with Lytton [...]

In hinting at 'strange times' at the Mill, and expounding on the complexities of love, Carrington was both enticing Gerald to join the dance and revealing that she, Ralph and Lytton had moved into a closer relationship. Ralph was fundamentally straight, but an element of sexual play is revealed in Lytton's letters to and about him. For a while, all three of them were precariously happy, sometimes shared a bed and were accepted in their world as an established, if curious, threesome. Carrington had achieved another triangle; Gerald Brenan was waiting in the wings.

1920

To Gerald Brenan

The Mill House
2 January 1920

Dear Muchacho,

I've not sent a Plum Pudding yet. But I will this next week.[1] This is to wish you a happy New Year, & to answer your last letter which now is restored to me by le oiseau Partridge [...] And in April I have the greatest hopes of seeing you in Spain. You must write often so that we shall know where you will be & your plans. R. P. has stayed here all this winter. He has become great friends with Lytton now, which is an immense improvement all round. As Lytton delights in teaching anyone literature, it's made R much happier, & less diffident, and I can have him here as often as I like. I am doing a large oil painting of him every day which gives me greater pleasure than it does to the unfortunate victim. Here he comes stamping along the passage, so I must stop till after tea. It's odd to sit here in front of a roaring log fire in my little library with those prints of flowers on the white wall, & wonder what your evening is like. And if you are by a fire with white walls [...] I send you a small P. Pudding by tomorrow post. I made it myself for you. So forgive me if it tastes queer. I wish I could get you straight in your house. It is the one thing I love, buying saucepans at old ironmongers or foreign earthenware in markets [...] R. P. lies exhausted on the sofa in my little library reading the *Athenaeum* like a confirmed dilettante. I make him wear such nice clothes now, leather jerkins, & knee breeches so that he looks like some lovely serving Elizabethan man. Lytton has lately read us Restoration Plays – *The Relapse* by Vanbrugh,[2] & poems by Pryor[3] – I read M. Keynes' Finance Peace Report when I am not painting [...] I've no news of people as I've only been in London for a few days the whole of this winter. I've become rather ambitious about my painting lately. I want frightfully badly to so arrange my life that I can paint a great deal more. At present I am so uncertain of myself, and have so little confidence in consequence. Directions re plum pudding will be attached, in case this letter goes astray. R. P. insists on reading my letter to you, so it's impossible for me to write anything about him! This as you may perceive is merely put in to jibe him.

1 She did. It got lost in the post.
2 John Vanbrugh, (1664–1726) wrote *The Relapse, or, Virtue in Danger*, in 1696.
3 Matthew Prior (1664–1721), poet and diplomat, said to have composed poetry while sitting on the Wittenham Clumps in Oxfordshire, a significant place for Lytton and Carrington.

Next week Clive Bell and his consort come here for 4 days. I always grudge visitors rather, as they involve me leaving my painting & doing fatigue duties which I detest. How true is what you wrote about happiness. I almost scream sometimes to watch it stealing away from me. I hate drabness so much. Lately I've been able to say often 'this hour was happy'. But in writing this one feels perhaps it is because one is easily contented & perhaps one does not analyse it, & so calls satisfaction & pleasure 'happiness'. I say this because when other people tell me something gave them incredible happiness I think their standards are not very high. We had a great argument on Christmas afternoon at tea. The mathematician Norton, James S. Lytton & R. P. on happiness. I thought of you. I wished you could have been of the company. If I was a better writer, & could remember things truthfully I'd like to write you what they said. But I am neither.

Now I must go & put some CHOPS on the kitchen fire to grizzle [sic] for Mrs Legg does not come on Sunday night to cook ... CHOPS CHOPS Fizzle Fizzle while the old dilettante reads to young dilettante. Lytton sends you his love. He likes you very much. And so do I. So I send my love & best wishes
    Your Carrington

To Gerald Brenan

The Mill House
12 January 1920

Dear Muchacho,
    A letter for Partridge has just come five minutes ago. But he is in London, so I impatiently opened it, to know your news. How sad it all sounds. I am upset by it. I know it all so well. The difficulties of moving in a house; the expenses and feeling ill. And Malaga with its Victorias. How that one day we spent in Malaga comes back to me. I had ten blisters on one foot and six on the other. The agony was exquisite. The roads hard and hot. Then I was too hot to eat the lunch they gave us, and the afternoon burnt one's face and made me hungry. Then we walked along that long road to Velez Malaga. It got darker and darker and I was so hungry and my feet hurt so I nearly cried. Then all we could find was a little fishermen's Inn for the night. And the people were hostile and pressed on us and smelling children crowded round and still we had to sit waiting for a dinner; 10 o'ck at night, and trying to be amiable. Then R. P. started wrangling with his sister, Noel became gloomy and I hoped the end of the world would come, as you did. Never have I felt quite so wretched as that night. Oh Brenan I wish I could be out with you to make things better. One can get faint amusement out of such despairing situations when one has another with one. But I hope

now it's passed, and you are installed with books in your cottage and happy.
I think the lack of money is perhaps more sordidly grim than anything. I've
known it in London, walking from Waterloo to Hampstead because I hadn't
a penny. Eating twopenny soup packets, meal after meal, in a smelling studio
in Brompton Rd – and for you, removed even from the chances of meeting
people to lend you money, really it must have been despairing.

[...] Lytton I found this morning in bed, studying a Spanish Grammar.
Which I took for a hopeful sign. I shall bring some money for you in case
you are very poor. Tonight I've got a vile throat, all thick with horrid blisters
and boils inside. It makes me feel rather cheerless but I cannot go to bed
for that would upset Lytton. R. P. has been down in Devonshire with his
father since last Thursday. Do you mind these vague remarks. Yet I am not
wholly material. I should like to know more about your imaginings, and
mental travels. Sometimes with Lytton I have amazing conversations. I mean
not to do with this world, but about attitudes and states of mind, and the
purpose of living. That is what I care for most in him. In the evenings
suddenly one soars without corporeal bodies on these planes of thought.
And I forget how dull and stupid I am and travel on also.

It's rather a responsibility having someone in love with one. One's behaviour becomes so much more important and it ties one to the earth in a
curious way. But the interest is enormous. Do you know even at the most
intimate moments, I never get the feeling of being submerged in it. I find
myself outside, watching also myself and my workings as well as his from
the detached point of view. I confess it has made me much happier, his
affection. For owing to the fact that I deserted almost everyone, except Alix,
for Lytton, there were moments when he did not want me, when I recognized the isolation of it all, when one turned in despair for some relation
with a mortal to assure one, that one wasn't entirely cut off. Now it is good
to tell one's feelings, and feel his fondness at such times. I hope you got the
plum pudding I sent. I am slightly doubtful, I had to fill in so many forms
and I could only think of 'La Fruita Pan' to express the contents of the
parcel. But we'll bring you stores with us in March. Lytton won't walk, so
that we can bring baggage. Perhaps you'll meet us at Seville, or Cordova
and so have a change of scene. But if we set foot in Spain I promise you
we shall see you. I write tonight because I feel too degraded to do anything
else; my throat aches worse and worse. The thought of eating is agony. Yet
if I don't, Lytton will notice and tomorrow R. P. will be here, and I shall
have more than ever to conceal it. Clive Bell and Mrs Hutchinson came here
last weekend. They aren't my style. Too elegant and 18 cent. French; for
that's what they try and be. I felt my solidity made them dislike me. Then
I had to make their beds, and empty chamber pots because our poor cook
Mrs Legg can't do everything and that made me hate them, because in order

Tidmarsh Mill, c. 1918.
Carrington placed two
imaginary birds on the water
by the house she found for
herself and Lytton Strachey

At Garsington, 1920:
Michael Llewellyn Davies,
Carrington, Ottoline
Morrell's daughter Julian
and Ralph Partridge

A labour of love: Lytton Strachey reading,
painted during the winter of 1916

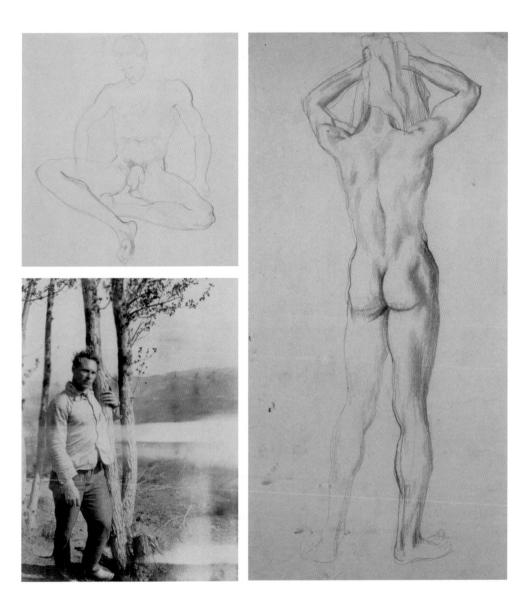

In 1919 and 1920 Ralph Partridge was often at the Mill, modelling for Carrington.
These two drawings of him naked were sure to delight Lytton

Ralph with his clothes on, 1920

Carrington and Gerald Brenan,
August 1921. Gerald, Ralph's
wartime friend, had fallen in love
with Carrington, and romance
blossomed at Watendlath in the
Lake District, where she also
painted his portrait

they should talk so elegantly, I couldn't for a whole weekend do any painting and yet they scorned my useful grimy hands [...]

    My love to you
    Carrington

In the middle of January, when Carrington and Ralph were in London, Lytton bought a four-poster bed.

To Lytton Strachey

41 Gordon Square
Thursday [20 January]

And shall we really find you listening to the birds under the moon, or the morning sun in the Great Four Poster.

[*From Ralph Partridge*]
What a triumph about the bed. You might of course just leave it in the garden and build the New Wing around it. Tchekhov is all finished now and

being taken to the printers today. I shall be ready for some typing during the weekend My love to you Ralph.

To Lytton Strachey

St Mildred's Hall, Turl Street, Oxford
Tuesday, 10 o'ck, 10 February 1920

... What a pity you didn't come to that tea party of generalisers yesterday. It was such a nice one. I liked Michael Davies. He looked more interesting than the average young man up here. But unhappy and moody. Perhaps that is just the gloom of finding Barrie one's keeper for life.[1] Then Russell, a cousin of Bertie. He says B.R. has gone back to Cambridge again. And Neil Little, rather vain-glorious, and a superb generaliser! But they all agreed that Imperialism was monstrous and we ought to give up India and felt very fine gentlemen at having discovered this all in one afternoon over tea. Then a supper with a bottle and a pork pie – and a dance at 8. No new young men. All rather dreary Etonians. Perhaps they aren't underneath but it's damned hard work turning the sods to discover the body. (This is only to be read as a figurative speech!) Lovely Alan [MacIver] glanced in for a brief moment in the evening, with a shining wet face after rowing. I thought he looked, again, very beautiful. I danced most of the evening with our Ralph, and in between dances we retreated up here and ate cakes and pies and sat over the fire. The 'missies' were incredibly dull. Really it's difficult to see how mother nature could with lumps of dough, and a carving knife, have contrived such heights of perfect dullness in their faces. Lust hid her face in her orange mantle, and withdrew after the first ten bars of music and a respectable two headed middle aged muse called 'Healthy and Jolly' appeared, and sat with us solidly for the evening. One young man, a Jew called Baring, discussed Psycho-analysis with me and dreams! but managed very skilfully to steer off P's and C's! [penises and cunts] I have lunch with him today, and a tea party later with Ralph, at Neil Little's rooms. One watches lovely red-headed, curly-headed, striped-headed youths gliding down the street below. How far away! Now we are going to look at the library, and the Ashmolean till lunch. What a damn'd muggy place this is. Tidmarsh is a Brighton in comparison. This is also a dull letter, but that can't be helped [...] An absurd notice in *The Times* today on Duncan saying that the painting of the open window

---

1 Michael Llewelyn Davies (1900-1921) was one of four orphaned brothers who became wards of J. M. Barrie. Peter Pan was inspired by him. He drowned in 1921, along with a friend, possibly a lover.

was the best picture in the show. And even more stupid things about his vagueness and lack of intention. My love to you dear.

Your Mopsa

To Lytton Strachey

In train to Oxford, approaching Bletchley
10 o'ck [13 February 1920]

My Dearest Friend,

The pleasure of coming back to you tomorrow almost makes it worth while going away. Really it is the best possible of lives in the best possible of worlds – ours at Tidmarsh. And lately it has seemed happier each day. I am now in a slow crawling microbe moving towards Oxford. Yesterday morning was simply Milton in its fairness. Ralph loved your Cambridge, and confessed he found it more sympathetic than Oxford! I saw your Willow Tree by Kings Bridge and thought of you. He was full of appreciation over Trinity. It certainly looked its very best with the willow pale green, and so new, and the sun shining cleanly on the pinkish stone library. But there wasn't really time to linger and many colleges, and gates we never saw, as his train went at 4 o'ck. I went in after seeing him off at the station and saw Sheppard. There were two young men there, [T. H.] Marshall[1], and [Patrick] Blackett[2]. The former looked rather intelligent and dominating. Mr Blackett an uncouth Bedalian perhaps, shy creature. Sheppard is producing *The White Devil* on the 9th March. Don't you think you, and your children might have a prolonged birthday treat and go there for it? After the beauty of the music, and the songs had faded from my mind, I reviewed *The Fairy Queen* less enthusiastically in bed yesterday morning. The scenery was really rather unpleasant, arty, and all pale purple and green like some Suffrage tea-room. But I forgive even the most mincing young lady because of the loveliness of that music. Sheppard was delighted because the Newnham Authorities have forbidden the young ladies to act in Webster, so that the female parts can now all be taken by the young men! The young men I thought however, didn't show the same enthusiasm at the abolition. Fredegond [Shove][3] came in yesterday evening. And was very entertaining. Full of whimsical bawdy

---

1 Thomas Marshall (1893–1981) was a Fellow of Trinity. One of his sisters, Frances, was then studying at Newnham; another, Rachel, was to marry David Garnett in 1921.

2 Patrick Blackett (1897–1974) was studying physics. He won the Nobel Prize in 1948.

3 Fredegond Shove (1889–1949), a cousin of Virginia Woolf and Vanessa Bell, was a poet living in Cambridge.

and scandal. And gave me an amazing description of Virginia and Vanessa
when they were young. James, I gather, isn't going there for *The Fairy Queen*
as he remains in Paris. And Alix alone has returned. So shall I write a review
for the *Athenaeum* instead? Ralph is incredibly happy to have shaken off those
Oxford Eight people finally. It was a dreadful scene, when that enthusiastic
blue came into his rooms and appealed to his sporting honour and vanity.
I really thought he was very good the way he politely but with great firm-
ness stuck to his lie and got out of it[1] . . .

Yr loving Mopsa

*Carrington now started a tradition of writing a poem to Lytton on his birthday
each year.*

To Lytton Strachey

1 March 1920

To G. L. S. on his Fortieth Birthday
Now Forty wishes do I bring,
To you on this day of spring,
The first day that the joyful hare
Skips across the farrows Bare.
Happy, Happy, hare of March.
Nibbling at the budding larch
Do you know that Lytton dear,
Now has reached his fortieth year?
Do you know you Blackbirds gay,
That this is my Lord's birthday?
Sing you thrushes, sing sweet wren,
Lay snow eggs you yellow hen,
Sing on Bullfinch, sing your best
And Daffy show your yellow vest
For soon our Dearest one will pass,
Walking on the happy grass.
Apple trees come out in Bloom,
And Bring the gorse, & yellow Broom
None must stand aloof today
All must sing, and none may pray,

1 Ralph turned down a place in the Oxford boat for the Boat Race against Cambridge, preferring to go
  to Spain with Lytton and Carrington.

Lytton, dear, I have no song.
I cannot join the Birdies throng,
I have no scent, no petals bright,
To lay before you to delight.
Only this little wish I give
That you for eighty years may live,
But that's too short! Pray let it be
Forty Thousand years WITH ME.

Soon afterwards, the trio set off for Spain, taking a boat to Lisbon and trains on to Seville, Cordoba and Granada. It then took them three days to struggle up to Gerald's house at Yegen, by carriage and mules; Lytton suffered agonies from piles, the food disagreed with him and Carrington and Ralph felt the strain, as did Gerald.

To Gerald Brenan

Hotel Terminus, Madrid
18 April 1920

Dear Geraldo,

At last I have time to write you a letter so warm of thanks that your fingers would get burnt, if you knew how much I loved the Yegen life, those four days. I shall always look back on them as some of the best visionary days I have ever spent. And in a curious way so interesting, combining so many delights of which your company was one of the greatest. It's strange but I feel like apologising because I feel I didn't 'show up' very well. I was rather tired, and anxious, and selfish. I'm afraid you didn't enjoy our visit as much as we did. I shall, I promise you, come out with our dear R. P. next September, in a different frame of mind, armed with pots and paints and no grief. But you will keep well till then? And eat properly? I know it's a dreadful nuisance but truly you know you weren't looking very well in spite of your red face, and you shouldn't get boils on your feet in good health [...]

Tomorrow we go to the Escorial, and then on Wednesday I shall see the Prado again. These pictures make me want to give up everything and become an artist entirely [...]

R. P. I think is enjoying himself. I was sorry you saw his sorrow. I wanted our visit to be entirely happy with you. But it is a great thing that the beauty of your landscape and your life sent us all away purified from cares.

Your honey still graces our breakfasts. And your figs are yet with us. It was such a good time. Thank you so much. I send my love

Yr Carrington

To Gerald Brenan

The Mill House
Started on 5 May 1920

Dearest Gerald,

At last I am back in this valley of green grass, and a wilderness of weeds. How much has happened since I left you. But what a difference it makes writing to you now, when I know the face of the postman who will leave your letter (this very letter at your door), and your library. I believe if you were to cross-examine me when I was 80, I should remember every detail of Yegen and your kitchen! So much did I love even the smallest details. What shall I tell you of first? But please be very lenient to my shortcomings as a writer. I've even a greater respect now than I had before I came to see you, for your character, therefore I'd like to please you with my letters, since I can no longer charm your stomach with delicacies. (PS By the way was that a good marmalade pie I made you.)

[...] Oh Gerald I wish you were here, such afflictions have fallen upon us. And Ralph would give a good deal I think to have you with him. There is nothing new. It is only he is very unhappy which makes me in despair also. And as far as I can see there is no solution. It seems appalling that in this world when one gets on with so few people, when one does care for someone as much as I do for him and he does me, one must part because of these difficulties. It is impossible to go on being perpetually unhappy and worried which is what he is doing now. Yet I know, even if I did not think of myself, to marry him would not make it any better. Because one cannot change a spirit inside one. And it is that he cannot possess. But I will not burden you with all this. I think it is aggravated by his being at Oxford, with no real interests to occupy his time when he is away from me.

Lytton came back to Tidmarsh yesterday. We spent the evening reading poetry. But it was rather depressing because one missed Ralph and I cannot bear to know such good people are miserable.

Friday

I write now in a train to Oxford.

It's delightful being back at Tidmarsh. We have a new housekeeper which is rather tiresome. But otherwise the joy, after so much travelling and beastly

Hotels, and finally LONDON, of waking up in that big bedroom and seeing the sun outside shining on the grass and to hear cuckoos in the fields beyond is very great. The beginning of this sentence is so removed that I've underlined it. It appears that the root of all my diseases: throats and colds – is a defective nose. I went to a specialist in London, who discovered I had bent the cartilage in the centre, and that until it was straight I would never get better. So next week I have to go into a hospital in LONDON and have it cut out. I confess I am not looking forward to it. As it will make one rather weak and also increase, and ruin, my already too large nose. But if it really does rid me of these infernal throats I shall not complain [...] Lytton will write to you soon. He loved Yegen so much you know. It was a pity he got so tired at the beginning of the visit. But in spite of that he said he would be always glad he undertook, for him, such an amazing experience.

Do you know sometimes I almost feel like flying with my paint boxes and leaving all these complications and simply changing my life and settling at Yegen. But I suppose it would be fantastic! From the train now I can see Wantage downs and the tops of those woods where we picnicked last summer.

Ralph was angry and bewildered that although Carrington would sleep with him she would not marry him. He was becoming aware that it was Lytton she really loved, not him, and was threatening to destroy their triangle.

To Lytton Strachey

St Mildred's Hall, Oxford
2 o'ck, 7 May 1920

My Dearest Lytton,
   He has just gone off to row. He is quite happy again. I just teased him about being unhappy, and behaving so badly, and he was charming, and didn't talk about it any more and said: 'Do you know for a moment I was so cross, that I nearly kept Lytton here last night, as I didn't want him to go. And I wanted for a moment to make you suffer because I was cross with you. But then when I thought how you would miss him not coming I let him go. Because I wanted after all to make you happy.' I am going up to Ruth [Selby-Bigge] whilst he rows this afternoon and we dine with them tonight. Dear one, I dare not say it hardly. But I think it may come alright. He is so friendly. And quite happy and talking about Tidmarsh and you. I think yesterday must have been a pent up outburst. Oh I am so sorry you were so unhappy. I think it best to stay here the weekend. I will come back early on Monday. I only hope James will

come and that you won't get depressed. Everything today seems to have disappeared. I expect that in spite of everything you said, you really comforted him a great deal. I have every hope by next week we will have him back at Tidmarsh. Will you accept my insurance on it? For – thirty pounds?

Please dear, will you burn this letter? As he reads everything he can find when he comes to Tidmarsh. And we will remember these days without reminders. I want to buy either a little fox, or a snake which I saw in an arcade this morning. Would you mind a little dear fox?

I am just going to send you a wire and go up to Ruth's. I thank you so much.

Yr most loving Carrington

To Lytton Strachey

St Mildred's Hall, Oxford
Saturday, 6 o'ck, 8 May 1920

Dearest Lytton,

I was so glad of your letter this morning [...] My dear one, all is for the best, not a trace of unhappiness in him today. I think you must be responsible for it because he is so happy now and never refers to anything, or makes those announcements about the future. We had tea with Ruth yesterday and then went [for] a long walk in the country. And talked about things. But he was perfectly calm, and happy. I told him that I wanted him to realize when I gave you affection it didn't rob him of any, and that one ought not to give affection to him, at the expense of making other people unhappy. When really one had so much love inside and enough to give to so many people. (But it's impossible to explain now in this letter.) I think he saw how fond I was of him and that it was important to concentrate on the happiness we had, instead of all the time aiming for something we hadn't [...] And coming back across the fields by Marston at seven o'ck he said shyly 'Do you know I thought it might be rather nice to go to Tidmarsh this weekend perhaps', 'or even if we can't this weekend perhaps next week'. I could have cried for pleasure at hearing him say it. But as he had to row this evening till 7 o'ck, and as your letter said you had asked someone else and Ottoline had asked us out tomorrow, I thought it might be better for him to come over one day next week. But it's such a great relief to have him as he used to be, perfectly happy, and so charming all day long [...]

Yr most loving
Carrington

To Lytton Strachey

Royal Free Hospital, London
Saturday morning, 7.30, 22 May 1920

Very dear Lytton,

I am feeling much better today but I've not been allowed to get up yet [...]¹ Today I've got the other disease so I am more complacent lying in bed. I am thinking over everything very seriously and when I get back I'll give you six ultimatums and then off with your head! Like the King I sit on horseback reviewing my past life and the future. Today I decided it was a very happy one and mostly, can you guess why, because of a friend I have? And you'll be going off to Oxford very soon and sporting yourself, perhaps in white flannels, and a Trinity blazer, along the tow path arm in arm with Alan. I suspect you of the vilest vanities when my back's turned!

The nosey is recovering its shape to my infinite relief. But do you know I weighed myself this morning and I was only 8 stone 8 lbs. Which pleases me. It looks as if it will be divinely fine this weekend at Oxford, I am glad [...] And really I suppose young men aren't as nice as one imagines they are, lying in a sage green ward. Positively my heart leapt up to see a man in trowsers yesterday enter the ward, although he was a miserable spotty doctor. But to think of a world of females as one lives in here, chills the blood. I think I shall draw today. I see rather good compositions lying in bed of white nurses and bedclothes, and green green walls. I wish I could have seen Virginia. Did you tell her how sorry I was it couldn't be arranged? How nice it is to think of the summer coming, and no more cold and rain. But of course you are hardly the person to write that to! I am much happier today and feel ever so much better. But what a long time it seems since Thursday. My first sneeze has just taken place. Very extraordinary sensation! Now goodbye to my dear one
    Yr Mopsa

While Carrington was staying with the MacIvers with Ralph, Lytton's sister Dorothy visited Tidmarsh with her artist husband, Simon Bussy. He admired Carrington's recent paintings, including one of the Mill with two black swans on the millpond.

---

1 Carrington was recovering from her sinus operation.

To Lytton Strachey

Wanlass How, Ambleside
Wednesday, 21 June 1920

Dearest,

Your letter made me so happy yesterday I read it over so many times. It is only I do care really so much more than I pretend to about what people think of my work, and I value the opinion of Simon particularly as he hasn't any axe to grind. I meant he didn't have to say something kind because I was present, & also because he has seen so many pictures in France. Thank you very much for making me so happy. You know in a curious way one feels what one means to do, & then when nobody sees it in one's work, & when Duncan & Vanessa liked not what I tried for, but for something else, I was confused. I tried so hard when I painted that Mill picture, for a certain vision, & I felt depressed afterwards because I thought I must have failed completely, as no one saw. Only a small part of it did come off, but that Simon should have seen that delighted me.

Yesterday it poured all day until four o'ck, so I read Dorothy's journal.[1] Sometimes it is too intimate & exciting. 'William read us "Peter Bell" in the orchard', 'William wrote late, & read me "The Rainbow" before retiring', imagine it! What days they must have spent together, & those moonlight walks by the Lake! I am glad I know now her bedroom, I have even seen her wash stand, & the old cracked yellow jug & basin, and the little seat of stones that they built near Rydal where William used to compose his poetry. Yet I have had a Poet read me his poetry! I thought in many ways it was so like our life. And I loved them both so much, for the way they sowed Broad Beans & she darned socks, & he read Shakespeare to her. But I fear I cannot recall that I even baked bread, & pies & copied out neatly your verses! Alan took us a walk after tea yesterday up a Mountain, just near the house, & we had an amazing view of Windermere from the top, but the Langdale Pikes, where we went the other day, were all buried in mists. It was wonderful watching the rain driving across the big lake, & the light piercing the mists far off like rays from the Holy ghost in Heaven. When we came back we helped him clean his motor car until dinner. Then afterwards they taught me billiards, which interest me immensely. But I find it rather difficult to control my cue, & my excitement. Ralph was very good. I played with Alan's married brother [...]

---

1 Dorothy Wordsworth (1771–1855) was the sister and close companion of the Romantic poet William Wordsworth (1770–1850). They lived together in the Lake District, and she described their life there in her *Grasmere Journal*, first published in 1897.

Did you read Gerald's postcard? How typical to have written a letter which has got blown away by the wind! It looks better today, but the sun hasn't come out yet. Still I think we shall climb a combe, sun or no sun. The portrait of Alan went better yesterday. Mrs MacIver is a woman of understanding & has given me a little library for my own to paint in, undisturbed. Ralph read us *Peter Bell* whilst I painted, & some English Essays. I am glad the weekend was such a success, & that you are keeping well. I wonder if I shall ever settle down to a life without motorcars! But if one couldn't walk this would be an awful country. The roads are absurdly unbearable with traffic & hearty Manchester people in tweeds with sticks. When one reads of Dorothy Wordsworth's life on these very same roads, & the occasional beggars & pedlars who passed their cottage ... & then views the same road with its unending processions of cars, coaches, buses, & pedestrians one groans. Life is very chaste here, very, and when do you put spice in your cake & eat it?

Love from yr Mopsa

To Lytton Strachey

The Mill House
Friday, 12 o'ck [3 September 1920]

Don't leave my letters lying about. It may be childish but I rather hate those grown up people knowing how much I care for my Dearest Lytton [...] I've invited the Nashes over for the weekend rather vaguely. His wife is attractive, German.[1] It's a pity we haven't a piano she plays so well. But I hardly think somehow they will come.

All this decision business has upset me. I feel rather unhinged by it. I hate so much (a) to be responsible, and make my decision in any direction (b) perhaps even more to hurt a human being and make anyone unhappy. It seems wrong that with a surplus of affections for so many human beings that there can't be combined happiness for more than two people at a time. But I shall leave it now, and see how things work out. Do you know how extraordinarily happy that conversation you had with me on Wednesday evening has made me? I care so much. I hope you'll get really rested down in Sussex and quite forget that old Hag Victoria. I wish I could be with you in spirit, sitting invisibly by the fire tonight watching you talk, and listening to all the fun. Perhaps I shall be there, so you had better be careful. No, really it's lovely here now so hot that one can sit with pleasure out of doors and birds chirping, just because you've gone away. What a damned cynic

1 John and Christine Nash, Carrington's great friends from the Slade.

this old clerk of the weather must be. How I miss you already. The last few days were such good ones [...]

Lytton dear, do you know what comfort you are to me. I feel as long as you live on this earth I can never mind anything.

Yr most loving Mopsa

Carrington was now under great pressure from Ralph, who had left Oxford and was looking for a job in London, to live with him in Gordon Square during the week. She dreaded being forced to abandon Lytton, who did his best to reassure her:

My dearest, I am sure that all is really well between us, which is the great thing. Some devil of embarrassment chokes me sometimes, and prevents me expressing what I feel. You have made me so happy during the last 3 years, and you have created Tidmarsh, as no one else could have – and I seem hardly to have said thank you. But you must believe that I value you and your love more than I can ever say. It seems to me that your trying the G. Square experiment is probably right. But whatever happens you must rely on my affection.

Faced with Ralph's emotional blackmail, Carrington gave in. Her correspondence with Gerald was increasingly an outlet and a comfort.

To Gerald Brenan

The Mill House
30 September 1920

My Dearest Gerald,

I have not written to you for a long time. Yet it is not because I have not felt affectionate, on the contrary your letter accusing us of treachery threw me into a great state.

Often when the sun glimmers out for a few moments & I am reminded of your real sunny land I say I must leave this vile misty bleak place [...] and when visions of your roof, & the many coloured mountains, & those poplar groves come up before me, I feel I can't bear the flatness & greenery of England a second longer [...] Often I feel the only thing is to lead your simple life in that most exquisite country. Yet you see I do not move – I suppose partly because I am too female, & partly because my affections are so involved. Now R.P. has taken a job in the Woolf Printing Press, & become Leonard Woolf's secretary so he can't leave England. And I have committed myself to living with him at 41 Gordon Square this winter, as a sort of trial to see how we get on together. I feel it's only fair to him after I have made him so unhappy up till now. Fundamentally I can't believe I shall ever settle down, & be domestic, & responsible. The whole reason why I have lived so peaceably here with Lytton is that he never controls me, in fact he takes no interest in my movements, & never intrudes into my life [...] I loved the mountains, & the wild valleys in Westmoreland but I hated violently the rich Liverpool un-intellectuals with their dull tepid minds. But I've been on several expeditions since Westmoreland – one week-end to the Woolfs at Rodmell on the Newhaven & Lewes Downs – with R.P. – Virginia is a most extraordinary woman, touched with madness but so full charm and wit. I am very glad R.P. is going to work with them. It would have ruined him to have entered an enterprising business, & made money. And Leonard is very much connected with international politics, & yet they lead a most simple life at Richmond in a house full of Books, & printing presses. Eventually R.P. will control the printing Press, & if it's a success perhaps run a book shop for them in London also to sell the copies [...] I work very hard now, Gerald. I think one loses all respect for oneself unless one does paint seriously.[1] Lytton is busy writing *Victoria* every day. I think it's better than his last book. R.P. comes down for weekends, & splits the wood, & saws it, with a naked torso. It was a wonderful vision to watch his huge marble body, with the great muscles swinging the hammer in rhythm yesterday in the garden. He is quite happy again now. I feel so often sorry Gerald that we weren't at our best for our visit to you. That you should have seen the worser side of all our characters ... Promise you will write to me very soon. The flat R.P. has taken in London belongs to James Strachey (& my friend Alix Florence who he has lately married. They are now in Vienna. He is studying under the great Freud.) It has one of the best librarys, over six thousand books. R.P. now leads a very proper life reading the Russians until the Woolfs return from Sussex and start work. I shall have a studio in one of the rooms & paint there this winter, when I leave Tidmarsh. What a stupid disconnected letter this is. But you won't mind because it carries so much love with it to you. Now write at once to me in great detail all your doings. My love to your good Maria. I would like a poem from you also.

    Yr Carrington

---

1 Carrington was turning against woodcuts and printmaking.

To Gerald Brenan

The Mill House
6 October 1920

Amigo Gerald,

Do you know I just wrote to you & posted the letter, when lo, the socialist postman who wears a green tie at funerals, & doesn't believe in a God, rang the door bell, & gave me the best of letters possible to receive, with a post mark from Spain. I wanted to sit down & write at once. But then after all I had nothing to sit down & write because I had just written, only I was so extreemly (as Queen Victoria would underline) delighted with your letter. Do you know I just whisper this praise for it is for you alone, Lytton said after he had read your letters 'He certainly has a talent for writing. What good letters ... He certainly will be a writer.' There. Now you mustn't be too puffed up. For really it's the very highest praise possible [...]

I must protest in being coupled with Ralph. That's the danger when people appear together, & talk with the same mannerisms ... But it is not true ... I am not frank. It is often a burden to me my deceit. Like you I had an awful childhood, and honestly when I escaped & came to London at the age of 17 I couldn't speak the truth if I wanted to, I had acquired such an art of self protection, and even to Ralph I find I never can give myself completely away. But these people with whom I live, Lytton, I mean, Alix, and Lytton's brother, & their friends all assume a frankess of conversation which (as you were at our conversation) appalled me at first. Then afterwards I saw it was a kind of technique, and behind it all there was a great reserve. I think I've caught rather these habits of conversation, but I never feel I give anyone except perhaps Alix my complete frankness. Do you know I have one character with Lytton, with one set of reserves for him, and another with Ralph, & then another with the general world. I think Ralph is really a frank person. I fear I must now conclude that I undoubtly come under 'the nondescript' heading 'without intellectual or moral capacity to be either' which isn't flattering, but probably the most truthful remark I've yet made in this letter.

I wrote to you about a week ago. What has happened since? Very little except I've been lain low with a most vile cold, which I caught from that wretch Lytton. Last weekend, Marjorie Strachey came, Lytton's younger sister, and Ralph. Marjorie is a most interesting person, like one of those violent student females that suddenly appear in [a] Tcheckov story. She has a curious witch like appearance, & makes sudden violent movements which start one out of one's skin with terror. She imitates everything she speaks about with gestures. Once at tea she imitated an angry hen & I was terrified.

Her knowledge is immense, on every subject, and her views always extreme, & violent [...] She attacks Lytton, and refuses to be whimsical to his whims. Yet she is very amusing, full of stinging wit, and with so much conversation, & good bawdy jokes. Her profession is that of an educationalist & she teaches female children in Debenham & Freebodys continuation school. She also writes stories, translations of folk love stories, which I didn't quite see the point of. Ralph was very charming and sat for a portrait. I am painting very hard now. My complaint is, that I so easily get despondent, & dislike my picture, and then abandon it without finishing it.

Lytton is insisting this month, on penalty of a great breach of affection, that I must send a picture to the London Group Show, so I suppose I shall have to. But the mere thought of seeing my half hatched efforts displayed in public almost makes me sick, & suicidal. But I shall not see them, even if they are accepted. For I shall never go. I am dear Gerald going to do you a Book Plate for a Xmas present. So tell me what device you would like. I shall do a wood cut with your name underneath it and an inscription in Spanish if you like to say that you are willing, or not willing, as the case may be to lend your books. But you must tell me soon, or otherwise it will not be done by the anniversary of our Lord's death [...]

Always write here, as I am rather vague about when I shall take up my abode in London. I hope so much you will soon be well again. Give Maria my love. And write me another letter immediately.

Yr loving Carrington

To Lytton Strachey

41 Gordon Square, London W.C.1
12 October 1920

My Dearest Lytton,

The young men have just taken them off to Heals![1] There. Now give me a kiss & tell me I am a good girl. I could not write yesterday. I was so busy painting smudges, and making new smudges, which the journey up had made on the wet portions of the pictures. Vanessa yesterday rather disappointed me, she was so vague, and didn't seem to know anything about the prices, or even which of the three I should send, or if I could send three. But she came in this morning, and was much more awake, & helpful & suggested sending all three, and seeing what happened, and brought an

---

1 Carrington submitted three paintings to the London Group Exhibition at Heal's. Vanessa Bell had encouraged her, and advised her on prices.

introduction for me to send with them. She told me £15 for the big mill picture and £10 for the others. So I put £30 on the mill, as you said that, and £10 & £15 on the other two, which I thought would be alright either way. It's a great mercy to have them shipped off, and to have been so brave. Bless you dear, for spurring me on. You know I was so grateful, & I didn't mean to be tiresome. Mark and Brett are not sending. I went up yesterday at 6.30 & spent the evening there. Mark looked dreadfully white and worn, but was completely cheerful and very amusing, talking the entire time, until we left at 9.30. Kot [Koteliansky] was there when we arrived. He seems very sensible, and capable. Brett hopelessly vague of course, and talking about her tennis with Murry most of the time. As Mark says she seems to find her sexual outlet playing with tennis balls with Murry, instead of Murry's balls. But I'll tell you all about Mark when I see you tomorrow [...]

Having agreed to live with Ralph in London during the week, Carrington found the separation from Lytton hard to bear. Ralph's efforts to make her happy only made her feel guilty and miserable and his constant presence brought out her devious side.

To Lytton Strachey

41 Gordon Square
25 October 1920

My Dearest Lytton,

I feel dreadfully depressed now, installed high up in this gloomy grey Square. The beauty of that walk made me long to be in the country again. To sit on the edge of the river and paint those barns against the red stained woods. But all these thoughts are backsliding – and Bull of Bashanish. I love the smell of fallen poplar leaves and the loveliness of the coloured trees and Tidmarsh so passionately: I can't write what I feel, because I cannot trust you to tear up my letters, and Ralph will read them. Will you burn this one? I won't write another one ever again like it. Perhaps you thought I didn't care leaving you this morning, and when you told me you were depressed last week and had not written *Victoria*, that I did not mind. Oh God. You said the middle of the week would go so quickly, but the weekends, they go quicker far. And I saw so little of you ... Yet I must try honestly to forget now that I have given my promise to stay here with him. Perhaps in a few weeks I will either numb some senses or realize I cannot bear it. He is so good to me. He tries to make me happy. But I have to hide my pain, which makes it harder. For I do miss you so frightfully. Promise this, dear, to me, if you feel it matters to you, my being away, if you feel ill, and worried to write and tell me [...] I shall not tell you this again, because if he knew it would only make him wretched so please directly you have read this burn it in the fire. It is just an admission that I feel I must make to you, and that it can be the secret of an afternoon between us ... The secret of my grief at leaving – Next weekend we will talk a little together. You will tell me how you feel. Oh wasn't it a wonderful talk this morning. I see you now crawling under the fence on your hands and knees like a mild red bear in spectacles, in the orange leaves.

You mustn't think I am not happy here. It's only I had to tell you and you alone, how much I cared. Oh Lytton, why should it be so difficult? Write to me, but say nothing of this.

My dear one goodbye. This week I will come on Friday afternoon. Tell me if the Dog[1] is coming.

Yr most loving Carrington

To Gerald Brenan

41 Gordon Square
End of October 1920

Amigo Geraldo,

How I will do my best to live up to your insidious flattery and write you a good letter. How shall I give you a great discourse on marriage and the folly of your sentiments? One cannot be a female creator of works of art & have children. That is the real reason why so few women have reached any high plane of creators. And the few that did become artists; I think you will admit, were never married, or had children. Emily Bronte & her sisters, Jane Austen, Sappho. Lady Hester Stanhope. Queen Elizabeth. And even lesser people like the French female artists Berthe Morisot, Le Brun, Julie de Lespinasse & Du Deffand. There has been a controversy lately in the *New Statesman* between Virginia Woolf & Desmond MacCarthy, as to the reason why females have never produced great writers, poets or artists or even musicians. Virginia gave bad education, and upbringing as the chief reason, also prejudice, and child bearing. I am sure it is impossible unless one is so rich that one need never look after a child which would mean one would be very insensible to bear one's child brought up by others – or so supremely impossibly competent that one can control a house, children, & husband &

---

1 James Doggart (1900–89) had served in the war and was a recent graduate in medicine from King's College, Cambridge.

still preserve the concentration, and singleness of purpose that is necessary to all artists. These seem to me good reasons if one wishes to be an artist for refusing to marry or bear children. My real reason however is that I dislike merging into a person, which marriage involves, and I do not care for children. They seem so tedious, & interrupting. I prefer the friendships of grown-up human beings.

If when I am 30, I am not an artist, and I think it is no good my persevering with my painting, I might have a child. But I doubt if I shall ever had maternal feelings enough to go through the bother & tedium of childbearing. Amen.

Then your 'two in one organization' how can you write those words, and then favour marriage. I hate those little self-centred worlds which married people live in. But enough of this sermon. What is Virginia Woolf like? Well I will send you when I get hold of one a photograph of her. That will be a truthful outside representation. Inside it's rather difficult to describe her. She has been mad, seriously, twice. The last time for three or four years. One always feels this a little with her, as if she had lived a life one had not lived, and as if she had visions one could never see. She is the most imaginative person, always attacking people from odd angles, full of curiosity and very thorough with her analysis of characters. Her simplicity is her great charm. She has no snobbery but a real dignity because she recognizes her own value honestly. I am sure she would charm you. She has the manners of a man, unaffected, and earnest, & yet is very graceful & full of a woman's competence. She cooks wonderful home-made bread, & makes country preserves, & pickles, and knows such names of plants, & enjoys friendships with such various people as her servants, a chemist in Richmond, old women who she reads to, authors, and young educated women. She has no prejudices, and is always absorbed in her immediate surroundings. Then she has a classical background which one feels in her conversation. She is a great reader of Greek. I always when I am with her feel overpowered with her brilliance, & charm. Then I like her husband also. He is a Jew, but very interesting and simple & free from the limitations of most Jews. I feel they were quite the best people for Ralph to be with and he is doing good work with them. Will you really let them bring out your first book? Think, Lytton said 'I am sure Brenan will be the coming author of this century'. That is actually what Lytton said, after reading your letter, and he is always crushing in his criticism. But perhaps you don't revere him and his praise quite as much as I do!

Do write to Lytton sometimes. I am sure he would so like it. Secretly he feels a little sorry he didn't write to you when he got back from Spain & now he feels a little ashamed of not having written, and yet could not apologise, because it is not his way. Of course he never told me this. But I surmised it ... He is writing *Victoria* at Tidmarsh now. Those that have read *Victoria* think it is a great deal better than *Eminent Victorians*. I will send you *E.V.* out by J.H.-J.[1] if you tell me if you would like it ...

I've been in London at 41 G.S. a week now. Oh how I miss the autumn country. But I've promised to stay here, so I mustn't cry! But do you realize what it means to leave Tidmarsh after living there for three years, & being intimate with almost every leaf & Bird in the garden. Last weekend we went back very early on Saturday morning to Tidmarsh. Ralph the sloven was loath to get up at six o'ck & catch the 7.30 train down there, but I insisted, & how it rewarded one, the beauty of the walk from Pangbourne at nine o'clock, with the mists rising from the little river was indescribable. Then there was Lytton over his fire, & little Annie in the kitchen with a smiling face [...] I planted rows of tulips for next spring, & coloured irises in the garden on Saturday morning.

On Sunday afternoon we went an amazing walk up to Sulham Woods. It was most beautiful in the great Forest of Beeches. Their smooth green trunks, & underneath soft crunchy carpet of coloured leaves like some Titian painting, varnished reds & browns. On the way back we saw dangling in the sun, on the bar of an old rusty field-roller two adders, which some game keeper had caught and killed, and hung there. They were the most lovely creatures. I had never held an adder in my hands before. The feeling was amazing, the soft pliant bodies with the cold smooth scales. All mottle black & ivory. I opened their dead mouths and saw the big black fangs, and do you know even although maggots were breeding in their jaws, the tail of one of them still wriggled in a hand, and curved up & down, as if in pain. We stood for a long time in the sun, on the edge of the big Beech Wood looking at them. I wanted to take one back with me to draw. But Lytton was against it, as they were long dead. Then crossing the Fields near the Mill, we saw a cow give birth to a calf in a field, and almost the minute afterwards she rose up & walked across a little river ditch, with the absurd little white calf, with its knees rocking together, and its natal cord dribbling in the sun, stumbling after her, like some clumsy big dog. On Sunday morning instead of coming up to London from Pangbourne station, we walked along the edge of the Thames, along the tow path to Tilehurst station, some six miles. It was 11 o'ck in the morning, & the sun shone furiously through the clear frosty air.

1 John Hope-Johnstone (1883–1970) was one of Gerald's closest friends. He had encouraged Gerald's rebellion against convention, introduced him to Augustus John and to Bloomsbury. In 1912 they had attempted to walk to Bosnia together. He also tutored the John children and edited the *Burlington Magazine* from 1919 to 1920.

The woods mounted up on the Whitchurch Downs, & looked all stained with red ink like a water colour picture which has run. Really the beauty of the scene made me feel exhausted with emotion. I saw a king-fisher some lovely coloured ducks, a big kestrel over the downs, and six grey cygnets gliding along the river, like dignified ships. Then I like those Stately Homes of England which grow by the edge of river with their sloping lawns & cedar trees. They are so English. We got lost in the end of our walk in a private estate and had to climb a high wall to reach Tilehurst station. Lytton was so gay on this walk, and he and Ralph looked so well in the English landscape [...] Then at Tilehurst we parted. Lytton back to Tidmarsh in one train, and Ralph & I up to Gordon Square in the other train. I suffered great depressions when I got back here. The beauty of the country rends me inside ... and then Tidmarsh is such a wonderful place to me.

Well dear Gerald I must stop now, as I've got to earn some money and do some Book Plates. Write to me very soon please. I love your letters so much, more than anyone else does. I write this in a great hurry so forgive its faults. Please take care of the fever & don't get ill.

   Yr loving Carrington

To Lytton Strachey

[41 Gordon Square?]
2 November 1920

Dearest Lytton,

   What a perfect day! The sun even penetrates old London, and now shines in my window. What a number of curious things seem to have happened since yesterday. Perhaps just as many have happened to you! Hope-Johnstone arrived to tea yesterday with an invitation to a party at his studio in the evening. He is a regular kiosk of gossip. Roger's [Fry] success in Paris, intrigues, and rumours. But I dislike him, and his methods. Nothing he tells one seems genuine. I think he is a very affected bore. I suspect he has qualities which he only shows Gerald. I can't believe Gerald would tolerate him as he is in London. Ralph was very cheerful, and worked away for Leonard. At eight o'ck we went into Karin's [Stephen]. We started at once discussing psycho-analysis and the topic never varied once! Ralph got on very well with them. Adrian is certainly less grim than he used to be.[1] Whether it's the result of psycho-analysis or not I don't

1 Karin Stephen, née Costelloe (1889–1953), was a philosopher and fellow of Newnham College, Cambridge, married since 1914 to Adrian (1883–1948), younger brother of Vanessa Bell and Virginia Woolf and former lover of Duncan Grant. Like James and Alix Strachey, both Karin and Adrian Stephen became Freudian analysts in the 1920s.

know. They both swear Mr Glover (the doctor who anylises [sic] them – PS
I have a complex about spelling this word) has improved their characters
enormously, their memories, and spirits. I almost believed them. They have
rather nice rooms. Also an early Duncan which interested me, of boys on
horseback, a decorative painting in monochrome. I quite enjoyed the
evening, a good deal of wild gossip passed, concerning the mad and the
semi-mad.

Then at 10.30, after we had dressed up, Ralph in a blue French blouse
and his cords looking very charming, your Mopsa in blue silk pyjama
trousers, and a frock affaire on top with a shawl, we went to J. H. -J. How
it brought back another world! These familiar Bohemian figures. Some
new ones, but mostly acting the traditional parts. John very drunk, lurching
about like a Cossack in *Petruschka*, from woman to woman. Two Bohemian
Fitzroy artists playing guitars and pipes in the corner, a mêlée of dancing
people, little syphilitic harlots from the Café Royal, with faces like chewed
india rubber, when you looked at them closely [...] Dorelia [John] like
some Sibyl sitting in a corner with a Basque cap on her head and her cloak
swept round her in great folds, smiling mysteriously, talking to everyone,
unperturbed watching the dancers. I wondered what went on in her head.
I fell very much in love with her. She was so amazingly beautiful. It's
something to have seen such a vision as she looked last night. And 'How
is Strachey? Is *Victoria* nearly finished? Tell him I really will come and see
him in the country ... yes quite soon ... I'll bring some food with me ...'
Then a mysterious smile. Ralph also fell in love with her. But was too shy
to approach the Deity. Then Sylvia Gosse[1] completely drunk looking more
vicious that it is possible to conceive. Dancing recklessly with her thin
loose legs flying like a marionette figure in every direction. A great many
revolting Café Royal girls, who made one almost sick. A group of dingy
artists from Fitzroy Street who looked like road sweepers. Even Morgan
[E. M. Forster], who I saw in an interval eyeing Ralph.[2] Chili [Alvaro
Guevara] who actually, so Ralph said, accosted him! A very perfect tart of
a young man who you would have loved, very slim, one of those fair
semi-Greek Henryesque faces, but probably riddled with disease. He came
with Lord Berners and Chili. We danced all the time, and quite enjoyed
it. I had some very entertaining dialogues with John, who was like some
old salt in his transparent drunkenness.

1 Sylvia Gosse (1881–1968) the daughter of the writer Edmund Gosse, was a painter and printmaker
  who ran an art school with Walter Sickert.
2 Forster was to conduct a flirtatious correspondence with Ralph and make a characteristically tentative
  and unsuccessful pass at him.

'I say old chap will you come away with me.'

D.C. But you know what they call that?

'Oh I forgot you were a boy.'

D.C. Well don't forget it or you'll get 2 years hard.

'I say are you insinuating,' drawing himself up and flashing his eyes in mock indignation, 'that I am a Bugger.'

D.C. My brother is the chief inspector of Scotland Yard.

'Oh I'm not afraid of him.' But in a whisper. 'Will you come to Spain with me? I'd love to go to Spain with you.'

D.C. This year, next year, sometime.

John 'Never.' Then we both laughed in a roar together.

Ralph was very entertained. He hadn't met John before. We left with the musicians, who packed up their instruments, at 1.30. Some more horrid upper class whores came in and I saw it would become a vast party of slobbers, and as I was tired, I hardly thought it worth while to linger. I thought we had what little cream there was off the top of the jug.

This morning we got up un peu tard. A parcel of woollens from my demented mother which I am wearing now. Then a journey to Birrell and Garnett[1] to get some addresses of book shops. I was looking in the shelves whilst Frankie [Birrell] and Ralph were talking shop. Suddenly I smelt something very vile, turned round to discover the armchair in flames. Frankie suddenly saw it, looked very surprised, and just gave it a kick or two expecting it to go out. In the end I had to smother it with gloved hands. The cover was completely ruined, and most of the chair burnt. What a character Frankie is! Then glory be to God R.P. went down to Hendersons and managed to sell 125 copies of the Hogarth productions! He was wildly delighted, as it was his first venture into a bookshop as a pedlar.

Would you like 2 vols of memoirs of Marguerite de Valois from B. and Garnett's shop as a little present? They were rather charming books. I am just going to tea with Faith [Henderson] today, and later to Brett's for dinner.

1 Birrell and Garnett was a bookshop set up by Francis Birrell (1889–1935) and David Garnett in 1920. Francis was the son of Augustine Birrell (1850–1933), a prominent Liberal Party politican, writer and wit. In love with Garnett, and like him a pacifist, they worked together for the Quakers in France during the war.

To Lytton Strachey

41 Gordon Square
24 November 1920

Dearest Lytton,

A properly dated letter! I hope you are keeping well, and that *Victoria* goes well also [...] Alan gave us a super dinner at the Café Royal upstairs. Really when the food is so good and rich I unfortunately always feel rather sick [...] Afterwards we went to what is called a musical comedy at a theatre in Drury Lane. It was interesting. The herd instinct of the sham-upper-class audiences and the tendency of modern humour. A young man called Leslie Henson was the chief actor in the play. He was a very skilful combination of George Robey, little Tich, and almost every comedian on the Musical Halls, including Charlie Chaplin. In painting, such a wilful 'crib'of artists, blatantly mixed up on a canvas would produce an outcry. I don't think anyone notices the lack of originality in a comedian. There was one French actor in the play. And it was amazing the difference. He only had the part of a waiter.

But the point he gave to his acting, the completeness of it, was astonishing. It was a play adapted from the French. One saw the indecent situations, the indecent suggestions, and yet they had so covered it up, that all South Kensington could watch without a blush. Really I do think the English are appallingly stupid to laugh at such jokes and applaud such hideous vulgar scenes. This morning I went at eleven o'ck to paint her Ladyship [Lytton's mother].[1] She is superb. It's rather stupid to tell you this. But I was completely overcome by her grandeur, and wit. I am painting her against the bookcase sitting full length in a chair, in a wonderful robe which goes into great El Greco folds. It is lined with orange. So the effect is a very sombre picture with a black dress, and mottled cloak, and then brilliant orange edges down the front of her dress. She looks like the Queen of China, or one of El Greco's Inquisitors. Pippa[2] was superb. For, do you know, when they heard I had captured her as a model, Roger, Duncan, and Vanessa then stormed the castle, and asked her to sit for them. Pippa valiantly pleaded that as I had asked first I must be allowed to paint her first, and alone. They had suggested my joining them in a quartet! It's all very well for a nude model as a back is as good as a front. But I didn't like the idea of painting her Ladyship back view in a confusion of easels and conversation! [...]

1 Lady Strachey, née Jane Maria Grant (1840–1928), married Sir Richard Strachey, soldier and administrator in India, in 1859. She bore him ten children and was a leading campaigner for votes for women.
2 Philippa Strachey (1872–1968) was one of Lytton's five sisters and a passionate suffragist and feminist.

Gerald wrote me such a long letter on Monday. I am still trying to digest it. I wish he wouldn't write a letter continuously for two weeks as its volume quite overpowers one when it does arrive! Six pages were devoted to you, and a criticism of your work. And I thought Gerald showed remarkable intelligence in his remarks. But as he has asked me not to show it to you I don't very well think I can. There was one remark however which Ralph must have found difficult to swallow.

'As to his being a master of English prose there is no possible question. Gibbon cuts a small figure beside him, in spite of the greater "weight" of the *Decline.*'

I will bring you, however, the letter and his poems to read next weekend [...] I cannot but help being lonely without seeing you, and I feel so often perhaps you miss me, and that you aren't comfortable. *Victoria* matters so much to me. That's what Ralph doesn't feel. The importance above everything that a work of art, and a creator of such works, has for me. And yet do you know, this morning I felt these conflicting emotions are destroying my purpose for painting. That perhaps that feeling which I have had ever since I came to London years ago now, that I am not strong enough to live in this world of people, and paint, is a feeling which has complete truth in it. And yet when I envision leaving you and going like Gerald into isolation, I feel I should be so wretched that I should never have the spirit to work. But this must sound childish to you [...] Dearest be happy till I come back. And write to me sometimes.

Yr loving Carrington

Although Carrington's complex emotional life and her dedication to Lytton and their Tidmarsh life did get in the way of her painting, her own diffidence and the knowledge that her style was very different from the Charleston painters and not much admired by Roger Fry also held her back. Lytton himself always encouraged her, while also relying on her ruthlessly as his housekeeper and hostess.

1921

To Lytton Strachey

41 Gordon Square
[3 January 1921]

Dearest Lytton,

Yesterday I went with Brett to the Burlington Fine Arts and saw, what I still even on cool reflection, think the best picture I ever have seen. By Piero di Cosimo – a picture completely of wild animals, and the most beautiful birds, in a landscape of bushes, and a distant sea.[1] I shall go again tomorrow to amaze over it. Really in these famished days of pleasure, it was a joy to see such a picture. You I am sure will adore it also. Afterwards we went to the New English. It was too awful and depressing to describe. Even Chili's pictures were a disgrace. Brett spent the entire day with me. In the evening we both drew Ralph. Brett was so excited however, that she said she couldn't draw properly!

Thursday

Yesterday Barbara arrived at lunch time very delighted to be back in London. In the afternoon we talked, and at six o'ck Faith and Hubert came in to see Barbara and a few minutes later Leonard. Then we had the greatest of dinner parties. Virginia clothed in gold brocade and scarlet as an Eastern Prince, looking very beautiful and tremendously gay, and lively. Saxon, Leonard, and us three. Mrs Sneddon produced a four course dinner, ending with an additional course of cheese straws! Then at 9 o'ck we went to the party at Bunny's shop. The Anreps came, and a young lady of Bunny's from the floor above.[2] And Oliver and Inez [Fergusson]. Most of the company spent the time reading books from the shelves! And discussing business, and printing. After the Wolves left, we danced, listened to the gramophone, and played hunt the slipper, which old Anrep and Ralph enjoyed naturally, pinching the ladies' legs looking for the shoe. On the whole I think it went off alright and Barbara enjoyed it very much. Now I must go to the post as I am going to paint Margaret Waley at 11 o'ck.

---

1 Piero di Cosimo (1462–1522), a leading painter in Renaissance Florence, renowned for his portraits and for mythological scenes. Carrington's description fits *The Forest Fire*, 1505, now in the Ashmolean in Oxford.

2 Bunny's young lady was Rachel (Ray) Marshall, who married him in 1921.

I will come down on Friday evening. Barbara, Saxon and Ralph are coming down on Saturday. No more news.

[*From Ralph Partridge*]
Have to dance among the fishes on Friday – will be down as early on Sat. as I can. Fond love R. D.C. has broken my nose. SHAME.

To Alix Strachey

The Mill House
15 April 1921

At last I have an evening completely to myself, dearest Alix, so I'll commemorate it with a letter to you. The Major and Lytton both went back to London this morning and left me here alone. I started a still-life yesterday of tulips, and I was so pleased with it that I stay here alone to finish it. After all London's a slight fraud! Lytton is now on the crest of his wave and lunches and dines with the shipowner's wife 'Maud'¹ and Chelsea pseudo aristocracy, daily. So I hardly ever see him except in the evenings when he totters into 41, almost dead with exhaustion and high society. Partridge, Christian-named Ralph now, is on the crest of the Woolf's back, or the Hogarth wave. They have just produced Tchekhov's note-books which are very masterly and amusing. Short stories of the East by Leonard ... which I've not and never will read although wood cut cover by yours truly humbly. R.P. is so busy tying up these books and typewriting that I get rather merged into it and find it interrupts my painting. Also my enthusiasm for tying up books was rather curbed as all the parcels I did tie up were returned to Leonard disintegrated in a pulpy mess. I heard rumours that Woolf growling was fearsome, so I hid from his wrath. [...]

Lytton's *Victoria*² has been a great success in every periodical and paper in England and Scotland. Even *The Times* and *Daily Mail* bow before him! Many say it can't be so good as *E.V.* to receive this adulation. But it is I think, much better. His fortune will soon be immense, if a revolution does not come and cut short his life. For he is definitely joining the Upper Classes I regret to say. He's charming to me. I think he is walking on air for the moment and can't be disagreeable!! Last Tuesday he hired a private motor and took Ralph and me to Hampton Court. It was fun whirling

---

1 Lady Maud Cunard (1872–1948), also known as Emerald, was a leading hostess and admirer of Lytton's.
2 Lytton's biography, *Queen Victoria*, was published by Chatto & Windus in 1921.

through London pretending to be one of the idle rich. Hampton Court is an amazing place. I much prefer it to Versailles. I think it is probably the greatest achievement of architecture in England. The colour is so remarkable.

We had lunch in an inn over-lapping the river, and then motored back to London, dropping the private secretary at the Woolves' Lair on the way back [...] Did I tell you at Easter Bunny and Mrs Bunny turned up here for one day on a walk they were making to Goring. She is – Heavens, what a face. What a character DOUR and SILENT. No one can understand it. R.P. thought her breasts rather attractive but that was all he could see in her favour. Perhaps Bunny is losing his eyesight, as well as his wits. Francis is distinctly cut up about it and weeps on one's neck whenever one goes to the shop.

I have hopes of going to Italy with Lytton, but I see the finances are rather black for me. Lytton goes on the 7 May to La Berenson in Florence for 2 weeks. Then, D.V. [*Deo volente*, God willing], I may go out with R.P. and Pippa and join him. But it's rather vague as R.P. may not escape from the Wolves [...]

My love dear one,

Carrington

PS My beautiful friend Phyllis [Boyd] is shortly to marry a French Vicomte, a farmer in Normandy.

To Lytton Strachey

To L.S.
The Mill House
Sunday. Precisely 9 o'ck. But more vaguely morning, 8 May 1921

Dearest,

I have no idea what you are doing, what you look at, whether you glide in the rain over alps, or shiver in an Italian station room in your great cloak. You know what the sitting room looks like, and the view from this window: your visions I can't even guess! It's Monday morning now and I am writing sadly. So forgive the tinge of melancholy, if it creeps into these pages. I will tell you anything which has happened since you floated away with your hats, & boxes in the rain from Gordon Square – I dashed almost at once in a taxi to the Grosvenor Gallery with a nameless picture just in time, as Roger had started hanging. I took the tulips, I didn't much like it. But I hadn't anything else small enough [...] Some how I feel rather despondent about the painting! It never seems to be anything like as good as what I conceive inside.

Everything is a failure when it's finished. They start off so full of life – I hope Giotto & the Florentines may brisk up my powers. Lunch with Ralph at G.S. and then a five o'clock train to Pangbourne. We found Barbara & Nick busy gardening & very happy [...]

Ralph has had a mania for getting married lately [...] He thinks it will be easier to go to Italy à deux & make things easier living at G.S. afterwards. There is something in it of course. But if we are going to be at loggerheads when I want to live here alone, perhaps it's better to not be married! Au fond the real difficulty is he likes me always to be with him, and sometimes I prefer this life here. This morning he went off in a rage & Italy seemed to vanish with him. Now you know dear he only first told me this weekend that you are going to pay for our tickets. I cannot thank you, you are too good. So charming that I'd like to serve you all my life. Thank you very much indeed. 'Too kind, too kind' she murmured xxx and forty hugs for Blue Beard.

Dear, there is so much to say to you, yet I can write nothing [...] I want to tell you that I miss you very much, yet it sounds so weak without the exactitude of feeling which I'd like to express. I hope you will be very happy in Florence [...] And keep well. Please when there is time send me some jottings, about the people at the villa, the view from the windows & the pictures you see in the galleries. We must come! And I'll give up everything to humour that Barbarian if only to bask under Italy's sun. But he is a savage you know and I am a stoopid little mopsa I suppose & you, the wisest, best, loveliest bearded poet alive xxxxx

To Lytton Strachey

The Mill House
Saturday morning, 12 o'ck [14 May 1921]

My dearest Lytton,

There is a great deal to say and I feel very incompetent to write it today. Last night I composed a great many letters to you, almost till three in the morning. I then wrote an imaginary letter and bared my very soul to you. This morning I don't feel so intimate. You mayn't value my pent up feelings and a tearful letter. I rather object to them not being properly received and left about. Well there was more of a crisis than I thought when I wrote to you on Thursday. Ralph had one of his breakdowns and completely collapsed. He threw himself in the Woolves' arms and asked their sympathy and advice. Leonard and Virginia both said it was hopeless for him to go on as he was, that he must either marry me, or leave me completely. He came down to Reading yesterday and met me at the Coffee tea shop. He looked dreadfully ill and his mouth twitched. I'd really made my mind up some time ago that if it came to the ultimate point, I would give in. Only typically I preferred to defer it indefinitely and avoid it if possible. You see I knew there was nothing really to hope for from you – Well ever since the beginning. Then Alix told me last spring what you told James, that you were slightly terrified of my becoming dependent on you, and a permanent limpet and other things. I didn't tell you, because after all, it is no use having scenes. But you must know Ralph repeated every word you once told him in bed; that night when we were all three together. The next day we went for a walk on the Swindon downs. Perhaps you remember. I shall never forget that spot of ground, just outside Chiseldon, at the foot of the downs, when he repeated every word you had said. He told me of course because he was jealous and wanted to hurt me. But it altered things, because ever after that I had a terror of being physically on your nerves and revolting you. I never came again to your bedroom. Why am I raking all this up now? Only to tell you that all these years I have known all along that my life with you was limited. I could never hope for it to become permanent. After all Lytton, you are the only person who I have ever had an all absorbing passion for. I shall never have another. I couldn't now. I had one of the most self abasing loves that a person could have. You could throw me into transports of happiness and dash me into deluges of tears and despair, all by a few words. But these aren't reproaches. For after all it's getting on for 6 years since I first met you at Asheham; and that's a long time to be happy. And I know we shall always be friends now until I die. Of course these years of Tidmarsh when we were quite alone will always be the happiest I ever spent. And I've such a store of good things which I've saved up, that I feel I could never be lonely again now. Still it's too much of a strain to be quite alone here waiting to see you or craning my nose and eyes out of the window at 41 Gordon Square to see if you are coming down the street, when I know we'll be better friends, if you aren't haunted by the idea that I am siting depressed in some corner of the world waiting for your footstep. It's slightly mythical of course. I can pull myself together if I want to and I am more aware than you think, the moment I am getting on your nerves and when I am not wanted. I saw the relief you felt at Ralph taking me away, so to speak, off your hands. I think he'll make me happier, than I should be entirely by myself and it certainly prevents me becoming morbid about you. And as Ralph said last night you'll never leave us. Because in spite of our dullness, nobody loves you nearly as much as we do. So in the café of that vile city of Reading, I said that I'd marry him. And now he's written to his father and told him. After all I don't think it will make much difference and to see him happy is a rather definite thing. I'd probably never marry anyone else and I doubt if a kinder creature exists on earth. Last night he told me in bed everything Virginia and Leonard had told him. Again a conversation you had with them was repeated to me. Ralph was so happy he didn't hear me gasp and as it was dark he didn't see the tears run down my cheeks. Virginia told him that you had told them you didn't intend to come to Tidmarsh much after Italy and you were nervous lest I'd feel I had a sort of claim on you if I lived with you for a long time, ten years and that they all wondered how you could've stood me so long and how on earth we lived together alone here, as I didn't understand a word of literature and we had nothing in common intellectually or physically. That was wrong. For nobody I think could have loved the Ballades, Donne, and Macaulay's Essays and best of all, Lytton's Essays, as much as I. Virginia then told him that she thought I was still in love with you. Ralph asked me if I was. I said that I didn't think perhaps I was as much as I used to be. So now I shall never tell you I do care again. It goes after today somewhere deep down inside me and I'll not resurrect it to hurt either you, or Ralph. Never again. He knows that I am not in love with him. But he feels that my affections are great enough to make him happy if I live with him. I cried last night Lytton, whilst he slept by my side sleeping happily. I cried to think of a savage cynical fate which had made it impossible for my love ever to be used by you. You never knew, or never will know the very big and devastating love I had for you. How I adored every hair, every curl on your beard. How I devoured you whilst you read to me at night. How I loved the smell of your face in your sponge. Then the ivory skin on your hands, your voice, and your hat when I saw it coming along the top of the garden wall from my window. Say you will remember it, that it wasn't all lost and that you'll forgive me for this outburst, and always be my friend. Just thinking of you now makes me cry so I can't see this paper, and yet so happy that the next moment I am calm. I shall be with you in Italy in two weeks, how lovely that will be. And this summer we will be very happy together. Please never show this letter to anyone. Ralph is such a dear, I don't feel I'll ever regret marrying him. Though I never will change my maiden name that I have kept so long – so you mayn't call me anything but Carrington.

I am not going to tell my mother until the day before, so she can't make a fuss, or come up to London. I think we'll probably get united by Saint Pancras next Saturday and then drift over to Paris and see Valentine.[1] If my Fiend comes on I'll linger there for 2 days and then Italy ... Nick and Barbara

---

1 Valentine Dobrée (1894–1974) was the artist wife of the literary critic and man of letters Bonamy Dobrée (1891–1974) and a lover of Mark Gertler, who painted her in 1919.

are still here, and this weekend Saxon, and Alan and Michael come this evening. We'll pay off all the books before we leave. Now I must leave you, and paint the other side of the grey hound.

Later

Nick has just mown the lawn and it is now as smooth and short as a field of green plush.

All the ducks and chickens survive and Ralph spends his time lying in the sun on the lawn trying to persuade them to swim in a pan of water. I thought you had been clever to escape the thunderstorms and rains, but today the heat is more wonderful than anything in your land of the Romans. Saxon is an extraordinary character!! I am telling no one what I have told you. It will remain a confession to a priest in a box in an Italian church. I saw in London Group catalogue a picture by Walter Taylor called 'Reading Lytton Strachey's *Victoria*' – such is fame. I shall do a still life of a dozen Victoria's arranged in a phalanx for the next London Group. My dear I am sorry to leave you. I'll write again tomorrow. It's such a comfort having you to talk to.

My love for a dear one
Yr Carrington

3 o'ck, Saturday

PS I've just read this letter again. You mustn't think I was hurt by hearing what you said to Virginia and Leonard and that made me cry. For I'd faced that long ago with Alix in the first years of my love for you. You gave me a much longer life than I ever deserved or hoped for and I love you for it terribly. I only cried last night at realising I could never have my Moon, that some times I must pain you, and often bore you. You who I would have given the world to have made happier than any person could be, to give you all you wanted. But dearest, this isn't a break in our affections. I'll always care as much, only now it will never burden you and we'll never discuss it again, as there will be nothing to discuss. I see I've told you very little of what I feel. But I keep on crying, if I stop and think about you. Outside the sun is baking and they all chatter, and laugh. It's cynical, this world in its opposites. Once you said to me, that Wednesday afternoon in the sitting room, you loved me as a friend. Could you tell it to me again?

Yrs Carrington

This last letter took six days to reach Lytton in Italy. She kept on writing to him and others as usual, and broke the news to Gerald Brenan.

To Lytton Strachey

Driftway, Middle Wallop, Stockbridge, Hants
Thursday, 19 May 1921

Dearest Lytton,

I am staying down here for two days before we whisk over to Paris. My mother bore the shock very well, and is fortunately making no fuss over it. So little fuss indeed one is apt to think perhaps she has known all along my wicked ways! She is mercifully not coming up to London which is a great relief. Dear, I've had it on my conscience that I wrote you rather a horrid letter last Sunday from Tidmarsh, but I was rather 'beside' myself, as they say. I hardly saw, or knew what I was writing. Now I am quite happy again and calm and I love my Lytton. Ralph is such a dear and somehow so child-ishly happy that I don't feel it's a plunge in any direction. In fact I suspect it will make practically no difference. Ralph is coming down here today to be inspected. Then we'll glide off tomorrow to London, have a joy day looking at Max's [Beerbohm] pictures. (I see they charge 5/- entrance today! Private view was yesterday.) The Nameless show[1] and in the evening *Bulldog Drummond* with Alan, and Marjorie. Saturday 10 o'ck St Pancras' Registered altar, then your 11 o'ck train, and Paris. I have asked Valentine to get me rooms at her hotel, and perhaps will stay till Monday before we move on to Italy. I believe I feel all these proceedings very little because I am so excited about ITALY! It's almost too exciting sometimes, and already I am depressed about coming back, and the end of the month being up! It's wonderful to be in Wiltshire again, and see the downs and the juniper bushes and the rings of beech trees on the tops of the hills. The cuckoos are cuckooing to despair almost. Bees buzz in the garden which is full of big poppies, and flags. Italy will have to be in fine trim to equal the beauty of Middle Wallop. So tell her to muster up her birds and flowers to greet Queen Mopsa next week. I've just been reading the History of Vanessa and Swift and their letters.[2]

I didn't know it was like that. It touched me strangely. How lovable was Vanessa, rather like Alix I thought. On Tuesday evening we went into 51 G.S. after dinner, and talked to the family. Simon and Janie [Simon Bussy and his daughter Jane] were there, the latter I thought very attractive. Marjorie was in one of her most hectic moods. Ray was there also and her ladyship. We played bridge afterwards, and gossiped with Ray, and Marjorie. I had an awful time over my passport signing 'D. Partridge' on every line,

1 Roger Fry's latest show, where the paintings were anonymous, included Carrington's *Tulips*.
2 Jonathan Swift (1667–1745), the Anglo-Irish cleric, poet and satirist, had a long and complicated romance with a much younger woman he called Vanessa. His letters to her were published after her early death.

and making a thousand mistakes. I got Noel Olivier to sign for me as she is a doctor. She thought Mrs P. was an excellent joke and fairly roared over it! I didn't tell her it was nearly or would soon be a grim truth. Unfortunately in her merriment she signed it wrong so I had to forge her name. Which may yet land me in jail instead of in Paris! But I trust they'll not discover it. I am bringing my spy glasses, an air cushion, and a camera, and a drawing book. C'est tout. Here's a little blue flower for you. I'll write if I can tomorrow.

Dearest Lytton, love me always as much as you do now and I'll be happy.

Yr Carrington

To Gerald Brenan

Driftway, Middle Wallop, Stockbridge, Hants

20 May 1921

Dear Gerald,

Isn't Middle Wallop a good name for a village, and it's as good a village as you could find south of Andover. – I am again full of absurd emotions writing to you! Because no matter how prosaically I sit down to write to you, instantly, a vision of you in a blue cotton suit, tall green poplars, coloured mountains, and your house float into my head, & destroy all my literary talent & coherence [...]

I would like to paint like Uccello & I never shall, because as you say he is highly 'intellectual and conscious' – It has something – this desire – to do with my wish to have Lytton as a lover, a wish that the veriest goose could have known was impossible.

I am obviously a simple painter. Simon Bussy once saw 'the quality of Rousseau' in my work. I have more feeling really for signboards & very simple 18th cent. English painting than for modern French. But I appreciate these Intellectuals almost to a pitch of worship. Matisse is exquisite. I love him too. But he's not quite rich enough. Or tight enough for me. A little too – how shall I say it, water-coloury & pale muslin dresses for me. But perfect in his own way.

I hope to see more Ingres very soon in Paris. I saw some at the British Museum about 3 weeks ago. They are astonishing.

Yes, I agree also about Raphael but I always feel there's something lacking in oneself if one doesn't appreciate him. When Roger Fry talks about 'the fullness of the lines' and 'the massive drapery' I strain every wit & muscle to grasp what he means, but I always find honestly, I am cold and feel nothing. He never seems to me to be 'peculiar' which is what I love in artists [...] Piero de Cosimo is my Saint at the moment, I burn all my candles to him [...]

[...] Shall I answer your letter or break my news, like a cart belching out its stories on to the poor road, & burst it on you now, & then proceed with your letter.

The latter course is obviously more civil and the first wiser, as perchance if I answer the letter, which, you may remember is a long one, the post will come & carry my letter away without the news.

But after all what news is this? If I'd painted a masterpiece, made £100 to share with you, written a poem, that would be news ... But this news is merely like any other, a passing fact, a slight alteration of names

DORIC CARRINGTON PARTRIDGE

Is it hateful to you? You, the connoisseur of names!

Next Saturday morning at 10 o'clock at St Pancras shrine I shall change my beloved name of Carrington to a less noble one of Partridge.

You smile & say 'how are the stiff necked fallen, where are her grand principles!' They are still here young man, locked in my amazon breast. 'I never will change my maiden name that I have kept so long' rings a good song – to you I shall ever be Carrington & to myself ...

I sent you some books as a present did you ever get them? And I sent your letter to Lytton to Italy.

Oh, I am very glad you think so highly of *E.V.* Lytton has not received such high praise, as that, from anyone.

[...] The reason? Ralph was very unhappy & said if I didn't, he couldn't bear it – He is too good a man for a little wretch like me to make unhappy. Besides I had inward reasons, a devil, a plague to destroy inside me, he will help in the destruction. And he makes me very happy, & helps me bear the brunt of this tiresome world. It won't make any difference, for we'll not 'set up' in a house, with a neat maid in black & white & have napkin rings, we'll live at the good Mill & keep a little room in Gordon Square & always a bed for Geraldo.

He is so charming, such a good companion, I couldn't have married anyone else, unless perhaps ...

But you shall never know that perhaps. G.B. Perhaps? Or perhaps not!

I am sorry the neuralgia plagues you. I will send you some excellent flat tablets for the same, 3 of which hurt no man or woman. I read Vanessa's letter to Swift. It almost made me wept. I understand it so well. Dear Gerald never cease to remember I am still your friend Carrington & you can rely on my help if ever you want it.

My love dearest one.

D.C.

To Noel Carrington

41 Gordon Square
21 May 1921

Dearest Noel

This morning at 10 o'ck punctually I married R.S.P. at St Pancras Registrar. Please R.S.V.P. & tell me you are pleased.

A little gold ring now adorns that hand that once stood brown & bare
a wreath of orange blossom twines around her once so golden hair
oh dearie me oh dearie me
never again a maid shall I be!

Rex is very happy, & that's the main thing. We had an entertaining time breaking the news to mother who took it in a proper spirit & wasn't too overcome. She professed a great liking to him & was very obliging not coming up to the wedding.

Alan & Marjorie Strachey alone supported us. Alan is a charming creature. Very soon in a couple of hours we glide to Paris, rest a day there, & then Italy. Then fresco tours like Assisi & Siena & Ravenna & then Venice where we join Lytton & Pippa Strachey.

Then we travel in the north, pay a visit to Mrs P & Dorothy & come back to London & paint pots on June 20th.

Everyone is very nice to one on such occasions I always find.

Lottie [Carrington's sister Charlotte] even sent me a wire. I only told her in a letter this morning. Mother only knew two days before so she hadn't much time to get agitated & secretly I believe she was vastly relieved I wasn't costing her a penny in clothes, or a cape even. You must be happy also as I know you will [...]

Why did we do it after so many years of brazen sin? Mostly to please Rex, who has a slight mania – entre nous – to behave properly! and then it made him happier. It's cheaper also and deception is rather wearying year after year.

Mother hadn't even heard of R.P. in connection with me apparently!

I've no more news as now I must pack. It's a superb hot day & I am very happy. A cable cost too much for Rex has spent most our money on shoes & a new shirt.

Send us your love soon.

Yr devoted ever to you

D.C.

*After some days, Lytton's long reply to Carrington's letter about her marriage arrived.
He was as loving and reassuring as he could be.*

> Oh my dear, do you really want me to tell you that I love you as a
> friend! – but of course that is absurd, and you do know very well that
> I love you as something more than a friend, you angelic creature, whose
> goodness to me has made me happy for years and whose presence in
> my life has been, and always will be, one of the most important things
> in it. Your letter made me cry [...]
>   [...] if your decision meant that I should somehow or other lose
> you, I don't think I could bear it.

*As for 'the physical part', he suggested that Virginia was not always to be believed,
and that what he said to Ralph might well have been 'a passing phase'.*

*The Italian honeymoon journey was a mixed success. Carrington lost her wedding
ring and they fought a good deal, but they met Lytton in Venice and were happy
walking in the Tuscan hills. She wrote Gerald four long letters about art and landscape.*

*Back at Tidmarsh, it was not long before Gerald came over from Spain and
hurried down to see her. They picnicked and kissed on White Horse Hill. Soon he
realised he was 'deeply, irretrievably in love'.*

To Gerald Brenan

The Mill House
Friday, 8 July 1921

I feel absurdly happy today, what a lovely day it was. Really you are one of
the best companions in the world ... and when I got into the train I thought
about all the things that I wanted you to talk to me about. Bosnia, Yegen,
your writing, so many things which we never reached [...] Isn't exploring
the most exciting thing almost in the world, yes in every direction.

This morning I feel everything so acutely. The smells in the garden, the
sounds of the flies & the bees, & the warmth of the early day, for it's not
yet nine o'ck.

I feel so full of affections and happy ... And I look back every few minutes
on yesterday & feel happier & happier until I want to start again, so I put
out of my head the vision of White Horse Hill & then after five minutes
recall it again. I hardly feel it was you I was with, the same person I am
now writing to.

How very perfect to have one such day a year in a lifetime.

You couldn't have enjoyed it quite so much as I did. You don't love those downs & the colours quite so much, confess? Then you didn't feel a shepherd's toothbrush burning a bristling into your face.

Ralph was very cheerful, we played Bagatelle most of the evening. He loves you also so much.

Goodbye Gerald for a little.

Come & stay here before the 28th please for as long as you can. You must come very soon.

My love

Your Doric

To Lytton Strachey

The Mill House

[n.d.]

Dearest Lytton,

[...] We reached the Woolfs rather late for tea but of course they are so charming they never really mind and the tea was delicious. Really Virginia does make heavenly jams. Then, after tea, Leonard went for a walk over the downs with Ralph, and Virginia and I trailed behind gossiping and croaking. Mary, you and your writing (of which I knew nothing), Vanessa and Mary, Ralph and THE SITUATION, the merits of Rodmell against Asheham, composed our conversation. I came back full of enthusiasm for Virginia. It's impossible not to fall in love with her I find. She was so friendly to me I couldn't help but collapsing completely. Dinner. Then a sogjourn – which I know is spelt wrong but I can't make it look better – to the summer house. Leonard very grave after a terrible silence. 'Well I think we had better perhaps discuss the situation.' Then he started. Really he is superb: so logical, fair, and intelligent. Then Virginia gave her point of view. Then Ralph rather tentatively returned the fire. And I summed up the proceedings at the tail end of everything. Ralph is writing to you and will talk it all over when we meet again. Leonard and Virginia will also talk it over. So I will not now repeat it. We slept like logs on the Rockeries but I doubt if your back bone will hold out! Really Tidmarsh is the Carlton in its comforts. Why do we ever fuss? The next day Wednesday was divine wasn't it? So lovely at Rodmell I longed to stay on. It was terrible to have to leave. Leonard gave us masses of apples and pears to take back with us. We spent most of the morning picking pears for him at the top of a ladder. Then we raced off before lunch as La grand Loup et fille were appearing in fact did appear at a quarter to one [...]

[...] Lytton dear, I love you so much today. We talked for a long time over the fire last night and a great deal about you. I feel much happier today. Ralph is so fond of you and Tidmarsh. Bless you my dearest one. I hope the good weather will go on, and that you will enjoy Rodmell. It's perfect here today. This morning Mrs Wright united two families of bees with great success. I wasn't stung and I had no glove on one hand.

I wish dreadfully that you were here just because it's so warm and beautiful.

Your Mopsa

The 'situation' under discussion concerned Ralph's future at the Hogarth Press. He was frustrated at being a mere dogsbody and the Woolfs found him idle and temperamental. Virginia also disliked what she saw as his histrionics and his bullying attitude towards Carrington. 'We have had a mad bull in the house' Virginia wrote later, 'A normal Englishman in love.'

To Noel Carrington

The Mill House
Sunday [15 July 1921]

Dearest Noel,

As this elegant figure below, which some old gentleman at St Pancras tells me is my husband, clad in familiar and dirty pair of white shorts and a rowing vest is writing you a letter by my side I feel I cannot do less than imitate his excellent Sunday example.

But what can I tell you? Life is happy. The sun is as hot as India now in England. R.P. works hard now all day at the Hogarth Press and returns ravenous

and wolfish at 7 o'ck for his evening meal. Lytton comes down every weekend and often Oliver and Inez and sometimes good people like Brenan, who is back from Spain on a holiday and various friends. Tidmarsh is still a communal nest for breakers of the law so the Partridges escape having a home to ask in-laws to stay in and refrain from silver teapots and cradles.

I've become signboard painter to the county of Berkshire. I've done and finished one signboard for the Tidmarsh Inn and now I've three other commissions given me on the strength of it. If the Brewery will stump up £10 a sign I'll be content to be their painter for the rest of my life, and when you come back my humble efforts will greet your eye at every pub you tarry at! I will do the Phoenix bookplate and one for you very soon, tell Cumberledge.¹ Tidmarsh is so lovely this summer, full of charming animals, geese, ducks and hens and a yellow cat and such good company. We have a gramophone now and it really is getting quite a vast library as Lytton is becoming reckless with his wealth in buying books [...]

[...] I had one long day on those Wantage Downs alone with Brenan a week ago, very near where we three spent a day with Brenan just before you set off to India. It was baking hot and we cooked our lunch under a beech-wood and basked on the downs and talked about Spain and people we knew. I think you must get out at Gib. on your way back from India and we'll meet you and then go and stay with Gerald in his cottage in the mountains.

You know of course mother has left and sold Driftway [...] It's good to think you'll be with us in the spring and the daffodils.

Your loving sister D. C.

Early in August, Carrington set off with Ralph for a holiday in the Lake District, along with Lytton and James and Alix Strachey. Gerald, struggling with the realisation that he was in love with his friend's new wife, was about to set off back to Spain.

To Gerald Brenan

41 Gordon Square
Friday morning, 8 o'ck [5 August 1921]

It's just eight o'clock and I have packed up my clothes and look out on a grey sky with plane trees waving, and lurching in a cold wind. I've rather a hollow sort of feeling inside about going away to the Lakes. Already I see

1 Presumably an OUP colleague.

the rain, uncomfortable wicker chairs, a linoleum tablecloth and discomforts on every side – and I am so sorry to leave you.

But perhaps it wouldn't have gone on being so very happy if we had lingered! [...] But how very perfect it is that we have with so little restraint been able to understand, to a hair's breadth, our fondness for each other.

Please keep very well in Yegen, and don't get ill or I shall worry.

If you ever did and wanted someone, if J. H.-J. doesn't go out, you must always wire. R.P. and I would come at once. Please remember this.

This letter is dull, and explains nothing but how can one write? I think that you know that the discovery of a person, of an affection, of a new emotion, is to me next to my painting, the greatest thing I care about. I shall think of you very often dear. Please say nothing in your letters. I shall know in spite of their nothingness. G-rrrrrrrrrr 'how difficult life is'. Yet G-rrrrrrrrrrr how exceedingly and excessively happy the same life can be.

You've not got the camera! I'll leave it wrapt up and addressed to you on the hall at 41 G.S. Please call for it today, or some day, and do go and see Birrell. A chemist photographer will explain the camera to you.

My love my very dear one. Goodbye till the spring.

D.C.

To Gerald Brenan

> c/o Mrs Wilson, Watendlath Farm,
> nr Keswick, Cumberland
> Sunday [7 August 1921]

Well, two days have passed, as the postman only calls once a day for letters, and as my letter is seldom ready when he does call I will start one now to you, with an exquisite fountain pen belonging to Alix and try and get it finished by tomorrow afternoon. A scene of our sitting room in the farm house. Our daily life is dominated by Mr Wordsworth as we call the amiable stuffed ram who is attached to the wall above the window.

Lytton sits muffled in overcoats reading 'Family Life' by E. F. Benson[1] looking infinitely depressed, Alix plays chess with an invisible James, who has crept out of the picture. They take twenty minutes over every move, and never speak, and I sit as you see at the corner of the table. It is black night outside and rains. On my right twenty photograph frames face me, north country rustics in their hideous Sunday clothes.

1 E. F. Benson (1867–1940), prolific author and champion figure skater, best known for his Mapp and Lucia novels, had published an autobiography, *Our Family Affairs*, in 1920.

The two most cherished relatives have mats of sheep's wool to perch upon. They really deserve a still life or a sonnet to themselves. I would like to, if I could, write a novel introducing these twenty human beings, with their portraits, as they appeared in my novel. Still Mr Wordsworth glares down on me with his glassy yellow eye and moth eaten countenance. Yesterday I went a long walk with Lytton, some 10 miles, before supper.

Alix and James arrived at 8.30 in the evening. It's delightful to have Alix with me again. I love her very much. She is so unlike other women, so impersonal, more like a man. This morning we went a walk by ourselves to Rosthwaite, and talked of everything that had happened since we parted last September. They give one the most stupendous meals here. So big that I've ruined my digestion with sheer greed [...]

1

C/o Mrs Wilson
Watendalth Farm
near Keswick
Cumberland

Sunday
about the 8 Aug 1921

Well, two days have past, as the postman only calls once a day for letters, and as my letter is seldom ready when he does call I will start one now to you, with an exquisite fountain pen belonging to Alex, I try & get it finished by tomorrow afternoon
— a scene of our sitting Room in the farm house.

Our daily life is dominated by mr words worth as we call the amiable stuffed ram who is attached to the wall above the window

To Gerald Brenan

Wanlen Hall, Ambleside
Wednesday, 9 August 1921

I've not heard from you once yet, because I've left Watendlath & joined
Ralph here for 5 days. – I hope I'll find a letter when I get back there on
next Saturday – Ralph came over on Monday afternoon for me in a car with
his friend MacIver. It turned out that unless I went with them they couldn't
come over again. Ralph rather made me feel it was impossible not to go ...
so here I am with the vegetables of Liverpool. They are so 'hearty', so
conventional & very amiable. Why should one so constantly be depressed?
I really don't like living aimlessly and I now definitely feel it's a waste of
time to talk banalities with people I don't care for.

Yesterday I went fishing and caught 2 perch. They were so beautiful.
We put them in a bucket so I could watch them closely. Windermere lake
is a fraudulent affaire. Hotels, boarding houses & horrible people in boats.
I feel Wordsworth's melancholy spirit in my bones. It doesn't suit these
lakes to make them into imitation Blackpools. In the afternoon I went
sadly with Ralph in a yacht with MacIver. Rushing through the water,
and sitting under the bulging taut sail has a delight for one unlike any
other pleasures.

Ralph after tea made a feeble attempt to convert me into a country house
lady & tried to teach me ping pong! But unimpressed after a few minutes
it was hopeless because I don't care for winning or playing seriously. I really
was sorry, as he enjoys games so much.

The evenings are the worst part of this house. The men play bridge &
the females sew & talk to each other. I can do neither. Grrrrrrr.

Protect me from such society in my old age, children, babies & golfing
men & females.

Today Ralph & I went off alone to Langdale valley and climbed the
Langdale Pikes and walked in the Watendlath direction. We were to have
met Alix, James & Lytton but they didn't meet us. I suspect it must have
rained too much for them to start.

The beauty of the mountains quite restored my temper. Ralph borrowed
a small car & drove me to the foot of the mountains & back again. Now
he has gone fishing & I sit & write to you alone in a magnificent Liverpool
drawing room – and you are still in England ... Ralph wished you were here
today with us on the Langdales ... and I?

I've been reading a life of the Benson family by C. F. Benson, Lytton had
it from the library. It's almost impossible to read because C. F. B. is so stupid.
But it's rather interesting as an insight to an Archbishop's life.

Soon you will leave England. I wish you had gone. You can't think how different it is ... to remember there is nothing really which prevents me from seeing you except a few hundred miles. You must write to me often please. Because I am so absolutely fond. I thanked you, when I met Ralph, that you were as Koteliansky the Russian says 'a güd man'. Bless you.

Your loving Doric xxx

PS Did you see in *The Times* last Friday, that 'Gerald Brenan & an accomplice, were arrested & reprimanded for assaulting the Dean of Westminster & his son, in their garden late in the evening. The Dean did not wish to prosecute so the proceedings stopped.'

Well? Surely there are not two Gerald Brenan's in London? And what did you do to the Dean or was it his son? And after all what were they doing in their garden after dinner?

Grrrrr you are NOT what you pretend to be, you Brrrrr.

PS I will not have any children, ever.

PS There are 12 children & 3 babies in this house.

Urged on by Carrington and Ralph, Gerald changed his plans and joined the Watendlath party on 18 August. For the next twelve days he and Carrington hid in barns and behind hedges to kiss and talk of love while Ralph fished. He tore himself away on 30 August and headed for London and Spain.

To Gerald Brenan

Watendlath Farm
Tuesday evening [30 August 1921]

Dear,

You can't think how I minded sending you away. But I felt a shiver when R suddenly came over that mound. It might have been different. It seemed a warning from the heights. I think one can't keep things at a certain pressure indefinitely. I felt you were becoming slightly strained, was I right? The whole relation was shifting to one of trying escaping alone. Yet you must know my heart was almost breaking and my eyes crying when you left. Ralph unfortunately made it worse. He became instantly depressed, you wronged him when you said he did not care very much. He clung to me and burst out 'I always feel something may happen to Gerald, and perhaps we will never see him again.' I think he thought of Michael Davies, who was drowned. He became suddenly so sweet, and lonely and talked of no one but you, and how he cared for you all the way back. Then he turned on me, and said it was my fault because I had made you go, by not persuading you to stay, and if anything happened to you he would never forgive me, and said it was my selfishness that made you go. It was dreadful because I couldn't tell him anything and I couldn't tell him I cared fifty times more than he did, that you should have gone. Yet, I feel now it was best. All the same I think it is about as fine a torture as could be invented to force a loved one to leave one when there was no necessity for a departure.

The beauty of Watendlath is the same as last night. I have just been for a walk with Lytton and Ralph right round the end of the tarn. But its loveliness made me sad. Lytton also is going tomorrow. Maynard Keynes wants him in Sussex on Friday. This adds to our gloom. We both miss you so much, very much. You know Gerald you mustn't pay too much attention to our wrangling, and disputes.

Really I love Ralph so very much. That is why I am a little discontented he isn't rather more to me. I would so like to find all I want in him. I fear you thought we were rather a disagreeable couple. But really I think he is very happy with me and I with him. What a wonderful time we had. I also go over all the pleasures we enjoyed with our eyes, and our other sensibilities. I could not suddenly bear to hazard such pleasures for a few moments more, which might have marred everything. Ralph loves you so much, he would have been wretched even if he had only dimly guessed we cared a little more than ordinary friends. Now, we neither of us feel any guilt. And who can tell what may not have happened by next spring? But we will have the pleasure always now of remembering this short very perfect span in our lives. And we will write conscious of it, all this long winter – Promise you believe me when I tell you I did want you to stay?

You mustn't think that I ever do not care as much as you do. I believe I know your feelings to a hair's breadth – Write to me from the Pyrenees.[1] I shall give Lytton this letter to post tomorrow, and I hope you will get it before you leave London, otherwise I trust God it will be sent to you unopened [...] I've given up my painting this evening to write to you. Alix told me she saw you in Keswick and she took my breath out of my cheeks by saying you all but ran into a big motor bus in Keswick street. Please be very careful. What can I tie on your finger to make you remember not to run into motors, or sit on railway lines? It seems gloomy without you. Ralph is fishing before dinner. And I've fetched your picture from the barn. Now there is no reason to ever go there again. I was sorry not to show it to you. I don't want you to see my work unless it's to my satisfaction. I am rather vain after all I find, to have your good opinion.

Your train will soon be rushing into London.

1 Gerald was to stay with the Dobrées at Larrau, their house in the Pyrenees, on his way to Yegen.

Please write to me very often Gerald. We leave here on Friday. Write to
Tidmarsh always please; not 41 Gordon Square.

Now you are gone I remember all the times I might have been more
friendly. I pour coals of contempt on my head for not taking more risks, for
not being more adventurous, for not spending more time with you alone.
Grrrrr. But this always happens. Why have we these predestined lives of
inaction?

Gerald your sympathy, and friendliness made me happier than I can quite
ever tell you. Don't let Valentine and her coal black charms obliterate
Watendlath and

Your Doric xxxxx

To Gerald Brenan

The Mill House
Thursday, 12 o'ck, 8 September 1921

I had to send off your letter yesterday without reading it over again, so you
must forgive me if it was ungrammatical or ill-spelt. There was a slight scene.
All was nearly lost. After all our care I nearly ruined ourselves. I thought
Ralph was writing to his parents & not paying any attention to me sitting
the other side of the room writing to you on the sofa. I put three crosses at
the end of my letter & then looked up & then saw he was watching me 'x
x'. He instantly said 'who are you writing to'. I lost my head slightly and said
that I didn't see that it mattered who I write to, he had no right to ask me.
He then became suspicious. An argument blew up. Then I lied, and said I
was writing to someone else. It was all rather horrible. I said that if he treated
me as my mother used to, I should deceive him. He said unless he investigated
me I was so childish I was capable of doing anything. Well, the argument
went on, I refused to give up my principle & he purported in his authority
to control my letters & relations with people. By the end of the argument
he had forgotten the reason of it, so I rushed upstairs & posted my letter to
you before he remembered his curiosity. For it is only that [...] But I paid for
it last night. I couldn't sleep. I lay in bed when the room was pitch dark
listening to the rats gambolling in the mill, trying to forget you & trying to
go to sleep. I think I must have been awake at least 6 hours. I went over
everything and wondered if it was now over or just beginning. I hated myself
for having these affections & for deceiving Ralph. At last when it was light
& the hops showed pale green against the blue sky I fell asleep.

I thought of you this morning still in England. Now at 12 o'ck I suppose
you are on the ship. Leaving Newhaven behind you.

I was jealous of H.J. [Hope-Johnstone] yesterday going away with you. Suddenly Spain seemed to be the most perfect place, & I envied you your liberty. Yet how lovely Tidmarsh is, and who am I to complain today! Yet I feel I have lost a friend & it's a day of mourning [...] I write now as Ralph is out of the house & I am quite alone with you. You must tell me all you do. I am even curious to know how you spent Wednesday after you left us in Gordon Square? And every detail of your voyage to France.

I lay in the Roman Bath yesterday under the cold water and you weren't there to see me in my loveliness. Can I write at random to you? Have you pockets enough to contain all my nonsense? No one but you may read my thoughts today.

In the cool green bath yesterday I lost all the greyness of London & became a Watendlath character again.

'But where are the dancers the dancers all in yellow,

where is the sweet music & where the green hills O.'

The heat is superb here and the garden is full of singing birds, and exquisite flowers ... and yet one wants more ... why? Why?

Give Valentine my love again today when you get this letter. Will you be as fond as I am of you & write so often? Tell Valentine I will be with her. I am going to live very economically till then to save up enough money for a long stay with you.

Forgive me, if for a little I write rather restrained letters. You will understand. I cannot at the moment live deceiving Ralph & having the burden of writing to you with my doors bolted. Not just now. It adds too much to my depression. You will know I care still, as I cared, in our Yew Tree house.

In a few weeks I will write unrestrainedly.

Oh I wish you were here on this most perfect of days. It is such another day as two people once spent on White Horse Hill.

It's three o'ck now, and you must nearly be in Paris. I am making rare pickles in the kitchen & putting my house in order. In a few days I will paint my sign boards. I am full of a new picture now. Your figure in the olive green stream at the ford last Tuesday made me think of it, you looked so lovely in the water. Like a Piero della Francesca figure.

Gerald how can I thank you for making me so happy – I loved my herb book you gave me. I am going to do some herb pictures for your walls at Yegen this month.

Now goodbye, this letter tells you nothing, but I find it's not possible.

I shall be glad when I've forgotten you a little! This loneliness makes me restless.

Goodbye dear one

Xxx Yr Doric

To Gerald Brenan

The Mill House
Friday, 6 October 1921

You alone have made me alter my slovenly habits and put numbers & dates at the top of the sheet.

Dear, how good it is to write to you again. Yet you have deserted me shamefully. You reached Yegen 2 weeks ago next Monday and I haven't had a letter yet and who was to going to write first? Who indeed? I am all alone today. Ralph is in London & Lytton with his old mother in Gordon Square. My day has been one of which you entirely disapprove. It has been spent since 7.30 this morning entirely in useful labours. Every minute of it. But that is the only way that I can do things. All laziness one day. All painting another. And concentrated virtue and industry on the third. The results are the sitting room has been re-wallpapered for the winter. The carpets cleaned, the floors washed with Annie's help. And 6lbs of red apple jelly in a store cupboard and now I lie exhausted gasping in a chair at 3.30.

Valentine wrote me a charming letter last week. I feel in love with her, just for her letter, all in a moment. She appreciated you properly and said many delightful things about you. Oh Gerald, I wish you were here. That such remarkable days should slide away unseen by you – because after all it can't be quite so exquisite in Yegen – and not spent with me – is lamentable ... I can't write properly as I am literally lying down in a new chair Lytton has installed. It looks a vulgar chair but once one falls into its velvet caresses it is impossible to sit up right and one forgets all one's aesthetic taste for shapes.

Lytton will never write again unless we seriously keep him from ever sitting in it.

Now I've had my tea woken up and sit properly upright in a chair. Shall I tell you again how extremely fond I am of you? But the curious details of my fondness cannot be told bleakly with a pen and I cannot really be very fond of a person unless I see them. Already you are beginning to fade away and I have to go back to Watendlath to see your face. My brain is scattered today so you will not have a good letter.

We have burnt sienna curtains now in our sitting room. I bought the canvas for 8 lira a yard in Venice, it is the same material they use for the sails of the ships. They completely alter the room making it very rich and autumnal in effect. You would approve I think. Do you know this morning as I lay in bed at half past six watching the starlings eating the red apples on the tree in the orchard, I saw an exquisite bird alight on the top most branch. I thought it was a hawk at first, I jumped up and ran into the pink room and fetched the spy-glasses to view it better. It was a green woodpecker with a most lovely face & beak and a yellow bar on its green coat tail. It stayed some little time eating the apples and then flew off. Wasn't that an honour for our garden?

Yesterday Ralph didn't go up to work, and as it was so hot, too hot to work indoors, he climbed to the very top of the big apple tree and picked the apples. He looked so lovely against the blue sky, his head and shoulders above any branch, swaying like a fat quail on the slender branches, Annie & I held a big sheet below and he rained down apples into it. We carried in baskets & baskets of apples. I give a great many away & the rest we bake and make into jelly. They are such lovely things, I lie in the wet grass looking up at Ralph amongst the shining red fruit – I want badly to use it in a picture. But I can't quite conceive it. We have a big attic now full of apples. It smells so heavenly when one steals in there, in the dim light, with a new load [...]

I go back in my week to you because it is the only way I can remember what I have done. On Tuesday Annie and I went into Reading for a treat. A short Tchekhov story, as we sat in the baking sun on the little platform bench I heard a bell ringing, so I said to Annie 'that must be two o'ck' she said 'no it's John Low's funeral today'. I thinking John Low was someone I ought to know said rather vaguely 'oh is he dead?' she said 'I told you Sunday he was. They brought his body all the way from Bournemouth in a glass hearse. I saw it pass through Tidmarsh this morning, they are going to bury him this afternoon at Pangbourne. He was only ill 5 days. His father is a gardener. Isn't it sad, he was only 19. And he looked so well in the summer.' Then she stopped. I felt rather embarrassed for she remembered how I had caught her with him under the lilac bushes in the evening & how I talked to her and she cried. And I thought of it and remembered how much more upset I had been than Annie and then the bell tolled again and our train came in & we left the station and the bell and the funeral behind.

I shopped in Reading. Tried to find a kitchen dresser for the dining room. Saw a marvellous beautiful picture of Tibetan mountains, equal to our Niagara fall masterpiece. Found several good furniture & old china shops then met Annie again at 4.30.

Had tea with her in a cheap little shop where the market people drank their tea from saucers & then went to the cinema and saw Charlie Chaplin in *The Kid*. Annie loved it and laughed the whole time. It had a curious interest apart from its brilliance but that would need a discourse. We came back by a 6 o'ck train & Ralph got in our carriage at Reading, he had been to London all day. I thought of poor Johnnie Low when we reached

Pangbourne but I saw Annie was only thinking of Charlie Chaplin & the glories of Reading.

Last weekend the genius Saxon Turner was here! And a young Cambridge man, a doctor. On Sunday Lytton hired a motorcar & we drove to Savernake Forest & ate cold chicken in a grove of green bracken under the great beeches.

The desolation and wildness of Savernake always surprises me afresh. It looked particularly beautiful last Sunday. We then drove back, the most lovely journey in England. Round Chute Causeway, through my old village of Hurstbourne Tarrant. Past our old house (where Jane Austen once stayed) & then over Combe Downs. I got out and looked at Combe House and wished Headlam had never lived to steal that most beautiful of all houses from me.

When you come back again we alone will go to Combe & my Hurstbourne and on your bended knees you will confess you have never seen such country. All evening we gambled at poker. Now I must stop my letter or the post will vanish.

Alix & James sent me the most superb book on Spanish architecture & china from Munich. It has marvellous photographs in it. Will tell you more of them in my next letter.

Bertie Russell has married Miss Dora Black. She staggered to the Registry office heavy with child, just in time, to save the Earldom of Russell from sinking to illegitimacy. For Bertie's brother has no child.

Bunny Garnett's wife, Ray Marshall, who J. H.-J. knew, had a dead child born to her.

I have had bad colds & throats but I revive today. The heat is still amazing. I still have baths outside in the Roman Bath in the mornings –

My love dear one
From your Doric
xxxx

To Noel Carrington

The Mill House
8 October 1921

Dearest Master Noel,

[...] We live in an old mill lodge consumed like old cheese by the rats. My husband is still kind to me and I hope when you next come back we will still be the loving pair that we are at present.

Which are loving doves in case you don't recognise the sweet birds.

I am only writing to you as I see Mister R. is doing the same. I once met Tagore,[1] but I doubt if he remembers the honour! It was at Rothenstein's house in Hampstead. He was a great friend of Albert R's little brother.[2] I thought he was slightly too self conscious and precious. His voice rather charmed me and his exquisite manners. I thought he showed up compared to the crude English very well. But I dislike people who suffer themselves to be iconized ... one shouldn't be vague about such matters, one should say 'clear out' to Mr Andrews & his kind and only keep good company.

After all more intelligent and able men than Tagore have moved in the world as human beings. Tolstoy for instance didn't suffer such 'reverent' admiration.

I've no news. We live very peacefully & quietly down here.

R. goes up to London not every day by any means, in case he is writing his life too blackly to you, in a most luxurious arm chair over a log fire. He spends most of his day when he isn't working adoring his geese & counting his apples & talking to his ducks. Lytton thanks you [...] Write again soon please.

My love
Your Muchacha

To Gerald Brenan

The Mill House
18 December 1921

An old variety of handwriting born of a new china inkpot and a new Ladies' nib. A Happy Xmas and a Happy New Year.

It's a pity after three years that mellow plum pudding should have been devoured by the heathens of Malaga! Now I'll answer your letter. What fun it sounds, masons, masons everywhere. I have built 2 new fireplaces since you visited Tidmarsh, and I have a big box of cement in my larder with which every day I bung a hole to keep the rats out.

We also are preparing for Xmas, and for the great Shah of Persia, Maynard Keynes and his attendant slave, Sebastian Sprott.[3] Yes, that is really his name!

---

1 Rabindranath Tagore (1861–1941), the Bengali writer and educator, spent time in London in 1912 and won the Nobel Prize for Literature in 1913.

2 Albert Rutherston (1881–1953), a painter, teacher and art book publisher from a rich and artistic family, who changed his name from Rotherstein in 1916, was another admirer of Carrington's at the Slade.

3 Walter John Herbert Sprott (1897–1971), known as Sebastian, was a Cambridge graduate and budding Freudian psychologist in love with Keynes.

Boxes arrive, not on mules, it is true, but on a carrier's cart from the station, by every train. Boxes from Fortnum and Mason, a large bacon from the Jew Waleys of Essex, crates of rare wines from Soho, and vast cheese from Jermyn Street. I have just made two silk dressing gowns, one for myself and one for Ralph. Mine is speckled like an eastern sky and Ralph's deep sea green. Then he is also having a pair of yellow silk pyjamas. By the way you never sent me a pattern of your silk. I can easily get it for you at Liberty's. For it is awful to think of you night after night lying naked from the knee to the toe! I saw some superb handkerchiefs in Liberty's. What a mixture of horror, and taste is mingled together in that shop.

I went up to London last Thursday. Had tea with my super-refined sister in Finchley Road. No, you couldn't imagine such a perfect specimen of horror if you thought for 20 years. She talks disparagingly of the whole world. She is very refined and superior and constantly says 'I can't think why she married him, he only has £700 a year.' 'They must have come in for some money lately they have 2 cars now.' It was the most hideous house I've ever seen. Such good drab taste. Two footmen like the footmen one sees in West End plays. In fact she looked very like Irene Vanburgh[1] sitting at her writing table when I entered the room. She gave me a petticoat for a Xmas present and a pair of stockings. As they also have a house in Portland Place and a car, I expect they must have £3,000 a year. Her saggy discontented face still haunts me and to think for 10 years we lived side by side and slept in the same room together. Now I feel she is more removed from me than Mrs Lloyd George, or Princess Mary [...]

[...] In the evening Lytton, R, Alan MacIver and I went to a play, Charles Hawtrey. It had a curious merit. One had to laugh all the time. It combined the pleasures of Gilbert and Sullivan and a music hall melodrama. I slept at the MacIvers house in Kensington. They are marvellous those respectable houses. One ought to be preserved intact every 10 years to show to future generations. They should be on view. How lovely it would be to spend a day in one, when we are about sixty. I always fear some ghastly revolution will sweep them all away from us, as they were swept in Russia. How nice it is when the year is nearly over. Already I am tired of these grey drawn out days, the stale memories of this year. I long for a new blank year, with no regrets, no sentiments. Clean, and entire with 365 days to spend.

Tragedy. An unknown friend sent me a lovely Treacle Print.[2] *Prudence and Justice*. It arrived in a paper parcel completely smashed. I pieced it, tearfully, together only to see it had been one of the best Treacle Prints

---

1 Irene Vanburgh (1872–1949), a fashionable leading actress.
2 Treacle prints, reverse printed on glass by hand and so called because of their rich colour, were popular in the late eighteenth and early nineteenth centuries and rare thereafter.

ever made. I have not the heart to throw this broken image of loveliness into the dust bin, and yet it is impossible to stick a thousand pieces of glass together. And all my life I have longed to possess a Treacle Print. What irony! Death haunts me, I think of it at least three times a day and last night I dreamt of the dead. It is menacing but I hope if I put off writing my will, God out of decency will wait till I have done so. Of course one of these days out of sheer idleness I shall make a will, and then he will have no excuse for delaying. I hope you will write to me soon and tell me about your visitor. Is Hope-Johnstone as good at Spanish as you are now? Lytton bought on my advice a most lovely bedspread, Queen Anne embroidery with a big sun flower in the middle, very pale colours, with flowers embroidered all over it. It is a vision of delight. You will be envious! I will write to you after Christmas and tell you of our feasting, and the conversations. There are so many things for me to do. A lampshade to design, a dresser to paint yellow; Lytton's bed also to paint. Two wood cuts to make and at least forty letters to write before Christmas. I am old fashioned enough to love writing letters at Xmas. I suppose it's a complex because I really love getting them back. Not a complex to investigate certainly. My poor mother hates Spain. It rains; it is cold; and my brother and sister in law are unkind to her. So the poor woman returns again next month. Bringing an Andalusian hen and cock for our establishment.

Ralph has become a hen-maniac and secretly I have a complex against them, because I don't like the taste of eggs. If you had read Mr Aldous Huxley's latest book you would realise that a certain young lady called Mary Bracegirdle always talks about complexes. But it's a book which makes one feel very very ill. I don't advise you read it. [...]

Please don't write anything in your letters, as it's not so easy as it was to get them from the postman and Ralph always wants to read your news. Give J. H.-J. my love

Yr Doric

1922

To Gerald Brenan

The Mill House
27? January 1922

[...] This week we had Barbara to stay with us, and she brought her little girl aged 3. The visit was a triumph for me! For Ralph said when they left 'Well that's cured me of ever wanting to propagate my kind. I'll never have a child if I can help it.' I must say I had no idea children could be such boring teasing creatures. And this one was very pretty and well behaved. But it never gives Barbara more than 1 hour to herself and in her cottage she has a baby aged 1 year as well. I thought she led a life which was little better than that of any illiterate cottage woman – and then what an end to a lovely little creature who once held nearly every man who ever looked at her captive in love. Our relief when they departed was almost hysterical. Poor Lytton suffered most perhaps ...

Pray God, I will never go through what poor Barbara has suffered, the degraded torments of pregnancy, child birth and then perpetual sordid boredom with children to bring up. Grrrrrr. Let us pledge ourselves dear Gerald not to propagate our species ...

Carrington was not a great fan of Clive Bell, and composed a hoax reply complete with forged signature from George Bernard Shaw after Bell had criticised Shaw's writing in the New Republic.

To Clive Bell

10 Adelphi Terrace, London
[February?] [n.d.]

Dear Clive Bell,
   Thank you for the numerous compliments you have paid me in this week's *New Republic*. I am sorry I cannot return the compliment that I think you, or your prose, 'Perfectly respectable' ...
   You do not, it would appear, lead a very enviable aesthetic life; to me it seems dull.
   Yours Bernard Shaw

To general glee, Clive Bell was completely fooled.

To Lytton Strachey

The Mill House
15 February 1922

Dearest Lytton,

   Thank you so much for your letter. We shrieked with laughter under our canopy of blue very often as we read it ... Especially about Clive and Shaw's letters. Really he was a greenhorn. Did it never occur to him Bernard Shaw wasn't likely to type the address on his note paper? Perhaps he does. Perhaps God inspired me, and the first letter was the image of the second! Poor Shaw I wonder what he thought of Clive's apologies! 'Clive Bell completely ga-ga. Never wrote him a letter in my life.' I see a new aspect: a new avenue in life now! Forgery between lovers, enemies, dukes and duchesses [...] I sit writing to you like Nelson's Column with lions on every side, with a cat on either arm of my chair, with an untasted tea before me on a chair.

[…] I painted my roebuck [inn sign] all today. I want to get rid of it and start some serious work. I've put him in the snow one side with a dutch snow landscape in the background. It's simply pouring with rain now I write very quickly because it's nearly six o'ck. I hope you haven't been forced into Bunny's shop yet. Can't you get Pippa to be a little more precise and if she will come, what will she like to do? Did you take Aldous's book of poems to Davis? I see Penrose[1] has been decorating an opera at Cambridge. The Ibsen play sounds rather good at Oxford. I suppose you wouldn't like a matinee with R. and me on Saturday afternoon? I didn't know Mark's pictures were so dear. No don't buy one unless you like them. He might do something more lively this year. £40 is too much to spend unless one really likes a picture very much.

My love dear,

Yr devoted Carrington

In late February, Carrington and Ralph rushed to Vienna where Alix Strachey, studying psychoanalysis under Freud, had become dangerously ill with pleurisy. Ralph soon went home, leaving Carrington anxious and frustrated as her friend was thought too ill for visitors.

To Lytton Strachey

Hotel Hammerand, Wien
Later: Pension Franz, Wahringerstrasse 12, Wien 1
28 February 1922

Dearest Lytton,

I will just start a letter to you whilst R is paying the bill. We couldn't go to Pension Franz until Willie Sargant [Alix's uncle] left which he did yesterday evening. First I will tell you about Alix. You know it was the most serious operation. I hadn't grasped that, when we left England. They had to cut a big piece of rib away to clean out the lungs and she can use only one lung to breathe now. But ever since the operation she has been getting a little better. The temperature has been more steady and lower. Poor James is very exhausted and I think he has never left his room except for a few hours and until Sunday he could hardly tell me of her appearance.

I have not written to you since a postcard in Nuremberg. I put on the postcard that I thought all the architecture in Germany hideous. But later I

---

1 Probably Roland Penrose (1900–84), from a Quaker family, who had driven ambulances during the war and returned to study architecture at Cambridge.

retracted just as I was posting the postcard, so I rubbed it out with a wet finger as a false statement! For the old part of Nuremberg is indeed very remarkable [...] What charming people the Germans are! They enjoy their life so tremendously. Their plainness, their stoutness never depresses them. They all sat drinking weak wine, laughing and smiling at each other. The little girls danced with gauche young men, with beaming hot faces. I made one conquest: a fair German youth came and asked with a click of his heels and a stiff bow, if he might have 'the honour'. Unfortunately I was so hot I really couldn't, but I appreciated the compliment. We were sorry to leave such a clean, sunny town. Vienna is indeed the grimmest city I've ever been in. Much, much worse than Madrid, worse than Manchester. Everything is deep grey. All the houses are either old and crumbling, or new and cemented Baroque. The roads are grey and cold with slimy mud.

Heaps of grey snow piled up on the sides of the roads. The plaster peels of the houses. Nobody smiles. All the faces are grey and the boots covered in mud. We nearly burst into tears on Monday. We both became so depressed in this fearful prison of a town. At first I was so surprised why James never stirred outside his nursing home. Now I do not wonder. Life here is just as expensive as England and the food is horrible. Everything has an overcoat of batter. The meat often wears two waistcoats and 2 mackintoshes to conceal its identity. The very cakes wear macks. The butter is ashy pale and tasteless. I had chicken last night that tasted of mongoose and then one's lunch costs 4/-, each bed and breakfast 5/- each, and the room had stained glass windows, and was practically a dentist's waiting room. The Pension Franz is much better. The rooms are light, and James and Alix's untidiness is human and the sight of books makes one happier. Madame Philip Florence has one room and we share the other. She is very pleasant and we all get on quite well together. We always see James after breakfast, and again for tea. The nursing home is a most extraordinary place. Nuns in sweeping dresses with flowing head dresses are nurses. For it is an R.C. institute. Baroque dominates, and sham tapestries. The appearance of cleanliness, James says, is only superficial. He lives in a little white bedroom, just opposite Alix's door. Nobody but James could have borne living in that bedroom for 2 weeks day after day! If you could only see the vision that greets my eye as I write to you now. What can I compare it to and make you see it? Perhaps a flat in a high building in the Strand, near Waterloo Bridge. Only it is greyer and trams run below! But let us leave the Pension Franz and go to the gallery together.

This morning we were happy for the first time. Two divine Giorgiones; one of those Three Men and the big rock landscape, a tremendous picture. Then the head of a boy, also Giorgione. Too divine. A superb Raphael, of a Madonna and children with landscape, a lovely nude by Bellini. At least 20 Canalettos, so amazing you ought to come to Vienna just to see them. A superb Tintoretto

of Suzanna and the Elders, perhaps the most remarkable picture in the gallery.
A great number of Breughels, only one good one, the famous *Snow Scene with
Dogs*. Two good Cranachs. At his worst he is awful. Some lovely Rembrandts
and some Italian pictures. I shall go back again tomorrow and make a more
thorough inspection. There is a riding school which James says I shall like, and
tomorrow we see *Figaro* together. Unfortunately the good music season seems
to be over. Really I am amazed every hour how James and Alix could stand life
in this Pension and this city! The hideousness of the rooms is not to be imagined.
We travelled on the train with Mrs Riviere,[1] who made friends with us. R rather
succumbed to her charms [...] But R will tell you all our adventures. James
says he is fairly well. I think Alix's recovery will make him better faster than
anything. I thank you darling Lytton for making it possible for us to come.
Keep well till R gets home to you.

My love, Mopsa

*By mid-March Carrington was back home, having not been able to see Alix, who
gradually recovered. Meanwhile Gerald had been staying with the Dobrées in Larrau
in the Pyrenees, where Valentine had become his confidante. He and Carrington
were trying to arrange to meet.*

To Gerald Brenan

The Mill House
Tuesday afternoon, 14 March 1922

Darling Gerald,

Yesterday Valentine gave me your letter and I was overcome when I read
it [...] Oh you do not understand if you think I do not still care or if I haven't
cared just as much since Watendlath. But you have conception how difficult
it is with Ralph. He is so suspicious in a queer way & I do so dread if I write
as I would like to you you may reply ... and I shall not be able to show him
your letters.

The truth is I am quite happy with him & I need not tell you what a
charming creature he is, but I want more ... and I find it impossibly hard
to control friendships so that he can always peer in them.

That is my reason for preferring Larrau to Yegen, we shall be able to be
alone more naturally. We will not have to manoeuvre it. I see Valentine

1 Joan Riviere (1883–1962) was another early disciple of Freud who became an analyst and later collab-
orated with the Stracheys on translating his writings for the Hogarth Press.

understands ... not that she said much but she understands enough to make it far easier for me to be alone with you than if we were cooped up in Yegen with J.H.-J. & Robin John.¹ I love Valentine very much. She is a marvellous person – yesterday quite made up for the rather disappointing first meeting on Saturday. We had lunch alone together & then talked in the afternoon. Before she left she gave me your letter. Oh Gerald how good it will be to be with you again! I will be very fond of you. Do you know your 'Bestiary' struck me as so very good I asked R to show it to Virginia Woolf – was that wrong? – and they are so struck with it they want to publish it! So perhaps you will have to come back to England to see to the publishing of your book.

May I please do woodcuts for the animals if they publish it. Lytton is very enthusiastic. There! You have at least pleased 2 Partridges, a Lytoff and two lean Woolves! – and you wrote it for me. I am so happy I keep on saying 'it's mine' 'it's mine' because I love it so much. I haven't time to write today & tell you in detail how much I like it. I just went up yesterday to London. Last night we spent at Gordon Square. Lytton took us out to dinner, such a lovely dinner and to *Pinafore* afterwards which I had never seen. I thought it most lovely & the music was charming. How dreadful never to have seen it before [...]

I am going to start the wood blocks of your beasts this week – why do I never tell you of my painting? Because I am often sad about it and I think and think & draw picture after picture & then so little is ever painted. Tomorrow I start a picture of the 'Horse Riding School' in Vienna, of which I made sketches. This is a hurried letter just to tell you how very very fond I am Gerald – you don't know how difficult it is to bottle up feelings. To know one might have cared so much more if one hadn't been prevented. As you say everything proves this to be a cynical & idiotic world. I have loved Lytton for 6 years. He might have had my love for the rest of his life if he wanted it. He might have made me his boot black or taken me to Siberia and I would have given up every friend I had to be with him ... and now it's all been melted down, smothered with pillow after pillow of despair and finally put away in an envelope the day I married R – and R can make me care for him in every way except the way he wants me. And we who perhaps only want a month together on the mountains of Yegen to get thoroughly tired of each other have hardly been alone 6 hours [...]

I have a feeling we might achieve this at Larrau. Valentine's diplomacy will count for much.

Gerald darling if I have made you unhappy it was never intentionally [...]

My fond love xxxxxxxxxxxxxx

Yr Doric

¹ Robin (1904–1988) was the third son of Augustus John.

By early April, Gerald, Ralph and Carrington were all staying with the Dobrées in Larrau. The plot thickened when Valentine started an affair with Ralph, who was still in the dark about the developing relationship between his friend and his wife. In Larrau Carrington and Gerald's romance deepened, though they were still not technically lovers. Gerald went on to Spain, but by the end of April, all four were back in England. Ralph continued to see Valentine whilst Gerald longed for Carrington, who in turn clung to her happiness with Lytton.

To Lytton Strachey

[29 April 1922]

Oh why are you not here to enjoy the loveliness of The Mill House, Tidmarsh, Pangbourne?

Really today Saturday its beauty is unparalleled. [...]

The Charltons [recent tenants of the Mill House] really are amazing occupiers! They weeded all the footpaths, cut the hedges, cut the box hedges and left the house shining with cleanliness! Annie was here to greet us last night more exquisite and seductive than ever. R was more than moved. She is a coquette. Fires crackled on brick hearths. The wallflowers' sweet scent pervaded every room. Tulips shone on a clean yellow cloth in the dining room. An exquisite French dinner à la Tidmarsh greeted us on the table.

We are overpowered by eggs. Two huge buckets in the larder already.

The little ducks are monsters, all the chickens alive and a garage complete in the paddock! Thousands of letters, bills, papers, and packages of books for you! All is very beautiful, and I've come to the conclusion we must never never leave this earthly Paradise. Really I think Annie was very clever to keep the livestock so superbly when we were away. I've given her a new print dress as a reward.

Please bring back a Duncan [Grant] for our walls.

The heat is really almost too much today in the garden. Ralph has a great deal of news about the Hogarth Press to tell you, so do hurry back. Dear Lytton I hope Pippa will bring us good news, and that I shall see you on Monday.

There are so many *Country Lifes* to look at, I feel almost bored with old houses. Our sitting room resembles a dentist's waiting room today.

My fondest love,

Yr Carrington

[*From Ralph Partridge*]

I love you so much, do come down like the wind, the wonderful Charlton aftermath will all too soon disappear. The Hogarth is in the clouds, to rise or fall!

Your Ralph

To Gerald Brenan

The Mill House
Tuesday, 2 May 1922

Kunak,

Which in Georgian means a superb and superior kind of friend, in fact a friend who has reached planes of friendship and love, only reached in Georgia. How can I thank you enough for the plates and the ruggery?? They are so lovely I rush into the dining room every five minutes to gaze on their beauty, ranged in rows on the yellow dresser. (You ought to get our village carpenter to paint you some furniture I am sure he would.) Oh but Gerald the weight of that chain! You really carried it on your back all those miles over those Pyrenees? Do you know I could hardly stagger with it from the station on my bicycle to the Mill House, and you carried tents, sleeping bags, and personal baggage as well. If you had known of my joy over the plates your burdens would have seemed feather bags. I feel I wasn't half grateful enough, but you never told me how terribly heavy they were. Bless you. Bless you. Bless you. Lytton is in almost equal raptures and even the stoical Ralph is moved into frenzies of delight. They were only both very sorry not to see you. But I felt for you in your 'cold' distress so acutely that I thought it sheer selfishness to ask you to stay when you sniffled so wretchedly. You only seemed fit, to tell you the blunt truth, for parental closes, and I hope they will soon restore you to a presentable condition.

[...] Ralph was so sorry to miss you last night and hopes you will come back here soon. Here is a letter from Valentine, full of affection, and so many apologies. I am sure, that you will soon be in love with her again. Please write me a detailed account of your family life to amuse me. Lytton thought the photographs even from a photography point of view very very good. No one else will ever see them.

Mais il est un très exquise jeune homme, et, je suis très rongé avec la desire pour lui. Hélas. Je voudrais que j'étais un jeune et jolly fille aussi. Hélas.[1] I've

---

1 'But he is a very exquisite young man, and I am ravaged with desire for him. Alas, I wish I were a young and pretty girl too. Alas.' Here Carrington is speaking for Lytton. The photographs were presumably of Gerald.

nothing to tell you. We simply eat tremendous meals, talk like kings, and laugh like jesters. Lytton has bought me some amazing books from London. A novel by Middleton Murry and a superb book of some aged Victorian peer, which is simply an attack on Victoria. But what an attack! The old peer triumphs over Lytton by sheer brilliance of sentiments. It will delight you beyond any book at Tidmarsh. I am so happy. I feel filled with Russian feelings of goodness and love for everyone. I could kiss the old butcher who brings the meat to the door, I feel so spiritually light hearted. Gerald dear, I was glad to see you again. Only your collar slightly abashed me. I believe collars are the mainstay of virginity. Valentine once told me of a young woman she knew who always wore stick-up-white-stiff collars. One day she accidentally left them off. The change was extraordinary, she suddenly felt very randy, rushed off, started a new life, had lovers, even Sapphic affaires, took to drink, drugs, and never returned to the path of virtue! Which a white collar had supported for nearly 30 years impeached. Now I must stop. I've so many things to do. The tapestry you brought looks lovely on the bed in a pink room. I do hope your cold is better. I love the plates very much indeed. They are almost too lovely to be possessed by such a creature as your D.C.

Dear Gerald if I ever have moods of being tiresome do not despair. I am so fond of you. I value friendship higher than anything. That is why sometimes I am a little nervous of in any way threatening our present very happy relation. Burn this letter, or all may one day be in the kettle of fish. Here's a pretty kettle of fish! Bless you again.

Your most loving Doric

It was Bloomsbury's habit to share letters, which Carrington, as her correspondence with Gerald became more intense, found increasingly alarming and took steps to avoid.

To Gerald Brenan

The Mill House
Wednesday [3 May 1922]

[...] R doesn't see my letters. I always get them in the morning before he comes down. He has been so friendly and charming since France. Perhaps that is partly why I've had this reaction of virtue!

No, but really all I meant was: please don't dwell on it, and please don't expect anything from me. I can't give you anything worth much, except my friendship. Don't let us spoil the pleasure we get from being friends by having complications and too many secrets from Ralph. But we'll talk about it some-time. It's not very important in any case. What would be fun would be to walk from Swindon to Pewsey and take a train back here. I promise you'll be very happy with me because I am so fond of you; so don't feel gloomy. It will be lovely to have you here. We'll go long walks, and we'll out talk these birds. And Wednesdays we'll make expeditions to London on cheap tickets, and see the great world, and the intelligentsia of Richmond and Hampstead.

Please write to me often. I've an aching back, a sore throat and a cold so you must forgive me this diseased letter. Don't quarrel with your father.

Grrrrrrrrrrrr Bless you.

Your loving Coldrinda

To Gerald Brenan

The Mill House
5 o'ck [early June 1922]

I have reached Tidmarsh and now tea is over and we sit on the lawn where for nearly a month every afternoon you have sat with me. Lunch was awful: the weather had turned everything bad. My most lovely steak and kidney pie had to be given to the hens and it was such a delicious pie full of eggs, rare spices, kidneys and steak. Then Lytton thought the cockerel which we had the minute the pie vanished from the table, was bad, so that had to be whisked away. Then we felt so exhausted and our noses so weakened by smells that we only just managed two eggs, and a little salad. Then Pippa arrived and for hours I sat on the lawn and talked to her of Alix and Vienna. I miss Annie almost more than Ralph! I never realised how much work she must do every day, until today I had to do it myself. Lytton is reading a big book on Mount Everest and the expedition. Some of the photographs are marvellous. It makes one almost want to rush off there. It's almost worth your while coming back here to see this book. The Tibetans look the most intelligent people. You are rather Tibetan you must know at moments. Ha! Ha! What a subtle compliment. Lytton likes you. He talked of you a long time. I forgot all about your cheque, and in the morning I looked out of a window and saw a rook carrying it off to its nest, I suppose for bumphf, so that's that, a complete rookery on your part. Rooked by rooks for rook shit. They have expensive taste in Bromo, as I told them this morning when one fluttered onto the lawn. I love the animal book so much. Too much. I will give it back to you, as really I am not a fit person to possess such a rare treasure. Even Lytton was delighted with it. Bradfield College acts *Antigone* in the open Theatre this month on the 24th. I was so excited.

I wish Lytton could have been here to go with me. The wind was awful last night. I couldn't sleep, so today I feel just as tired again. I wonder what has happened to R since I last saw him at 6.30 yesterday [...] Unless one is uncritical and allows affections to overlook the follies of one's friends no friendships can survive.

No, you aren't a load round my neck, or if you are, I miss my load and would be glad of it soon again. Bless you. I agree, confusions when one is with other people made intimacies difficult. Believe me I shall manoeuvre the ≈ all right.[1] I have written today to Ruth Selby-Bigge. Tomorrow or very soon I will make plans, and give you more positive days. Be frightfully careful of my letters. You must burn these. Don't leave them in your pockets at Rodmell, as V reads letters recklessly and she is the worst possible person to know anything. [...]

I've so many letters to write before the post. Gerald you mustn't think I don't care. But I have lost something which seems to prevent me giving myself away completely ever again. But in some ways I can give you everything and I do give you a great deal of love.

Your Doric

To Gerald Brenan

[The Mill House?]
[5 June 1922]

[...] Must I shout my remarks in the evening to Lytton on the lawn for you to hear.

I LOVE GERALD VERY MUCH, AS MUCH as prunes, as roast duck and peas, as Venice, as crown imperials, as tulips, as Devonshire cream and raspberries, as walking on Combe Downs, as Padua, more MORE MORE than all these things do I love Gerald.

How happy your letters make me! Very, very, happy. I sing like Annie as I brush the rooms this morning, for has not my Charlie a nice face? I would I could write to you, all day, but breakfasts must be cooked, hens fed and a hundred and one other things done. I say when do you leave the Cotswolds????? 'Cos could I not cram in a day, a pure day, just this week? It seems rather a pity if you pass this way to London not to have one day this week together, if you don't go to Sussex after all.

1 This symbol was used by Carrington to indicate sexual activity. By this time, probably because she knew Ralph was sleeping with Valentine, she had been to bed with Gerald, or was promising to do so.

Darling Gerald I'll never call you Kunak again if you dislike it.
KANUK or Kobjek or KOTNOB.
Yr Doric xxxxxx

*Within days, Valentine had told Ralph that Carrington and Gerald were making a
fool of him, had been lovers since Larrau and had asked her to distract him.*

*Despite his own open infidelity, Ralph fell into a jealous fury and what became
known as the Great Row ensued. Gerald was summoned for a confrontation with
Ralph; at Carrington's request he admitted to being in love with her but not to
having sex with her. Tidmarsh rang with tears and anger.*

Lytton tried to pick up the pieces.

To Gerald Brenan

The Mill House
Thursday, 5 mins after you have left, 8 June 1922

I cry so much I can hardly see. Oh Gerald I saw you thought I didn't care
[...] I couldn't trust myself to talk to you of myself and you because I only
cry when I think of you away from me, and this end to our happiness. But
you mustn't be unhappy. Remember even if I can't write I am your fondest
friend, and all I ever said and felt towards you was true & nothing that was
between us wasn't real – I've not slept since Tuesday and I've hardly eaten
anything so you must forgive me if this afternoon I was so unhappy & did
not show much feeling.

I could not dare to let myself talk of you much. It broke my heart
completely and made awful moments of despair and misgivings rise up.
Lytton has been our only true and just friend.

He is so sorry for you. Really he felt deeply for you because he knew you
cared so much for me. Oh Gerald I write to you because I must. It's harder
for me than you think losing you, you'll never quite believe what your
friendship was to me and how terribly I cared today when you left. I will
write again if Ralph will let me when I am calmer. You have been such a
perfect friend I cannot and will not believe it is all gone. Do not ever think
ill of me. Fate was against us that was all.

[...] If I have made you wretched forgive me, you know I never did it
willingly and the choice was not made in a moment. Remember I cared and
all that was real & that I still care for you very very much.

Your loving Doric

I shall sometimes write you letters which years after perhaps I shall send you. It will be easier so because I shall not miss writing to you and telling you a little what I feel. But I shall lock them all up & not send them this year.

Oh my dear Gerald Goodbye. X

Burn this letter and all my other letters please.

Gerald ignored this request. They exchanged many anguished pages.

To Gerald Brenan

The Mill House
Friday morning, 7 o'ck in bed, 10 June 1922

Dearest Gerald,

Do not think I shall write anything that can matter to any of us or R now. It is simply I cannot bear having these conversations in my head any longer with you. I have resisted a hundred times since you left, the impulse to go to Cirencester and see you. But I know it will only make it worse for us both if I did. Yesterday I hardly looked once at your face or your body because I did not feel strong enough. Now since you have left I have only thought of you. Lytton was so kind when I told him of all your misery. You mustn't think for a moment he was against you. He said he was so touched by the way you behaved in coming to Tidmarsh, and your gentleness, only he thought perhaps after all this may have been inevitable. That you could not have lived always, as we have lately lived, in a strain, deceiving Ralph – But that the cruelty of it all ending, so appalled him that he could hardly bear to think of you separated from us. He says he is sure when R gets over the shock of it, he will not wish never to hear or see you again. His affection for you will return, and he will let me write. But we know somehow that something is lost that cannot be altered now.

I did not discuss anything else with Lytton. He was terribly shattered. He has had to bear everybody's unhappiness. Last night he read me Hardy's Poems. Some of them are almost too real for one to bear. Ever since you left the house I have thought of nothing else. Oh Gerald please please remember how I cared, and still care. That you alone acted just as in the worst moments I knew and wished you would act, has been my only happiness in this nightmare. You alone did think of me, and remember that a friendship was more worth than anything else. I never until then only for an awful moment, when Lytton said (after he saw Ralph yesterday morning), believed you could forget my affection and my feelings, and everything we had said to each other.

It was trusting you in that one thing that kept me from breaking down, from rushing away wildly and at moments from ending my life. If when I first saw you I was cold it was not from ill feeling. The second I saw you in Pangbourne I knew you were my friend. Oh Gerald I moon in the orchard looking at the seat where we two sat, at the flattened grass where you lay. And I wish that I could have told you then how I cared, how great my misery was when I knew I should not see you again. I could not simply trust myself to speak. I knew it would hurt you more to see me cry. I longed to have your affection to cling close to you and tell you all my thoughts and talk of Valentine and Ralph as I did, and not to talk to you of what I minded most and felt so cruelly. But I could not bear our last meeting should be one of senseless grief. Yet it was best so. And I feel, you must have, even if I behaved coldly, you must have felt my pent up love go out to you with every sudden look, whilst we sat on the grass. You will care for the little picture; I gave you so much more, as I gave you that.

I am crying now again. I cannot see the paper. Oh I have cried since you left until my eyes ache. Even Annie knows I am unhappy and tries to be kind to me. She speaks so gently, and I saw last night she had cried also. The last straw was when I was trying to plant some lettuces in a despair of wretchedness, the cats both came and sat beside me, and rubbed my hands with their faces. Lytton's pale face, and affection makes me break down every moment. Gerald, my dearest friend you mustn't think it wasn't worth while, for you know it was. That I mind so terribly is awful. That you care even more is worse still. The irony, the superb irony, was that no good could come of it. I was tied, I could not leave with you. I should have felt for ever an exile, with a ghost between us. I couldn't have left with the memory of that face in the orchard distorted with rage, and horrid threats of murder. Our relation was so very perfect. It was never marred by callousness, or too much intimacy. It never faded into something casual. Every day I learnt more to be fond of you, found new pleasures. That no one now will notice what I wear, or how I feel, that I shall no longer rush down to get letters from the post, that no longer I can plan to see you in Spain is more awful to me, than anything else. If this happened with anyone else, if only I had had the outlet of being able to write to you my feelings, my griefs, and my happinesses I could have borne it. One never knows until one loses a person exactly how much they mattered to one. You may think (you are so humble in remembering I care for you) I could decide easily to live this altered life here? Do you not know it would have been far easier to rush off with you? Not to endure this pain? But I could not. One does owe something more than the enjoyment of life to a person like Ralph. How superb he has been, only Lytton knows. You will forget me, you will in time simply look back on me as something that was very good, and perfect for a few short years. It would have been different for Ralph. Do not ever quite forget me however. You MUST burn this letter, dear please. I have said more in it than I meant to when I first started to write, but the agony I have been through since you left has left me less brave.

Please remember my last wish and your promise to me. Do not see R or Valentine before you leave England [...] I remember everything. You must also. Your friendship was one of the most perfect I ever had. We never once quarrelled. And I never liked you less; only more, as we knew each other better. Remember that. You mustn't please tell J.H.-J. about this, for if he comes back to England he will tell others, and it may make it harder for me.

Remember dear I gave you a great deal, for I loved you, for that if you can, not to talk of this to anyone. I think the Woolfs will still go to Yegen. And Forster would also. I am sure of that. You must write to Virginia please from Spain. I will give you Forster's address at the bottom of this letter; if I don't you can always write to his publishers.

Every word now recalls a joke, a happier mood when we were such friends only a week ago. Tidmarsh pervaded with you, memories.

Do not hate Valentine. I think she did it unconsciously, she did not mean all this pain. But I never think of her now. It is better not to, otherwise one gets thoughts which hurt one's head to contain. And you mustn't rebuke yourself for anything you did or said. Because I've never once rebuked you. I forgive everything. It was simply misfortune. Gerald I've never once turned against you. And still care as much as I did a week ago.

I hope it will make you a little happier to know I still love you. Gerald I still don't realize quite what I've lost in you; my one happiness is that you never deserted me, or thought ill of me, and our affection wasn't killed, only forcibly divided. Forgive me this letter, I write in such misery. I only hope you will soon forget, and please never reproach me. I could not bear that last blow. Will you try and write again. Remember I think more of your writing than of anybody's but Lytton's and could you send Lytton sometimes the things you write, for judgement? Then I can read them also. I shall think of you not only today but for weeks and weeks and only with love. Goodbye. If you knew how brave I am at not asking to see you again, you would be happier. Bless you, my very dear friend. Your Kunak

To Gerald Brenan

Sunday morning, 9 o'ck [11 June 1922]

Gerald, I see R has written to you. Please even if he begs you, do not see him again. I will some day send you a letter telling you every thing that happened since you left. R has now been hardened and is cynical. I am treated rather like a peculiar variety of imbecile! It may be too difficult, but Lytton begs me to be patient for a little. He says Ralph's hardness is just the reaction after all this [...]

My Dearest Gerald. Bless you. Goodbye again.

Your Kunak

Later. Sunday, 5 o'ck

I did not mean to write another time, but now I must.

Ralph has today for the first time talked to me. He admitted he nearly didn't come back because I hadn't told him everything at first on Wed. morning. When I told him the reason I think he believed me. But I see Valentine is determined to push matters as far as she can, even now. Really the things she told him, unnecessary things that she had heard from Gertler. And when I asked him how I had behaved 'treacherously' to her to deserve such treatment, the only treachery she could produce was my questioning her motives about her telling me not to see Gertler. Now everyone is against me. You are let off as being 'vague', and well intentioned. I am a deliberate villain! Yet I can see R really believes me a little, and when Valentine leaves he will grasp we were fond of him, and we didn't behave quite so elaborately as he now believes. The sordidness of it all and the lack of necessity for all this, wearies me. I feel perhaps more than anything the hardness of Valentine's heart. The meanness of all this conduct. You will go away soon please? I want to think of you away from all this. Lytton is superb. Today I am perhaps less unhappy than yesterday, that is all. You must always let me know where you are in case I want to write.

The uttermost indifference is shown to all my actions now. But R is so unhappy I don't think he realizes quite how I feel. Gerald dear, you must forgive me for having made all this bother and having caused your pain. What a misfortune it has turned out! You mustn't regret anything that you did, nothing matters now. I shall never regret knowing you. I will tell you later how everything goes. Please remember not to tell J.H.-J. very much for my sake. I hate it all so much. I'd like to feel it wasn't going on any longer. Again goodbye. I am going to try and be an artist and paint very hard this summer. But I will write to you sometimes unless you would rather I did not. Only you must not write until I tell you. My love dear from

Your Kunak

To Gerald Brenan

Written in my bedroom
Wednesday afternoon, 3 o'ck, 14 June 1922

Gerald, I simply couldn't come up to London today. You needn't think I didn't want to come, for I did! [...] R still sees V although he never tells me he does. But he isn't coming back tonight or tomorrow night. I shall be here quite alone till Saturday, as Lytton goes away tomorrow for 2 days. I am going to change my bedroom into a studio. For now I shall have a great deal of time to paint. Lytton will tell you if I am ill, or if I die. I hate myself for being so strong [...] We are all so tired and unhappy, and yet we can't go away, because where can one go to? I think Lytton must long for next week when he can get away from us all, and be in Venice. He hates these sordid 'repeatings' as much as we do.

Let us forget all that part of it, and this last week. And think of a friendship which, while it lasted, no one but we two knew the texture of it. How far V was from ever understanding us. I am glad that the intimacy of our friendship was never dragged out into this shattering daylight. The most important thing to us both they never bothered to ask about! I alternate between despair and hatred of myself and my character, and a hatred against the irony of the whole situation.

I shall read your letter very often. It was dear of you to write me such a long one. And one which gave me so much pleasure. You are right it wasn't 'inevitable' until Valentine knew. Then it was. And perhaps if I had been wiser, and less fond of her I would have seen it. I repeat what you say: 'I cannot regret having known you.' [...] I feel a captive now. My spirit has gone. When one is forced to choose one can't go back and face the torment of choosing all over again, or tempt oneself. I feel very altered, so tired. Thank goodness our friendship was never sordid, that while we lived we were so superbly happy. I feel as if I am in a tomb today. I hear the wind, and the rain but I can't move. I wonder what you are doing [...] You will have forgiven me by now for not coming today. I was too worn out. I haven't a particle of rashness left in me. In a few years I suppose I'll be tamed. I am more aware of everything than you suppose, or anyone supposes [...] This is goodbye. I am firmer than you think. Nothing will make me write again. But I wanted you to know why I couldn't bear meeting you today. It wasn't I didn't care just as much as you did. I simply couldn't stand any more unhappiness, for I also want to be now removed from all these scenes, and scandals. My dear Kunak goodbye. I tell you very little but I cannot. Besides there is no use in it now.

Your loving Doric
FINIS

A little later [15 June 1922]
Gerald, you see I am completely unmoral still. I say I won't write another line, then I open the envelope again, and write line after line ... I want to rewrite all I have written but if I do you will never get it. I mustn't write any more. One must remember the play is over, the audience has left; the epilogue has been said. The tailpiece and FINIS written on the last page. These are just fly leaves, blanks, then the solid Morocco cover and the book is shut and is put on its shelf. In secret we may write a second volume. But we must not read it until we are very old, and hideous and impotent. Please remember dear that it was harder for me not to see you yesterday than you can possibly imagine ...

    Goodbye now. Grrrrrr.

As the following letter shows, for all her misery Carrington was able to stand back and give Alix a calmer account of the episode, in which she made her priorities quite clear.

To Alix Strachey

59 Finchley Road
(Only for one day in London) 19 June 1922

Dearest Alix,
    Your postcard came this morning. It was exactly as I had conjured, your superb sanatorium. No it's not true. I am NOT interested in the tubes, only you mustn't take the breath out of my lungs by descriptions of operations which are not going to take place [...]

Oh! Alix dear, would you were in England now that Despair is here. Never, never have I been more wretched and less able to know the truth, or my mind or anybody's mind. R now says I am so incorrigible in my lies, deceits and delusions, he will gladly pay for me to go to Freud to be cured. Lytton will give a rather cynical story I expect when he sees you in the Lakes. I am so worn out with scenes, explosions and tears that I can only give you the serial headings without comments. Only the bleakest serial sketch because I still doubt if anything is true or if I am capable of speaking the truth.

At Watendlath perhaps you observed Gerald Brenan conceived a passion for me. It had started before Watendlath really. However we both knew it was hopeless because (a) I wasn't in love with him and (b) because R would be in a state if we went to bed together. So nothing happened except embrassades. Then he went off to Spain and it all faded away. He admitted himself it faded rather when he left me, and he really only enjoyed writing me long letters and being friends.

[...] They [Ralph and Valentine] wanted to spend Whitsun at Tidmarsh. Annie was away. Pippa was coming and I honestly could not face cooking for 5 people for 3 days and having to see R making love under my nose [...] Lytton was superb and tried to smooth it out. I am afraid he must have found it terribly boring and nervy work. I made a great many miscalculations and errors of course. Gerald went off to Spain and I am never to write or see him again. I didn't care sufficiently to go off with him. I wish I could have to get away from it all. Lytton says R's complex about my virtue is almost insane. It has made him dreadfully wretched and reduced him to a man of nerves. You of course, will be cynical and say 'why do I put up with it?' Well, I suppose it's because I care a great deal more for living with Lytton and R and Tidmarsh, than I do for occasional affaires and Gerald's friendship, and I really am very fond of R. Incidentally I must add I had begged Valentine never to tell R about this absurd affaire with G because it would so upset him, so she knew quite well what she was doing. I like to see other people live with honest relations to each other – this has reduced us all pretty completely. R now says he can't face living with me at moments because I am such a fraud etc. Lytton thinks it will be alright in time ... but that I mustn't if I am going to live with R have any more affaires. As they were not even affaires, romances I suppose is the only word for this one and as I have had no others, it isn't much of a sacrifice to give up this imaginary life of rouée. I am now feeling as you will see rather grim – I mean now to paint and become very serious. So perhaps the end of this rather wretched business will be I'll paint and be some good as an artist. But it means Alix, unless the explosives become too much for me, I'll not be able to come off to the Lakes to see you. It was always rather dim and now it's dimmer. You must understand – should I get too much for R's nerves and he for mine then I'll fly to you in Italy ... Lytton was an angel – my only support – really I could not have survived these scenes without him. But to you who haven't seen or heard this, you must find it I suppose like every other domestic quarrel.

Forgive this tedious letter but I want to tell you a little and I shall promise you if I am not happy I will come to you and James. I shall try and find you a cottage in Dorset, Devon or Cornwall for August. Lytton goes to Venice today so I feel rather sad. You mustn't think I am in despair. It's only I've been sleeping badly and feel rather ill and Lytton's going makes it rather worse today. How I look forward to you two coming back to England.

Bless you, my fondest love,

Yr Carrington

PS Only for you and James, this letter and don't write back a hymn of hate against R.P. – in fact don't mention it. But tell me about yourself.

To Lytton Strachey

The Mill House
Friday afternoon, 23 June 1922

Dearest Lytton,

R came back last night. He was very friendly & did not talk about it anymore. I think he has almost over talked himself with Virginia & Leonard & he seemed pleased to be back here in the quiet Tidmarsh.

I believe Valentine disappearing has made him more settled & calm. Anyhow whatever the reason it was all much more cheerful last night & he said this morning he would spend the weekend here instead of going to Virginia & Leonard at Rodmell as he had previously arranged to do [...] Barbara comes tonight with Judith! Ugh! Almost a good thing as the 'Baby remedy' is gaining ground. Alan supports it. I say, give me one year to paint. If I've not reformed by then, or if I've not painted one decent picture I'll give in ... But I can't see why plunging one into complete misery should make us both happier and who should know better than I, whether I like children or not?

But I feel things aren't worse. This morning he was far more cheerful. Slowly I understand a good deal ... and frankly I don't believe we'll ever be happy again if he goes on with this friendship with V. She does belong to another world. I see it more & more & she will always ridicule me slightly to him now. She doesn't want him to love me again. I believe she'd like him to be her lover, who at intervals in the year she could see ... Rather as she keeps Gertler. Well I may be too gloomy about this side of it, [but] on the whole I don't think I am [...]

[...] I am trying to be good. And I don't think I've been untruthful yet [...] Darling Lytton you are my best friend, I realise that more and more. When you come back I will tell you a great deal that I wanted to tell you before you went away, which because of many things I couldn't manage to speak about.

Bless you. I am much happier. Ralph grows I am sure less hostile to me [...] no, I am not over cheerful I assure you [...]

Green peas from the garden & you are in Venice. UGH! My love to your patron saint. And burn a candle for me on the altar of the Lady of Pity.

My love to you
Your devoted Carrington
Barbara sends her love.

To Lytton Strachey

The Mill House
Tuesday [27 June 1922]

Darling Lytton,

The state of your patients? Monday was a black day. Even bright little Barbara collapsed under the gloom. He [Ralph] went off unhappy, and returned even more silent. He was friendly to Barbara, and markedly hostile I thought, to me, so all my feelings of thinking things were progressing fell with a thud. After dinner I went upstairs and painted as the light was still good and R went out for a walk with Barbara. Suddenly he came into my room after I had gone to bed and talked to me. I tried to tell him things he wanted to know and told him frankly of my affection for Gerald and what our relations had been. Ralph after this talk became infinitely happier and remained so this morning until he went off to London. Whether this change means anything, or not, it's difficult to say, but I felt this morning he had shaken off something, perhaps his pride and that things were changed in a way they hadn't been since the crash. I must tell you just these feelings because I know you care. Barbara is really very understanding and I think her calmness and simple affection has a wonderful influence. A sinister budget [a letter from Valentine] came from Paris this morning. So I said 'wouldn't it be a good thing not to read it until you get in the train.' To my surprise he said 'Yes I think it would' and put it away in his case. Barbara thinks that once he gets fond of me again, and Tidmarsh, he will see things more in perspective and will turn against the 'repeatings' and intrigues.

Anyhow today is happy and that is all one is certain about. Bless you. I forget when I last wrote. Did I tell you Alix and James wrote to me? There is real friendship! Their portraits will be framed and hung on the wall as the perfect example of 'Good Friends' [...]

Bless you my dearest my love and love to Sebastian.

Yr Carrington

To Lytton Strachey

The Mill House
Wednesday, 5 o'ck [12 July 1922]

Darling Lytton,

I do hope you'll enjoy London very much, I miss you today ... I do love being with you and it makes me happy in a very real way. I wish that I could forget everything. I try to, but some things it's difficult to get over. It isn't easy to lose a friend. I miss Gerald's letters, and his friendship more than I ever thought in my wildest moments I should; and when one mustn't talk of it, it keeps on tormenting one's head. But I won't talk of him because it only makes me remember him more; then, after all, no one else can mind except me. Only if I am grousy, and sullen you mustn't think me altogether selfish. I've read *The Watsons* today with my meals. It wasn't very good. But perhaps it was because it didn't end and one felt rather angry at being defrauded.[1]

I haven't kept my Reform Bill. Today I've not yet, and it's nearly 5 o'ck, painted a stroke. But there are two sweet boys mending something in the bath room, a senior builder forbade me to forth in any W.C. except the garden, the bricklayer crashed broken glass on the wall with all violence possible, 2 men repaired drains outside, Mrs Stiles whisked and broomed about inside, so I became restless and rushed off into the orchard and bashed and nailed away at the fence. Now it's all repaired and set up again on its feet until the next storm. An organ grinder played this afternoon and brought melancholy to me. It plays the gayest of tunes but I always feel like crying when I hear it. It has played every afternoon that I have been particularly unhappy here. The day I wrote to you when you were in Florence and told you I should Marry R. The day I wrote my last letter to G and many other days, all black days. So today which was so lovely, and smelt so good, suddenly by an organ grinder made me all despair.

[...] Lytton dear, I loved my walk with you so much yesterday in the fields. You are more to me than I can ever express to you. I wish I could

---

1 An unfinished novel by Jane Austen, published in 1871.

make you as happy as you can make me. I write in an absurd humour, so forgive the stupidity of this letter. My fondest love,

Yr Mopsa

To Lytton Strachey

The Mill House
Tuesday, 5 o'ck [25 September 1922]

Darling Lytton,

I am still at Tidmarsh, and you will read this in Berlin! You can't think how sorry I am that we can't be with you. You must forget nothing and you must come back laden with surprises: German sweets, post cards of Russian actresses, boots lined with fur, cigars for the Majora, and German picture books and honey cake! That is the most lovely cake in the world! Beg James to find you some. I felt very inadequate in my thanks this morning dear one. But you must know behind my trivial verses I meant a good deal. I knew how awful it would be, even for a few minutes last night facing that sort of conversation. But I am so glad you craved it. I almost thought that perhaps you thought I had been nonsensical to be so alarmed since when you talked to him you found him so calm. But you know he does change very rapidly, and partly because of my position, and partly because I dislike these scenes, I know and ask very little of his present feelings now, and of what has happened since she [Valentine] came back. But I do know a great deal of his past feelings, and her conduct. So my moments of alarm aren't quite groundless. But Lytton how can I ever thank you for all your support and your conversation? When you are here a creeping paralysis seems to come over me and I can say nothing of what I feel. But when you leave me I want to rush after you and hug you for all your goodness. You are almost too good you know. Sometimes I feel almost embarrassed. You must always tell me if you aren't quite happy, and if I could make anything more comfortable in any way. I think Ralph is immensely relieved at having talked to you. I think he felt there was rather a gulf growing up because she was never mentioned. And yet, up till now, I think he would have resented any approaches from you; I believe you chose the one and perfect moment to speak to him. Later perhaps he will be able to tell me more of his feelings. I am only so glad that you are happy. I rely so entirely on your judgement. I haven't painted today as I am rather stuck until the chair arrives. So I tidied up my room, and arranged my paints and cleaned my palettes. It's even a dirtier business than your book cleaning!

I do hope you didn't have a very 'ruff' crossing. It thundered here this afternoon. The house seemed very dismal and sad without you. No more jaunts when you come back. Promise? I hope Alix will come on Friday. Perhaps James will come down here with you and then will go back with Alix to Lord's Wood the next day. Already I am making plans for your return you see. This is a stupid letter but I write very quickly to catch the post, only I felt you hardly knew how much I loved you this morning and I want you to know.

Bless you und der gut Gott nach Du etwas sehen. Eure Liebe,[1]
Mopsa

By the autumn, Ralph's time at the Hogarth Press was coming to an acrimonious end. His affair with Valentine petered out, but he continued to have other flings without a qualm while watching Carrington like a hawk. Gerald was back in Spain writing her immensely long mournful letters.

To Noel Carrington

The Mill House
10 October 1922

Dearest Noel,

Your last letters gave us both great pain. For why should you also be plunged unto sad love affaires & why should you be so far removed from us that we cannot weep with you.

No, but I am sorry you are sad & I hope soon the sorrow will be less acute [...]

Alix has been staying here a week whilst Lytton & her husband James were in Berlin. What arguments she & Rex had to be sure. Conception, conscience & objections to war. The ceiling almost fell, but we enjoyed her company. She talks a great deal about Freud & sex which is always fascinating especially to R.P. Lytton & James had a wonderful time in Berlin. They saw the *Three Sisters* by Tchekhov acted by the Moscow Art Theatre [...] Why not have your holiday en route to England in Germany? The cheapness will not occur again in our lifetimes probably and the Germans are nice people. Margaret Waley spent her summer holiday there & enjoyed it tremendously.

R's career [at the Hogarth Press] is still in the balance. A House of Commons will sit on next Thursday to decide his fate.

Mercifully he decides through thick & thin he will remain at Tidmarsh wiith Lytton & me & he refuses to live in London. I love the country so

---

1 '... and may the good God look after you. Your love.' Carrington's German was even worse than her French.

much I don't feel I could face London again. One spends so much money in London & wastes so much time, & then the intrigues wear one's spirits away.

I am painting a portrait of R attired as a boxer, a most striking picture.

But I fear I shall not carry it through, it's becoming rather difficult to manage. The paint gets too thick & the colours dirty after one has worked at the picture for very long I find [...]

We do like your letters, so much. I feel in no good mood for writing letters this morning. Yesterday's sweet calm seems to have vanished. But I hope it will return tomorrow when R comes back. He is away today in London & all tomorrow interviewing Leonard, another crisis, so I feel un peu grey until he returns with the verdicts. It really is extraordinary how complicated one finds life for no apparent reason, when everybody might be friends, love & share each other – everybody intrigues & fumes & continues to make everything difficile. One does it oneself in spite of all ones principles [...]

I am sorry you've been unhappy. The only mercy is one doesn't remember every thing as acutely each day. They gradually fade away & one becomes cynical & hardened I suppose.

My love

Yr devoted D.C.

To David Garnett

The Mill House
Friday, 26 October 1922

Dear Bunny,

I must write to you and tell you how much I enjoyed you book last night.[1] I read it breathlessly at a sitting in about 3 hours! Really I believe you must have written it especially for me it pleased me so much! Lytton says the style is superb and I agree with him, as in all things but I think the story is so beautiful and fascinating [...] I suppose you will soon be worn out with flattery and praise if you are not already. But I doubt if any can be as genuine as mine because I am sure no one except a few people could like your book as much as I did. Once I had a lovely dream about a fox and very often buzzards are my night companions. But it is a rare pleasure to find a book to read by day so entirely to one's taste. The people in England will be idiots if they don't all read it as quickly as they can, for it makes one so happy. Will you tell Rachel [Ray Garnett] how much I liked some of her woodcuts. The very small one on the front page of the Reluctant

1 David Garnett's novel, *Lady into Fox*, was published to great acclaim by Chatto & Windus in 1922.

Mrs Fox behind the bush with her husband I think I liked best. I am just going to write and tell Alix what a good book it is. Will you please send G. Brenan a copy. Reg: post. And put it down to my account as soon as you can. G. Brenan. YEGEN, Ugijar, Prov. de Granada, SPAIN in case you have lost his address.

I am sorry to write such a bad letter, but this is the first one I have ever, (except last week to Virginia), written an author in praise of his book.

You must be very excited and proud to have made such a book! I feel now one has mismanaged life. Surely nothing could be nicer than that life in the woods with Madame FOX. I am sorry Hudson[1] died before he could read it. But I can't help feeling very glad I am alive to have read it. You mustn't think because I am rather a flatterer I say all this without meaning it. Because really I do love your book so much and not simply because you wrote it.

Please remember me to that exquisite sister in law Frances.[2] Perhaps if one can't hope to have tea at Tidmarsh with a Fox, sometimes a Rabbit will grace our board.

Your affectionate and most admiring

Carrington

Frances Marshall had left Cambridge in 1921 and found a job in Birrell and Garnett's bookshop. There she met Ralph on Hogarth Press business.

To Lytton Strachey

The Mill House
Monday afternoon [6 November 1922]

Dear, I posted your letters which I found on the table.

I feel very vacant headed today after all those arguments of yesterday. I do so want Ralph to keep in the Press if possible because in so many ways it is such a good job for him. On the other hand it's intolerable if he really doesn't suit them, from both points of view [...] I wish you weren't in London. After all these mental crises one longs to sit over the fire, and read *Shandy*, and shut out this world of activity and crises [...] I do love you so very much. And you make my life a very happy one. I am feeling rather extremely today in my solitude how much you matter. Ralph agreed yesterday that nothing mattered compared to our Triangular Trinity of Happiness. Even expulsion

---

1 W. H. Hudson (1841–1922) was a successful novelist, naturalist and ornithologist.
2 Frances Marshall (1900–2004) was Rachel Garnett's younger sister.

from the Garden of Paradise Road is nothing if we three are together. My dear, you are so good to us, and I love you terribly sometimes. Please take great care and don't get any colds. I am looking forward to Suggia!

Yr most loving
Carrington

To Gerald Brenan

The Mill House
Monday, 14 November 1922

Kunak, your letter has just come. I feel I deserve your reproaches. One does get into states of mind similar to those of scullery maids over this business. It's true what is this absurd frankness which we all talk about, and do not keep! How can we tell what our feelings will be when we see each other?

Oh Gerald you will never know what it was to be on the battlefield. If you have a nausea for these past events you can guess a little what I feel. But mercifully you aren't associated in my head with all these nightmare days and nights. I never connect you with them. Thank god I never saw you except once under those hideous clouds. Ralph has been the person who has in a way ruined himself for me in some curious way by being associated with all that ugliness. I learnt to dread him, and to fear him. Which are rather difficult sensations to recover from even in six months. My God, you know I do sometimes blast and curse Valentine for all this havoc!

To Gerald Brenan

The Mill House
20 December 1922

Dearest Gerald,

I am so old fashioned that I keep Christmas almost as seriously as Annie does. So I must write and wish you a Happy Christmas and a Gay New Year. I have nothing to send you. I meant to paint you a little picture, but it was never done. Perhaps I will think of some book that will please you when I will send it to you.

I had a wonderful visit to Normandy.[1] The beauty of the country still makes me a little discontented with our flat marshes, and these insignificant hills. I

---

1 Carrington had been to visit her friend Phyllis Boyd.

saw the forests of Eure (probably spelt wrong) that Ralph knew when he was in Normandy. Did you ever go there with him? It was fascinating living with people so strangely different from oneself. I only wish I could remember all the stories Phyllis told me. A wonderful account of Lady Munster her grand-mother who lived at Brighton and had 40 clocks all going at the same time in her bedroom. But of course you with aunt Tiz will not think much of such tales. I left just a week ago today on December 13th. The sea was very rough, and a French woman vomited all over my luggage. A just reward for my selfishness, as although I knew she wanted a basin I refused to go and get it for her. However I had some slight revenge when a custom's officer at Newhaven insisted on opening my suitcases 'something damp in this case mam', suspecting brandy or scent leaking over my clothes. 'Yes, a woman was sick on my box.' He shut it up very quickly and gave me a look of rage.

Ralph met me at Victoria. We had so much to say, after a week, we talked until we became tired of talking. And soon forgot all we had important to say and talked about absurdities. We had dinner at Ralph's mother's flat, in Francis Street. I wish you could see them and the flat. For pure Anglo-Indian plus sham Jacobean taste it is unrivalled. Mrs P is a pretty good example of a provincial missionary's daughter, full of false pride and ignorance.

Dorothy [Partridge] is much more human. She sings so beautifully and has learnt many lovely songs simply to please R and me, Mozart and the Ganges song and many other good old English songs. Mrs P I think thinks we are very heathen not to like the Italian songs that Dorothy used to sing in Milan. After dinner we rushed off to a lecture by Roger Fry. He is giving a whole series of lectures. Tracing the development of design, and 'significant form' in painting. He has amazing slides, Giotto, and the Sienese school. He always shows one a great many that one has never seen before. The last lecture brought one up to Uccello. Tout le monde is at these lectures. The females are characterised by their plainness and serious countenances, and males by their long hair and pasty spotty faces. Everybody knows everybody so before the lecture begins, the babble of conversation is not to be described in words. Chelsea meets Bloomsbury, Hampstead bows to Richmond and even ladies from Mayfair talk graciously to Logan Pearsall-Smith and Mr Tatlock.[1] If J.H.-J. was only there nobody you could possibly think of is not there! After the lecture Barbara, Ralph and I went to Duncan's [Grant] studio above J.H.-J.'s old room, to a sort of informal party. It was rather a classical party, with an air of a French studio in 1889. Arthur Waley's mistress Miss De Z[oete][2] played Bach on a harpsichord; the room was lit by candles, young earnest Cambridge

1 Logan Pearsall Smith (1865–1946), an influential man of letters known for his wit, was the brother-in-law of Bertrand Russell and Bernard Berenson. Robert Tatlock (1899–1954) was a friend of Roger Fry's and editor of the *Burlington Magazine*.
2 Beryl de Zoete (1879–1962) was a ballet dancer who later taught and wrote about oriental dance and theatre. She took up with Arthur Waley in 1918, to the dismay of his old friends.

men twisted and twirled on their toes and shrieked in high nasal voices. Vanessa drooped like a flower with a too heavy head over some coffee boiling on a stove. Duncan moved about with sprightly steps with trays of biscuits and beer in glasses. I talked to Miss Margery Fry about Vienna and the poverty of the Germans and behind me I heard Ralph discussing Spain with Arthur Waley. The next day Thursday we came down here. Tidmarsh looked wonderfully beautiful after an absence of a week. It is so snug and warm, lined with its walls of coloured books. In the winter when it's so dark one can't see the rat holes and the dust; one curls up in it like a fox in its hole, contented. We had a very social weekend, Sebastian Sprott, a young lecturer in psychology at Cambridge, Morgan Forster, and Roger Fry.

So you didn't like *Lady into Fox*. Morgan told me he had heard from you and repeated everything you wrote to him! And I liked it so much. Ralph is more on your side than on mine. He didn't care for it nearly as much for it as I did. But then again, Lytton likes it! Morgan is a charming character. He is so amusing and has good ideas when he is serious. Roger's vitality never fails. He talks from the moment he appears at breakfast till he goes to sleep murmuring his Coué chant. For he is a devoted disciple of that French Christ. They all left us on Monday. Tomorrow Ralph's holidays begin. I am glad, secretly I admit, because I want to finish a picture of him.

The yellow cat has passed away. Dead as a ducat. Maynard Keynes, and Lydia Lopokova come here for Christmas. I hardly know Lydia; opinions seem to differ very much about her character.[1] After Xmas I will tell you what I think of her. Ralph will write and tell you all the Hogarth Press developments. I will not encroach on his domain. Roger's lectures (on the Italian pictures) have inspired me to start some big compositions. Suddenly reviewing my last year's work it seems disgracefully amateurish and 'little'. So I shall now start this Xmas after they have all gone a composition of an interior scene in this kitchen.

Only I shall paint it very big. I do not want to tackle anything too difficult, or I know I shall then despair and give up the composition before it is finished [...]

I am so sorry you have not been well. What is the matter with you? If it is serious and continuous, do go to Seville and see an English or a German doctor. Please don't get decrepid like J.H.-J. and all those Fitzroy people. I have the greatest contempt for people like Middleton Murry and Katherine Murry who think it is 'interesting' to be ill and who sniff up their noses at any writer who hasn't cancer in the stomach, or violent consumption.

---

1 Lydia Lopokova (1892–1981) was a leading Russian ballerina who, to the amazement and initial displeasure of Bloomsbury and the sorrow of Sebastian Sprott, took up with Maynard Keynes and married him in 1925.

I've got such a good book on Rousseau. But I refrain from sending you any book, picture, verse, or prose after your severe 'Vixenish' rebuke.

My mother has just bought another house, this time in Minchinhampton. Poor woman she already writes, even before she has moved in and asks me if I know anyone who would like to buy it! The shady eldest brother has returned from Spain bankrupt, and now lives fast and loose sponging on my sister in London. Mercifully I have not yet seen him.[1] Do write to Ralph soon and send him some MSS. This was meant to be an interesting letter to cheer your Christmas feast. It seems to me on rereading it to be about as stale as that Christmas pudding must be which probably still sits in the poste restante at Granada. Would you like the *New Statesman* and *Nation* every week or do you take them up yourself? Answer N. or M. Now I must stop, as the paper is all used up. I send my love and best wishes that next year we may all be happier: bless you.

Yr Kunak

To Virginia Woolf

The Mill House
Thursday, 21 December 1922

Dearest Virginia,

I send you this little casket of sweetness as a token of my affection for you and Leonard. Please honour me by accepting it with my best wishes for a Happy Christmas, and a successful New Year. Well, well. So now it's over.

I thank you for trying so valiantly at Tidmarsh to come to a happy ending. But perhaps reviewing everything now it will all turn out for the best. Ralph is rather disconsolate at the moment but I expect his feelings will soon revive. I am sorry of course, because I cared so much for the Press that I couldn't help wishing Ralph to be in it also. But that's not quite a good enough reason for his staying in it when there are so many complications on both sides. But we are still all friends. I must say that seems to me a most important issue. In January I will come and see you again at Hogarth. We had a very gay and talkative weekend last Saturday, Sebastian, Morgan, and Roger. On Saturday Maynard and Loppy arrive. We are all slightly trembling at their approach. Today we went to Reading. The male element were very crabbid and wouldn't let me spend any money on Christmas presents, so I am busy making toffee, and converting bromo boxes into Italian letter cases this evening [...]

1 Carrington's eldest brother, Sam.

I hope you and Leonard will enjoy Rodmell. Ralph sends you his love and best wishes. Lytton also send his.

Carrington sends even more.

As this last letter shows, after a series of awkward discussions Ralph finally left the Hogarth Press. Both the Woolfs had found him an unsatisfactory employee.

To Gerald Brenan

The Mill House
25 December 1922 – Christmas Day

Dearest Gerald,

[…] Christmas Day. One can hardly see the country sky, the smoke of a thousand plum puddings & turkeys soar up to God. We alone insult his omnipotence. Cold saddle of mutton & baked potatoes, salted almonds & cold white celery – But tonight … we shall be Englishest of the English. Maynard Keynes & the lovely Princess Lydia Lopokova are with us. She is almost a dwarf only 4.8 inches high. But exquisitely made. I cannot but help being the slightest bit in love with her. She talks charmingly … using wonderful English words. 'I smell a great beast in the oven, coming into my bedroom, I like it. Smell very good.' She is always gay & laughing.

She adores Maynard and listens whilst he is telling Lytton & Ralph some utterly boring facts ('Mexican Eagles & Industrials will go up after Christmas') with an exoteric [*sic*] expression on her face as if he was Shelley propounding some new philosophy. She dresses beautifully in a Russian style. Her stupidity is far greater than Barbara's. But her charm and high spirits make it almost unimportant. One wonders when looking at Maynard with a cold detached eye, how she could fall in love with him … Except that he is bald, pot bellied & lascivious & resembles a high official in a government department in one of Tchekhov's stories one can see little attraction in his appearance! His intellect seems almost entirely to consist of economics and stocks and shares, & his long accounts of his successes in diplomatic & political circles. She can talk of nothing else but the Russian ballet & Sir Oswald Stoll![1] Yet they are enchanted by each other's company and in spite of the cynicism of Bloomsbury spend all day … perhaps discussing Sir Oswald Stoll. Perhaps the revision of the peace treaty … at the moment lying upstairs together … in connubial bliss?

1 Sir Oswald Stoll (1886–1942), a leading theatre manager.

The question is whether Maynard is so far gone and disssolved that he will have to marry her or whether he will be able to avoid it. His more intimate friends in Gordon Square are considerably agitated as she is without all higher conversation, very boring to talk to after a little & quite insensible to any atmosphere of hostility.

However I can't see that it matters if Maynard doesn't find her limitations boring. And if he can't disentangle himself from her to see his friends alone he can hardly be worth saving [...] I think women of real intelligence are as rare as Hoopoes or Hoopoos in England, so that it is better for them to be lovely & charming in character than boney-faced, vulgar & half intelligent as Inez Fergusson & young Cambridge ladies. Lunch is over, the lord has sent me as a special present ... The Fiend.

So now I really am provided with an excellent excuse for any dull wittedness. I hope we shall hear from you soon.

Please now let us write every week to each other. There are some things I like to be even methodical about, & one is a regular letter from you every week. Lytton has a new German philosopher in the house. Perhaps he would suit you. He is very crushing, & gives no hope, or false promises. I like what Lytton has read to me because he supports my Hume. That there is NO cause & effect. And there is no reason unless one is superstitious to believe the sun will rise the next day. Yes, I will send you this new philosopher. He was once at Cambridge, & Bertie thought he was so great, even in his youth that he went down on his knees & adored him. In the war this philosopher fought for Germany & was captured, imprisoned in Italy where he wrote this book I speak of. – He has now retired to a mountain & forsaken the world.[1]

Ralph has been so friendly to me lately. Really it is not true that we are not such good friends. I think we are better. But you must write often to prove to me you are also my friend [...]

Last night at dinner Maynard entertained us with a whole bag of conjuring tricks. Lydia shrieked with laughter. It was just what she loved. False eyes, & teeth & a plate which jumps mysteriously on the table is happiness to her. After dinner we played cards till bed time.

Today I am still rather crotchety. So I am browsing over the fire thinking of you. Last night I dreamt I met Valentine & Bonamy. I turned as I left the room & said I thought with extreme cleverness 'I hope I shall never see either of your hideous faces again!' I was enraged this morning that I had not been really sarcastic ...

I can't help minding a little that Christmas brought no letter from you. Please write to us soon. You can't think suddenly how happy I have grown

1 Carrington is describing Ludwig Wittgenstein (1889–1951), the Austrian philosopher, and protégé of Bertrand Russell since he arrived to study in Cambridge in 1911. His presence in the house was in a book, not in person.

now that there is no more enmity between Ralph & you.[1] I think Barbara is almost too stupid. I tell you this as a slight warning. Her indiscretion appears some times ... and much as I love her irritates me. I think her denseness makes it rather difficult to reach any higher planes of friendship with her. Yet she is so charming inside one hardly notices it generally.

It is Wednesday. And Maynard & Lydia have just left us. Lytton lies exhausted in his chair after the strain of so much weighty conversation with Maynard. I painted Lydia yesterday and today. Damn but it wasn't what I meant to do of her. That's so awful when conflicting ideas crowd into one's head. The model is before me, one must paint, one throws away the first & chases the second. I meant to do a very large head side view boldly like a Matisse almost, against a black background painted extremely quickly & simplified with no modelling, I did instead a rather spottist painting of her in a Chinese dress, rather elaborate & down to her knees. But she has promised to come again & stay with us & sit for me. I liked her very much in the end. She is exactly like a little girl in *War and Peace*, I forget her name – so excitable & young, always happy & absurdly serious listening to old Maynard holding forth on stocks & shares. She is a year older than I am. But she looks only 20 ...

Tell me a great many things when you write, what you read, what you do all day & how you are in health.

You can now give up all your other correspondents & devote yourself entirely to me & Ralph. Because I don't mind telling you in confidence although I've never exactly heard it with my own ears, that everyone, but we, find your letters very LONG & TEDIOUS. Rumour has it so.

Annie has gone to the pantomime so I must go and grill the turkey's legs in the kitchen for Ralph & Lytton's supper. Annie is becoming a perfect cook & now I hardly ever put hand to brush, or nose to saucepan.

Bless you Gerald dear & write back to me soon please. I send my love & wishes for a Happy New Year.

1) Tell me if you would like the *Nation* & *N.S.* weekly.
2) If you want any books to read.
3) If you keep well.

Yr Kunak

With the Great Row of 1922 now behind them, and the Tidmarsh ménage intact, Carrington was able to joke with Gerald about his letters. But although the affair with Valentine was over, Ralph was now openly pursuing romance in London, and Carrington had no intention of discouraging Gerald's devotion.

1 Gerald and Ralph had also been writing each other long explanatory letters.

1923

The Mill House
[1 January 1923]

Kunak,

Write please to me soon. Now that is all over, and we are free again, are we so chicken-spirited that we have no affections left?

I tell you Ralph has completely altered. I told him both times I wrote to you, and asked him if he would like to read my letters to you. He never bothered to, and then simply laughed at me when I said I had posted them two days later. Is all this to have a Tchekhov ending? 'That after months of self denial, and anguish, when they could write they found all desire had vanished.' Or you may be ill? Or perhaps on a ship bound to Buenos Aires, or the West Indies? I send you all my love for this New Year. Lately, perhaps because I have nothing of you now, I have been living in a ghostly world of memories. I can't help being very fond. I am now so grateful that I had the little of you that I did have. It might have been even less. Here is a book on El Greco. I don't know if you have one on him already. He is almost my favourite artist. I am reading Hogg's life of Shelley now by myself in the evenings.[1] Please, unless you feel disinclined write to me, or Ralph soon, if that (disinclined) I can wait. My dear, I wish I could see you again soon. I send all the love you want, and my best wishes for your work.

Your loving Doric

To Gerald Brenan

Tidmarsh-in-the-snow
Sunday, 14 January 1923

Your last letter was perhaps the best you have ever written. I take it as an honour that I should be a Fanny Brawne ... I read Keats' letters last night. They gave me a pleasure I cannot describe, one of great affection for a dead human. Now I sit over a grilling red fire. Lytton reads Dante in an exquisite first edition which he has just bought, in the big chair, Ralph is absent in the library typing for his Master, outside a cold wind howls & the ground is white with snow [...]

1 Thomas Hogg (1792–1862), a close friend of Shelley, wrote an unfinished posthumous biography of the poet, published in 1858.

I am rather feeble mentally & otherwise, so you must forgive this sluggish letter.

I always write to you in this moment of my life it seems – is it symbolic or merely an excuse for writing badly. No, it is because there are only two idle days in every month with me!

I have little to tell you. Last week I went up to London & saw my mother. It makes me very sad every time I see her. I see a doom – a vision of myself perhaps at the age of 70 – she had an awful time in Spain with my eldest brother. He has married a young Irish lady who leads a gay life, riding, balls at Gibraltar, combined with a most sluttish life on their farm in the stables & mud. My poor mother was forced to cook, clean & darn for them & then was continually cursed by her exquisite Irish daughter in law because she couldn't pay them more than 2½ guineas a week! & because she couldn't lend them any more money!

They run their farm very badly, spend the money as soon as they get it, cheat & lie to their customers. I spent a dreary morning with my mother listening to her sad experiences. The only thing she enjoyed was the journey to the ship. She loved the ship-cooking. The rough sea & the Anglo Indians returning from Bombay!! She was quite sorry when the ship reached Portsmouth. – She bought me a good earthenware bowl with holes in the bottom for chestnuts & a good earthenware dish. I bought a scarlet jersey at a sale & an infinitely respectable coat & shirt, so respectable you wouldn't recognise me if you saw me walking down Yegen in it! This is because next Thursday I go to a grand wedding in London. My most exquisite friend this Phyllis Boyd, by name, is going to marry a French man Henri de Janze of Normandy & I go to the function & elbow the duchesses out of the front pews. Phyllis writes me very good letters, very upper class and immoral, but full of character & she has a very special character. She will live in Normandy & perhaps I shall go and stay with her. She is a direct descendant of Mrs Jordan[1] on her mother & father's side as they were cousins and she looks it. I have known her since she was 17, a scraggy little girl at the Slade. It's rather fascinating to have seen a Rake's progress in real life and now I shall see the finish of her, carried off by a Norman Vicount or Viscount. – I can't spell some times very well as perhaps you notice – I wish you could have seen Phyllis. She gave one a standard of beauty that few women have ever attained. Then she is clever also, in a curious way, reads 18 cent. French literature, Tchekhov & very up to date scientific & medical books. But she is too rich & immoral to have insight or sympathy into many people's lives. Now we are going to read *Troilus & Cressida*, so you must be put away.

---

1 Mrs Jordan (1761–1816) was the actress mistress of the Duke of Clarence, later King William IV, by whom she had ten children.

Wednesday, 12 o'ck

You have been away into your grave for three days now and much water has flowed under our mill as well as under London Bridge.

On Monday morning the wife of John, the man that works at the mill died. All Sunday she lay a-dying & John, refused to speak to her, on Monday morning they rushed up to the mill & begged him to go back to the cottage as she was dying, 'canna come, must see to this hay n the waggon.' The old cronies were staggered, they went across the fields to the cottage, in a few hours she was dead [...] John never speaks to anyone. And all the neighbours shake their heads. I stay indoors, so that I am not forced into either camp. Once a week I visit the old miller's man Dan, who lies in bed with his toe rotting off & we discuss 'life' & old times, & other very boring topics. He never gets worse or better & I've now become a 'lady visitor' & I suppose I shall remain one until he dies. And that's all the news in Tidmarsh [...]

On Monday at 11.40 I set sail for London & stayed with the mysterious Hon. Dorothy Brett who you don't know in Hampstead. Now she really is a queer character.

We talked over the stove in her studio, as only females can talk. Then I looked at her pictures which weren't very good. Then we walked to Finchley Road & took my poor mother out to tea in Oxford Street. Afterwards I went to Liberty's & bought some silks at a sale. (If only you had sent me a pattern I would easily have matched your silk. Do send it & then I'll get it for you.) I bought a pretty handkerchief for myself & one for Lytton & Ralph. In the evening I had dinner with them [Lytton & Ralph] & Boris Anrep in Hampstead. They have a charming house, only beautiful in its china & arrangement. Talked to them & the consumptive sister in law who lives ill in the bed up stairs. I have a great affection for this lovely sick creature. To look at her is to fall in love.

I rather enjoyed this escape from my husband & the freedom of being alone with my friends and companions again.

Grrr was it a pity to change? To be so cowardly of facing the hardship of loneliness & poverty ...?

Who can tell ... Freedom perhaps would have lost that sweetness that I find in it now.

Went with Brett on Tuesday morning & looked at some Degas at the [illegible] Galleries. I wasn't very impressed. But they were all very slight efforts. Went to the National Gallery & paid homage to my Bellini and Poussin again & examined other Poussins, Constable, Crome, & Gainsbrough very carefully. Had lunch with Ralph & MacIver & an old Slade female friend of mine who unfortunately has developed Brights disease & a mental madness, so it was rather a painful reunion, than pleasurable. I can't bear to see what was once as lovely as Juno, strong & virile, now a wreck of nerves & aged – She used to sing to me in the fields at Hurstsbourne – what songs! I shall never hear her sing again and her beauty will be seen no more.[1] Went with her after lunch to the wedding of my beautiful Phyllis Boyd.

It was in a Catholic church and Priests with Robes & a Bishop with a mitre married them.

It was a fitting end to her gay life. The bridegroom is a charming young man. I met him on Monday evening in her bedroom. (I left out that visit, for before I went to the Anreps to dinner I spent 2 hours with the lady of charms in her bedroom. She was lovely, I actually suffered torments because I longed to posess her in some vague way. To make her realize somehow, that I was important to her. But she only prattled away in her bed about her chateau in Normandy, her parents, her past lovers & the scandals of London.) She looked very lovely in her white, given away by her terrible old rake of a father, stout with grey curling moustaches & the figure of a comic French roué. It was like some lively scene in a Ballet. The voices of the choir boys, the smell of the church & the flippant society audience, mingled with the devout governesses & Catholic nuns, who hope to save the soul of this lady of charms.

Then Ralph & I went off to the Strand & bought chicken houses & a bicycle pump ... & came back to Tidmarsh in the evening.

Lytton read us such a good dialogue that he wrote whilst we were away. But I shall tell you no more. It will appear in his essays in the Spring.

> A BAD COLD
> DULL letter
> But we live in a
> BAD DULL COLD
> Climate
>
> And I've a cold, Bad, Dull character
> Oh to be my Persian cat
> Lying snug upon the mat

To Gerald Brenan

The Mill House
Thursday evening, 29 January 1923

Mi guerido,

Your epistle to the lady of Tidmarsh arrived last night! I was so delighted with it that my French lesson which begins at a quarter past six, just after

---

1 This friend was Christine Nash, nèe Kuhlenthal.

the post man comes, went ill. I could hardly pay attention and my mind wandered from La Malade Imaginaire to un letter non imaginaire.

I am progressing with my French. Every evening as punctually as hen lays its egg, Lytton and I open our Molière's over the fire. He reads it aloud in English & I follow the French [...]

I snatched your mystic P.S. and concealed it in my corsage. I cannot write today about the white fawn. I must think a little then on Thursday when I am alone I will write a long letter.

I write every day, a short letter, because then the many things I want to tell you, do not vanish from my head [...]

Yesterday Ralph asked to read your letter. Then he said 'You evidently have a great many jokes & intimacies of which I know nothing with Gerald.' He then carried on the conversation later at night. He said I always evaded discussing my feelings for you, and he thought perhaps these letters which we are always writing might be leading us on in that direction. He said he did not mind (except as a friend he hated to see you in pain), you being in love with me, it slightly flattered him, but if he knew you were, he would then know I would probably return it, & that is what interested him. He wanted to find out my exact feelings for you. For even if he knew we were quite loyal (or whatever the expression is I can't think of it) to him, if he knew I felt physical feelings for you, it would enrage, or make him unhappy, just as much, even if we never indulged in them. – He admitted his affection for Frances [Marshall] made him more indifferent to my feelings & relations with you. But he said that if he suspected I had more than friendly feelings for you all his old jealousies would come back.

As it was he had no hostility at all towards either of us.

I tell you this, because I realized rather acutely how important it is we should not in letters betray our feelings. You must not write more affectionately than your last letter [...] It is so perfect at present being able to care for you, that I cannot bear the thought of it ceasing, and it will be our own folly if it gets into those complicated bogs.

Because of this I do not ask you to send me your treatise. If I think of a plan that I could be certain of receiving it alone I will tell you. I am rather loathe to ask any third person to negotiate for us. It at once makes things complicated.

Ralph is so charming most of the time & so friendly towards you, that I do not want to risk a reversion of attitude [...]

N.B. It is rather important if you leave Yegen that my effects & letters should be absolutely safe ... You must know that the inhabitants of Bloomsbury are not above tampering with locks, or bursting boxes ... Today I meant to paint, but I had to find a canvas in my little attic. I discovered whilst I was searching for the canvas that mice & rats had crept into my wooden boxes of old letters & had played gay games with them.

They were shredded into confetti, chewed into flakes of tissue. Whole bunches of letters had vanished to make little nesties for the mousies.

Well, it was rather a relief. There were far too many of them. And this mice feast gave me an opportunity for burning all the half munched pages [...] They stopped short at a packet of Lytton's letters. So there is snobbery even in the rat world!

The total effect of all this made me gloomy & cynical. What a life I saw before me stretched on the floor! What letters! What friendships! Some of them made me positively uncomfortable but I laughed & preserved one example of every friend & lover & tied them up in neat packets [...] I found your first postcard & the first letter you ever wrote me ... one wouldn't have guessed much would have come from them.

Tomorrow morning I shall finish tying up the packets & then they will be put in a mouseproof box & locked up until we move. – I burnt over 500 hundred I should think this afternoon!

[...] I found some old m.ss. in a book amongst the letters, one's affections when young are so depressing. In fact I am now very glad I shall be thirty next month & forty ten years after. I detested my ingenuousness today exposed in these letters.

Goodnight my fondest love.

Yr Cirod

By now, Ralph was in serious pursuit of Frances Marshall. She was attracted to him too, but unlike Ralph's other lovers she had no intention of having a casual affair with a married man. Highly intelligent and very pretty, she had many more eligible admirers. Unlike Carrington, she was already part of Bloomsbury: her mother, a keen suffragist, knew the older Stracheys; her sister Rachel was married to David Garnett and her sister Judy to one of Lytton's nephews, Dick Rendel.

To Gerald Brenan

The Mill House
29 January 1923

Amigo,

I wrote you two tiresome letters but what of that – I can't be proud with you. I have to confess my affection & ask for your pardon.

Grrrrr so Virginia & Leonard will see you in March!!! That makes one chomp one's teeth. There is a project on foot for us – a visit to North Africa coming back though Sicily, Naples, Rome, & Florence in March & April.

But whether anything will come of it I don't know. At the moment we've no money left & even Lytton is rather reduced in wealth. He has been spending so much on books lately [...]

Last week I spent a whole day with Brett in Hampstead. She told me the whole account of Katherine Mansfield's death.[1]

Brett was in her curious way in love with Katherine, she was very broken by the suddenness of her death.

Katherine had retreated to a mysterious priory at Fontainbleau, a community with mystical tendencies run by a Russian whose name I forget [George Gurdjieff]. Men & women of all nationalities live in this priory. The Russian Seer is all powerful & all wise and a complete dictator ... There are no servants, everyone has his particular task allotted to him. Everyone must work. Then they have a theatre in the grounds which they built and decorated themselves where they act plays & do Delacroix-sort-of-dances. They garden & milk cows and build when they want out houses. There are sixty disciples – Brett gave a very good description of the community! – She disliked the Grand Seer who apparently is so busy firing orders and devising tasks that he is never seen to work. Katherine had been there two months as an invalid so she was allowed a servant & kinder treatment. Fortunately Murry was staying with her. He had arrived three days before she died.

She suddenly had a haemorrhage after walking upstairs & died in ten minutes.

Brett went over to the funeral with Sullivan. I am sorry Katherine is dead. I hadn't seen her since she lived with Brett and me in Gower Street. But she was a great life enhancer. Her writing was the least interesting part of her.

You take a dark view of that remark? – But if you had known her you would have seen she was no ordinary woman. Even Lytton was impressed by her. She was so witty, and had such courage. She lived every sort of life. She knew every sort of person. It was queer that she wrote so dully. For she was the reverse of that when one talked to her. I always think she was doomed through her connection with Murry. I think he ate her soul out of her [...]

At last the curtain is down and the orchestra has gone home. Even the bills are torn down & never more will La Bella Valentine Dobree grace the boards.

She returns to England today [...] She wrote a characteristic letter to Ralph saying she never wanted to see him again & wished to avoid meeting him in London ... Ralph said unmoved 'if she wishes to avoid meeting me there wasn't any need to tell me she was coming to London. I can't say I

1 Katherine Mansfield had been suffering from tuberculosis for some years.

think she is very sincere.' But the farce is over. I confess when I saw her familiar writing on the French envelope I shivered.

I wonder in two years time how she will tell this romance to her intimate friends.

You will hear of the Hogarth Controversy when you meet the Woolfs in Granada.

One thinks Ralph is absurd not to stick to such excellent people, but really he is right. The whole difficulty is working under anyone & receiving orders. Leonard & Virginia are perfect people to know as friends, but rather difficult as overseers & business people.

The Tidmarsh Press[1] will be better because then Ralph will have a free hand to do what he wants. He will work for himself at his own hours. He can hardly make less money than he did with the Woolfs [...] And after all poverty with complete liberty is worth more than a safe income of £300 a year – (not that he got that with the Woolfs) – in a business in London, with the dreary prospect of 2 or 3 months freedom every year ...

[T. S.] Eliot brings out every quarter of the year an amazing periodical called *The Criterion*[2].

Ezra Pound excelled himself last week in an article enumerating the few writers since Isaiah that were worth reading! In fact I am sure you will agree with him in everything he says ... So I will send it you, if I can get Lytton to give it me. Gertrude Stein has a novel in it. Far far more advanced than Virginia, about as much like a novel as Picasso's cubist painting were like Giotto's painting [...]

Please write to me soon unless you feel unpleasantly towards me. Then on the whole I would rather you waited until you felt amiable.

I am painting fairly regularly now. I found Roger's lectures very inspiring – they fairly set me on my lost tracks again.

I am in love with a South American or Spanish cinema hero. His name is Valentino. He is more lovely than Robin John. I have seen him in three films now. Once he was a Toreador. Really he fought Bulls in the ring in Seville & looked divinely beautiful with tight breeches.

Last Wednesday I went with Marjorie Strachey in London to a film called *The Sheik*, an amazing film of the Arabian desert with my Hero as a Sheik riding an arab horse. I also saw Charlie [Chaplin] on the same afternoon and a 'close up' film of Locusts and a Badger Hunt. I only wish there was a cinema at Pangbourne. – Even Ralph confessed he was slightly taken by Valentino. I have a picture of him. But unfortunately dancing in the arms & legs of his wife who is equally ravishing [...]

1 This notion of setting up another Press came to nothing.
2 T. S. Eliot had started *The Criterion* in 1922. Early contributors included Gertrude Stein (1872–1946), the experimental novelist and art collector who lived in Paris with her lover Alice B. Toklas.

After all this you may expect to see 'yours to a cinder, Mary' at the bottom of the page. On the contrary you will see the familiar name of
Your
Kunak
Doric

To Gerald Brenan

The Mill House
19 February 1923

[...] You know I really think it would be lovely to spend next winter at Yegen. I should escape this awful cold and rain and I would really get some painting done away from all the distractions of Tidmarsh. You must start in the summer writing to Ralph week after week to persuade him. If he isn't involved in any business in England I see no reason why we shouldn't come [...]

It's true one loses a good deal by marriage. The privacy of one's bedroom after all the house has gone to sleep. But really the truth to be faced is one loses one's privacy the moment one falls in love, or even more when another person falls in love with one and one allows them entrance to one's chambers of secrecy. But one gains something also [...]

Bless you Gerald, I send you my fondest love
Your amigo
xxxx

To Gerald Brenan

The Mill House
20 February 1923

Gerald,
A Mere Postscript to yesterday's letter.
I was very clever, as clever as Irene Vanbrugh in one of those society plays. I almost heard the hushed thrill of the audience below. – The usual debate who should run down & fetch the letters ... they arrive about half past seven in the morning now.
I invented an ingenious rule. That we should fetch them on alternate days. I starting in today. Tuesday ... Ralph had some dull letter from his mother, as I opened yours I saw the postscript, it fell from my hand onto

the floor. Ralph turned round & said 'let's read Gerald's letter together'. The audience sees the postscript lying on the floor – my side of the bed – what does it not contain? (I confess I saw the word 'Wittgenstein' & hated the idea of an 'economy' lecture so that was why I dropped it.) Then came my cleverness, as I got out of bed, as a bare foot reached the ground it pushed the letter under the flowered curtains below the bed. It was a pity after such a feat of foot manoeuvres it shouldn't have contained a plot to poison Ralph or a proposal to take ship to China ... still to me it is exciting because I can read over the fire a letter from you only seen by me.

How glad I am you liked Wittgenstein, you know I know nothing of such books. I only sent it you because Lytton & other people talked so much of him. The Tacitus I didn't even choose, I simply asked Bunny Garnett to send it you.

You thank me best by not thanking me ... and by writing to me often please.

Don't load poor Virginia with any presents for me. For to begin with she is human, & if they are lovely she will certainly keep them herself or give them to Vanessa Bell!

Bless you Gerald, I send you my fondest love.

To Gerald Brenan

The Mill House
6 March 1923

This letter was started on March 1st – Lytton's birthday to be exact – It is now March 6th [...]

On Lytton's birthday Mary Hutchinson came for lunch, she surprised us just as we were eating our omelette. She bought Lytton a lovely bottle of Madeira as a present. In the afternoon two exquisite American girl friends of David Garnett came to look at the house with a view to taking it whilst we were away. One of them was lovely. Very tall with an olive skin, dark shining eyes like jet beads, & perfect slim figure & short black curling hair. Her friend was my style, pink with a round face dressed in mannish clothes, with a good natured smile. Her name was Henrietta. Mina Kirstein however did all the talking. Henrietta agreed with everything she said. I felt a little sad at such lovely creatures wandering around the house taking about as much interest in me as if I'd been the housekeeper! 'Say Henr-ie-t-ta aren't those dog violets just too lovely I haven't seen them since I left Massachusetts.'

I looked out of the yellow room window, I couldn't see a sign of a dog violet ... So I said 'do you mean the yellow celandines' – 'yas, we call them dog violets in America, you seem to call a good many of our flowers by different names' [...]

I wonder how long the Woolves will stay with you? I can hardly bear it [...] That Virginia should see your new room before me. That they should see you before I do. That I shall have to go to them & ask them for news when I return. Ugh! Grrrrr ... Say, at risk of your displeasure, may I ask you to be very careful what you tell Virginia – Really she can't resist reckless gossiping & all is fuel for her tongue. She is very anti-Ralph at the moment – They both are – It's not worth discussing – It's simply they don't care for him & he gets on their nerves. They can't state this fact and leave it but they discuss very minutely his shortcomings regarding the Press, his failings in relation to them, etc. etc. – I only mean Virginia will very likely egg you on to talk about last summer. She will be sympathetic & try & draw you [...] It's only, if she comes back & starts talking about it again & against Ralph it will soon come round to Ralph & then he'll think you've been siding against him with Virginia.

So although I see it's inevitable there should be some wild talk (& Virginia is not a woman to be failed if she does not want to get anything from you) still ... Remember my dreary words of wisdom & moderate your confidences.

I could hardly bear any more clouds to come across our sky.

I was discovered! Birrell & Garnett sent me a bill the other morning, I couldn't conceal it – so Ralph asked me at once if I had sent you Wittgenstein. I confessed I had. There was nearly a row. It just shows how friendly we are now, that there wasn't quite a row [...] My dear, I am so sorry because there is so little else I can give you. But I suppose that it's rather mean to spend Ralph's money, which I do when I've used up all mine.

I am so glad you've abandoned M.[1] Really I was rather terrified. For if she allows you to have her, the chances are she lets other men and confess now you take no precaution – or only sometimes rather vaguely – against S [syphilis] ... & really I can't believe any right possible man can be worth the humiliation of that particular disease.

For that reason I think m[asturbation] is better than c[opulation].

I don't get over my affection for you Gerald. I still spend far too long thinking of you everyday.

Do you know on March 29th I shall be x years old, or perhaps n years. I am never quite certain. It's pretty serious. I used to think people who were n years old were practically [...] to be pitied.[2] I think the secret to keeping

---

1 Gerald was sleeping with his Spanish housekeeper, Maria.
2 Carrington was about to be thirty. She hated getting older.

one's spirits up is never to meet lovely young American ladies of 23 or gay young men of twenty. If we all move along together, taking care to only meet elderly consuls, business men & old widows, moving in a bunch to our Doom the chances are we will keep up the illusion even at forty that we are not antiques in an art school class room [...]

Gerald, dear I send you so much love.

And don't part with any of your mss to Virginia. Remember you belong by a previous bargain to me & after that to a possible Tidmarsh Press. I care so much.

Your loving Doric

The possibility of letting the Mill to the 'lovely young American ladies' while the threesome were away came to nothing; Lytton took against them and forbade it. But Carrington had been genuinely smitten by Henrietta; her playful admission to Gerald, very much in the idiom of the Mill when a new attractive young man or woman appeared on the scene, was only partly a tease.

Henrietta Bingham (1901–61) was visiting England with her friend, former tutor and first love Mina Kirstein. She was the wayward bisexual daughter of a rich Kentucky family; her father wanted her 'cured' of her homosexual inclinations, for which she was soon being 'treated' in London by Freud's leading follower, Ernest Jones.

The journey to North Africa began on 21 March. Carrington spent a week ill in bed, but wrote many long descriptive letters to Gerald. They returned via Sicily and Rome.

To Gerald Brenan

Written in the train between Tunis and Constantine
[About 23 March 1923]

Last night after tea which I brew in the hotel on a spirit lamp, Ralph and I went for an exploration into the Jewish quarter of Tunis. At first we only saw the curious Yiddish eating houses and souks; there seemed no definite distinction between the Moslem quarters and those of the Jewish people. Suddenly we came to a very narrow little alley with only room for two people to walk abreast. In front of us walked a little girl of ten, very gaily dressed, a short frock above her knees, white socks, enormous fat pink legs, walking in little wooden pattens very slowly, picking her way through puddles, as it had been raining all day. Her hair was short, yellow tied with a big bow. We felt we had reached the 'nymphs' quarter!

Suddenly she turned around. Her face was that of a hideous harlot old and jaded, covered with thick paint, terribly made up. Then we saw more and more of those horrible FAT creatures, the alley grew narrower. Some in chemises just below their parts, all with bare legs, except for the low white socks. They lay on little benches at the door of their little houses, which seemed to consist of a single room, and hung about in groups at the doors. They shrieked at us. I couldn't make out if they were French or Jewesses. I think French. But you can't conceive the effect it had on one, seeing these creatures, touching them, for the alley was so narrow. They were painted as pantomime girls are painted for the stage and all in these ridiculous 'little girl' dresses with fat doll-like legs. Ralph was excited at these apparitions. I confess I was filled with a curious terror. One awful thing was that the men, some Moslems, some French, walking down the alley looked at them perfectly calmly and cynically. We saw some amazing scenes in the other alleys. Bake houses; a huge negro with a great tray of little cakes which he was putting in a huge oven. His face and bare top of his body lit up by the red furnace. Little coffee houses with Moslems sitting around on high shelves against the walls, cross-legged and smoking. Basket and rope shops with huge monster moham-madans and lying on heaps of plaited rushes, like great sheiks in some Arabian Night's Dream. One in a little eating house suddenly leered and made a most dreadful face at me like one of those lecherous Chinese masks. As a rule they hardly looked at one, or if they do, scowl.

Coming back we came across another Jewish quarter, with dark olive skinned women all painted and bedecked with earrings, long greasy black hair and Eastern trousers and shawls. They were obviously harlots; one saw inside little rooms with divans, and old hags equally painted.

It's queer leaving these little alleys and souks to come through a big archway and find trams, civilized French women and men in Paris clothes. Bon marchés and post offices [...]

To Gerald Brenan

[Kairouan, Tunisia]
27 April 1923

I will write a more orderly letter soon. I hope you keep well. I long to have news of you, and hear all about the Woolfs. You can't be too enthusiastic, to please me, over Virginia! I always feel she is one of the few people it has actually been tremendously good fortune to have known in this life. I am sure few women since the beginning of the world have equalled her for wit and charm, and a special rare kind of beauty.

This will be one of the longest holidays we have ever made. I doubt if we will be back in ENGLAND until the middle of May now. We spent a whole month at that curious place Hammam-Meskoutine. I don't regret it. For one never really enjoys a place utterly to its fullest until one has been there a long time. The last evening there was perhaps the most perfect. I had not been outside in the fields for nearly a week as I had been in bed. Everything had a peculiar vividness for this reason. I fell in love with olive trees again. The blue borage, orange marigolds, yellow daisies, and purple gladiolas seemed to me more brilliant and wonderful than I had thought before. We sat in a little grass valley, looking down a steep bank on to a little stream, which ran dark, and cold like some black snake beneath the oleanders, heavy palm trees, and tropical oaks. The gnats flew from flower to flower shining in the sun which was just sinking behind the great mountains. The asphodels looked ghostly pale and transparent and their stalks were invisible against the green grass, only their pink-grey flowers were lighted by the sun. Lytton read us Keats: 'Endymion' and 'The Nightingale'. The air was very still and hot, and I thought Keats and this world had never been so exquisitely beautiful before. The sun sank and we walked along the ridge of the hill through the olive trees, and asphodels listening to the nightingales and croaking frogs. To feel such ecstasy seems to me to make life, even if all the other days were dull and tiresome in the year, worth living. Someday you must go to Meskoutine. I am sure nowhere so much pure beauty is contained. I cannot forget those fields of flowers, and the amazing beauty of the mountains.

To Gerald Brenan

Kairouan
Monday [28] April 1923

This is a superb town! The raging wind had gone down, and the sky is completely blue. We have just seen the great mosque. One is allowed inside, for in 1840, the French stabled their horses inside, and so defiled the mosque for good. It is far more beautiful than Cordova, with a vast marble courtyard outside surrounded by a colonnade of marble pillars, which I think were taken from Carthage. Lytton has been buying leather morocco skins in the souks this morning. They are absurdly cheap, even although we are swindled, I expect, by these crafty Moslems [...]

Yesterday we had coffee outside a little Moorish coffee house, and watched the sun go down. The good Moslems eat nothing from sunrise to sunset now for 40 days. It's very simple and rather extraordinary to see them sitting in rows outside the eating houses with oranges and cakes in their hands waiting until the muezzin from the minaret cries out. Then they all fall on their food, and drink up their cups of coffee.

Kairouan is far more Eastern than Biskra. There are only 500 Europeans in the whole population, and no French buildings, and only this one hotel.

One sees no great sheiks or chieftains or Arab horses. Do write to me. We won't leave Rome c/o Thomas Cook until the 12th of May about and then Tidmarsh. My fondest love.

Doric

To Virginia Woolf

The Mill House
Sunday, 20 May 1923

Dearest Virginia,

We are back again [...] One expected a crowd of enthusiastic friends at Victoria, a budget of letters at Tidmarsh. There was nothing! Then I read last night your account of Spain and I felt you were the only person who understood the immensity of travelling to Timgad and Segesta and returning to England. Perhaps Hogarth didn't disappoint you. I confess I was depressed the moment we climbed on board our ship at Boulogne (yesterday afternoon), and saw Bonar Law's[1] dreary yellow face on the deck, and the crowds of dull English travellers. I even turned traitor to Kent and Sussex and despised them. The Clapham back gardens with the hens. But still I felt we were travelling to Tidmarsh and that the moment I saw its beauties my spirits would revive. Do you know for the first time in my life I turned against our Mill? I suddenly felt, as I suspect all our visitors feel, how very flat and provincial it was and that the ducks, and chickens were just as dull as the ones in the Clapham back gardens. My mother was here and had put new covers on all the chairs and made the insides of all the rooms look completely hideous. But even she did not entirely account for my depression. One didn't realise what an exciting and beautiful life one had led these last two months until last night. You will suspect me imitating your travels in Spain if I tell you of all our adventures in Italy in this letter. And although I know you will accuse me of flattery I must tell you I thought your essay was amazing! Everything came back to me. Every word you wrote gave me a vision of scenes I had quite forgotten and I loved you for writing it. This letter is all

---

1 Andrew Bonar Law (1858–1923), Conservative politician, had been Prime Minister Since 1922. He resigned through illness and died later that year.

a prologue to a cadge for an invitation to Hogarth. Will you ask me to tea
with you. So that I can talk to you alone, of all your adventures, and Gerald?
I can easily come up for a day, or will you both visit this rather despondent
Mill? Gerald alone did not play me false, last night and wrote me a long
letter. But he simply omitted to tell me one word about the last month
because he said you would tell me everything.

This is such a stupid letter. But I feel so excited and at the same time
depressed that I can do nothing sensibly.

The cold here is dreadful after Rome and I can hardly bear the way the
elms seem to press against the windows, after living in an Archbishop's
Palace at Ravello that looked across the Bay to Paestum.

Lytton comes back tomorrow and then perhaps by murmuring the mystic
words Segesta ... and removing the chair covers one will gain a little of
one's lost happiness. Dear Virginia, I do so long to see you again. Please
give Leonard my love. I send you a little present which I brought you in
Rome. Perhaps round your garden hat?

My fondest love
Yr old Carrington

*Although their relationship was increasingly fractious, when travelling with Lytton
Carrington and Ralph were in harmony, both of them dedicated to his welfare and
enjoyment. Back in Tidmarsh, she found herself discontented, especially after Virginia
Woolf gave her news of Gerald.*

To Gerald Brenan

The Mill House
Sunday, 28 May 1923

Amigo, I put off writing the long letter that had been fermenting in my
head since we left Italy because it is so difficult to write letters off hand,
and then when I got back to England I felt the most violent depression which
has only just left me. We have now been exactly a week in England. It was
madness to return. Rome is a far better place in which to live than this flat
greenery. The cold is awful in England. I was going to write to you this long
letter after I had seen Virginia but then something she told me when I went
to tea with her last Wednesday made everything vanish out of my head.

I wanted to go to tea with her alone, but that wasn't possible, as R was
in London with me. Still it didn't really make any difference really. Virginia
said just as I was putting a piece of stale ice cake into my mouth, 'You know

Gerald is going to get married; he has just written and told Leonard that he is engaged to that American girl.'¹ I think it was the word 'engaged' that made me feel that it wasn't true and that made me rather angry. I felt Virginia couldn't know you very well to use such a word in reference to you, or perhaps everything had changed. I quickly argued that my feelings were absurd, all words are absurd and 'engaged' is just as good a word as 'bedding'. Then she said: 'I thought he probably would get married very soon, but of course it may be one of his jokes.'

I wish I could have the definite feelings that Ralph has, he was plunged into a profound gloom, and felt he must go out and see you at once.

All the way back from Richmond, he talked about you and saw all the horrors of marriage, the end of our friendship and every possible disaster. If it is true that E is going to live with you, or marry you, Gerald, I am so very glad. Because at any rate for a certain time, a few years, you will be happy, or happier than you have been this last year. No one but a fool imagines that he can be certain of achieving happiness for more than a few months. If it was only one of your passing jokes to Leonard which he misunderstood, then all I have written is unnecessary. But I wanted to tell you, because I think I probably care more for your happiness than anyone else, that I am very glad if you are going to be happy with E.

Will you please write, and tell me soon. It does in a curious way make rather a difference. I am not going to write a long letter today. In a few days I will.

In any case I refuse to believe our friendship was so ordinary that if you take a new friend, or a wife, to yourself, our relation ends. Ralph couldn't understand why I wasn't 'hurt'. Really he understands very little of my feelings for you. Perhaps I shall be more contented if you remove finally all possibility of my ever coming to Spain alone. In spite of growing older I still find I have lapses. I am often very stupid. I hate facing certain things as impossibilities and seeing the limitations of our life.

Your letter is in my hand. It is not true that R is more human than I am and has no feelings about classes. You only know such a small portion of my life. You do not know the number of 'ordinary' friendships I make and my attachments for such people.

I told Virginia I wasn't surprised and that I guessed you would soon marry E. it was only half true. I wanted to gain a little time to hide my feelings from her. Then it is partly true for ever since you first told me about E I had faced this probability.

Perhaps if you have her with you, you will be able to regard me more easily as a 'neuter' friend. It's pretty depressing what a mess I made of your feelings and of mine this last year. I always thank you for not reviling me.

---

1 The identity of the American girl Gerald called E is unknown.

Virginia was so charming. But it was a slight nightmare. I longed to talk to her about you, ask her hundreds of questions. But I felt as if there was a glass window between us and that she couldn't hear what I was saying.

The flowered cottons were lovely. They looked so beautiful in the sitting room at Hogarth. Ralph's without a job. I hardly think we will ever get a Press. There seems no money to start it with. Perhaps something will turn up soon [...]

If you are happy, or unhappy it matters to me. It will be a relief if for a change I am not responsible.

I think Ralph is writing to you. His agitation over your fate shows how deeply he cares. I have seldom seen him so upset. In a few days I will write sensibly of other matters. Even if you become a Moslem and marry four wives I am damned if I will stop writing to you.

Gerald dear I send you my love.

I can hardly bear Barbara going out to you. It's intolerable. Why do you allow it! Why can everyone go to Spain and stay with you except your rejected, and deserted

QUEEN OF NOTHING

PS Tidmarsh seems incredibly squalid and cramped after Ravello. And I hate these backyard hens and ducks. Ugh! Perhaps we will leave it soon. It is too green and stuffy.

The strength of Carrington's and Ralph's reactions to the rumours (which turned out to be unfounded) of Gerald's engagement shows how emotionally involved they were with him. Both felt he belonged to them. Unsettled, Carrington began to think of moving on from Tidmarsh, which had started to feel claustrophobic and had been tainted by the Great Row of the year before. There was no question of breaking up the ménage, which remained central to their lives, but with Lytton increasingly pursuing romances with young men and Ralph falling in love with Frances Marshall it was clearly changing.

To Gerald Brenan

The Mill House
31 May 1923

Amigo, I will make some attempt to fill in the gaps now, the interval between Rome (two weeks now) and Tidmarsh. But it shows how dreary everything is, travelling, London, gossip, all dreary compared to friendship. Because in spite of my head being fuller than it's ever been full before of things I want to tell you, I can only remember Virginia saying: 'Gerald has just told Leonard that he is engaged.'

I remember so accurately what happened a year ago today. You probably can't remember. The gloomy days of despair didn't begin until June 7th for us. How I sympathise with those aged women who suddenly say over the cold mutton on Sunday evening: 'exactly twenty years ago, I and my dear husband ... ' 'It was just this time of the year, I remember the apple blossom on the grass, and the organ grinder ... ' I used to wonder how my mother remembered. I see really it's one of the forms of masturbation, self-indulgence. One doesn't want to forget. I went up to London yesterday. I telephoned Virginia. I wanted to go and see her alone. I wanted to hear more about you. But she was away from Richmond. You can't tell me anything. So don't bother to write me a sermon of reproaches and explanations. If you tell me anything at all, I shall understand. I know you couldn't have remained a hermit for ever and I have said every time I read a letter from you that I didn't deserve such luck to have your letters. And when you said our friendship was futile and probably doomed from all the circumstances, I knew you were right. But I thought perhaps because nothing ever happens as I expect it will happen, that perhaps we might always be friends. Perhaps you were really as curious as I thought you were. What I regret, and always will regret, is I didn't know you better when I might have known you. And you never knew how fond I was. I concealed that. I can't think why I did now. At the time there seemed some reason for it.

But I will refrain from more masturbation of the spirit. And I will go back to my old philosophy that one need never be gloomy about the future, since it is never what one thinks it will be. I wish, so very much, I could come out with Barbara to Yegen. I find one doesn't care for new people. And when I hear news of you indirectly, all my old impatience to see you again and laugh and joke, comes back to me. I am going to do my best to prevent Ralph getting involved in a business which prevents him having holidays. Then unless you lose all your money, or become a hopeless family man, we may meet more often. Shall I tell you what comes into my head. I don't really see that it matters. The difficulty is, without making a letter as bulky as the Bible, to describe one's exact feelings. The reason why your friendship matters is because you are nearer to me in spirit than anyone else. I agree so very closely with your views on life. It gives me a support, and a self respect for myself. Lytton has the effect of making me feel so stupid and hopeless about myself that I wish to avoid the world and retreat. It isn't that he thinks this about me, it's grasping his standards and preciseness, his truth and the way he is 'himself' so entirely. Ralph has the opposite effect. I feel it isn't a very serious matter after all and that one had better face oneself and then leave it alone. When

I talk to you, I am not conscious of all these struggles, I feel clearer when I read your letters but not gloomy.

How badly I express this. It seems complete balderdash when I read it over. And yet when it came to the point I couldn't face giving up Ralph and Lytton for you. All I want to put forward to you is my point of view. I can't give my reasons for caring for you. Although it's illogical and impossible I do still care [...]

It's curious but no matter what you do, or say, I never for a moment feel angry or criticise you. If you marry: in you I see it's perfectly sensible and even courageous. If you don't marry I think you are equally original. Alix would say I've a complex about you. Probably, I often suspected it. I am in love with Shelley and so I pretend Shelley lives in you and you can never do wrong for me. In any case I should make the most of your rare advantages, and trounce me and bounce me since you cannot turn me into a vixen!

[...] Yesterday I went up to London to my dentist again. I spent all the rest of the day with Alix. She is amazing. She never disappoints me. She always has some amusing new mood. Yesterday she had developed an aesthetic mood, and bought two carpets of great beauty for her rooms and told me the Cambridge gossip. Morgan Forster spent last weekend with us. I always feel that I know him so well before he comes, but when he is actually here, I feel rather shy with him [...]

I hated Switzerland. We passed through the Simplon tunnel and saw all the grand mountains, and lakes, complete with sunset, Swiss cows, chalets, and glaciers. It seemed to me a monument of all that was pretentious, and vulgar in the Victorian epoch. The country between Naples and Rome was lovely. Wonderful fields of corn, and vineyards, with distant blue mountains. It reminded me of that lovely blue picture by Poussin in the Louvre, *Ruth and Boaz*. Beautiful women with bare legs and feet, broad straw hats and blue pinafores were heaping hay on to great carts in the fields.

They looked so gay, but at the same time classical. One returns to England and finds wet green fields, cold winds, and perpetual rain and females in the fields wearing artificial silk jerseys, with hideous young men in navy blue serge Sunday clothes. You have no idea how I hated Tidmarsh when we came back [...] It's better now. Two weeks have dulled my sensations. I still hate the ducks and the bees, but I no longer think of Ravello, and Rome.

I am contemplating buying a studio, and putting it up in the garden. I find the room-space is too cramped. But perhaps we will leave Tidmarsh next year; then it won't be worth while. I want to find a house on the Lambourn Downs. I think it's a mistake to become sentimental over any place and I can't quite get over my hatred for this garden and the dull green fields since our return from Rome [...]

I advise you to take a ship to Naples and inspect Amalfi to Ravello. All the country from Amalfi to Calva seemed to me very good. My mother now lives near Newbury in an old Georgian cottage. Ralph and I go over and see her once a week and loot her house of eatables and clothes. Today Ralph found in the old cellars beneath her house 8 very old wine flasks. They must be some 300 years old. I have washed them and put them on the dresser. They are amazingly beautiful. Dark olive green. One has a glass seal on it with three wild geese, and a hand rampant.

Next week we will see Duse act in *Ghosts*.[1] Lytton has just read the play to us. We are now reading *Othello* in the evenings. Lytton acts the moor superbly whilst he reads. I am sending you Middleton Murry's new magazine [the *Adelphi*] It really is very good reading!

Can you imagine a man of education could sink so low? You must read the story of Mr Joiner and Rosie. It is thought Middleton Murry himself wrote it. It should be called 'The Servant Maid's Adelphi.' I am going to write them a little story about a charwoman and a lost hairpin in a drain. I promise you it will be accepted. Let us lower the *Adelphi* until even the scullery maids reject it!

Friday, 1 June 1923
Lytton finished reading *Othello* last night. It is almost too moving [...]

Reading *Othello* made me realise last night that a year is not long enough to forget some things. Ten years is a more suitable interval. Bless you. I send you my love. Don't answer this letter. I write it in a particular mood. By the time you answer would reach me, I should feel differently. I think I only just want to hear about you. For the moment I am bored by myself. I will send you some photographs soon. Perhaps Barbara will take them to you.

Your loving Doric

Reading this over before I post it, it seems to be rather a dismal wail from a cast-off mistress! But I didn't mean it to be that. I merely want to ask you to write to me, since no matter what the news was that I received through Virginia, if you were ill, if you were going to America, becoming a sailor, marrying an American, I should at once want to hear more about it from you. Anyway she told me nothing except extolling your virtues, which after all I knew about better than she did. I really only want to have a letter from you. Nothing more. I've long realised my life will never change much. If you marry, you will join

1 Eleanora Duse (1858–1924), celebrated Italian actress, came out of retirement to tour Europe in 1921. Mrs Alving in Ibsen's *Ghosts* was one of her greatest roles.

the fixtures, fixed gas brackets. I would persuade you eloquently against the few years of loneliness and isolation that I lived through after I left the Slade.

The great thing I am sure is to realise the grotesque mixture of life, the pleasures of being loved and loving and having friends, and the pains and sordidness of the same relations. The pleasures of freedom, and isolation, and the despairs at the same time which beset one in that state. One year I would like to take an average of the days one is happy against the wretched days. Perhaps it's absurd to ever think about it. If one painted pictures it wouldn't matter and one probably wouldn't think about it. But I can't see the use of painting pictures 'as good as' those at the London Group. I think except for a few French artists, and perhaps two English artists there are NO important LIVING artists. Painting hasn't advanced, there are very few inventors and original artists alive now. They reduce painting to the same culture as architecture, and furniture, always reviving some style and trying to build up a mixture with dead brains. The French cover their tracks better than the English do. But really I don't think much of this revival of Rembrandt, nudes à la Rubens, imitations of the naïve artists, Poussin. Matisse seems to me one of the most definitely original artists alive now. I think all this 'culture', and 'groups' system perhaps is partly the reason of the awful paintings produced. Then the intelligence of most English painters is so low. They are only fit to be house decorators.

Do you know, plain and aged that I am, I made a conquest just before I left England, at a party given by David Garnett?[1] An American girl. I only know her name is Henrietta. She has the face of a Giotto Madonna. She sang exquisite songs with a mandolin, southern state revivalist nigger songs. She made such wonderful cocktails that I became completely drunk and almost made love to her in public. To my great joy Garnett told me the other day she continually asks after me and wants me to go and see her. I am sure she is far more beautiful than your E! And if you think I am imitating you I tell you I am not. Ralph cut my hair too short last week. When it has grown longer and my beauty restored, I shall visit the lovely Henrietta and revive our drunken passion. Gerald dear I care so much for you. Forgive me for whining and write to me soon.

D.C.

---

1 For his thirty-first birthday. He was to pursue Mina without success though they became great friends, and had a brief affair with Henrietta.

After a holiday in France with Lytton, Sebastian Sprott and Barbara, Carrington, to Lytton's alarm, began to pursue her plan to visit Gerald in Spain. Ralph's father died in August, necessitating a reluctant visit to his mother in Devon.

To Lytton Strachey

Cofton, Star Cross, Exeter
Thursday morning [September 1923]

Dearest Rat-Husband,
    I wish you'd play your pipes and lure your two Mopsämen home again. The cold here is terrible. LISTEN, with all this wealth we have NO FIRES in any rooms in this house. I was simply frozen to a block of salt last night sitting round a table in a large dining room with the rain and wind beating against the window pane, and NO FIRE. Give me our poverty stricken life with rats, and a FIRE. The conversation is entirely about money and investments. Poor Mrs Partridge is in a great flutter because she saw Mr Sparke's estate announced in *The Times* and she realised her estate will have to be exposed to every curious eye. She is terrified someone will snatch her money if they know how much she has. Really it's Tchekhov it's so mad. Père Perdrix left over £38,000 in England, the India estate isn't settled yet. And yet they are too poor to have FIRES. GRRRR. We only just bear up. Thank goodness escape will soon be here. The port was superb last night. But the females hardly sipped it. It might have been medicine. Cider is 1910, and more delicious than any cider I've ever tasted. A dreadful poor relation is staying in the house with a face like the fish footman in *Alice in Wonderland*. She sews curtains, and occasionally murmurs 'in Cornwall I've often noticed ... ' But no one ever listens, so she never finishes her sentence [...]
    Ralph looks very beautiful in his velvet jacket. It would be good to get back to our Lytton again and fire. I hope darling your cold is better, and you aren't feeling depressed [...] The weather is quite as FOUL here as Tidmarsh. My fondest love and a kiss from the
    Mopsa

To Gerald Brenan

The Mill House
Sunday evening [15 September 1923]

It's all settled dearest, we BOTH will come!!!!!! Ralph has written you a letter swearing he will come. Today he had a talk with Lytton on a walk and told me afterwards that Lytton relents and so I shall come. So WE BOTH will come some time the end of November and stay at least a decent lengthed month with you at Yegen [...]

Virginia and Leonard are really superb people. We visited them on our way back. I always choose the Newhaven crossing, it's such a good place to see England at its best. We drove straight to the Woolves in the car. They are only a few miles from Newhaven; Sussex is a wonderful county!

That part round Newhaven is filled with queer memories for me. We always went to Seaford or Brighton every year. And as I hated the sea, and bathing with family groups I used to walk on the Lewes downs, and paint. Within a stone's throw of the Woolves'old house. Little did she think that L.S. would kiss her on those downs. And turn her into a poetical dormouse. But that's a long story [...]

I like the Woolves far more than they like me. Ugh. I have a queer love for Virginia which fills me with emotion when I see her. They talk better than any people I know. How quickly the conversation becomes intelligent and amusing when Virginia talks! We slept at Lewes in a superb old English Inn. The beauty of England, even although it is so vulgar after France, makes one's heart warm with an inside joy. It soon vanishes, but the first two days are always remarkable to me for their vividness.

Tidmarsh was exquisite with its rows of shining books, and the dresser with your plates.

Again I thank you for those plates. It's an achievement to have given me two presents which I literally look at every day and then think of you. The little picture on my mantelpiece and the plates. I wrote this morning a frantic letter telling you we are coming in December. It's true unless I commit some incredible act of folly, or unless Ralph changes his mind ... We are now on the most amiable terms. And I can't see any reason why we shouldn't go on being sensible like this, at any rate until December.

Ralph's carrying on some intrigue in London at the moment, so I sit alone in the dining room. Looking out not on anything as poetical as your mountains and blue skies, but on dark sombre elms and privet hedges [...] Don't get ill on your travels. I dread these months before November. My dear I am so happy.

Your, elated
Princess of Georgia

Carrington hoped that Ralph's 'intrigue' – his pursuit of Frances Marshall – meant that he would be more easygoing about her relationship with Gerald.

To Gerald Brenan

In the top attic, Tidmarsh
Tuesday afternoon [about 8 October 1923]

My Dear, I can't write you letters when I don't know if you are at Yegen.
Then I keep on saying one more month and I will be at Yegen. That makes
it seem absurd to tell you what I am thinking in a letter, when we will talk
to each other so soon. You can't think with what restraint I behave. I hardly
ever mention Spain, even to Ralph. I feel if I pretend outwardly that it is
very improbable I shall go, God with His white beard who dominates our
lives from the top of the apple tree won't be able to frustrate us.

Are you really excited, as excited as I am? [...]

I shall buy painting materials at Granada. I know where there is quite a
good shop, on the hill, on the left hand side. We won't stop at a single place
on the way until we reach Granada. I long to come by Lanhiron, you know
what I mean, the way we came with Lytton, or will the river be too full?
Ralph is up in London today book binding. He lives a very gay life with
intrigues, and love affairs, after his book bindings shut up. He is much happier
now he is working for himself, and not under Leonard [...]

Do you allow me to admire Mr Norman Douglas? Lytton was so taken
with *Alone* he bought an entire set of all his books. I was very delighted
with *South Wind*. It seemed to me so interesting. But after that *Fox into Lady*
faux pas I hardly dare venture an opinion.[1]

Just to annoy you, I tell you Garnett has been awarded two of the grandest
prizes in literature this year amounting to several hundreds [...]

My fondest love.
The restored
Princess of Georgia

To Lytton Strachey

102 Ridgemount Gardens, London
Saturday [17 November 1923]

Lying low, very low, very low indeed.

Darling Lytton, I lie low with the fiend, and lower still after an entire
glass of sherry. So forgive my wandering wits [...] A curious evening here

---

1 Norman Douglas (1868–1952), writer and hedonist who made little secret of his predilection for boys,
   lived in Capri. His best-known novel, *South Wind*, was published in 1917. *Alone*, a travel book, had just
   come out.

last night, Marjorie S your sister, Frances Marshall your niece-in-law, and Missie Partridge. Marjorie S was at her wildest. She sang us song after song. Dorothy P who had never heard, or seen anything like Marjorie before was completely bowled over! It was an extraordinary merry evening. Missie sang Mozart most beautifully. Even Marjorie was very pleased I think with her voice. Sweet Frances sang Purcell, Ralph sang Spanish songs, and only the Monster Mopsa was silent [...]

I saw James yesterday. I lunch with them today. James says we must get Ham Spray and supports every extravagance! But then he is already bankrupt. What are we to do? I feel in terrible despair! I can hardly bare to let it fade, and yet it seems impossible unless the other client turns out to be a straw scare-crow. Lytton you are a darling. Perhaps I might see you next Tuesday for a moment ... I love you Lytton more and more, and you can't think how much I miss you although it's only yesterday that we parted [...] I hope you will enjoy yourself very much. The car is a great boon in London. We went for a drive in it this morning. It is such fun. Bless you a thousand times for being such an angel to me and to us.

Your loving and most intoxicated Mopsa

Ham Spray was a handsome farmhouse with eight bedrooms near Hungerford beneath the Berkshire Downs, where Carrington had long dreamed of living. Ralph had inherited some money from his father, and the plan now was that he and Lytton should buy the house together.

To Gerald Brenan

The Mill House
Thursday, 20 November 1923

Amigo, a despair has fallen over me. Not a reason that will draw forth sympathy from you.

I am in love with a house ...

For the last week I have been in the depths of misery. For it is apparent that I will never posess this enchanted house. My hatred for Tidmarsh, for love, for everyone has reached a crescendo – I feel nobody sympathises. Ralph is in love with a blackhaired beauty and thinks life perfect. Lytton thinks life what it is, and is not surprised at our failure to posess this house [...] So I keep my griefs to myself and only sulk outwardly.

How I hate Mrs Partridge and her idle thousands. A mere five hundred pounds would gain for me my Elysium.

We come to Spain.
Today even that sentence doesn't make me happy ...
Bless you, your weeping
Queen of Georgia

A month later, with Ham Spray still in the balance, Carrington and Ralph set off for Spain. Ralph was trying to persuade Frances Marshall to meet them in Paris on their way home; Carrington was hoping that Lytton would also join them there.

PART THREE

Ham Spray House,
Hungerford . Berks.

The Erosion of Happiness: 1924–1932

Two places, Carrington wrote, were written on her heart: Watendlath (where her romance with Gerald really began) and Tidmarsh. Ham Spray was a larger and more distinguished house, with its classic Queen Anne front and veranda looking across fields to the hills. She turned it into the perfect setting for Lytton, somewhere he could arrange his library and write his books and see his friends, and where she herself had a big studio. But the happiness and ease of the early days at Tidmarsh were not to be recaptured. There were many hilarious gatherings and good times, but the best times of all for Carrington were when she was alone with Lytton, and this never happened quite often enough.

At Ham Spray the ménage a trois was never settled. Gradually it expanded to include other lovers for all three of them. After the crisis over Carrington's attachment to Gerald, Ralph's own affair with Valentine Dobrée faded away, but he had other lovers before falling in love and finding a permanent partner in Frances Marshall, which Carrington minded more on Lytton's behalf than her own. For herself, she could only accommodate lovers who understood that her love and loyalty were fundamentally Lytton's. Apart from Gerald, they all did. She accepted Lytton's series of relationships with young men, several of whom became her close friends and correspondents; only his last serious attachment, to Roger Senhouse, with whom he hoped to set up house in London, unnerved her. Her own dalliances with women, apart from one, were less serious, more a source of fun and distraction than anything deeper.

The greatest threat to her happiness at Ham Spray came after Ralph and Frances came back from a journey to Spain in the autumn of 1925 announcing that they planned to live together. Carrington's great fear was that if Ralph withdrew from Ham Spray life Lytton would not want to carry on. Her concerns were not unfounded; Lytton was very fond of her, but he had always feared her emotional dependence, and worried about their companionship without the influence of Ralph's reassuring, practical, familiar masculinity. After a short but painful period of negotiation the situation settled down; but inevitable tensions remained. Both Lytton and Carrington, while never disliking Frances, found her constant presence difficult. It was not easy for her, either; as she later wrote, at Ham Spray she felt neither guest nor host. The women did their best, but by 1928 the situation was making them both wretched. Frances became depressed and ill, while Carrington, whose tormented relationship with Gerald was finally coming to an end, began to write in her diary of her loneliness and fears for the future. She also began to drink rather too much. The diary which she began in January 1928, when she found herself alone and unwell (writing on the cover, in a typical but somehow significant slip of the pen 'D.C. Partride. Her book'), gives an impression of increasing unhappiness. 'The year ended rather melancholy', she wrote. 'The great distinction suddenly seemed to appear between couples supporting each other – & isolated figures unattached [...] If one becomes detached there seems a danger of becoming eccentric, and old maidish. A dislike against the melange of living too closely against other people'. She had ominous dreams, about Mark Gertler and about Ralph. In one, she was frightened by strange shadows on the lawn 'so I called to R who I knew was talking upstairs, I could hear his voice but I couldn't make any words carry, so then I crawled because I was so terrified on my hands and knees indoors to the foot of the stairs, & cried Ralph ... and tried to cry louder, but only made noises in my throat...then I heard quite clearly his voice arguing with F saying "the point about Ibsen is" and I realised with terror it was no good, I couldn't interrupt and I woke up trying to cry loud'.

For all her deep ambivalence about men, something in Carrington still needed a male presence in her life. She also found to her surprise that she missed sexual contact. She had a brief affair with the bisexual and sexually voracious sculptor Stephen Tomlin, who was also a passing lover of Lytton's and might, according to Gerald Brenan, have been a substitute for Ralph in the Ham Spray triangle, but this possibility evaporated when he took up with Julia Strachey. She had an even less serous fling with a Cambridge academic, Peter Lucas. Then, a handsome younger man from a family long connected with Bloomsbury entered her life. Bernard Penrose, known as Beakus, became her lover, and proved to her and to those around her that she was not just an eccentric old maid.

Although she was always thinking about painting, and regretting her lack of dedication to her art, she exhibited only once more, in Salisbury in 1930, and sold no paintings during the Ham Spray years at all. Instead, she took up making decorative glass and silver-paper pictures, designing tiles for friends kitchens and bathrooms, and decorating walls, furniture and cupboards. Ham Spray, and the life she made there around Lytton, took up almost all her creative and artistic energies. When he was away, she relied more and more on the Augustus John clan, who had come to live nearby. Her greatest fear remained that of losing Lytton.

1924

In Yegen, it proved difficult for Carrington and Gerald to be alone together and tensions simmered. Carrington, who needed Frances to join them in order to keep Ralph happy, sent her glowing accounts; the two women realised they needed to be friends, not rivals.

To Frances Marshall

Yegen, Ugijar, Prov. de Granada
Monday [January 1924]

Dearest Frances,

So many letters seem to have been written to you that I can't think of anything to tell you. I do wish you were a little rasher. Why didn't you abandon all and follow us? The sun alone would have been worth it, and who would live off coffee in Gerrard Street when she could eat persimmons, grapes, oranges and turkey stuffed with chestnuts? And why do people eat breakfast in the cold shades of Brunswick when they might bask in the sun, munch on toast and cherry jam on a roof gazing on the sea and the green mountains of Africa? And who would go to parties in Fulham Road when she could sit over a log fire and watch the dancers of the Alpujarras and hear exquisite shepherds sing ravishing coplas?

I have seldom been so happy continuously day after day. In the afternoon I generally go out with a little village girl of 12 and paint the mountains. She talks to me the whole time in Spanish. To everything I reply 'si, si' occasionally I vary it with 'no intendo'. She sits behind me and holds my paint box for me. R.P. spends most of his day arguing with Gerald. Yesterday we spent an entire day in a village haggling over jugs, and dishes. You would have laughed to have seen the finale: a small upper room in an inn, with about 80 females, children, weeping babies, crowded round us, every few minutes a new person pressed in with a plate. Sometimes terrible little Victorian rosebud horrors, which they were amazed when we refused. At last a small girl brought a broken china duck! The bargaining was terrible. Gerald and Ralph are the most adamant characters. We feel in despair at the thought of ever packing up these objects and getting them to Almeria and then England. I fell off a cliff yesterday into a ditch full of Spanish chestnuts so my hands are engrained with prickles today which is an excuse for writing so badly. I hope in secret you will escape your overseers and come to Paris. Partly I confess because I would like to linger in that town and I know I shall have very little chance unless the Gerrard Street siren is there. Another time Frances you must come to Yegen. It is a unique Arcadia. I am always so fond of you. I was sorry at Tidmarsh I was so distracted with packing, but you will come again when we come back and admire sympathetically all our carpets, and dishes?

My fondest love
Carrington

To Lytton Strachey

Yegen, Ugijar, Prov. de Granada
Before breakfast on the roof, 8 o'ck, 2 January 1924

Dearest,

Do you know we nearly sent you a wire yesterday 'Silence is brutal.' If only you knew how I am tormented in my dreams. Last night a letter came from you saying you had bought Ham Spray for £2000 and were moving in next week! My only correspondents since I left England have been one letter from N.L.C., [Noel] and Mr [Raymond] Mortimer and one from you. Ralph is in a dudgeon because his young lady has only written once. Your fate hangs on today's post. SHOULD the postman NOT bring a letter with the Tidmarsh mark we have resolved NEVER to return, but to live for ever in this TROPICAL heat eating persimmons and listening to the sweet guitars. We had another party the night before, not quite such a large assembly. But some new characters which made it interesting. A lovely Shepherd boy with a much better voice than any we had heard before. To make our presence less royal Gerald asked the young man to dance with me. I had one exquisite dancer he was so pink, and beautifully mannered. I really believe he was at Oxford! The young men are far better looking than the females in this particular village [...] Today is a great 'fiesta'. Already a brass band and a procession has been twice, or even thrice, round the walls of Yegen. Last night they carried, with lanterns and torches, the Holy Virgin round the village. All the windows of the houses were lighted with candles. We watched from our roof. Spanish fire works were sent off. Those that reached the stars were very gorgeous, but far more never left the earth. We live like princes, eating cold turkey and ham every day and drinking Spanish wine.

Yesterday we all walked to Valor and had lunch lying in a grassy grove under some slim grey poplars. How I longed to have you with me lying on the hot bank, gazing up at these exquisite bare poplars against the most delicate of blue skies. A butterfly flew above my head and bumblebees searched for flowers. In the bank we found wild smelling violets. Ralph and Gerald on the way back from Valor after 'tea', i.e. black coffee, bathed in a mountain stream. We then climbed some mountains and came back to Yegen by another way. Gerald reads early Spanish poetry to me and one evening I had a French lesson and read Baudelaire. He has far more books on Verlaine and Rimbaud than you have, with a great many new portraits. He has one book with a facsimile of Rimbaud's poems in manuscript. Have you ever seen it? Ralph is reading the *Arabian Nights* and Proust [...]

Oh Lytton, so often I have longed to have you here, to share all these delights with me. You could not feel Spanish was 'antipathetico' in this weather and with such material pleasures. We have all been very well ever since we came. I do hope Tidmarsh is not uncomfortable for you in any way. I now have a great many new plans for furnishing H[am] S[pray]. All hideous furniture is to be sold and there are to be far fewer objects in the rooms. The pleasure of having so much space and so many rooms is very great here.

We lead very idle lives here. It is impossible to get over the continual pleasure of lying in the sun. But now I go, and paint my landscape.

Must
shall
ought
My love and xxx from your very happy
Mopsa

On 9 January, as they were about to set off for home, Lytton wired to say the purchase of Ham Spray had gone through.

To Lytton Strachey

Hotel de Cataluna, Madrid
[10 January 1924]

My very dearest Lytton,

Your letter has just been given to us by the chief cook [of Thomas Cook & Son]. You are too good, too kind. What can we do? You can't think how moved we are. How terrible the agitation must have been for you all alone. But a triumph I think, for after all we did bring old P down a little. We must hope that the perfection of our lives will be so great in the sun and on the Downs that we will never regret it. I feel certain myself that we will master the situation.

The real thing that matters is the indissolubility of our affections. The addition of hot sun, a veranda and the most beautiful country can only add to an already existing state of perfection. We love you so much. I do not know what to write to you, the past, the present, or the future. I can't also remember how much I told you at Granada. Already I've planned all the rooms at H S, painted them a hundred times, planted the garden, and cut down the fir trees. You were the dearest person in the world Lytton to send that telegram. Please don't be despondent; we will be back very soon now. Did it look lovely in *Country Life*?[1] I always feared the cunning Mrs P would do something to finally break down the spirits. Never have I ever been so full of sensations. They rush through my head like flames up a chimney. But my predominant feeling after reading your letter is to be with you [...]

D. V.[2] Sunday 13th at 6 o'ck we reach Paris and go to the Pas de Calais [hotel].

A little explanation. Ralph told Frances M before he left England that he would be returning to Paris and if she cared to join us for a few days we would be very pleased. (She thought it doubtful so nothing was fixed.) She has just written to Thomas Cook saying that she has been able to get a holiday for a week and will come over next Saturday the 12th. Now the alternatives are

(1) That you will come over and join us for a few days or a week after Clive and Mary have left you on the Monday or Tuesday. In which case a wire from you would summon your faithful attendant spirit to the station to meet you in Paris.

(2) That you won't come because of the storm and the beastly weather. In which case, I will (if F. M. does not object to my departure) come over on the Wednesday by myself and reach you and Tidmarsh as soon as possible. R is compromised, and will have to stay until the end of the week, but he has been such a dear he really deserves a little rest from the fatigues of looking after me, and the crates of china [...]

The Louvre will be shut on Monday, so I would like to spend Tuesday in Paris, so that unless a wire comes, (and unless F. M. objects in which case I will of course wire) I will come over on Wednesday. If a wire comes, we will meet you at the station. I so fear the cold will wreck your health that I do not put our real feelings foremost [...]

If you only knew the agonies we have been through!

Another time we will manage better. But when one is abroad the expense of everything makes one try these curious methods of transport. Ralph has been terribly heroic and sympathetic over it all. We bought 2 lovely chintzes

---

1 Ham Spray had been advertised in *Country Life*.
2 Deo volente (God willing).

in Granada. If we want more, Gerald promises to buy them for us in April and bring them back with him. He was so good to us Lytton. Really, next to you, he is the kindest person I've ever known. He simply heaped presents on us at Yegen. And refused to take any money for our stay with him. He gave us all of his most beautiful plates, and jug. His kindness on the journey to Granada was typical of him. [...] I don't think I've ever been quite so gloomy in my life as on our second day in Granada. The mud in the streets was indescribable and it poured all day. Gerald of course after his gay spirits on the motor bus journey, collapsed into deep sadness. Ralph was rather gloomy; but calm. I felt the change from the beauty of Yegen and the perpetual sun almost as if I had entered a grave in Finland [...] I hope you have kept well all the time we have been away, since you say nothing I hope you are well. You can't think how I long to see you again. I think of you very often. My dearest you are almost too kind to us. I only hope you are as happy, as you have made us. Bless you. Une mille baisers.

Your Mopsa

Later [...] It's wonderful, Lytton, to have Ralph and you, and H.S. altogether to enjoy this year! [...]

After they reached Paris, Frances Marshall arrived and Carrington fell ill. Her spirits improved when Lytton joined them on 12 January, but she was still unwell on their return to Tidmarsh. She confided her reservations about Frances to Gerald.

To Gerald Brenan

The Mill House
Tuesday, II o'ck, 22 January 1924

Dear,

I think R enjoyed Paris very much. He is of course fascinated about his lady. He tells one everything. And goes into her most menial actions. I feel personally a slight gulf of age between her and myself. She has so obviously never loved or felt anything passionately. She has also never suffered. She clearly thinks we make rather a fuss over life. I think it's too big a difference between us. Even Ralph admitted it made a limitation to her understanding. She is also rather egotistical, that is rather terrifying. If you were here I would talk a great deal to you, but I cannot write now. I have not the energy with this aching head to write clearly. But I shall not forget to talk about her when you come in April.

Ralph as I knew he would of course had a reaction on Sunday when he came back here. He tried to make out I wasn't friendly to his liaison, and that I hadn't tried to make friends with her. This was too childish. For I was only twice alone with her for a few minutes and it was perfectly clear she was engrossed in R and hadn't the slightest desire to be my most intimate friend. My sadness in Paris was entirely inside myself. I confess sometimes they annoyed me when I wanted to lie alone in my room by their high spirits, but that was merely my moodiness. I saw underneath R wanted me to object, or be a little difficult to him ... because he saw he had made it rather difficult sometimes for me at Yegen ... but it's only we have different characters. There's no virtue or vice in the matter ... R said 'I tell you all about my feelings for Frances, and go into detail of our relations, and what we discuss, and my lust for her. And you never tell me anything about yourself and Gerald. Whenever I ask, you give me a sort of communiqué. If I want to find out what happens between you and Gerald I have to ask G then if I tax you with what he has told me, you suddenly remember and either deny, or admit what he has told me. For instance, I never know what your physical relations are with G. Would you, if I said I didn't mind, like to go to bed with him? For I would much rather know what your real feelings were, than know you conceal your feelings so as not to hurt my feelings. Why can't you discuss your sensations with G and his feelings for you quite openly?'

I said we did care very much for each other as he knew but that we did not think of going to bed together because we knew he would not be able to bear it. That if he changed his mind completely then possibly we might realize we might like to, but to continually think of something that wasn't possible and agitate our feelings by wanting it, seemed madness. We were quite happy as we were if we could go around together, and the only thing that could spoil our happiness would be if R was injured and made unhappy.

R then said 'But surely even if you know you can't live together, you must know if you would like to.' I said I don't think we ever think about it too much. R said 'You are queer people. Of course you clearly think it spoils something if you describe it in detail to me, and you incidentally find it impossible to analyse your feelings for Gerald, as I do mine for Frances.'

I tell you this because I think it's important. What one has to remember with Ralph is that he has reasonable moods, when he would even perhaps go so far as to think he didn't mind us living together, but I know [given] a reversing of his fortunes, (if F. M. deserted him,) he would then remember my confidences and use them against us. It is of course a temptation because one is interested in truthful discussion to confide everything but I thought it would be folly. I could see no possible purpose, and it would probably be used as a reason for curtailing our liberty in the spring. I tell you in detail what I say to Ralph, because he sometimes plays us off against each other to make us confide in him. Also I have another reason for my reticence. I find it impossible to confide my most intimate feelings for you, to anyone but yourself, and even that is sometimes difficult ...

To Frances Marshall

The Mill House
[23 January 1924]

Dearest Frances,

It was charming of you to think of writing to me. I must confess at once that you are one of the very few young ladies I would ever again chaperone because your behaviour was so perfect! In short you require no chaperoning! I am only sorry I was such a decayed pumpkin the whole of our jaunt in Paris. I now feel rather more decayed, in fact I doubt if I shall survive, my headache grows worse and worse, although I drink purge after purge and drug after drug. I expect every moment Lytton and Ralph in a rage will drive me out of the front door with the cats (who were both sick yesterday) and then throw me and them into the stream [...]

Really Frances, I was a little afraid you might have thought me churlish and green tempered in Paris. But I promise all my glooms and despairs were entirely within myself. I felt far iller than I dared confess because I didn't (a) want to bother Ralph and (b) to bother Lytton after he so nobly came over. I had a suspicion Ralph thought I hadn't been as friendly as I might have been to you. But I really felt too dim to show any signs of life except killing both the Madames at the hotel [...]

I am so sorry you have to go to work every day. And you will come and visit me here in my swamps and bogs one weekend? For I see I shall never reach London.

Give my love to yourself.

Your Carrington

To Gerald Brenan

The Mill House
[3 February 1924]

Dear, oh why did you write that letter to me? Do you want deliberately to end everything or make things difficult? I have told you in every letter I write that I may always be asked by Ralph, that he may read your letter. If you write as you did yesterday you make it impossible for me to show your letters.

He did ask, I refused, and said I was sure you would prefer, and so did I, that he should not read it. He at once became suspicious. So I showed it him. Minus two pages which I was able to extract. He then said 'No wonder you don't want me to read Gerald's letters to you, because he is so obviously in love with you, otherwise why should he be in this state?'

The whole morning has been given up now, to what I most wish to avoid, discussing our relations. Dear, I am not angry, only I feel rather hopeless. Is it not possible for you to realize how difficult it is for me to read your letters in private? That we can only be intimate in our conversations? If you admit you are in love with me Ralph then says he knows it will end in my either giving way to you, suppressing feelings, or making you very unhappy [...] If you must at any time write something indiscreet although I beg you not to, please put it in a small PS so I can show Ralph half the letter.

Yesterday you wrote me a huge package, with one sheet which it was possible to show, and a PS eight pages long. How could I conceal it all, or pretend your envelope contained one sheet? If all this is too tiresome, I feel it may be sometimes for you, tell me. I can't alter it at present [...] One day I shall be forced to tell Ralph simply in self-defence, more than I want to tell him. Please wait until April. I will send you memoirs, letters every day, if only you will not make our friendship impossible. I am to blame you know. I am terribly sorry. Please forgive me. I write on Tuesday next intimately. My very fond love.

Your most loving Doric

[...] **Later**

You mustn't dearest amigo, think I was angry. I couldn't be with you. Also no great harm was done, Ralph was slightly agitated but nothing more only please do not make your letters a source of agitation to me directly I see the outsides of the envelopes!

I must tell you the riveter at Reading has mended the plate so perfectly, not a trace of the breakages remains. So our weeping was imaginary. Your lovely pink primitive house dish stands on the dresser. I do love you for giving it me. We go tomorrow to see Ham Spray House. I write the day after. Please write to me very often, only no gloomy emotions. [...]

I love you very dearly.

Your Doric

To Gerald Brenan

The Mill House
Tuesday morning, 11 o'ck, 4 March 1924

Dearest Gerald,

I hope you will soon write to me. If it wasn't that there is a decree out against protestations and scenes, I could tell you, that I almost wrote off a frenzied appeal for a letter yesterday when no letter came from you.

The last letter you wrote me reached me on Thursday and today is Tuesday.

I feel very gloomy, so do not expect anything but wails, and dismal howls and mia-owls. We went up to London on Saturday morning leaving Lytton fairly well. He has had slight lumbago in his back all this week, but I thought he had practically recovered from the influenza. When I got back on Sunday morning I found he was much worse. Mercifully his sister Pippa was here with him on Saturday, and sent for the doctor. The doctor says it is a relapse after the influenza and that he has fever and must stay in bed some time until he is quite strong. You can think of my feelings when Pippa said: 'I thought it was pleurisy from all the symptoms, but the doctor assures me it is not.' Last night Lytton was worse, and felt new pains in his side. Soon the doctor will be here again, and then I shall know what these pains mean. Although I suspect the doctor is rather an owl, and probably isn't very expert. What a curse diseases are! I feel exhausted with rage against a universe that seems designed to torment people with fevers, or worry people with agitations over sick friends and now of course this train of thought has led me to think of what I have been trying to avoid thinking about, that you may be ill and perhaps that is why you haven't written. I won't let you spend another winter out of my reach.

The Yegen 'landscape' has been held up again by Lytton falling ill. But I am going to start painting again directly I have finished this letter to you [...]

I saw on Saturday afternoon D. H. Lawrence and his fat German spouse Frieda and the great decaying mushroom Middleton Murry and an attending toadstool called Dr Young at Brett's house in Hampstead. I went up there to say goodbye to Brett, but found to my dismay this dreadful assembly of Adelphites. Lawrence was very rude to me of course, and held forth to the assembly as if he was a lecturer to minor university students. Apparently he came back this winter expecting to be greeted as the new messiah. Unfortunately very few saw his divination. The great Dunning almost denied it. A few critics called him a genius but that wasn't enough. 'England is rotten, its inhabitants corrupt.' Mexico is the only country where prophets, and great writers are appreciated. So tomorrow Lawrence, and Frieda and Brett set off in an ocean liner for Mexico.[1]

Of course on examination it comes out it is New Mexico that they go to, which is a state of U.S.A. But they speak about it as 'Mexico'. 'We lead a very primitive life, we cut our own wood, and cook our own food' 'and Lawrence makes the mo-ost beau-ti-ful bread'. Frieda always comes in like a Greek chorus, the moment D. H. L. has stopped speaking. I nearly said he could come to Tidmarsh if that was all he wanted by 'Primitive'.

'And here is Carrington, not very much changed, lost a little of her "ingénue" perhaps, still going to parties, still exactly the same, except I hear you are very rich now, and live in a grand country house.'

I took the shine off his Northampton noise and his whining 'ingénue' accent. I told him I had £130 a year which I had always had.[2] 'Ah but yer married a rich husband!' – 'He has £80 a year.'

'And yer don't mind the change, that's very fortunate.' I report his conversation so you can have an idea of the greatness of our present day geniuses.

He then gave a description of Mexico, with some fine literary passages at which all the assembly looked up and took notes in invisible note books. My brother Noel was at this strange tea party and of course was delighted at talking to the great D. H. Lawrence. Whenever D. H. L. talked about the Mexicans, Indians, Noel made some absolutely boring remarks about Hindus. If D. H. L. described the Rockies and vegetation of the desert in Mexico, Noel at once described the Himalayas!!

The decayed Murry sat on a sofa and said nothing; he swayed backwards and forwards like a mandarin with hollow eyes, toothless gums, a vacant smile and watery eyes. Only once he spoke. 'Say, Brett your butter's bad. It's not good.'(D. H. L. They've scalded it Brett, butter should'na be scalded. They've boiled the milk.') Otherwise the great Murry never spoke. It is reported he has given up the *Adelphi* and is, in a few months, going to follow the Messiah, Frau Messiah, and Brett to Mexico. He said, when asked what it all meant, and what would happen to *Adelphi*, 'Oh, that's the last of my hypocrisies.'

[...] Later, 3 o'ck

The doctor thinks Lytton is going on alright. So my agitations are over. But I expect he will be in bed all this week. I've exhausted all my Yegen memories, so it is time you came back soon, and gave me some new ones [...]

1 The Lawrences were on a visit to England from New Mexico, where their attempts to set up an artistic commune with Brett and other friends had been a failure. They returned later in 1924 to try again. Lawrence had become openly hostile to his former Bloomsbury circle, their open homosexuality and their preoccupation with 'their little swarming selves'.

2 Carrington had inherited some capital from her father and an old family friend from India.

Portrait of Annie Stiles, one of Carrington's favourite
cook-housekeepers at Tidmarsh Mill, 1921

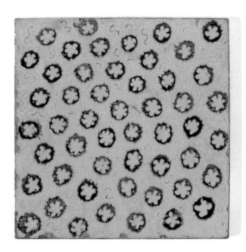

Two examples of the many tiles
designed and made by Carrington
for friends and clients from the
mid-1920s

She also liked to paint furniture:
cabinet, mid-1920s

Tulips in a Staffordshire jug, 1924.
Flowers, especially tulips were among
her favourite subjects

Cactus, c. 1924. This more exotic plant
was perhaps inspired by her travels
in North Africa in 1923

Larrau in the Snow, 1922

Mrs Box, c. 1919. Carrington's monumental
portrait of the farmer's wife and her landlady at
Welcombe, near Bude in Devon

I hope to go to Ham Spray on Friday to see my gardener. We are all going to plant trees. Lytton plans a mulberry, Ralph a medlar, and I shall buy a tulip tree. Will you bring me a small dragon's blood tree from Cadiz, and plant it in a corner of the garden?

Please write to me soon. Throw this dull mutton chop of a letter into the cat's plate, but put the £2 in your pocket. If by any chance you could buy two chintzes, of the same design, I would be grateful, as I want to make curtains for my four poster bed.

You are very dear to me. Bless you.

Your Princess Doric

To Gerald Brenan

The Mill House
Sunday, 23 March 1924

[...] Do you know if I was very rich, I should send telegrams. How fascinating it would be to interchange telegrams with you every few hours from Paris.

Gerald, I am so happy at the thought of you coming back to England that in spite of a certain unease that Lytton's illness gives me, inside, I lead a very happy life. It is alright about Lyme Regis. This elder sister has definitely promised to go with him, so I shall not be involved. Promise you shall send me a wire from Paris telling me when you arrive at Victoria?

Last Tuesday we went to Ham Spray House for a sale of relics. You never saw such objects. It was a fit subject for Virginia's pen. 'Ladies Shooting Boots' went for 2/-. Terrible bamboo furniture, little rockeries of ornaments, faded photographs of young ladies, a Turkish Bat made of india rubber, all these cast off objects were strewn on the lawn in small groups and sold by auction. Everyone pointed us out 'that's Major Partridge and his wife, who have bought the property'. I suddenly felt as if we were appearing in the first chapter of a novel by Morgan [E. M. Forster] [...] and they all saw us. I can't think what they thought. They little knew we were poorest of the company probably.

I've bought a few things very cheap. But most of the things were too horrible, 'gimcrack' to use my father's favourite word.

I am terribly excited over the house!

I was a thousand times right to insist on them buying it. Already I've invested it with a special beauty. The rooms, the arches, passage, have a very definite English character. The garden is romantic and yet very gay with huge bushes of lavender and red hot pokers.

You must be very enthusiastic or I shall be miserable. I know I shall want to show it to you before anything else. Perhaps you will help me paint the inside. I have chosen the colours for the rooms. I shall consult you about a great many things. And I am going to grow the most exquisite flowers [...]

Gerald had decided to leave Yegen for the time being and return to England, where he intended to write a book about St Teresa of Avila and win Carrington. She met him at Victoria Station and spent the night with him at a hotel. After this promising reunion, she was to prove once again that she did not like to be pressured, especially over sex. Moreover Ralph had made it plain that he did not wish to share Carrington sexually with Gerald, as her needs were minimal while his were strong. He continued to supervise her correspondence.

To Gerald Brenan

The Mill House
Thursday, 3 April 1924

Dear, I simply can't tell you how happy you made me yesterday, I am only sorry I was so agitated and rather tiresome over the telephoning.

But that was not our fault. It didn't really matter. I only feared this morning, in the cold light of the Belgravia Hotel, you might think I was rather boring with my perpetual telephones!! Ralph quite understood, and didn't mind of course in the least. The truth was, I was rather tired and exhausted. I only saw, and felt, when I met you, how very much I had been looking forward to yesterday. It made me so happy, that really I minded nothing, not even the post office, or the Belgravia Hotel.

How very fond I am of you.

This morning I looked at all our treasures. I love my white shawl. You will see this summer how beautiful I will look in it, for you. I will see a little figure walking down in Inkpen Beacon; I will then rush into the house, and in a moment, a Botticelli nymph, in a flowered shawl will fly across hedges and dew ponds and treading softly on gentians will meet you [...] Do you know you were very charming, and looked, to me, beautiful.

[...] I could write to you all day. xxxx Don't for mercy's and Miss Moffat's sake write back anything that my mother couldn't read! You are too kind, too kind, she murmured.

PS Oh happy I am! xxxxxxx
[...] Cirod

*Instead of the regular meetings he longed for, they decided on an exchange of long
'diary' letters about their daily doings and their past lives. Gerald wrote at inordinate
length; Carrington's attempt to write the story of her life stopped when she was six.*[1]

To Gerald Brenan

The Mill House
Saturday, 3 May 1924

I haven't finished your diary yet. I've only read one third of it. I read it slowly
because I shall have to give it you back I suppose and I would like to
remember it. I read your letter, it depressed me.[2]

You know I do a great many things, and say a great many things, for your
'good'. I know this will drive you mad. I can't help it. I believe in many
things I am wiser than you. I am more conversant with this world. I know
more than you do, the impossibility for some things. For these reasons I am
sometimes, what you term 'a governess' but I can't help it. And you make
it harder by protesting.

Do you know I really think I shall be glad when we grow up, and become
too old to be tormented by these passions, and emotions!

There! That will encourage you. But I feel it today. Here is a perfect
world. Birds that sing for our delight, veal and ham pies, and rare yellow
wine, for lunch. Fields of cowslips and primrose, tulips in the border,
magnolia trees. Shelley and Keats on the bookshelves. Volumes of learning,
and atlases to prevent our ever becoming bored, music in London. Pictures
in galleries, lovely creatures in the lanes, and streets. Exquisite painted plates
on the dresser, and yet in spite in all of these everyday beauties, we torment
each other, so that everything is useless [...]

But do you know I fail to do almost everything I mean to do. I mean to
write you very well thought out letters. Telling you what you would like to
read, and what would further our intimacy. But I never do. I simply ramble
like a rambler rose all over the fence, vaguely without point [...] Now
everything is put off to Ham Spray. Life will begin there. But perhaps it's
just a new cage I am walking into, a new maze of box hedges from which
I shall never find the way out.

I can't ever decide really when I am face to face with decisions. I find it
easy enough lying in bed early in the morning to plan out wisely my day.

1 See the introduction to Part 1.
2 Gerald was protesting about her elusive and inconsistent behaviour. He was also becoming aware of
   her feelings for Henrietta Bingham, back in England for the summer season.

But then the mere sight of a thousand dandelions may determine me to make a brew of dandelion wine, or a letter from you may make me write verbosities in the attic all the morning, or an argument with Ralph may make me lie in an arm chair in front of the fire.

I would like you to be outside my confusions. I would like to come to you, as a ship into a new harbour, without unloading my perpetual freightage [...] You happened to meet me too late. My life was more or less fixed. We must recover from the irony of that, and evolve a new and extraordinary friendship from our limitations [...]

Do you know, I think I would rather you came the weekend after this – all my reasons? – a) I don't think if you are feeling depressed you will enjoy helping paint walls. And you will be angry with me for wanting to paint. b) the weekend after this H [Henrietta] will be coming, and I would like you to see her. c) I shall be now coming to London on Tuesday. So the gap next week will be less than if we see each other this weekend and Tuesday. And then a long interval. d) I am rather depressed. Paraqua? I don't know. I think the weather is enervating. And I don't feel very lively. e) Lytton is going away the weekend after this. f) I really don't know what is in my head, so decide whatever you like. I've been trying to pack up things preparatory to moving, which I think may be any day now. I mean in a few weeks, say 2 weeks. I've been tying up canvases. The sight of all my old pictures depressed me. What a useless artist I am!

Then I went and had a cold bath, and lay in the hot sun without my clothes. Now I feel limper than I did this morning and even more empty headed [...]

H has never written to me since I last saw her on Sunday. So I now imagine everybody has turned against me because I am such a detestable character, and I have even turned against myself! Lytton still writes under the rose tree, as if nothing was happening [...]

The air is heavy with the smell of elderflowers, how ridiculous one is! What does it all matter ... I love you very much, or I wouldn't write to you as I do.

Bless you. Very dear.

Your Cirod

After her return to London to continue her 'treatment' wth Ernest Jones, Henrietta Bingham proved her sexual versatility by having other affairs with both sexes as well as with Carrington, who now discovered what it was like to be in pursuit of an elusive lover. To Lytton and Ralph, both of whom disliked Henrietta, she played down her feelings. Gerald she tried to reassure.

At the same time as prepraring to leave Tidmarsh, Carrington was redecorating Ham Spray. Ralph and Frances helped her, as did Henrietta and other friends.

To Gerald Brenan

[The Mill House]
Friday morning, 10 o'ck, 13 June 1924

I want a superlative of Amigo mio. I wish I could conjure up one word to tell you how much I care.

Dear. And now I would write no more. Do you see that in 'dear' I say all I can [...]

I remember nothing of yesterday morning. I believe you spent it with me. I only remember a dark hall, and the shutting of a door. I woke up and found myself in a barber's shop with a female hairdresser washing my hair with a strange smelling verbena hair wash. Alix didn't notice my hair, but Henrietta did! [...]

Then I rushed off to Knightsbridge to Henrietta's secret house. A house which nobody knew of except us. She had taken it for her friend who arrives tomorrow. But not a soul knew of it. We had a lovely tea in the kitchen, of biscuits and garlic sausage and tea with lemon. Then she drove me across the park to Paddington. It is nice of you to be pleased because I am happy. I hope you will meet her soon. Perhaps it's all a delusion, she may of course be quite uninteresting inside. I hardly ever speak to her. We are the most silent of friends! But I feel sure she is very like her early Italian exterior. She also has a goodness that is unusual.

[...] Do you know James saw you and Frances at Wembley? Alix said 'is that an affair now?' James said 'no, I am sure it is not, from their backs, as they got out of the train I saw it was no affair'[1] [...]

Bless you, most dear amigo.

Your princess of Georgia. Cirod

To Gerald Brenan

Sunday morning, 22 June 1924

Dearest amigo, xxxxxxxxxxx –

I have had hardly any time to write to you. But I remember everything. You mustn't think I don't realize how good you are to me. I do see it. And then I behave badly. I get carried away by Kentucky Princesses who after all compared to my Amigo are not worth one half minute's thought [...]

1 Frances and Gerald were becoming good and lasting friends. They did not have an affair.

Write me a long letter please. I am never quite certain of your affections, so the slightest silence on your side can always make me feel you have turned against me. I wish I could write a long letter. But we are starting for Ham Spray in 5 mins. My head is full of images, so strange and exciting I can hardly believe they are real. I shall be more controlled and less thoughtless the next time we meet. I love you so much dearest Gerald. Remember nothing you do can ever offend me and I forgive you for any of your vaguenesses long before you have committed them. My dear dear amigo bless you.

Yr Cirod

To Gerald Brenan

Monday afternoon, 23 June 1924

Amigo Mio, it's such a beautiful day here, a hot sun and the sound of hay cutting machines on every side coming over the brick garden wall ... I am afraid this last week I simply can't come up to London. I haven't enough money, I want to make before I leave Tidmarsh a painting of the Roman Bath. So now it is at last hot, I shall start my days of painting out doors. I have just been bathing in the deep green waters under the elder bushes, it was so cool, and dark after the glaring sun [...]

All yesterday we spent at Ham Spray. Henrietta came down with Tommy[1] to lunch, and helped paint the walls all the afternoon. After tea we all went for a long walk to the top of the Downs. And H and I went far across ploughed fields, through a little cornfield plantation until we came on to 'Shepherds Down' and far away in the distance the Downs of Tidmarsh.

She won me by being completely captivated by my Downs. I long for you to know her. I can hardly bear to care so much for anyone that you do not know also! She dresses badly, talks American, and has a hundred faults but somehow they don't matter, she is so beautiful, and so charmingly sensitive.

Sebastian Sprott and a Mr Ritchie[2] spent last week end here with us, and both came over to Ham Spray.

I am painting my bedroom pure white, as I like the effect that one gets in Italian and Spanish inns of cold cleanness. Henrietta was a wonderful painter of walls. Far better than I was to my surprise!

1 Stephen Tomlin [1901–37], known as Tommy, was a sculptor who did portrait busts of Lytton and Virginia Woolf, among others. Bisexual himself, he was having an affair with Henrietta, whom he wanted to marry; she refused. He later had brief affairs with both Lytton and Carrington, and was, unsurprisingly, disliked by both Ralph and Gerald.

2 Philip Ritchie (1899–1927) was a young Oxford graduate with whom Lytton was falling in love.

I have never seen the garden quite so exquisite, the rose trees were covered with flowers. Red hot pokers, moss in the bull rushes and many new flowers were in bloom. But nothing equalled the loveliness of those Downs, with the skylarks rising and falling in the air, singing their high transparent songs. I would like to know that you will sometime this summer either live near us or in the remote end of the house [...]

Please Gerald, remember that even if I am dstracted by Kentucky Princesses that you have only to murmur in the quietest whisper your reproaches and I forget them all for you ... You do not know how much I love your rooms. How I enjoyed our evenings together, and those most delicious meals of grapefruit, honey and coffee. I think I love those rooms in a way that I have seldom loved London's rooms before. I feel they are, in part, mine.

Please write me a long letter tomorrow Tuesday. And post it early so that I may get it on Wednesday morning.

I think of you so often. Do you know that?

This is a dull letter, but I am rather exhausted by the agitation of yesterday, the continual conversation, too much sherry, too much sun today and the coldness of the dark green water.

My love. Your princess

Your Cirod

Carrington's infatuation with Henrietta and the difficulties of finding time to spend with Gerald intensified. She had found sex with Henrietta a revelation, and was more reluctant than ever to spend the night with him.

To Gerald Brenan

The Mill House
Friday morning, 25 July 1924

I would rather know you didn't come because you didn't care for me, than you were prevented because you hadn't enough money. The fare is 10/3 return weekend. But I am glad at any rate you have told me you were poor. I should not have taken your present. The little right I had to ask you to do anything to please me vanished last Wednesday. So I shall not ask you to come again. I am only sorry I wrote those plaintive and rather unnecessary letters. You had much better conduct your life in future without considering me. I agree with you entirely. I am impossible. I say this in no particular mood of deprecation, but the result of a week's thinking alone. The solution

to all my difficulties lies upstairs in my studio. Henrietta repays my affection
almost as negatively as you find I do yours. In the end I think you will find
St. Teresa your best and most faithful mistress. I feel rather tired and dispir-
ited and perhaps I shall not write for a little. Bless you. I love you.

Yr Cirod

*Gerald had recently written to Carrington: 'I do not understand the possessive
instinct ... it is part of my philosophy that love is free and unrestricted and is
increased by being divided.' But he felt very differently when Carrington wrote that
she was coming to London but would not be able to see him. He replied: 'Do you
really think to behave like this is nothing? [...] If I could make you unhappy I
would; I should be dishonest if I pretend to any good wishes or gratitude. I simply
see in you an object which (for motives I don't understand) causes me the most
elaborate suffering.'*

*By the end of July, Carrington, Ralph and Lytton had moved in to Ham Spray.
Gerald had decided to leave London and to try to break with Carrington.*

To Gerald Brenan

Ham Spray House, Hungerford
Wednesday [6 August 1924]

Amigo Mio,

[...] I find it difficult to give up at a moment's notice, my affection for
you. I think too much about you. I can't tell you as I have a horror of writing
to you, if you are in another mood. On Monday morning Ralph found me
crying at breakfast alone. He was very sympathetic. But I couldn't bear to
talk about you at the moment, so I said I would talk about it later. Yesterday
I saw from something he said about you, he hadn't in the least grasped what
I was unhappy about and really had quite forgotten about it. This morning
he said, 'We must have missed one of Gerald's letters. He never said anything
to me about giving back the keys.' Then I saw it was too late. I couldn't tell
Ralph about your letter. It would mean endless conversations about you and
our relations and then on Thursday Frances would hear it all and I should
be treated 'sympathetically' by Ralph. So I said nothing. Now I shall never
say anything. I don't really suppose Ralph will notice until a few months
have elapsed that we aren't writing to each other! I prefer really to think of
you alone inside myself, than to have you discussed, even with Ralph. His
relationships are so easy, he never finds Frances lacking in any quality. He

can't understand our difficulties and if he does he simply thinks either you are mad, or that I deserve what I get because I behave so badly.

Henrietta came on Monday night with Mina and picked Tommy up, and carried him back to London. It was such a confusion I hardly had time to speak to her alone. She goes to Scotland for a month now and is engulfed in her father and brothers. So it's better to get her out of my head.

I am glad I knew her, as I did know her. It was an experience and I feel I have known the strange possibilities that some women are capable of. Alix was the only other woman who ever surpassed H in a peculiar variety of magical charm. I think Dorelia has it, but then I never felt it myself, for I never knew her. Lytton is still in Brittany but I hope he will come back soon, perhaps the end of this week [...]

On last Tuesday evening Ralph and I made a compact that we wouldn't quarrel, or argue, again. And that if we did the person who first made the quarrel be to blame. This was because we both became instantaneously bored and disgusted by our habits of wrangling.

And, will you believe it, that we have not bickered once since this magic compact was made. It is a great improvement. You are not allowed to be cynical amigo, because it is really quite difficult to break bad habits. Perhaps by October I shall be such a transformed Cirod that you will forgive me. But I oughtn't to say that, I am sorry. If you change your mind and would like me to come for a day secretly to Canterbury, or the Romney marshes, or London, will you tell me? It is true, I am trying a little to persuade you. I confess my thoughts nakedly. But I also know you are capable of doing what you like and this is how I prefer you to behave. Please give Helen[1] my love. Thinking of you, I see what a dear friend you have been to me. There will never be anyone quite so perfect in some peculiar ways. My rages against myself are almost unendurable.

In that we have something in common. Bless you. This letter is purposely flat. There is no point in writing anything else. And I shall not write again unless you expressly ask me. I'll be your ghost, you can conjure me to appear, or leave me in a grave, as you wish.

My love, dearest Gerald.

Your Cirod

And yet one has another self that shrieks GRRRRR half the day.

My love. C

---

1 Gerald had gone to stay with Helen Anrep (1885–1965) in Kent to tutor her children.

With Lytton in pursuit of Philip Ritchie, and Ralph of Frances (who was still not
prepared to go to bed with him), and Henrietta out of reach, Carrington was not
inclined to let Gerald go. She went down to Kent where they slept together, but
nothing really changed.

To Gerald Brenan

Ham Spray House
Sunday [19 October 1924]

Oh, but you did enrage me yesterday. Or rather I raged against Fate, and
flu and thin envelopes and curious amazon post mistresses and sensibilities
and everything I could rage against. You posted your last letter to me
unsealed. Really it was never glued, because when I examined it most
carefully I saw the glue was virgin – unlicked. The post mistress gave it to
me breathless with agitation and confusion. 'I promise you it arrived in this
condition. I hand it you just as it was handed to me,' etc. etc. In a terrific
loud voice so that R outside in the car, heard every word. Imagine my
feelings all the way back in the car to Ham Spray. Can you? Or does that
mean very little to you? I was so sick with agitation, that by the time I
reached my room I could hardly read what was inside. Please, please give
up thin envelopes. They are fatal to keeping stuck even if licked and please
remember to seal your letters, or I shall go mad. Don't think me absurd.
But it really is hideous to get letters, especially yours, after the whole village
has read them. Now I have over boiled like the stew in the kitchen, and
the whole letter smells like burnt onions and fat and am myself again, and
quite merry [...]
    The fair at Newbury was wonderful. Annie and I went by ourselves and
met R at the Newbury station. The streets were crammed with farmers,
boys and girls. You never saw such a gay scene. Flare lights with cheapjacks,
illuminating every face in the crowd. Boys stuffing confetti down the blouses
of giggling girls. Strange leering faces pressed against each other. Stalls
selling finger snaps, and sweets. Amazing gypsies telling fortunes. The pressure of the crowd was terrific. For the stalls went down the street on both
sides. Then in the square there were huge merry-go-rounds, swing boats,
lottery booths, quacks and astrologers. We went on a lovely swing merry-
go-round, that whirled one round very fast so one flew out into the dark
sky like a revolving bird on wings, higher than the houses, above the top of
the shrieking merry-go-round and below one saw, tearing round and round,
the crowd and the flaring lights [...]

I think all that is best in English life congregates at a fair. All the farm boys looked so gay and beautiful and once I saw, for a second, a face that was worth going to fifty fairs to see: a very pale young girl, with black eyes like sloes dressed rather respectably in tailor made clothes leaning on the arm of another girl, whose face was shrouded by a drooping veil. As they passed me, the pale girl turned around and made a most lascivious leering smile at some farm boys who were passing. I looked at them, they were bewildered by her beauty and excited, but couldn't make out exactly what she meant by her strange passionate look. Then she laughed in their faces twisted round and rushed off on the arm of her friend into the crowd and was lost from view [...]

Your letter, now I am no longer angry, was so charming. You are a dear to write to me Gerald so often. I have been painting very hard on my decoration for the cellar door. I don't know yet if it's any good. I worked the whole of yesterday morning from 10 o'ck till one o'ck. After supper I made Ralph sit for me, and I drew him. Today I will work again. It alters one's whole attitude to life, working hard, I find. I mind none of the vexations of life when I am painting [...] Would you like some apples?

My very fondest love amigo most dear.

xxxxxxx Your Cirod

To Frances Marshall

Ham Spray House
[October?] 1924

Dear, Dearer, Dearest, Frances,

[...] You are very charming to give me such a lovely present! I shall as the Queen in newspapers says 'treasure them always'.

Now I shall have to find something equally exquisite to give the princess for her travels. I cannot be put in such an indebted position. But will I ever find anything so lovely? I hope it rains a little this next weekend, on Saturday morning rather hard ... do you penetrate my design? I still maintain if that vulture wasn't so devouring, I should very quickly gain your attentions Miss, to say nothing of your bed – if it is fine think kindly of me. If it is wet I shall see you here, and show you, I hope, my affection. You say you like me more than I like you –? How can we provide such a delicate point? Ralph returned looking rather hollow eyed and worn but very gay and happy. For which I am to thank ... and full of scandal secrets and gossip. None of which poor Barbara was allowed to hear. In case I don't see you I hope you will have a very happy time with that curious trio in Italy.[1] But I know you will enjoy it. Bless you. And remember always that there are few people fonder of you than your Carrington.

Henrietta's acceptance of her complex sexuality appears to have enabled Carrington to be more open about her own. Her letters to or about women friends became suggestive, even provocative. This was a game Frances was not inclined to play. Henrietta was, and remained, Carrington's only female lover.

To Gerald Brenan

Monday morning, 20 October 1924

Amigo Mio, I am in the middle of my work. What am I to say? ... if I come up to London I know it will mean the whole of this good effort to keep working disturbed ... I think if you are working I shall feel the same about the importance of allowing you to work. Yet I am always so half hearted about myself as an artist that you have only to beg me, or tell me you are unhappy, and you know I shall come. But it is a little unfair if you wish me to ever be any good as a painter. I will come on Monday after the weekend [...]

Oh Gerald please don't make it hard for me to work. The whole of everything regarding myself I feel hinges on my painting. I know it's selfish of me to care more for my paintings than your unhappiness, but do you not sometimes when you are working feel the same? If you want to see me you can always come down here. There is nothing to prevent you. And Ralph is away on Wednesday afternoon till Thursday evening [...] And amigo mio, please be happy. When you write to me as you did this morning, I feel all my inside torn with unhappiness.

[...] Next Monday I promise I will stay with you. So will you wait till then! Dear Sweegie don't make me unhappy and it does when I know you are sad because of me. I will write a longer letter tomorrow. My love, dear one,

Your loving Cirod

---

1 Frances was going to Italy with her brother Tom, Harry Norton's sister Jane, who also worked in Birrell and Garnett's bookshop, and an admirer, Colin McKenzie, who was keen to woo her away from Ralph.

When Henrietta reappeared, Carrington went up to London to see both her and Gerald. Alix Strachey, who was herself in analysis in Berlin, knew all about Ernest Jones, with whom Henrietta was still in treatment for her sexual confusion; also bisexual but happily married to James, Alix was the one person with whom Carrington could be truthful.

To Alix Strachey

[Ham Spray]
[Winter 1924]

Dearest Alix

I saw my exquisite ravisher last Thursday in London, I met her a quarter to one outside Mr Jones. She was rather battered. 'He has been hammering away to get at my rock bottom, and I feel rather limp. For I put up a very [*word missing*] resistance.' 'Rock bottom' isn't what I should have described.

I've had a superb lunch in Soho, I find her taste so sympathetic. Grapefruit, cocktails, fish in mushrooms, fried ham and spinach, and raw pineapple. I really confess Alix I am very much more taken with H than I have ever been with anyone for a long time. I now feel regrets at being such a blasted fool in the past, to stifle so many lusts I had in my youth, for various females. But perhaps one would have only have been embittered, or battered by blows on the head from enraged virgins. Unfortunately she is living in London now with a red-haired creature from America, so as she tactfully put it 'You must wait, if you can. My passions don't last long, but at the moment ... '

H now goes to the London School of Economics every afternoon. I find her completely sympathetic. In other words nothing she does ever gets on my nerves. And most of the things she does charm me very completely.

She is a little terrifying, partly because I know her so little. I begged her to come to Berlin with me after Xmas. I told her of your sympathetic cafes. And she said she was 'distinctly attracted' and would do her best to come!

I spent two days last week in London. Most of the time I spent with Gerald. Lytton behaved monstrously and gave a party at Dadie's room in London on Friday night, and never even told R and I he was giving it, or asked us.[1] R came back in high dudgeon over it. But I composed myself, as I knew I shouldn't really have enjoyed it, and yet had I been asked, I should have found it hard to refuse. Lytton (entre nous) is making un peu d'idiot of himself over P.R. [Philip Ritchie] I mean I suspect P.R. isn't nearly so fond of Lytton as he pretends to be. Perhaps he doesn't pretend, and Lytton

---

1 George Rylands (1902–99), known as Dadie, academic and theatre director, was the latest handsome young King's graduate to capture Lytton's attention.

imagines it himself. He is staying here this weekend. Really his stories of perpetual rapes become rather boring. Helen Anrep is staying here also. I suspect she is very cynical over Mr R although she plays up with superb astonishment, and excitement over these endless stories of assaults! Of course I really always give way to Lytton, it's a habit by now so I almost think Mr R is one of the most beautiful and fascinating young men [...]

Ralph is getting on superbly with the bookbinding and orders rush in from every side. By mutual agreement we never quarrel now. Isn't that an astonishingly good plan! You see really Gerald always repeats (slightly inaccurately I suppose) all your conversations about me. R and Missie M [Frances] are more engulfed than ever. But really she is rather nice and fundamentally decent. She was here last weekend with James.

To Gerald Brenan

Ham Spray House
Wednesday [17 December 1924]

Dear amigo,

I send you this picture of Ralph. If you don't like it very much I can easily do you another. I never have any feelings myself about my pictures, they all seem after a few days equally as dull. All is confusion here getting ready for the [Christmas] party. Mercifully it is hot again and the sun shines, so one does not feel that awful depression that the rain and cold produce. I don't feel in a good mood to write you a letter, partly because I haven't heard from you, so I don't know what to say. I read *War and Peace* day after day, and live in another world, it is strangely beautiful in so many varied ways. Late last night I heard a fox baying with short barks at the moon in the field outside. The carter told Annie they are so tame here they are not frightened of the men and the other day a fox joined the work men at lunch in a field and had to be driven away, he was so anxious to join their feast. It is difficult to tell you when you ask me, how I am still fond of you. I only know when I see you again, I am overcome by a strange affection, which is different from the love I have for anybody else.

Yesterday I thought of Spain. It was just a year ago today we started for Yegen. Do you know I think there are very few hours that I cannot remember every detail of at Yegen. You will never know quite how much I loved staying with you. I can never forget, or thank you enough for letting me share your life there and for showing me so much. You know my life is almost entirely visual and no place ever gave me such exquisite happiness as last winter with you. I hope you will be happy, as far it is possible, at Edgeworth [Brenan's parents' house] this Christmas. You asked me not to have a lover when you saw me the other day. It is easy for me to promise.

May I ask you for a promise? Please avoid Valentine as far as it is possible, because I feel as certain, as spring follows winter, that only disasters to us all will come of it. I write purposely a little restrained, you understand why. Seeing you again made me so happy. My fondest love,

Amigo Mio, your Cirod

My Dear one, I send you all my love.

This was not the end of Carrington's romance with Gerald, but it was perhaps the beginning of the end. As with Mark Gertler, she could not enjoy sex with him but could not quite bear to let him go. Her sexual relationship with Ralph was coming to an end and she knew there was no future with Henrietta; her love for Lytton and her need of his companionship was as strong as ever, and their shared life at Ham Spray was her priority.

1925

Ham Spray House
Thursday evening, 6.30 [22 January 1925]

Amigo Mio,

[...] I must write in pencil as my pen is in Lytton's room and he is working, so I must not bother him. In half an hour I shall have to fetch Ralph from the station. There is a howling gale outside, a tiger of a wind, I wish I had not to go, as it is pleasant sitting over this blazing fire writing what ever comes into my head to you [...]

I was interested at meeting Henry Lamb. Mostly because of Lytton's past relations with him and partly because of Helen.[1] I longed to get him to talk to Helen, but somehow it wasn't possible. He looks like an Army doctor who has seen 'life' perhaps on the Tibet frontier or who has suffered from low fevers in Sierra Leone and also has a past murder, or crime, which makes him furtive and uneasy. He has a most unhappy face. But he is amusing and very charming sometimes. Did you ever meet him at Helen's house this winter? He promises to come over this spring with Dorelia to stay here. He is a most perverse man in his opinions. Almost as silly as Morgan sometimes, but sometimes extremely intelligent and inventive. I made two glass pictures on Tuesday and Wednesday morning. Did you like them? I always want to know if you like them. Will it not be wonderful if I can at last and by such a delightful occupation, earn £2 a week? I fear Ralph will have licked the sugar off my biscuit-of-a-letter by telling you all the Ham Spray news.

This morning, as I didn't feel in the mood for drawing I cut out my green grass brocade dress, it's going to look very lovely Querido Mio. It is a copy of my Persian dress, only made with slight differences. I shall take some weeks to finish it, as I only do needlework in the evenings whilst Lytton reads to us. But in March (after the Mystic Month of February is over) you and I have a party together at Fitzroy Street, only with no guests and I will wear my Persian finery. It's going to be very elaborate, green silk stockings and scarlet shoes and an underdress of fine red silk. The clock flies too fast, a quarter of an hour has gone and in ten minutes I shall have to get the car out of the stable.

1 Henry Lamb (1883–1960) was a successful painter, especially of portraits, who had studied under Augustus John and joined his circle. After an affair with Dorelia he remained devoted to her. Ottoline Morrell and Lytton had both been in love with him.

I will come up next Wednesday. I will try and stay Thursday night also. But I will not absolutely promise this. But I do promise all Wednesday and Thursday. There are pictures that I want to see, the toy shop at Hoxton and the London Library. But they are all occupations that I would like to pursue with a certain companion, if he will come with me. How can I tell you that I love you more than all the ~ some thing in you which I cannot explain? If you doubt this, you can easily prove it. We will spend our days in utter chastity, and I will still be happy.

Now I must go.

I will post this letter tonight, so you will get it very soon.

Lunch next Wednesday, at 18 Fitzroy Street.

My love, dear one. Bless you,

Yr Princess Cirod

There was occasional awkwardness between Frances, Ralph's new love, and Carrington, his wife and mistress of Ham Spray.

To Frances Marshall

Ham Spray House
[n.d.]

Dearest Frances,

You are an

(which is an owl)

also a

(which is a noddle)

also an

(which is an idiot)

When I say 'that depends' it is by way of a joke. A joke against Mr P [Ralph] insinuating of course that 'it depends' on nothing at all and of course she can come and wants to come, she must come and we shall be delighted. You knew this owl, idiot, and noddle and it's just because you thought it would be gayer to go off with Mr P. N.[1] gallivanting, that you excused yourself by pretending you didn't understand my little (and rather feeble) humour.

PS If I hadn't wanted you I should hardly have dared to have said so blatantly!

1 P.N. was Philip Nichols, a young diplomat who was Ralph's only serious rival for Frances.

PS Because my disease, 'that most prevalent of all complaints' [her menstrual period] causes me great torture, and produces a certain misery and despair, you flatter yourself if you think this unhappiness is caused by your presence! I ignore you Madame! I hardly notice your ghostly existence. In truth I wish, speaking for myself, you weren't so ghostly. Oh but I forgot you don't like advances from young, to be exact middle aged women. We've just been reading Norman Douglas. He is superb! My love dear lady. And please remember to come here when ever you want to, for it will also be reciprocated by your

Carrington

HAM SPRAY HOUSE,
HUNGERFORD,
BERKS.

I forgot you don't like advances from young —or (or scant middle aged- women. we're first been reading Norman Douglas. It is superb!

Dearest Frances

You are an

which is
(an owl)

also a

[which is a
noddle.]

also an

(which
is an
idiot)

your ghost) sentence. In truth I wish—speaking for myself you weren't so ghostly— Oh lots)

My love dear lady. and please remember to come here when are you want to, for it will also be reciprocated by your Carrington

When I say "that depends" it is by way of a joke. a joke against Mr P. insinuating of course

To Alix Strachey

Ham Spray House
4 February 1925

Now I've recovered slightly from my misfortune, and misadventure, I dream only once a week – instead of every night – of that wretch H and I think of her only 2 hours out of the 24. I've also used my self control to such purpose that I've not written to her since December the 10th. Someday – if ever you return you shall have the whole story. At least my side – she is still a mystery and I only know her version of my fall and disgrace through eavesdroppers but it's left me a warped, and gnarled old tree, with a pain in my head whenever I hear the name of 'H' or the word American. I did not lose her through pride as you suggested in your letter, but through excess of L ... [love?] I suspect she found my affections so cheap that she doubted they could be worth very much. And as she has an income of £8,000 a year I expect she thinks even L ... ought to cost a few hundreds. I'll give you one day a true history of the melancholy story from start to finish. I still can't help being a little embittered, as I feel, aged and dull witted that I may be, I can't be such an ass as her American female bitches that she consorts with. Also in the interests of truth she ought to have given me – not other people – her reason for abandoning our affaire. 'God's Neck – as Katherine Mansfield used to say –it is very mortifying. – Lytton curiously enough was the one person who sympathised. Although he was no admirer of that Lady.

You will be delighted to hear my ambitious nature is at last asserting itself. I now make over £3 a week selling little glass pictures at the Gerrard Street Book Shop. The pictures only take about 2 hours to make and some sell for 35/- or £2. So really the profit is enormous. My plan is to keep this minor talent in the winter as a means of making money, and in the spring and summer do my serious painting. I will do you a very lovely picture as a present on your return. In any style, on any subject. Flower piece, boxers, balloons, volcanoes, tight rope dancers, Victorian beauties, soldiers, tropical botanical flowers, birds and fruits, are a few of my subjects.

I cater for every taste. Ravishing soldiers in busbies for the gentlemen, and elegant ladies for the Clive Bells.

Ham Spray still remains very perfect. I am continuously happy here. The pleasure of my large studio, the Downs, and the garden continue, in spite of the atrocious climate, and the cold winds [...]

Norman Douglas has written a fine attack on D. H. Lawrence in a privately printed book. Aldous Huxley has written yet another novel on poor Ottoline. Henry Lamb came and stayed here after Xmas for two days – he played ping pong most of the time with Ralph! – brother Noel marries a Slade beauty the end of this month – which leaves me cold. Barbara and Faith are both

pregnant with child, and like Rachel fill the air with their lamentations [...]
Bunny has formed a 'Cranium Club', very exclusive, only the purest intellects.[1]
Dinners twice a month, discussions on only abstract and literary subjects,
no gossip, and no women allowed. Sherry, to be drunk – with great ritual –
from a SKULL ...

To Alix Strachey

                                                    22 February 1925

Thank you for your very friendly letter. Yes it was rather serious, (or at any
rate it would have been so had not that Lady [Henrietta] been too vague,
or unwilling to admit my seriousness) but now I have almost recovered. I
mean I only think of her occasionally, and only receive a few stabs in the
heart when I hear her name mentioned. In a few weeks she will return to
America. I shall be rather glad when I know she has definitely gone. Because
I still have struggles when I go up to London for a few days to resist trying
to see her. In time – I mean when one is 40 – I expect one will forget the
pain and look back with a certain pride on the adventure [...]
    Norman Douglas has written such a good attack on D. H. Lawrence.
Really very amusing. I'll ask James to send it you. It's very cheap. Lytton
has a fascinating correspondence with Norman Douglas [...]
    Frances M, who remains very charming, altogether nice, still comes every
weekend. She is rather a dim character. I mean she never behaves differently
– and one never gets to know anything about her. But considering how
lovely she is, and how spoilt by hundreds of young men, and the dullness
of the bookshop I think she remains very intelligent.

To Lytton Strachey

                                                Ham Spray House
            Monday morning, 7 o'ck in bed before breakfast, 30 March 1925

Dearest Lytton,
    Such a weekend! Such orgies! Such conversations! Why weren't you
here? [...] A wire from Henry [Lamb] and Dorelia to say they were arriving
for tea (and a wire from Tommy to say he couldn't come for the weekend).

---

1 The Cranium Club met over dinner at a Soho restaurant, to bring friends together across disciplines
   and foster good conversation. Lytton was a member; Ralph and Gerald were not. The club still meets
   and now includes women.

I just had time to whisk a few rockeries into cupboards and they were upon us. D looking very lovely, and in high spirits. H a little older perhaps, and a little balder, than the last time! I soon gathered they had come to spend the weekend. Mercifully we had some food in the house. They were both very sad at not seeing you and Henry has taken your address at Lyme and he said he would like immensely to come over and see you. I was completely knocked over by Dorelia and her beauty. She was very talkative and gay.

We played the gramophone most of the time, drank mead and sloe gin and bottles of wine, played ping pong and went to bed very late. Yesterday we walked over after lunch to Sheepless Downs. Poor Dorelia got very exhausted, so I had to support her on my arm. She has a fearful cough the whole time. She goes in April to Ischia, an island near Capri, with John. It sounds perfect, a little cottage on the edge of the sea, with a garden and an Italian cook and servant and a little sailing boat. It was interesting to see Henry and Dorelia together. She fairly raps him over the knuckles when he gets fussy and laughs at his absurd conversation and rags him when he gets sententious. Olive[1] is so far perfect. Far brisker that Annie, cleans and bustles about in a pair of squeaking shoes, and beams with pleasure when one talks to her. I think she will be alright in a few days. She is full of energy and common-sense. And already does a great many things on her own without being told.

Henry of course couldn't resist making up to F. M. [Frances] a little. But I fear his days of success with jeune filles are over. She couldn't see a trace of that former dazzling beauty in his battered face, she confessed afterwards. Noel and Missie A[2] came over to tea yesterday – we played poker after tea over the fire. Cream brulé came off and created a very proper impression. They [Henry and Dorelia] go back this morning to Alderney. Henry brought me a most superb Mexican Lily, a great red lily on the top of a thick purple stalk. I shall do a large painting of it today after they have gone. Dorelia promises to come again. She was delighted with our country, and properly enthusiastic over our beloved house. It was sad not to have you here and we kept all the time wishing you were staying at Ham Spray instead of at L[yme] R[egis] [...] We both miss you very much. I will try and find the cork of the hot water bottle this morning.

Love from your Mopsa

In an attempt to keep him close to her Carrington had found Gerald a cottage in Shalbourne, not far from Ham Spray. This did not, however, improve their relation-

---

1 Olive was their new cook-housekeeper.
2 Noel's fiancée was the beautiful Slade student Catherine Alexander.

ship. She drove him to despair by hardly ever seeing him alone and, if he spent a
night at Ham Spray, only reluctantly sharing his bed.

To Gerald Brenan

Monday night, 12.30 [1 June 1925]

Amigo Mio, I hadn't read your letter when I passed you in the car. I couldn't
read it till I got back here tonight. I am desperately unhappy and my head
aches. Last night was awful. I cried in bed because of the sadness and drear-
iness of our day together [...]

I felt last night you hadn't understood what I was trying to explain. I
mean I told you all my worst moods crudely. I let you see the horror of my
lowest days of gloom and nerves. But you are being unfair to both of us,
if you don't see the other side. I mean you mustn't forget just as some days
I feel removed and very distant physically, other days I feel the reverse. Only
it is quite true it is awful for you who mind so much what my physical
feelings are, never to know before hand, what mood I shall be in. I entirely
sympathise with your feelings. That is the worst of it. I am in despair because
I am against myself. I think about you until my head aches. But I do not
know what to say or how to alter things.

You see when you came over yesterday morning I was transported with
pleasure. I looked at you with the greatest happiness, filling the bottles and
talking. Then suddenly in the greenhouse, I could hardly bear the difficulties
and arguments which seemed to surround us. Just as I make you eccentric, you
react on me by your noticing me in some peculiar way and make me disagreeable and nervous. I am not like that usually. Directly I am away from you, I hate
myself for being so unfriendly. When I see you with Helen and other people I
see all your charms and love the humour and engagingness of your character.
But when we are together, half the time seems to be spent in this friction and
that instantly makes me intolerant not only to you, but far more to myself [...]

It is awful to care so much for you, to love your character, to be excited
by your mind and your writing and yet never to be in contact with these,
because of these other complexes which suddenly without the slightest
warning, appear. You cannot say I am incapable of physical feelings, yet the
last 2 weeks I felt as if I was without a body. Will you please not bear me
a grudge? Perhaps it's something which I will recover from. At the moment
I seem impossible. I quite agree. Dear, it is awful, after bringing you to
Shalbourne and getting what I had looked forward to for so long now, to
see you unhappy and looking ill. Why is it we cannot strike a sort of every
day relation that excludes these crises?

I showed Ralph your letters, for I was in such despair. I did not know what to do, and couldn't bear not to talk to someone. Naturally since he knows, perhaps even better than you do, the tiresomeness of my character, he could say nothing

[...] What can I say to you Gerald? I feel so utterly gloomy because I have made you unhappy. You will write to me? It's impossible for me, even although it's useless, not to go on caring very much for you.

My love

Yr Cirod

[...] **Later, one o'ck**

PS Don't let us make any decisions. Don't say you won't come back here, or you won't see me again in London. For I am childish, I always believe what you say. Now I must go to bed for I am so tired. Good night. I feel I've been so tiresome that I'll do exactly what you ask me. Write, not write. You must go to London thinking I've turned against you. It isn't against you. I wish I could explain. I care for you as much as I ever did, Amigo mio. You really mustn't think my distrait moods are to do with you, I should be like that if I was surrounded by beech trees and no men within hundreds of miles. Bless you.

Yr C

You shall have your birthday picture next week.

Tuesday morning

PS Please come over to talk to me today if you feel it will make things any easier.

With nothing resolved between them, nor likely to be, given that he wanted the physical and emotional commitment she could not give, Gerald went off to France. Carrington continued to write to him.

To Gerald Brenan

Ham Spray House
Sunday, 10 July 1925

Dearest Amigo,

You haven't answered any of my letters to Toulon. But as I know you treat writing seriously, and I treat writing as a mere pleasure, I will write you another. If however you don't answer this letter. I shall conclude you aren't in a mood for conversing with me. And I shall not be offended.

What do you want me to tell you? The summer glides by, without anything happening to me now. Tommy is still here, as far as I am concerned, as chaste as when he appeared. We go for long walks in the evening on the downs. And have endless conversations. He has just finished his statue for the garden. It's very classical and elegant, a nymph of the ilex tree with the cornucopia of fruit. It is to be cast in lead. I am painting a portrait of Julia Strachey, at the moment. She is a most amusing companion. She comes here a great deal nearly every week. But do not leap instantaneously to a wrong surmise. I have come to the conclusion that Henriettas are as rare as mandrakes. One great excitement in my life is that at last I have a horse of my own here – when I say my own, it really belongs to the little Japp girl.[1] But she has gone with her mother to Madrid, and has lent it to me. Everyday after tea I ride to the top of the Downs, and gallop along that grand track. The country is turning so lovely in England now. The tops of the Downs are pink with sorrel. And the edges of the woods are filled with small blue and pink flowers, creeping bushes and orchids. I ride very badly of course. But I daresay in time I will learn to do it better. I look after the horse myself, and feed it on lawn mowings. This week I shall have to ride it back to Lambourne, as I am afraid if I kept it too long something may go wrong with it.

Last week there have been two parties in London. Karin Stephen and Dadie [Rylands], and Douglas [Davidson]. And Philip Ritchie. That was a very strange affair. With Mary Pickford and Douglas Fairbanks, Margot Asquith, Lady Colefax and hundreds of celebrities, and exquisite actresses.[2]

My plan in life is to have so many things to do that I never have time to think about myself [...]

I send you whether you want it or not, my love,

Your loving C

To Gerald Brenan

Ham Spray House
Sunday morning [19 July 1925]

Your letter came yesterday morning. I have thought about you for a whole day. My detachment from us both seems complete. I shall always believe

1 Darsie Japp (1883–1973) was a painter friend of the Johns family.
2 Mary Pickford (1892–1979) had been married to Douglas Fairbanks (1883–1939) since 1920. Both were at the height of their film-star fame. Margot Asquith (1864–1945) was the outspoken wife of H. H. Asquith, the former prime minister. Sybil, Lady Colefax (1874–1950), was a leading hostess and interior decorator.

you to be one of the most perfect, lovable characters I have ever known. You contain more that attracts me in your character than I have thought possible for one person to contain. Thinking of you I forget all the difficulties and scenes and only remember other images of you.

But looking at myself I feel only resentment at my character. Most of your attacks are justified. I see my complexes only bring out your worst features, which probably if I didn't exist to torment them, would be invisible. I am only sorry you never knew, or so seldom, my better character. For somehow you also drag out something from me which I myself do not ever feel except with you. The irony of it is that H (who is a person of no importance and lacks all the proper virtues, for I can see even her, detachedly today) should have so completely altered my physical feelings for everyone. It was seeing her again that upset me so this spring. How foolish one is! To alter these things seems the hardest thing in the word. Yet with one's head one is perfectly logical, and sensible. Don't, Amigo Mio, turn on me and think it all a waste of time [...]

No one is quite happy. I know quite well, how much you really matter to me, but I agree with you, after one has one had a sort of perfection in a relation, one can't put up with something different [...]

Do not blame yourself that anything was ever your fault. I hardly think it was mine. It was simply an irony of fate, that drew out suddenly from a past bundle of suppressions, these feelings of mine for H, which are of course perfectly futile and senseless. My secretiveness has always been my own misery. But when I tell you I suffer literally, physically sometimes, when I hear my inside self discussed – but if you haven't these feelings it is difficult to explain. Will you when you go to Edgeworth send me back that diary I sent you. With you going away, my last contact with an outside world probably vanishes. I shall now retreat back into my self again. But I cannot bear to make you, (who in spite of all you say), I care for in a way different from my feelings for anyone else, continually unhappy. So I accept your letter. I will write to you no more and I will not come to London for some time. If I do, I will do my best to avoid any places where you may be. Dearest Amigo. You would forgive me if you knew how unhappy I make myself writing this. My fondest love to you,

Your Cirod

Later

PS [...] When Ralph said 'Gerald told Frances all about it and the letter he sent you, I literally felt sick with pain. You can never bind two intimates to secrecy. If I confided your secrets and feelings as recklessly as you do mine, to Ralph and Lytton you would have soon felt the stings of publicity. I know it's an obsession with me. But for a little I would beg you to remember it's part of a person you care for. Please don't write to me again; it simply makes it harder to behave as one wishes to behave. My love again,

Yr Cirod

Sunday evening, 7 o'ck
I could not after all send my letter this afternoon because there were no stamps in the house. I went for a long walk with Alix this afternoon to Shalbourne Hill. She talked a great deal to me. I think I admire her more than any human being I have ever known. Her intellectual, and moral honesty is so remarkable.

Gerald, I think I am unfitted as a human being to have a relation with anyone. Sometimes I think my obsessions and fancies border on insanity. As I haven't 2 gns [guineas] a day to spare to be analysed I had better put up with my complexes alone, by myself. In any case I think you are too decent a human being to be dragged into my mire. The alternative is to try and be a serious artist. You once said I couldn't face being alone. Don't you realize that unless one has intimate relations with a person, one is really alone most of the time? I think you think I don't understand your feelings. I understand them too well. Please do not turn on me [...] My love again.

C.

To Gerald Brenan

Ham Spray House
Tuesday, 21 July 1925

Amigo Mio, your letter from Rodmell, came yesterday after I had written to you. Oh my Amigo what an awful thing it is to be so divided, so unhinged. How much easier it would be if one felt definite and positive feelings, like other people. If only our feelings for each other coincided more often. You want perpetually something from me which it is not in my power to give you and I feel always a sense of guilt and depression because I cannot give it to you. Reasonably there is nothing to prevent me having a very intimate relation with you, except a feeling of secretiveness and an instinct to live away from the world which seems to drag me against all my reasonable inclinations, away into myself. I feel if only I mattered a little less to you, it would be less strained. But of course if I did, probably then you wouldn't want to see me. I torment myself with my own character. I envied Alix her independence from human beings and her concentrated interest in her work.

[...] I want so hard to try and be very exact. Because I know how easily you are depressed by misgiving. You know I have always hated being a woman. I think I mind much more than most women. The Fiend which most women hardly notice, fills me with such disgust and agitation every time, I cannot get reconciled to it. I am continually depressed by my effeminacy. It is true au fond I have a female inside which is proved by ≈ but afterwards a sort of rage fills because of that very pleasure. And I cannot literally bear to let my mind think of ≈ again, or of my femaleness. It is partly because R treats me not like a woman now that the strain has vanished between us. All this became clear really last summer with Henrietta. Really I had more ecstasy with her and no feelings of shame afterwards. You really pressed me out of myself into a hidden suppressed character. But when I returned, I turned against the other character that you had brought out and was filled with dread at meeting her again. I have been trying to make this clear, but perhaps it means nothing to you. (Suppose Seb [Sebastian Sprott?] persuaded you to go to the furthest point with him, can you not imagine although it was also part of yourself, you might be filled afterwards with feelings of terror?) It's really something nothing to do with you, but some struggle in myself between two characters. I think H although she gave me nothing else, gave a clue to my character. Probably if one was completely S [sapphic] it would be much easier. I wouldn't then be interested in men at all, and wouldn't have these conflicts. It's not true to say I don't care for ≈ with you. Because you know I did. But at moments these other feelings come over me, and I dread facing that side in my character. (It's not a dread against you, but against myself, against my own femaleness.) Somehow it is always easier if I am treated negatively, a little as if I was not a female, then my day-dream character of not being a female, is somehow pacified. I have tried to make this clear. I have never completely told R this, or anyone. It is a confidence I make only to you. Merely thinking of this makes me so agitated I feel I can hardly bear any relation with anyone again. In the past everything I believe went wrong for this reason. Always this struggle with two insides, which makes one disjointed, unreliable and secretive. I find it as difficult as you do to bear the strain of making each other unhappy. I don't see how I can ever give you up. Because there is nobody who for me, can ever be quite what you are to me. Perhaps this internal combustion will one day cease, and my torments with it.

I am going to try and lead a very regular life avoiding any personal agitations this summer and painting every day. I don't tell R about you and all our difficulties. You are wrong in writing this. I only talked to him this summer when you talked to him when you were at Shalbourne. I did not talk to him this weekend at all about you. Partly I confess because he wasn't interested. But mostly because somehow it is difficult to talk about one's inside feelings to anyone but the person concerned.

The pigeons arrived on Saturday. They were most lovely. This morning your mother sent me some plants; I am writing to thank her.

Let us calm down a little. If you want to write, or see me again, I shall not care less. You have been always dear to me Amigo, it's impossible to get over caring for you. Please don't answer this. I've simply tried to tell you something which I hadn't got clear until today.

My love dear one.

Your Cirod

[...]

After receiving this letter, Gerald wrote: 'Pehaps for your own happiness you should give up men and become a complete sapphist.'

That summer, Carrington was cheered by the presence of Julia Strachey, Lytton's niece and Frances Marshall's friend from childhood, who was now a frequent guest at Ham Spray and being pursued by Stephen Tomlin. Her letters to Julia were jokey and flirtatious.

To Julia Strachey

Sunday [summer 1925]

Darling Julia,

I am afraid you are a sad wretch. Because you go careering about in your Rolls Royce with a jeune homme of a Sunday and when asked to come here, don't come.

We all sat on tip toes waiting for the wheels of your new Royce up the gravel drive. But in vain, oh vain Julia. There were rows of young men on tip toes and yet you preferred to lie in the bracken, or under the gorse bushes, instead of coming to see your old friend. Well, well.

I hope you will come next Saturday in your Rolls and stay the promised week. I heard a great deal from poor Mr [Lamb] about you.

You breaker of Lamb's fry, or tails. Oh I wish you were here to do all these 'little jobs about the house.' But I'll learn yer when yer comes down my sweet honey. I'd let you tidy my drawers, mend my socks, and polish my boots. Had I but known you loved and so excelled at those hundred and one little things, I would not have let you lie idle in bed reading Galsworthy (or Tchekov much the same) a sleeping draught. One draught of your sweet lips: now I am becoming both sentimental and in bad taste, so I must stop this letter and run and put the peas on to cook. For it's Sunday night and the maid, my dear! I always think it's best, don't you, to let them have one evening out, and Sunday you know, for church, a week! [...]

Roger is a charmer. I was very melted by him this weekend.[1]
Darling Julia goodbye, my love
Your Tante Carrington

To Gerald Brenan

                                                              Summer 1925

Dear Amigo,
    Thank you for your letter. It is simply another proof of our fundamental
difference of character. I wish to bury the past; you have an infinite capacity
for investigating it. I do not believe any particular circumstances made our
relation impossible. It was rather my predestined inabilities, (which whenever
I think of my past life is forced upon me), to have any 'intimate' relations
with anyone. I believe I am a perfect combination of a nymphomaniac and
a wood-nymph! I hanker after intimacies, which another side of my nature
is perpetually at war against. Lately, removed from any intimacies, causing
no one unhappiness and having no sense of guilt I have felt more at peace
inside myself than I have ever felt before.
    I am only sorry Amigo, that you have been made so unhappy by me. At
present I do my best not to think about you. So will you please not write back
again. It was kind of you to tell me you have got over some of your resentment against me. Mine, against you, was always only for a few days; the rest was
against myself roused by you. I am glad you are happier now. I beg you not to
write again. I always shall think of you with great affection. With my love,
    Your C

PS It is quite alright about the diary. It doesn't seem to matter now, so keep
it if you like.

To Lytton Strachey

                                                         Ham Spray House
                                             Saturday [26 September 1925]

Darling Lytton,
    Your letter has just come. I wrote you a long letter on Thursday, and
Friday, but didn't post it. So now I will write it all over again. All Wednesday

1 Roger Senhouse (1899–1970), later a distinguished publisher and translator, was Lytton's new love.

was very hot, and exquisite, I spent the entire morning gossiping to Helen [Anrep] and inventing a dinner for our party. We drove to Hungerford before lunch; otherwise the entire day seemed to be spent in meandering conversation. The Japp world arrived at half past seven. The dinner was indescribably grand. Epoch making; grapefruit, then a chicken covered with fennel and tomato sauce, a risotto with almonds, onions and pimentos, followed by sack cream, supported by Café Royal red wine, perfectly warmed. (The cradle took Mrs Japp's breath away.) I shall repeat this grand dinner for our next weekend. We all became so flirtatious and talkative. Helen was a great support and was very polite to the Japps. We tippled sherry over the fire till after 11 o'ck.

The next morning I manoeuvred and got Dorelia to promise to come down, on her way to Alderney. She arrived at half past six. Henry came over. We again had a superb dinner ending with crème brule and two bottles of champagne and more sherry afterwards! Dorelia became completely boozed and very gay. Even Henry was less gloomy and rather amusing. We played Haydn, made endless jokes and talked without stopping. Somehow I thought it was the most lovely evening I'd ever spent. I wished you could have been with us. It was partly the loveliness of the femme Dorelia. I got a good many embraces from her, and one passionate rencontre with Henry in the hall. But I preferred the former. Henry stayed the night. He has given me some of his pills for going to sleep, which alter my life, as I now sink off into a complete snooze the moment I get into bed, until the next morning. I will replenish the sherry section of the cellar next week, as I am afraid I made rather a hole in it. Poor Dorelia was rather ill the next morning after our debauch, but I didn't feel any the worse. They stayed to lunch and then went off to Alderney.

Yesterday evening Helen's two children came down. Do not SHRIEK! They are very well behaved and they'll not be allowed look at any of your books. Otherwise Helen would have to have gone back yesterday. Now she will be able to stay till Sunday evening. The weather is rather wobbling here. Last night the bulls broke loose and rushed roaring round the house and blew all the branches down. No interesting letters, only a post card from Ralph from Toledo [...]

I have a lovely new cat. When I went to the Japps, they had ten exquisite cats of different sizes, tabbies, and blacks. So I chose a lovely dark tab, and brought it home. Poor Tiger had another fit in the morning and rushed in circles frantically round and round the lawn, and then had seizures under the laurel hedge. I fear I shall have to get rid of her. For she seems very neurotic, and sad [...] The little Anrepinas look rather charming running about round the lawn with bamboo branches. Helen and I go to Japp's tonight to a return dinner. Apparently Mrs Japp is renowned for her exquisite cuisine and was very agitated by our gorgeous display. So this is our rival party. I shall be glad to have you back again. Henry by the way made a long speech about you to me. So I assured him you weren't in the least hostile. He was pathetic in his curious way. He poured out a melancholy tale to me about Dorelia and John, and the lack of civilisation at Alderney. Now dear I must go and attend to my duties. Helen has a most corrupting influence on one. One does nothing but sit under the veranda and talk. I love you so very much. My fondest love,

Your most loving Mopsa

Ralph and Frances had gone to Spain alone together. During this journey they became lovers, and returned more committed to each other than ever.

Mark Gertler had been seriously ill with tuberculosis. While Carrington's artistic career had dwindled, his had been productive and successful. He was still unmarried.

To Mark Gertler

Ham Spray House
Monday, 27 September 1925

Dear Mark,

I heard the other day from Anrep that you were ill again. I felt suddenly so very sorry. I wished to write, and tell you so. I hope you will soon be better.

Hearing you were ill, my resentful feelings which I confess I have felt for some years, suddenly vanished and I wish only to send you my love and best wishes,

Your Carrington

To Mark Gertler

Ham Spray House
7 October 1925

Dear Mark

I was glad to hear that you are not very ill, and that you are recovering. It was kind of you to write, and tell me about yourself ... It's a little difficult to answer your letter – partly because I don't want to.

One of the comforts of being over thirty I find, is at last to know what one feels, and only to do the things one wants to do! So your letter will remain unanswered. But I assure you I've no longer any grudges, and I feel perfectly friendly towards you. I do not know what the mingled accounts of my brother, Desmond [MacCarthy] and Ruth [Selby-Bigge] were of my life! In reality I am very happy to live in this country and love it so passionately that I find nothing outside it seems to affect me very much. I do more painting than I used to do, as now I have a fine studio here.

Perhaps in five years we will meet, and then we can give each other a complete account of our lives since we last saw each other! – I know you will understand what I am going to say, so I shall not make any apologies. I don't really want to see, or write to you again. I know it's really impracticable and incompatible with my present life. My mind was set at rest by your letter, and now I shall return back into my mole hole. As a matter of fact I never go to London now, and I am too lazy to write letters. Half of one of course is always curious to meet again, and reluctant ever to stop a friendship but I expect you will agree with me. I hope you do not find the Sanatorium very tedious. I was so pleased to hear from you. I hope you will soon be strong again.

My love

Your Carrington

1926

After their return from Spain, Ralph and Frances decided they wanted to live together in London. Desperate to avoid this threat to the 'triangular trinity of happiness', Carrington suggested that Frances should move in with Julia Strachey in Gordon Square.

To Julia Strachey

Ham Spray House
[Spring 1926]

[…] I see no reason, as it is in many ways the only obvious person [Frances] you could ask to share a flat with you and it certainly would probably make your difficulties of housekeeping easier. But I love you Julia for being so understanding and giving me a straw to cling on. I will come and see you again soon, and talk to you and then, when the weather is a little less grim, I will ask you here. You will come? Don't write back to me, as Ralph returns next Monday and please burn this letter. If only one's feelings weren't so involved there is a fascination in intrigue and plots that is unequalled. It is so interesting to have a part laid down with one's words to learn. But I've very little spirit left. For which reason I've rather taken to the other 'spirits'. Now I shall live for a little in my nunnery, drink glasses of hot water and lemon, go for long walks, and read Proust in the evenings. Did you like my decorations on Alix's walls. Honestly? You see I've rather an absurd opinion of your taste.

My love dear Julia
Your Carrington

Later Friday
PS Lytton has just had a conversation with me. He says a dentist has now entered the arena. But that you put up a brave fight. Most dear Julia. But of course if F will come there is no reason why she shouldn't take the lower floor instead of the dentist, or an upper floor, in fact Gordon Square offers everything most suitable for the 'situation', general vagueness, tennis in the summer and company and nice rooms. However just because it would make life tolerable and prevent general disaster, I feel it won't happen. I shall always however love you for your kindness to me, even if it is of no avail. Meanwhile I hope the dentist will be prevented from actually taking the first floor until our fates are settled. My only hope rests with your diplomacy. I will write

next Tuesday when I shall probably know from Ralph the results of your letter. Please burn this letter.

My love again
Your Carrington

After this ploy failed, Lytton asked Frances to meet him to discuss the situation. He made it clear to her that he could not promise to remain at Ham Spray with Carrington without Ralph. Though no longer deeply in love with him, Lytton loved him dearly and relied on his strong, practical masculine presence. Frances, however, was not going to give in to emotional blackmail. The situation was painful for all concerned. Eventually it was resolved by a remarkable exchange of letters between the two women.

To Frances Marshall

Ham Spray House
Wednesday [early spring 1926]

Dear Frances,

This is a difficult letter to write. If it wasn't that I have grown very fond of you I couldn't write it. You will understand that, also since you are as unhappy as I am, you will forgive me.

I wanted to see you to talk, but I now feel it's too hard, because our feelings are so involved.

We each know what we have all three been feeling these last months. Now it's more or less over. The Treaty has to be drawn up. I have to accept that owing to a situation, which cannot be got over, I must give up living with Ralph. I simply now write quite frankly, to beg you to try, while these adjustments are being made, to see the position from my point of view and to try and see if it's not compatible with your happiness to still let me keep some of my friendship with Ralph. I can't get away from everything, because of Lytton. Even although the happiness of my relation with Lytton, ironically, is so bound up with Ralph, that that will be wrecked. I am obliged to accept this situation; you must see that. All I can do is to beg you to be, any rate at first, a little generous.

You see I've no pride, I write a letter which I suppose I oughtn't to write. You see, Frances, you can afford to be lenient because R is so completely yours in his affections. In spite of all your difficulties and unhappiness you are a gainer, we losers. And if you face it, the situation really is that Ralph can only give me what you can spare to give. My future does now rest with you. I can't ask you to understand what I feel because it's really impossible ever to understand other people exactly. I can't really understand all your feelings. But by putting myself in your position I have been able to see the inevitability of this situation and to sympathise with your misery.

I do love Ralph, only in a different way, just as you love him. It isn't any easier for me to give him up than it would be for you. As he loves you, he must care for your feelings before those of anybody else. That is rather an important fact, but I have been facing it for some time. The bare truth from my point of view is that if Ralph leaves me completely, or to all practical purpose completely, it really means an end to this life. I can't ask him to go on seeing me down here, because he really feels it depends on whether you can bear it. If you can't, nothing can be done. If you can, you must know it would mean everything to Lytton and me.

I don't suppose you ever realised that it wasn't easy for me a year ago to give up what I did give up, to you.[1]

In the next month a good deal will be settled. This is why I write to you. I am, you must see, rather outside everything, I can't alter anybody's happiness, or unhappiness. Ralph's position is much the hardest one to bear at present probably. Whatever happens, Frances, I would like to tell you, now, that I've never felt anything but fondness for you. I've no resentment because I regard it all as beyond us, in an odd way. I send you my love and I hope you are happier. Forgive me if I should not have written; perhaps however you will understand. It would be kind if you burnt this letter, for it was rather difficult to write.

I send my love to you.

Yr Carrington

Reading this over, I see I've expressed it very badly. And probably it's pointless. But I feel rather in despair, so forgive me and don't pay any attention to it, if you don't want to. There seems to be no answer, but perhaps you will write.

xxxxxxx

Frances wrote back to say that although she was not prepared to give Ralph up, she was prepared to share him. 'I never never never feel that if R should live with me I should want him not to see you very often and go on being fond of you ... Because I love R and want to live with him, and want him to share my life instead of being a visitor into it, I can't see how I could find this incompatible with his being fond of you and seeing you every day of his life.'

1 Probaby a reference to giving up sex with Ralph.

*And so it was settled that Ralph and Frances would move into the top floor of
41 Gordon Square with James and Alix Strachey (as Ralph and Carrington had
done five years earlier) and spend weekends at Ham Spray.*

To Julia Strachey

Ham Spray House
Monday [spring 1926]

Dearest Julia,

I am going to Falmouth this week with Lytton. So I shall not see you for
some weeks I am afraid. I wanted to tell you that things are rather better.
By a miracle James and Alix have stepped into the arena and saved the situation. Frances is going to live at 41 G.S., so you will have her as a near
neighbour to you. And a good deal of the horrors will be mitigated for
everyone I think by the new arrangement. It was so kind of you to be so
friendly to me. I felt you hardly realized how grateful I felt to you.

I stay at Falmouth a week. Then I will probably come back here. Tell me
about your mannequin job? It is amusing, does it help to gratify your passion
for dressing up in grand gowns? I feel rather better in the head now. So next
time I shall not be so boring I hope. May I come to your shop and buy
something from you? Or have you nothing under 20 gns in your department?
I will write again when I next come to London so that we can go on our
jaunts to the cinema. My love dear Julia,

Yr Carrington

*As the next letter shows, Ham Spray was not much affected by the General Strike
of 1926. Gerald was about to return to Spain.*

To Gerald Brenan

Ham Spray House
Thursday [6 May 1926]

Dearest Amigo,

[...] We live marooned on a green island here, cut off from the world.
Except for a charming lady at Inkpen Post Office, who rings up and gives
us 'the news' which she gleans from the wireless. You would fall completely
in love with her, for she gives one such a perfect selection. 'The Prince of

Wales has just come back by aeroplane. It is nice to think of having him back just now isn't it?' 'They say the hospitals will have enough milk and that there were 150 volunteers in Bristol this morning, before they were asked for. Oh yes, and the King is talking to Mr Baldwin, this afternoon, and two warships have taken food to Liverpool. I don't think there is anything else. No riots and everything much the same in London. Oh yes, trains run every 15 mins on the Baker Street railway.'

My mother is ill with pneumonia at Cheltenham. But I hope I shall not be forced to go over and see her. Lytton is reading Ford to me in the evenings: *The Broken Heart*. It is very good. This afternoon we have just been [on] an exquisite walk along the foot of the Downs. I found a wild yellow auricula, a cross between a cowslip and a primrose. The woods are filled with bluebells and all the birds sing great choruses in the little copses. It's difficult looking at the green wheat fields and the pale green woods to believe that anything unusual is happening in London [...]

I feel tired with the beauty of spring and too much internal enthusiasm. As the post takes 3 days to reach anyone this is probably the last letter I'll write to you. But I would like to send you my love before you leave England.

Your Amiga

PS Thank you for being my friend.

To Julia Strachey

The Owls' Retreat
Thursday [summer?]

My Dearest Julia,

[...] Tommy and I have just been off to Dorset on a spree. Ma foi quelle spree! We visited Mr [Lamb] on Tuesday after tea. Went for a dismal walk along the sea shore with him. Had a lovely supper of broad beans and claret and rather revived. Then he and Tommy played music all the evening. The next morning we woke up very exhausted as the cats made such a noise one couldn't sleep. We had then more music till half-past 10. Then Tommy and I went off to another region of Dorset and visited his old friends Mr and Mrs Powys of Left Leg fame.[1] I found them wonderfully charming. Mr Powys seems without a fault. He was so beautifully good, and gracious. It was rather like travelling with some dethroned King of Bavaria, returning to his long lost country. From every cottage old dames, and worthies, children and half witted hobbled out to kiss the hem of Tommy's corduroy trousers. Tommy insisted on reading me Marvell's poems all last Monday. 'Laments on Julia'.

---

1 T. F. Powys (1884–1939), writer, whose short-story collection *The Left Leg* had been published by Chatto & Windus in 1923.

'To my fair Julia' etc. etc. so I gathered from the expression in his voice, and the sadness of his eye, that you have indented his young heart with your cold imprint. Fie Fie. However it's a great consolation for me to have another lovesick bird to sing duets with on the loveliness of my Julia [...]

I love having you here. I will ask you very soon again. Most lovely Julia I send you my fondest love.

Your C

To Lytton Strachey

Ham Spray House
Sunday [19 September 1926]

My dearest Lytton,

Quelle Chaleur! Do you know one is forced to search out, positively, one's old enemy the wind today. Even in the shade and in the windiest corner of the lawn it is too hot. Faith [Henderson] arrived yesterday at 4 o'ck. She seems in high spirits and is very charming. We didn't get breakfast till 10 o'ck today and then went [for] a walk along the Downs to the mushroom field and didn't get back till half past two. It was twenty to four by the time we finished lunch! Faith is very vague and doesn't mind spending a whole weekend with beds unmade and no washing up. Which I have collected into a great Silbury Hill in the kitchen for poor Madame Slater tomorrow!

Do you know on the way to the mushrooms just at the top of Ham Hill I heard a plaintive mewing, and there, peeping out of a rabbit hole was a small cat, a rather half cat half rabbit. So I pulled it out, and carried it on our walk, and brought it home. It was a curious little creature slightly like a monkey with a dark face, feet and tail, and brownish fur standing up on end. It was terribly hungry. I shall try and find a home for it at the Lodge.

Belle¹ is very happy in her field, I pay her visits and she comes up, and lets me pat her – It is exciting to see from the top of the Downs a little white horse walking across Huth's² field and to know that it is Bellinda. We got a whole basket of mushrooms, but the heat was so great we only walked very slowly. Faith was completely exhausted by the time we got down to the bottom of the Downs and reached the Deserts of Sahara [...]

You can't think Lytton darling how much I've loved being with you alone lately and how much I love you for being so kind to me always. It seems ridiculous after 10 years to still tell you that I care so much, but every time you go away it comes back to me, and I realize in spite of the beauties of

---

1 Lytton had given Carrington a white pony called Belle.
2 Major Huth was their farmer neighbour.

the Ilex tree and the Downs, Ham Spray loses more than half its beauty robbed of its Fakir. My fondest love,

Your most loving Mopsa xxx

To Lytton Strachey

Littlebeck, Painswick Road, Cheltenham
[23 September 1926]

Darling Lytton,

Here I am plunged in the middle of Benares brass life, and Japanese screens, while you lie on Firle Beacons with Tommy, or talk over fires with Duncan and Vanessa. I can hardly tell you the horror I was filled with coming back to this life of dead ghosts again. The gargoyle side-board and the small details, the inkstand, and the sugar spoon with arum lily handle, and chipcarved photograph frames. If only there was a confederate outside so one could make some jokes. My mother lives with a grey mouse of a lady-help, and the refinement, and purity of life here is inconceivable! Home made lemonade, and cold blancmange and raspberry jam for the supper last night ...

I can't write you a letter, I am too depressed by the hideousness of this house, and the bric a bracs.

The awful thought is that one is tainted by the same blood, and perhaps my manias for treacle prints, and old tea pots is just as bad as Japanese vases, and Indian brasses! It's rather a charming little Georgian house but inside is now indistinguishable from every house we have ever lived in, so why my mother has moved so many times seems to me a mystery. I think however of Ham Spray, and our Downs and then this chimera vanishes. I love you so very much, and think of you most of the time and wish I had you here this morning to do a little 'pavement tapping boy accosting' – You had forgotten that line?

My love,

Yr most loving Mopsa xxx

To Gerald Brenan

Friday evening [17 December 1926]

Dearest Amigo,

Ralph has just come, and has brought the Christmas tree decorations and the toys. I love the snake so much I can hardly bear to give it away. The birds are exquisite. I now look forward to nothing but decorating the tree.

The party is to be on Monday afternoon. You were very charming Amigo to go to so much trouble [...]

Lytton reads. What does Lytton read? Not what you expect or what the world (which is Gordon Square) expects, for Lytton sits over the fire, the firelight playing on his red beard, his lamb skin slippers ('oh he treated Henry Lamb quite cruelly, I assure you') on his feet. The rug, (see Tate Gallery) thrown over his knees, surrounded by his library of books on every side (he collects mostly old books, especially 18th century French books) his three cats (Mr Strachey like Lord Kitchener and, or, Lord Roberts, cannot bear dogs) sitting on the hearth rug. His two companions Mr and Mrs Thrale in another corner of room, reading, as he sits over his fire; *Lord Raingo*, by Arnold Bennett.[1] There! Mr Crusoe. What a surprise for you! You thought I was going to say, *The Decline and Fall* of Mr Gibbon!!!! Mr Thrale reads his *Financial Times* and makes calculations. Miss Moffat, for Mrs Thrale has suddenly left the room, sits in her blue overcoat with brass buttons and a pair of striped socks to keep her feet warm, writing a letter to a commercial traveller. 'And pray what is his commerce?' 'Oh, he's a coffee importer, my dear.' 'Is that the same as an imposter?' 'Now, Barbara my dear, really you must not be so stupid, or ask so many questions.' And it is time Aunt Moffat went to bed for she is almost asleep. My love dear Mr Crusoe.[2] I am still and always will be your loving

Amiga Cirod

To Gerald Brenan

Ham Spray House
Monday morning [27 December 1926]

Amigo Mio,

[...] I wish you had been here this Christmas to put me in a good temper. For this morning I am in a very cross patch mood. Simply because I couldn't sleep last night and then, one gets so bored with looking after fires, coffee pots, and digging vegetables and making beds. That's just what you like to hear: Miss Moffat complaining, well I will complain but only softly to my dear Amigo! The Christmas tree looks exquisite. Those fairy balloons and the birds of paradise are my favourites. Ottoline telephones yesterday to say she was coming over with Mark [Gertler] and the Turners today for tea. But

---

1 Arnold Bennett (1867–1931), the leading realist writer of his day, had just published *Lord Raingo*, a thinly disguised portrait of his friend and patron Lord Beaverbrook (1879–1964).
2 One of her nicknames for Gerald, who admired Defoe.

today she telephones to say their car has broken down so she will not come. For which I am extremely glad, as I hate being responsible for those crushed tea parties, with everyone talking at the tops of their voices, or remaining gloomily silent. I haven't got your picture finished but there has been no time since the invasion arrived on Friday. I love having Julia here. She is a gay sympathetic character. Her turn of humour is very fascinating. How did you survive Xmas? I suppose by now your digestion is properly ruined and you are filled with gloomy vapours and a dislike for the human race.

Tommy arrived last night and seems in high spirits. Marjorie Strachey is very amusing and knits everyone together by her good temper and perpetual jokes. So one may say it's been a very nice Xmas party and everyone has enjoyed themselves.

Yes, I've been very happy except for this morning, when suddenly finding the stove had gone out and the water in the bathroom was cold, my neck was stiff and my head ached, I fell into a fine rage with life and Christmas and anthracite stoves. But already I've recovered since I started writing to you and now I feel very light hearted. This afternoon I shall go for a ride on Belle directly after lunch. Marjorie Strachey gave me the most beautiful Armenian boots and Julia a blue silk padded dressing gown. Henry sent me some marsala and James gave me a huge pot of caviar, so that for the first time in my life I've had the pleasure of caviar for breakfast, and caviar for every meal. I want to reform next year and do a great deal more serious painting and even writing. Will one? Simply to spite oneself and one's traditional character I think I will! You've been rather churlish not writing me letters, but I forgive you on condition you write me a long one this week. Ralph gave me a garbled and curious account of your affaires and conversations.

Dorelia sent me a most beautiful present. A box covered with shells, only not ordinary shells, but the most fantastic rare-coloured shells, that you have ever seen and inside the box, two charming figures of pottery.

Tonight we have a sort of dance, Japps, and Noel and Missie, I feel rather apathetic about it. I prefer these amusing conversations with Marjorie, Julia and Tommy over the fire to organised gaiety.

My love, dearest Amigo. Please write to me soon, if you are not too busy working. (Have you any news of Helen?)

From you most loving Cirod xxxxxxxx

1927

To Julia Strachey

Ham Spray House
[January 1927]

[...] I am sorry my lovely Poppet you didn't have a nicer Xmas. But the trouble was I was sleeping rather badly and couldn't pull myself together, and everything seemed rather disintegrated, but perhaps when I wasn't in the room the glasses clinked and all was in a roar [...] You have no idea how much I enjoy lying in my bedroom watching the fire on the ceiling. After the crises of last week it is a place of peace [...]

Do let's have ball. Dress you as an Empire oriental beauty. At the moment I am reigning Queen of Laplandia.

Your blue dressing gown is the comfort of my life.

My very fondest love,

From your devoted old Tante C.

is the pattern on which I base my life. The
style is to be an adroit mixture between Saint
Simeon — or mr Gerhardi. And the title. Ha
but you will cribe it. I shall not disclose the
title for therein lies the plot, the clue, and
the mystery. Give Tommy my love. who I
friend as I always do. the most sympathetic
companion. Do lets share a Ball
~~~~~~~~~ dress you as an Empire
oriental Beauty. At the moment I
am reigning Queen of Laplandia

from am devoted old Tanta

my very Fond & Lexie

Your blue dressing gown is the comfort of my life

To Gerald Brenan

Ham Spray House
Saturday [22 January 1927]

[...] What a life we all lead to be sure. Influenzas, mistresses, colds, and now I have fallen off a toboggan and bruised my bottom black.

Yesterday afternoon I went tobogganing with Olive on the Downs. It was a most lovely afternoon. The sun was just setting, and the sky was a most delicate green tinged with pink and little clouds rose up from behind the crest of the downs, like balloons liberated by some hidden hand and floated up into the pale opal sky.

The sun shone on the quarry, and lit up the snow along the ridge. I was so happy I could hardly bear to come back to tea. We had some lovely rushes down the hill. Olive had never been on a toboggan before. Unfortunately I took a ditch in my enthusiasm and bumped Olive's head and my bottom. But I feel better this morning. The country intoxicates me with its beauty, it fills me with the same sort of internal pleasure that one feels when the spring begins. Lytton read me *The White Devil* by Webster last night over a fire. Just as I was getting into bed, I looked out for the last time on the moonlighted lawn and there was my enemy the rabbit, who all this week has eaten up my lettuces and cabbages, so I knelt at the open window and shot him. He died at once mercifully in one shot. This morning it is snowing again. To my mind this landscape is at its loveliest in the winter, covered with snow. How appalling about your aunt. For although one at first laughs at her extraordinary behaviour, one soon remembers it is the end of everyone and how miserable underneath all her confusion of mind she must be.

Lytton came into tea yesterday, and saw the two cats lying embraced on his chair. 'Snakes in a sink, toads in a cistern' he said looking at the cats. For some reason with the expression on his face it was very amusing [...]

My fondest love dearest of Amigos. I am, in spite of all your prognostications your very loving
Cirod

To Julia Strachey

Ham Spray House
Thursday [about 24 January 1927]

Dearest Julia,

You are a fickle niece, find a comfortable bed and a kind uncle and poor Tante C is soon forgotten. Not so Tante C. She thinks perpetually of her Julia hence this letter. Well my dear you have no idea what an exciting time we have had here. Snow fights with lovely young men (or a man to be precise) with hair the colour of canary birds and the most heavenly blue eyes [Dadie Rylands] and Mr Peter Morris, his friend, with auburn hair and a 'quite lovely' nose. But his shoes were what won my heart. Under the excuse of examining the buckles, I gave them a delicate stroke, and the thrill that ran down my spine, my dear! I can hardly describe! [. . .]

That wretch Ralph will have told you all our news so what can I tell you? All yesterday afternoon I cleaned my studio and this morning, true to my word (for I had made Tante C who is rather a severe character, a promise to paint a picture today whatever happened) so I sat in my bedroom and painted a landscape of the snow with some cows. MacWhirter instantly rushes to your mind, with Scotch firs and lochs and Highland cattle. Which just shows you know nothing, miss, about painting. Most of my week has been spent motoring over to Shalbourne to see poor Helen Anrep and her children, who have influenza. Now they have gone away. So our hermitage life resumes its chilly course. Lytton is reading me *The White Devil* by Webster in the evenings. I can't ride Belle as the ground is covered with snow and very hard. When do you fly the country? Shall I ask Phyllis de Janzé to try and find rooms for you? Would you like a French maid to go with you to iron your frocks, and uncurl your hair? Unfortunately she don't speak French otherwise a most respectable woman. Not a word has reached me from London. So I suppose you are all deeply engrossed in intrigues, or parties [. . .]

Will you write me a letter? I hope you are happy, Julia. I have asked the cleaners to send your coat directly to 41 G.S. So you ought to get it by Monday next week. Lytton sits writing in the sitting room. The wind roars outside and the fire blazes up the chimney. Stump and Tinker lie in a lovers embrace asleep in the arm chair [. . .]

Last night I was chased by a huge black bull, in a dream. A tranquillity has settled on Ham Spray lately. Perhaps it is the snow. I feel incapable of anything but the very purest emotions. You have no idea how lovely the garden looks in the moonlight with the snow all glistening like diamonds. Tante C is becoming romantic, that will never do. My love dearest Julia. You know I love you a great deal.

Your devoted C

To Gerald Brenan

Ham Spray House
Thursday, in bed [27 February 1927]

Dear Amigo,

Thank you for your letter. It was like a cherry tart, one continually had to be taking stones out of one's mouth. I am no duller I assure you than I am usually. I enjoy reading enormously and I can do that all day long. Then I lie for hours making up imaginary stories and now that I cannot move[1] I no longer wonder if the stove has gone out, or if Olive has remembered to put on the potatoes [...] You wonder why I prefer my Wiltshire water closet to London? But where do you imagine I could lie in bed in London? I could not lie for ever in R and F's sitting room and the alternative was a nursing home and I would literally rather die on a dung heap than be scolded and fussed over by nurses, who allow one to see visitors between 3 and 4 o'ck as a great favour and charge one 10 gns a week for boiled cod and cornflour shape [...]

Lytton came back yesterday full of the most amusing gossip. I laughed for nearly 2 hours over his stories. Stump, my favourite cat, sits on my bed and drinks out of the saucer on my tray. It is very pleasant lying under the blue canopy hung round with the tapestries of Granada, with a Greek chorus of rooks outside. Yesterday for the first time I tottered three yards and sat in a chair over the fire. It's curious to feel so feeble. However Ellie [Rendel, Lytton's doctor cousin] when she examined me, gave me a very flattering account of my health. My blood pressure was only 118, and my physique was superb. She is a very charming doctor. She tells me very softly just what one most longs to hear. I have read all Gogol now. 'The Nose' pleased me as much as any story. And 'The Overcoat' and then the 'Diary of a Madman' is superb. But I can't write you a letter. It is a pity, for it is used to be one of the greatest pleasures. Your philosophy of life sounds almost perfect. I have plenty of books to read thank you; and I want nothing to eat.

But you will find the new universally admired genius will turn out to be the same Tomlin and that all the roads leads to Rome. That is one of the strangest phenomena of life. For a change, this year I will concentrate all my attention on my work and regard people as species of birds for my bird book, which I am making. I hope you will like your new room. It was kind of you to write to me. Forgive my stupidity but any sense I had has been thrown down the Wiltshire water closet in the bedpans.

My love
Your C

1 Carrington had fallen from her horse while riding with Henry Lamb in Richmond Park.

To Julia Strachey

> 51 Ladbroke Grove, London [a nursing home]
> Write to Ham Spray next time
> Wednesday [March 1927]

Dearest Julia,

Now you are forgiven only unfortunately you have whetted an appetite that can only be satisfied by another letter and very quickly. I am glad you are so happy. It sounds much more pleasant, and economical than London. I have been here for 10 days having my back massaged by a singularly unpleasant young woman with peroxide hair and the beauty of Phyllis Dare. She is terribly sadistic and hurts me very much. However I conceal my real character and lead her on to tell me all her innermost feelings. 'Don't you love Surrey Mrs P. I was down at Hindhead on Sunday giving my dog a run.' 'Don't you think dogs', violent slaps, 'much more', slaps, 'intelligent', bangs, 'and more capable of love', bangs, 'and affection than human beings', bangs. 'I think', slaps, 'something has been left out of human beings they are such miserable', bangs, 'mean', harder bangs, 'creatures', terrifying bangs, 'compared to intelligent dogs'. Today being the last day shall I reveal my true character and shatter her? But that is probably impossible. She is made of iron. When one thinks of what might have happened, lying smoothed tenderly by gentle loving hands. But I suppose there wasn't much chance of Ellie sending one a sympathetic masseuse!! This is a vile pen. I haven't been able to do much frisking about in London as I get so tired in the back. So I've decorated Lytton's sitting room at Gordon Square for him: very chaste. In pale green, white and cherry red, with decorations on the mantelpiece. Lytton bought a lovely still life by John B[1] which is a joy to put over the mantelpiece.

Am I cutting my throat, I often wonder, making Lytton's room so elegant and lovely? Will he now fly to Gordon Square with R [Roger Senhouse] every Monday and leave me desolee at Ham Spray? Then I've painted Gerald's new room in St James's street, apple green and vermilion. And Alix has commissioned me to paint her gramophone with pictures all over it [...]

---

1 John Banting (1902–72), a young painter drawn to surrealism.

Gerald was back in London for the summer. His relationship with Carrington staggered on.

To Gerald Brenan

Ham Spray House
Friday afternoon [13 May 1927]

Amigo Mio,
   [...] My head aches with thinking backwards and forwards about you, and myself. And I get more and more depressed. Yes, it's quite clear I am fit only to have relations with old plates and cats. I agree with almost everything you say. Don't ask me to make any decisions, or more promises. For I am incapable of both. I only will try and reform and please more and be less selfish. If you find me intolerable you had better give me up. I've such a poor opinion of myself. I can't argue about it. I am very sorry I have made you unhappy [...]
   My fondest love to you.
   Your loving C

To Gerald Brenan

Ham Spray House of Banging Doors
Saturday [11 June 1927]

Dear Mr Crusoe,
   I should be glad if you could tell me, since you are a seer, why doors bang instead of shutting or keeping shut? Why everything is green in the summer? And why Mr Robinson does not write letters? Phyllis is coming to lunch today so you can just imagine what a flutter Miss Moffat and her tuffet are in! [...] No visitors this weekend for a miracle, which is a mercy. For to tell you the truth, much as Miss Moffat likes showing off her wilderness of green leaves and her possets of sack, even more does she prefer dawdling away her time in her room and listening to *Mansfield Park* with Lytton over the fire alone. Do I see you next Wednesday? That would be nice, if you also thought it nice, and I will spend Thursday with you? No. Impossible! Yes. We'll spend all Thursday together; I'll not go back till the evening train [...] My love dearest Amigo,
   From your amiable Miss Moffatt

PS I've been reading a life of Sargent[1] the painter. It is almost unbelievable that such people can exist.

1 John Singer Sargent (1856–1925), fashionable American portrait painter.

Saturday evening
PS My letter never got posted today. Phyllis came this morning looking very dazzling like a grand Persian Wxxxe [whore] with a scarlet mouth. Really I could wish she didn't paint so violently. Lunch went off beautifully. Veloute sauce and carrots, cold chicken and cream posset. Lytton was very deign and friendly. After lunch we went off alone together and lay in the grass and talked. Very amusing gossip and conversations about lovers and lust. She has to go back at tea time. I must say she attracts me very much but I can't quite tell you why. She loved Ham Spray and was properly appreciative of everything. I wish she could have stayed longer, as there was so much to talk about that I simply forgot to ask her. Now I've finished painting my bedroom pale yellow and I've been for a walk with Lytton and discussed Phyllis's character with him. The day is not very agreeable, too sultry, and yet cold. I've got this pain in my back again, so feel rather distrait. And exhausted after the agitations of the Vicomtesse invasion. But it will be nice to see my sober Mr Crusoe on Wednesday evening. I'll try and be as good as you deserve.

Your very loving C

To Saxon Sydney-Turner

Ham Spray House
15 July 1927

I think if I enjoyed the party more than other parties it was perhaps because of your friendly wave as I started off in my ship (or cab) on my voyage. There was a very mixed gathering of nautical beauties. Lytton predominated as an admiral. Duncan looked very exquisite as a commodore. There was the usual contingent of male 'beauties', Douglas [Davidson], Dadie [Rylands], Angus [Davidson] and many others, all in white ducks. Julia was a 1890 middy. I meant to cut out the description in the *Evening Standard* which devoted two paragraphs to Lytton's appearance and the other notables. Miss Tallulah Bankhead the actress, Serge Lifar, Miss Todd etc. There was a professional cocktail shaker, who for 4 hours mixed 'side cars'and 'moon rakers' without stopping. I had a proposal from The Honourable Gathorne-Hardy, but unfortunately (or fortunately one never can tell) his original paramour a gentleman called Mr Ferriere, returned to the party, so he deserted me. And I ended up as I began with my old loves, Lytton and Alix and Dadie and returned with them to 41 Gordon Square. Alix moved me by giving me a passionate embrace half way up the stairs at 4.30 and said after all old friends were best and these new adventures really ended in dust and ashes. The next day I woke up with a terrible headache, for I had drunk nothing but cocktails the night before. Still as a dream and a vision of beauty, it still gives me great pleasure to think of these lovely sailors and sailoresses, all so very amorous, and gay. Julia and Tommy are to be married next week I think. They seem very devoted and happy so I hope it will (at any rate for some time) turn out successful. Oliver was to entertain the Judge and Lady Tomlin at a formal dinner at the Oriental [Club] last night! Unfortunately Lady T discovered about Paris,[1] so weeps all day and says if only it had been 'different' how pleased she would have been to have welcomed Miss Strachey into the Tomlin fold, but as things are, she can only receive her with icy drawn back arms. The dreadful scandal has been kept from the Judge, so Lady T has to bear 'the burden of this great sorrow' alone. I bought them a patch work quilt for a wedding present before I left London.

Lytton and I returned yesterday afternoon and at 4 o'ck the postman brought me your letter. I regret I am not yet old enough to be insensible to flattery. And I was very moved by your letter. But perhaps you also had been drinking old brandy for dinner? Topsy and Peter Lucas arrived yesterday and stay till tomorrow. Do you know them?[2]

[...] Tomorrow Olive goes to Brighton for the day. I feel slightly depressed as I can do my painting. There is no reason except that I feel I know what the result will be before I start on a picture, and the result is so dull always, it hardly seems worth while beginning. Lytton is getting on slowly with 'Elizabeth'.[3] He hopes to get it finished by September and then perhaps we may go away together for a fortnight. But I hardly like to look forward to it in case it doesn't come off. And in August perhaps you will pay Ham Spray a visit? [...] Do you grow happier or remain in much the same mood from one year to another? Lately I feel as if for the first time I've grasped what the general plan of one's life is, and will be.

My fondest love to you,

Your Carrington

A very notable black lily (the same variety as one Barbara had last year) is just going to unroll itself into flower so I am very excited.

1 Tommy and Julia had been living together in Paris.

2 F. L. Lucas (1894–1967), known as Peter, was an English don at King's College, Cambridge. He was an expert on Webster, a poet and novelist, and married to the writer E. B. C. Jones, known as Topsy. It was an open marriage; she was in love with Dadie Rylands, while he was to have a brief affair with Carrington.

3 Lytton was writing on Elizabeth I and the Earl of Essex.

Despite his mother's horror that they had been living in sin, Stephen Tomlin and Julia were married in the summer of 1927 and would soon move to a cottage in Swallowcliffe, not far from Ham Spray.

To Julia Strachey

[Ham Spray?]
Monday [mid-July 1927]

Darlingest Julia,

You can imagine, Julia, the load that has been lifted off my mind, and the hell I have been through and now all the loads are lifted, and one can see daylight again, and I am tremendously glad that you are so happy as I know you will be with Stephen who is a dear boy, and I am sure when you have both found yourselves as you certainly will soon, you will understand what a real married life can be. Oh Julia, I am very glad over your new born happiness.

Well well it's all been very fine but exit Aunt C. I fear now that her bird of a dove has found a nest.

I am glad seriously (exit Wogan for ever[1]) you are going to marry Tommy who if you didn't marry I should seriously think of marrying myself, for he is such a charmer. I loved our last weekend together (sobs and sighs) and I fear you'll incur a great many enemies, i.e. Lytton, by snatching the lovely boy into your Swallow's nest.

I am going to buy you a mirror for your blue spare room. I loved your cottage really, it looks very lovely, although what with the children and Barbara and one thing and another there is hardly time to look at it. Burn this letter, or we shall be disgraced and don't tell T as I am sure he will disapprove! May I be your best aunt at your wedding? But I suppose the crowd of sobbing, sighing lovers will be too thick and may I come in August and see you? I will whether I may or not. I wish I could come up this week, but I am afraid I can't. Tell me if you want a momentary loan of money to buy anything, a yard of brides-veiling for the occasion. Darling Julia, nobody can be as glad as your most loving

Tante C

---

1 Julia had been having an affair with the painter Wogan Philipps, who was married to the aspiring novelist Rosamond Lehmann.

To Julia Strachey

H. S. S. Owlscliffe, Wiltshire
Thursday [August 1927]

Darling, I fairly exploded with laughter over your letter this morning in bed much to the surprise of the little Tiberius who was about to eat my bread and butter (seeing it was a letter from you, and that my attention was completely engrossed.) 'But who are all those other letters from,' cries Mrs Nosey Tomlin? Ha Ha. If only you shared my double bed, and left your Swallow's nest for my snuggery you would be able to read all my letters, even those from the lovely R-s-m-on [Rosamond Lehmann]. Well, darling, if you really liked the spotted dog which was I confess 'knocked off' in two minutes to please a little boy of 4, I will do you a whole dinner service of: Pussy Cats.

'Really Julia, I must protest. I simply can't face eating my boiled sausage off a cat's back.'

'Believe me, Tommy it is only one of her jokes. But what shall we ask her to paint on our dinner service?'

There is a problem for you to solve and in two weeks please make up your answer, as I shall by then be starting on my new china enterprise. Oh dear I wish I hadn't a complex about earning money, and such a desire to have money at the same time. It's the same thing I suppose as my mania for wanting 'to go' to the W.C., and my dislike for being there, so that I rush out before I've even 'tried' as they say. I now take paraffin oil to assist Madame nature.

What fun your birthday party, with the blue cake, will be. I shall think of some very recherchez gift to stagger and I hope melt the granite heart of my perfect paramour.

We are infested by rats also. I use Rodine with some success. But it only lasts about a week. Then a new army enters the house from the farmyard and starts nibbling the books, the papers, and the cheese. The cats catch some, but they obviously are too many.

H. S. H.
Owls cliffe
Wiltshire.

Thursday

Darling, I fairly schloded with laughter over your letter this morning when I opened it

much to the surprise of little Tiberius who was about to eat up my bread & Butter, [seeing it was a letter from you, & that my attention was completely engrossed.]

To Julia Strachey

Ham Spray House
[17 August 1927]

Written *in haste*

Darling Julia,

Many Happy Returns of yesterday [...] I can't find your blue pettie-coatie my sweetie. What's to be done? I am afraid Stump must have stolen it and seized it for Sunday wear. Oh dear, I've given her a tail! What's to be done? [...]

At the beginning of August, Carrington visited Munich with James and Alix Strachey and Sebastian Sprott. She and Gerald were still exchanging agonised and repetitive letters.

To Gerald Brenan

Ham Spray House
Saturday [13 August 1927]

I haven't written to you because I have not known what to say. But I have been thinking a great deal about our relation.

The truth seems to be that I am almost diseased in the head over some matters and probably it's lunacy for me to try to have an intimate relation with anyone. Lately, I mean the last two months, I've had rather an obsession of the subject of copulation. The result is I sleep badly and get nervous about it. It seems out of my control. I mean when these feelings come, and go. However, I see it's maddening for you to have anything to do with me and the knowledge that my behaviour affects you so considerably and makes you bear me grudges only makes me feel disinclined to see you and depressed. I feel at the moment it's no good you seeing me. For I only irritate you. And I'm incapable of promising before hand what the mood will be, as I do not know about them myself. If however you want me to see you again later on, when your irritation has passed and possibly my nerves left me, you must tell me. Apparently I only get on with people and behave 'decently' when they have no intimate relations with me. It's no good 'going into it' and seeing for explanations in our conduct. I am only sorry that I was wrong in thinking last autumn that I was capable of sustaining a lover-relation. But I assure you there is no pleasure to be got out of finding oneself impotent, which is what it amounts to, and you might instead of heaping abuse on my grey head, give me a little pity. You know I am devoted to you, but these barricades seem to make it impossible at the moment. I will send back your keys by Ralph next week, as I expect you would like them.

I feel rather depressed so I can't write very intelligently. But I send my love. Your C

Philip Ritchie had died unexpectedly of septicaemia following a minor operation. Lytton and Roger Senhouse were deeply upset.

To Lytton Strachey

With J and T, Swallowcliffe
[21 September 1927]

Darling Lytton,

It was such a mercy to have your letter this morning. I am glad you were able to comfort Roger. I am sure it will make such a difference to him now, having your affection in this crisis to depend upon. I mean he has an excuse now for being natural and showing that he isn't self supporting. He wrote me such a charming letter this morning telling me all he had heard from Jennings about P's death. I thought of giving you that portrait of Philip I painted this spring and doing Roger a copy of it, or if you don't think you would like it, I'll give it to Roger. You can see it when you get back. I am afraid you must be rather worn out after Monday. I do hope your health keeps up.

As I thought, it was half past 11 o'ck before I got off in the car, laden with packages, and vegetables and black puss. I had a good drive to Salisbury. As it was market day, I lingered about a little and looked at the stalls, and farmers and bought some stockings. I reached the Cliffe about half past two. Tommy was busy drawing out plans of gates for Lincoln's Inn and Julia making scones in the kitchen. The cottage looks very nice inside. Really it's equal to Ham Spray in elegance and comfort, only cleaner and tidier. Puss leapt out of her basket and soon made herself at home in the kitchen, eating chickens' bones and purring in front of the fire. I have a grand bedroom with the new window that T designed which proves I think that he has a great architectural genius. Julia is in high spirits, and both of them seem very happy.

After tea, I drove Julia to Tisbury, and did some shopping. We found a marvellous postcard shop; I will send you a sample in a few days. Julia's vagueness about ordering is only equalled by your ignorance! 'How many potatoes shall we want?' in a whisper to me. In a commanding, imperious voice to the man 'Well send some potatoes, a good many.' Man 'How many pounds 14, 28?' 'Oh no not so many as that, about 2lbs would be enough I think.' (Two pounds being about 10 potatoes.) It was great fun. We laughed so much and even the man could hardly resist smiling. The cooking is really very good. Julia teaches the maid herself with Mrs Beeton sitting like an immense goddess on the kitchen table presiding. I am to paint a panel over a door, of the La Source a goddess lying by the water's brink, over the sitting room door. John B [Banting] has done an enormous 9 foot high (rather awful, for Venus is exactly like himself, I think, disguised as a female) Venus Rising out of the Waves in the bathroom. What Judge and Lady T must have thought as they sat on the W.C.!! I looked at a natural history book last night and T and J read, over a fine blazing log fire. I shall enjoy myself very much as it's exactly the sort of life I most love, talking and painting [...]

I send you my fondest love.

Your loving M

To Lytton Strachey

Ham Spray House

In the (sun) under the veranda

Monday morning, 12 o'ck [24 October 1927]

Darling Lytton,

... The weekend passed very merrily ...

After lunch we all went riding. Coker's horse (really a miniature cart horse) was more comic than Belle. And the spectacle of them both trying to prance together was so funny, we simply became weak with laughter. Lionel [Penrose] looked exactly like a monkey in the circus on Belle and Margaret Leathes [his fiancée] like nothing ever seen before. And when Huth's thoroughbred hunter pursued them across the second field it was like two walruses trying to escape from an antelope. We had some fine races on the top of the Downs.

The mouse ('quiet as a mouse' Mr Coker said to me) was egged on by Lionel into a gallop finally. There was a vast encampment of gypsies just near the Black wood. I have never seen such an exquisite girl. She had a thick silver necklace round her neck, and pale copper hair and a huge amazon figure. They all came running out of their ragged tents and begged for money. Dog gave her a shilling. In a field six children, very tattered, boys and girls about 4 to 10 years old, were dancing the Charleston together! [...]

My very fondest love to you most dear Lytton
Your devoted Centaur

PS Rosamond has sold 75,000 copies of her book in America! Love to Dadie.

Rosamond Lehmann had just published her first novel, Dusty Answer. *She was becoming a close friend of Carrington's, who admired her beauty and her wardrobe.*

To Dorelia John

Ham Spray House
[Christmas 1927]

Darling Dodo,
    ... We have had an awful time of it since you left. You were wise not to spend Christmas at Fryern.[1] I had 7 in this house for a week and then 2 for 4 days. And for a whole week no cars could get from Hungerford, so we nibbled ham and turkey bones like mice on siege. It was too cold to enjoy tobogganing (or am I too old?) and I seemed to spend my whole day lighting fires, thinking of new ways of cooking turkey bones and mincing ham and fetching my horse through snow drifts. Then on Christmas day there was a terrible scene. I rushed down in the ice cold one morning in a dressing gown and took a telegram on the phone for 'Partridge, etc. etc. Dorelia'. I was in high feathers and of course bragged to R. P. and he was cross because he hasn't been sent a message on the telegram. The next morning, 'a copy'

1 The Johns had moved to Fryern House at Fordingbridge in Hampshire, within reach of Ham Spray.

came to confirm the telephone, addressed to 'Monsieur Partridge'. Now if he'd been a nice sort of man he would have taken his revenge silently and not mentioned the subject. For of course I read the address on the wire and saw my, or rather the telephone girl's mistake. But the brute in front of everyone announces his triumph and rubs in the ashes. So my nose was disjointed for days. However your lovely postcard consoled me, and we are now on speaking terms again. Julia and Tommy were here. J very fat, and like a Veronese beauty. James S, Frances Marshall, and Lytton. We had to fetch food on sledges, and walk 6 miles across snow drift to get to Hungerford. On Monday everything thawed and we nearly lost the car for ever by getting stuck in a raging icy torrent in our lane. Since Sunday I've been in bed on and off with a chill and still feel very pretty mouldery. But it's very nice being here alone after the mob. Henry wrote me a letter with news of you. He seemed very pleased with Toulon and terribly embarrassed at having set foot in Cassis after his protestations that he would never go there!

Have you been keeping well? I was sorry to hear Vivien was in bed through over eating. I've some pictures for your R. D.s [Ravishing Daughters, Poppet and Vivien] but I can't get out to post them. I wish snow wasn't incompatible with pleasure, for the landscape looked exquisitely lovely. Mountain gales travelling 150 miles an hour now tear past the house, rattling all the windows to pieces. I feel very decayed in the head with this blasted chill, forgive a dull letter and please write me one to console me. And for what? For you having gone away. There'll never be such a lovely evening as Chambertin until you come back. Give my fondest love to Poppet and Vivien. Do you remember Raymond Mortimer? One of Lytton's Hoopoes, Henry called him. He is engaged to Valerie Taylor. Ah but will he marry her? Quite another question. What do you do? Stitch fine linen? Read Ethel M. Dell? But I shall never know. Poppet I suppose is cutting out a new dress. Peeled pears boiling in kirsch with a little sugar and then flambe as they come on the table, very good. But they must be Doyen de Comice. Everyone is in London, so I sit alone with Black Puss over the fire, covering the carpet with lettuce leaves, and salad oil. Tomorrow I shall go up and see the circus, and give the poor overworked Olive a weekend off. Now I must go to bed. I send you all my love but never dare if you love me, send a telegram, addressed to Monsieur Partridge in this house!

Your devoted most loving C

1928

On 1 January, Carrington began her new journal, writing on the cover 'D.C.Partride, Her Book'. Not only could she not spell her married name, if she noticed her mistake she did not bother to correct it. In its pages, she could admit what she concealed from her correspondents: her increasing feelings of isolation and loneliness. She was often alone at Ham Spray; Lytton and Ralph had found new lovers, Julia and Tommy were married. Her half-hearted affair with Peter Lucas was over, though they remained friends. It is perhaps not surprising that she soon fell into a new romance of her own. She was also not enjoying decorating Dadie Ryland's rooms at Kings, which required her to make regular visits to Cambridge.

To Lytton Strachey

The Pavilion
Tuesday [16 January 1928]

Dearest Toad in the Hole,

It's lovely here today. I wish you could whisk away and join me. A dazzling sun shines on the Pavilion. But where are the ghosts in white flannel? Only a large black cat sits staring into eternity on the window sill. Ach but I am in rage! That odious old camel writes to say he can't go riding today, or tomorrow and so there'll be no cantering along the Roman Road. I shall try and get Alec [Penrose] or Bunny [Garnett] to take me tomorrow if it's fine. A dreadful night of nightmares leaves me rather dim in the head this morning, but I shall hope for a cocktail when I get round to Dadie's to pull me together. Topsy is charming and in very good spirits and Peter [Lucas] in very good spirits and charming. And Steven as solid, and predominant as ever. Now I must whisk off to Dadie's room, and draw some plans. I shall console myself, for my defrauded ride, by looking at the owl books this afternoon. Please try and come back next Friday with us. Although I only tell you in a whisper, but it does make a great difference having a Ham Spray without a fakir. When I reached here yesterday evening I discovered I had put Tuesday on my postcard so they were rather surprised to see me on Monday.– Topsy was having a tete a tete with the mushroom growth Steven Runciman,[1] when I arrived.

My love darling Lytton and please get quite well by Wednesday evening. There is to be a very special concert on Wednesday evening at Ham Spray.

Your loving Mrs Snipe

1 Steven Runciman (1903–2000), historian, was then a young fellow of Trinity, Cambridge.

Snipe was Carrington's nickname for Bernard Penrose, known as Beakus. The youngest of the Penrose brothers, he was ten years younger than her, straightforwardly heterosexual and not bookish. He was a keen sailor with his own boat, and something about him reminded her of her lost brother Teddy. Her other nickname for him was Seagull.

To Dorelia John

Ham Spray House
8 February 1928

Darling Dodo,

It's a pity you don't emulate your daughter, and write some letters although the post cards have been lovely [...] I'm having a frantic struggle to alter the lawn under the Ilex tree, and make a more orderly garden. But the ground is solid willow herb, and nettles and fairly breaks one's back digging it. And the gardener has been so ill this winter, that now there's no time to plant the seeds in the vegetable garden, so I can't take him off, for my Ilex tree border. I've literally seen no one this last month, all our energies are devoted to writing Queen Elizabeth. We are reading a new novel by Norman Douglas in the evenings, tell me have you got it? It's rather Greek and very lecherous.[1] I've been drawing some designs for some rooms at Cambridge. Panels for doors. I think I shall go over there and paint them soon. It's a hideous gothic room in Kings, belonging to a sweet canary don called Rylands. So I'm doing hideous gothic pictures of Roman emperors heads, and Greek vases [...] Would you like a china plate? I'm going to very shortly, paint a lot of tiles and plates – Tell me what would you like a picture of, on your dish?

My love,
Your C

---

1 Norman Douglas's most recent novel was *In the Beginning*, published in 1927.

A Valentine

A Dove brought back to me
My Love on a Wave g the Sea,
A Dove brings my Love for you
Obscured in the Wool g a Ewe.

To Gerald Brenan

Ham Spray House
[9 February 1928]

I was lying in bed reading *Swann's Way* and two sentences make me think of you. Olive at that moment tapped on the door, and brought me breakfast and my letters. The coincidence of course is in your favour. I have (as you probably have) TWO minds about seeing you again. I had not 'no doubt guessed' you had long ceased to have 'unfriendly feelings.' I imagined to tell you the truth, that I had ceased to exist. But perhaps you've said and felt rather more than is compatible with being friends again? And then I have found curious pleasures in my isolation, and being exempt from any responsibilities, or blame. But it's also true, I seldom can think of anything more 'amusing' than having tea or lunch with you. So I daresay I shall ring you up one day. But not for some time, as I don't think I'll be in London this month.

Gerald – Well this is a nice encouraging sort of letter, and I wrote her such a friendly one.

But what can one do when one is a divided character? I still wonder of course what was your real reason for wanting to see me again. Curiosity? A desire to torment? Or had you also perhaps been reading Proust? Well, it's very nice to think that I can by putting 2 pennies in a slot and murmuring that mystic 8295 see you whenever I want to; very nice. I hope you are happy and working.

My love,
Your C

To George Rylands

Ham Spray House
14 March 1928

Dearest Dadie,

I am writing for Lytton as he is still rather worn and ill, to say how miserable he was not to come for the weekend [...] You have no idea how much I loved seeing you. I do hope you feel happier now. Ach, but I'd like to ring the neck of your late turtle dove for being such a ninny. One would think going to bed had no pleasures attached to it, or that having a lover was a positive hardship. When one reaches the slopes of middle age one is glad of the merest crumbs of affection, an eyelash of lust. I'm sorry I made such a

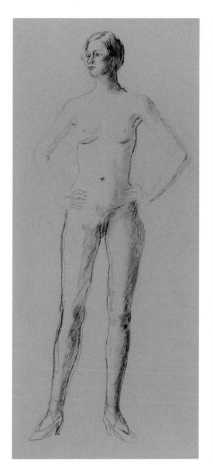 

Henrietta Bingham, 1924. Carrington's study of the lover of whom she wrote:
'no shame afterwards'

Henrietta with Stephen Tomlin, also her lover and briefly Carrington's,
at Ham Spray, 1924

Portrait of Julia Strachey, 1928.
Carrington was 'strangely moved'
while painting it

Drawing, possibly of Julia
Strachey, *c.* 1928

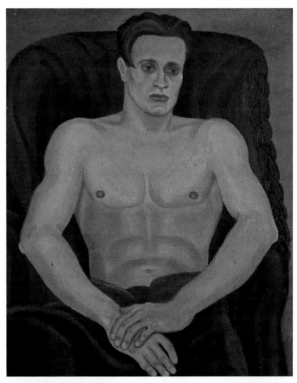

Portrait of Stephen Tomlin by John
Banting, 1925. Sexually versatile
and voracious, he married Julia
Strachey in 1927

Bernard (Beakus) Penrose (right),
Carrington's last lover, on the
veranda at Ham Spray, 1929.

Carrington's last painting: the trompe l'œil window at Bryan and Diana
Guinness's at Biddesden, 1931, showing Tiber, the favourite of her many cats

hash up of your door paintings, but I get 'over excited' about them, and so rather frozen ... But next term, I'll try and be a little less hysterical and paint them all out again and pull the whole thing together. The cold here is appalling, one longs – in vain – for a bedfellow to keep one warm [...]

Two enormous carthorses drove into the garden on Sunday, and tore through the lawn, and flowerbeds. So my enthusiasm for the garden has been slightly crushed, the tulips completely so.

My fondest love and Lytton sends his love also

Your loving C

To Sebastian Sprott

Ham Spray House
[14 March 1928]

Dearest Sebastian,

You are a snake of a man never to answer my letter. But I shall endeavour to turn the other cheek and forgive you. I write as Lytton's secretary, as he is rather ill, and worn, and unable to put pen to paper. Oh yes, no doubt if you were his secretary bird you'd write a much neater, better, more grammatical, and in every way superior letter, but as you aren't here, I must do my best to imitate your inimitable style. 'Would you care,' says le grand maître, 'to spend Easter chez Ham Spray?' If you would will you fill up the enclosed card with Yes or No, in the space provided for the same; an early posting, surely you can spare 3 mins to run to the post between Wilf, Will, and Edward? Will oblige your late master and the present correspondent, his present secretary [...]

I spent three days at Cambridge last week, but the agony of painting Dadie's walls, (which were a complete failure), ruined all my pleasures, except when I was drunk with cocktails. Of course I like despondent rejected lovers, so found Dadie very sympathetic and charming [...]

I keep fairly well, rather worn down by nightmares and the difficulty of reconciling myself to the fact that my painting isn't any better (if as good) as Douglas's [Davidson] I hope you keep well, and enjoy your low life with the blacks, and sweet Alice.

Morgan comes here next weekend. I still love my horse more than any man, but less than some women. Lytton enjoyed Norman Douglas and Paris enormously. But that's old cheese I expect to you, as I daresay you've seen Roger.

Now I must run to the telephone and ring up the doctor in London and ask for a tonic for Master and order some chops and feed the horse and –

you know the hundred and one little things that there are for a busy house-
wife to do after breakfast on Wednesday morning. So I must say goodbye
to my dear and rush off. Be a dear and say if you can come for Easter.
  Your most loving
  C

To Rosamond Lehmann

Ham Spray House
15 March 1928

My Dearest Rosamond,
  Although it is only a week ago since you sailed it seems much longer.
You have no idea how very much I loved seeing you again. I hope you are
getting stronger and more rested. It was rather awful to see you so thinned.
– What fun it was going to your dress shop. You know I enjoy these sorts
of expeditions more than almost anything. Watching hairdressers, tailors,
and bootmakers. I hope you didn't get too cold crossing. You escaped the
snow – since last Saturday the downs have been white and icicles hang from
the slates.
  Dadie was charming. I enjoyed seeing him enormously, but the painting
was sheer agony. It wouldn't come right, and I got hysterical, and fussed,
and then drank too many cocktails with Dadie, so the final results were
deplorable. However [...] it can easily be painted over again next term. It's
fatal if I work things out in detail first, and think too much about them. It's
rather maddening to have the ambition of Tinteretto [*sic*], and to paint like
a diseased mouse. But I daresay poor Douglas, whose panels I despised so
vainly, has just as lofty ambitions!
  I hope you bask in the sun, and are able to write. – You can't think how
I look forward to this summer and partly because I hope you'll be able to
come here very often. Do tell me how Wogan is, and if he is able to paint.
And which dress you are wearing when you write to me – if I dressed you
I should make you look slightly Russian, with an astrakhan pea jacket, and
a white woollen dress. It sounds a rather scratchy conception. And your hair
in a great knob at the back of your head
  Lytton overworked at *Q. E.* [*Queen Elizabeth*] and wasn't well enough to
go to Cambridge for the weekend to stay with Dadie. He was disappointed,
as he'd looked forward to it so much. All this week he is resting. It's a
nuisance, as he was getting along so well.
  Lytton sends you his fondest love.

Are the wild flowers lovely on the coast? My brain is numbed by the cold. So forgive a dull letter. Please if you have time to write to me sometime. Give Wogan my fondest love please. Please take great care of yourself and get stronger.

I send you all my love,

Your C

To Peter Lucas

Ham Spray
Monday afternoon, 19 March 1928

I am sorry of course that you are unhappy although I can't sympathise (any more than you do with yourself) with the cause. [...] I confess I am pleased if T [Topsy] is happy because after all that seems so rare an occurrence and she seems to me to deserve it more than most people – you wait till T goes off, and only comes down to see you if she brings her lover, and see how you like it! – I suppose you'd say you'd never put up with what I put up with. Yet what is the alternative? – and after a bit one can't go on minding day after day not seeing a person [...] T seems to me to be such an angel over your love affaires that I cant see how you can mind hers [...]

I admit I purposely go in the opposite direction if I think there is any affaire approaching me and on the whole you know I think it works out better for me living as I do now devoid of any relations except for my 'friendships' and Belle. If only one could stamp out a lingering envy which sometimes seizes one. Morgan was cheering at breakfast this morning, he told me about his childish fears. I wish we saw him more often.

[...] I wish I could offer you some panacea for your disease. But I know of none except reading Proust and so not thinking about it (my method). [...] I am sorry to be such a dull friend. But you know underneath I am very sympathetic, and I send you my love.

Your C

Lecture PS I believe one's actions ought to be as far as possible controlled by what is to one's own interest, and since jealousy does not enhance one in anybody's eyes it always seems to me good policy to stifle it, or conceal it. What do you say to that?

To Gerald Brenan

Ham Spray House
Good Friday, 6 April 1928

From pure old fashioned sentiments I send you my love for your birthday. For as you have so often observed fundamentally I am very conventional.

If I had not tetanus in my foot I should have written you one of my characteristic letters about the spring flowers, the birds, and my Ilex tree, but alas, striking an attitude this morning, as I surveyed my kingdom, I drove, in a triumphant gesture, my 4 pronged fork into the ground without observing my foot, in a white rubber boot, was below me. So typically, as Christ had 4 nails driven into his foot today 1928 years ago, or less, so I today crucified my flesh in memory of his death with four prongs. I go off tomorrow to that haven of fair women and Siamese cats. [Fryern House] If you were really at Broadchalke I might have dropped in on my way back and paid you a visit. But I expect you are already at Edgeworth's leafy glades ...

I send you my love for tomorrow.

Your C

Increasingly enamoured of Dorelia, and her two teenage daughters, Poppet and Vivien, Carrington was a constant visitor to the Johns at Fryern House.

To Lytton Strachey

Fryern Court, Fordingbridge, Hants
Tuesday [10 April 1928]

Darling Lytton,

As you may surmise this isn't exactly a good house for writing letters, or posting them. I hope you are having lovely weather and feeling better for your change of life! The polished silver, and white bear skin rugs, and hot water cans before lunch in your bedroom. Life here is very pleasant and to my taste. I sleep with Vivien in that big room you had. She is a most amusing bedfellow. After breakfast everyone sits on Dorelia's bed and talks. A strange spectacle the other morning like a scene in an African harem, this melange of recumbent females. But you can't possibly imagine what it looked like and I cannot draw it [...] After lunch today I went for a marvellous long ride with Henry [Lamb] on the Cranborne Downs. He was very friendly. The country was looking exquisitely beautiful. Long stretches of pale olive green Downs covered with little juniper bushes which look like misshapen black beasts bewitched and rooted to the ground. We came back about 5 o'ck and then sat with Dodo eating lovely honey and bread at the table [...]

I wish you could be here and walk on these ravishing Downs with me. It is so very much your style of country. There is such a perfect mixture of wilderness, and Wordsworthian loveliness here. The villages have little brooks with daffodils growing at the water's edge and charming pink thatched cottages. Tonight we go to the cinema at Fordingbridge and see a Wild West film!

Dodo sends you her love. She has given me a most lovely quilted counterpane from Provence as a present. Everything here is so lovely, the house, the garden, these females and the galloping horses. I am happy all day long. In fact if it wasn't for a bearded El Greco saint living in Ilex bower, I think I could spend the rest of my days here, painting pictures and riding. I made a Zambalione [sic] last night for dinner and just as it was finished, Henry stepped backwards and knocked the bowl all over the carpet into the fireplace! I was making it by the fire in the dining room. But fortunately there were masses of eggs, so I quickly whisked up another one. The foot is much better. I was able to get a shoe on today. Give Dadie and Topsy my fondest love please. I send you all my love.

Your ever and always loving Mopsa

When Lytton finished his book, he and Carrington went on holiday to Provence.

To Gerald Brenan

Hotel Negre-Coste, Aix-en-Provence, France
Thursday, 10 May 1928

Amigo Mio,

I was sorry to hear that the wind blows at Coombe Bissett and disturbs your inside. Here a mistral blows which fills one's lungs with dust and makes one's nose run. I reached here on Wednesday morning with Lytton. We came in a marvellous train out of which one never moved from Calais to Marseilles. I like Aix extremely. It is very beautiful and full of gay young men and women who parade up and down the Boulevarde Mirabeau. Lytton has an infinite capacity for 'flanning' and sitting in cafes. We looked at the market this morning. Tomorrow I am going to swim in the mineral baths. This is a very good hotel with no Americans or English. And the boots is a negre [Negro]. I think we stay here some little time, till next week and then go to Arles and Nimes perhaps. I'd like to stay in the country and paint. It looked very beautiful from the train before we reached Aix, high grey rocks, and olive trees. Are you able to write in the country? I went to a party with Alix the night before I left London and there I met Arthur [Waley] and had a long chat with him. 'Do you think Gerald will ever finish anything? I ask because one would like to read his books, as he is by far the most interesting writer I know.' It was a rather good party. I met the lovely Kathleen Dillon again. (Now no longer lovely.) And danced a passionate dance with Dorothy Varda.[1] But it seems very remote now I can't go back, and describe it to you. This is a fine town for cakes. I expect in a few days I shall be very ill. What a pity English towns have nothing like this life. One's head instantly becomes filled with a hundred ideas for painting. And even if one doesn't paint it is pure pleasure to watch these curious black widows, old men with white moustaches, and portfolios, nuns herding petites peuples in white dresses to confirmations and the students of the University of Aix arguing with each other outside the cafes.

You were so charming the other evening. I enjoyed very much seeing you again. I was only sorry I had to go off so early. I expect we'll be back after Whitsun.

My love,
Your C

While carrying on her sporadic affair with Beakus, Carrington spun erotic fantasies around the John girls.

To Poppet John

Ham Spray House
Thursday evening [summer 1928]

Darling Poppet Sweetie,
    Thank you very much for your charming letter. I do not know quite why this abandoned creature and Tiber have crept into this letter.

1 Kathleen Dillon is unknown. Dorothy Varda (1900–48) was married to the dancer and painter Jean Varda (1893–1971).

You were a dear to write me one so soon as it was a great consolation for the sadness of leaving you. I was miserable at that lovely party coming to an end. I longed to slip up stairs & hide myself in your bed. But we must have another very soon. All the best parties that ever take place happen at Fryern on Sunday evenings. Perhaps it is because it is such a Holy Day, that all Sunday parties seem blessed.

I've never seen Dodo look so lovely as in that Pink trowser-dress. And so you've turned your coat about little Beakus – changed your tune miss! – He was wildly enthusiastic about you & Vivien, & the party, & the house. He didn't know which, or what, he admired most! I wish I was young & lovely & could win a sailor's heart, indeed I do.

But as long as I can keep my Poppet, I am contented.

I woke up this morning with a longing to come to Fryern. But then a letter came from Vivien saying you were going to Highcliffe Castle for lunch so I thought it wouldn't have been much use. Also the rain came down again. So perhaps it wouldn't have been a very good day for a jaunt. Do tell me what you did with Sailor Beakus when he arrived that afternoon! And did he go off with May [unknown] alone? Or did Tommy sit behind! Nothing has happened here since that lovely Sunday.

I've been alone with Tiber. Everyone else is in London [...]

It's a pity I always spend half my time having hiccups in Dodo's little room. I really mustn't drink so much next time. Soon Darling Poppinjay I'll

come over & stay two days, & two nights. One night for P & one for V.
Now don't leave this passionate letter lying in the BATHROOM or I'll murder
you next time I see you. I went a ride on Belle last Saturday on the downs.
She is quite well again now. Alec Penrose is the funniest sight you ever saw
on Belle. He leans very far back & sits absolutely stiff with no expression
on his face! And charges along like Roman emperor.

My fondest Love Darling
From Your Loving C xxxxxxxxxxx

To Poppet John

Ham Spray House
Tuesday [summer 1928]

My Darling Poppinmouth,

It seems a terribly long time since we lay together in that sweet embrace
in the taxi on Monday. Although in truth it is only a week ago ... and pray
my little sweet what have you done since then? Please be an angel & write
me a letter. I came back to Ham Spray the next day after I left you only to
find Olive still ill, & no servants ... so I was distinctly enraged. However
Puss is much better. He lies in the sun in a bank of crocuses as I write to
you at my feet. Darling Poppet you can't think how much I enjoyed France.[1]
I felt afterwards I had been dingy dim company for you. But the truth was I
felt rather mouldy most of the time with a pain inside. But that didn't prevent
me enjoying myself terrifically & thinking you lovely.

Our car is still being mended so unfortunately it's impossible for me to
buzz over, & kiss my princesses ...

I suppose a hundred lips have pressed yours since I last drove in that
romantic taxi to Chelsea. But mine I assure you madame have been
surrounded by wire netting ever since.

My Fondest Love
Your Very Fond Carrington
xxxxxxx

To Julia Strachey

Ham Spray House
Saturday morning [June 1928]

Dearest sweet,

... [Tiber comes] through the open window carrying a large rat which
he lays at his master's feet. Master shrieks 'Horrid creature. Take it away.'

1 On her trip with Lytton they had called on the Johns at their house at Cassis, near Marseilles.

Poor Tiber. Life was ever thus. Take it away. How often has one's offering of love laid at the toes of our beloved been greeted by those cutting words 'Take it away.'

> But madam
> Keep my counterpane
> Let not in vain
> My gift from Spain
> or from Provence as the case may be.

So write to me again. My life is nothing but a whirl of carpenters, engineers and schemes for improvements. I'm getting quite a mechanic over the car now. But perhaps it would be better if I did a little less mechanising and a little more ... who can say? I wish I had a lover. Yes, just this morning I thought how nice it would be with the sun shining in my room and nothing to do, as it was 6 o'ck. But I read Borrow in bed and soon forgot and now breakfast is over and there are joints to supervise and raspberries to pick and no time for lovers.

To Sebastian Sprott

Ham Spray House
Saturday, Whitsun 1928

But 'any way my darling' it's very nice to get a letter from you. Even although you can't come and stay [...] Did you enjoy the Pavilion? Did you have 'heart-to-hearts'? I suppose Peter [Lucas] was in high feather now that Topsy is alone on her beach once more. What brutes men are! He-men I mean, my dear. I hope Arthur [Waley] told you what a success he was with all of us here, and how devoted I am to him now. He was rather crushing to my advances I thought, actually! But as faint lady never won Chinese heart, I suppose I mustn't complain. Lytton has just gone off to Sweden. It's queer how much I miss him. He's a tremendous prop you know to my existence. Ralph and Frances are here for Whitsun. No one else. Ralph came back this morning from Brittany, in high spirits. But it's slightly like going back to look at Tidmarsh. He brings back a sort of past life and makes me see that I'm rather 'out' of the present. I slightly resent for some reason, and obvious reason I suppose, feeling out of it and going off by myself and being unable to be enthusiastic about Brittany. Suddenly in the middle of tea this afternoon I felt cross I had no one to go to bed with when I wanted to. But then, if I had, I should probably be cross because it wasn't to my taste! I rather envy you your animal variety. My life is rather too untouched by human hand at moments.

Reading *Phèdre* with Lytton of course is a very good substitute, curious, as it may seem. I mean I get tremendous pleasure you know by living here. It's so lovely, and Lytton is such an angel to me. After Cambridge next week I'm going to stay at Fryern with Dorelia and their exquisite little sirens. That will be perfect. Then I come back here and probably linger while the central heating is put in and paint 500 tiles for Margaret Waley. Would you like a tile to stand your tea pot on? [. . .] I say you mustn't go to Rome. Norman Douglas wrote to Lytton last week and said it was so hot in Florence he had flown to the mountains. But of course it may have altered now. The cold here is icy, and one shivers in one's drawers. How was Jim? Not know Jim in his striped bathing dress, what do you take me for? My new studio is going to be lovely. I shall when it's finished, completely change my character and become a very hardened recluse and paint pictures all day. Then all these spinster ravings will no longer blast my letters to you. Now I must go and play badminton, or it will look as if I'm sulky, which I am not, or cooking the dinner, which I'm not either [...] I wish you were available more often. Really that weekend was one of the nicest we have had all year. I feel I never tell you quite how much I love seeing you dear Sebastian. But in a whisper I do enormously. What is Oundle life like? Any sprees? [...]

Lytton read me *Zadig*[1] last night, very much to my taste. I go to the Cricket Hut on Tuesday till Friday to paint Dadie's room. Oh why did I ever embark on that foolish business, mere agony to me and mere mumbo jumbo, as my father used to say, to Dadie. Do write to me and tell me how you are. I hope the health bears up.

Your most loving Carrington

To Poppet John

Ham Spray House
Tuesday, August 1928

Sweet Darling Poppet – there isn't anything to write about since I left London on Thursday.

I came down here on Friday with Ralph. Dodo will have told you about a fine dinner party she asked me to at the Eiffel Tour given by Stulick.[2] I got dreadful hiccups & drank so much!! I slept at Mallord Street in your sheets – very romantic! – and Dodo called me in the morning with a beautiful breakfast on a tray, in a Chinese silk dressing gown looking like a Mongolian Queen. I think she looks very, very lovely in that Chinese dress. Don't you? – The next morning I spent in the British Museum helping Lytton find pictures

---

1 *Zadig*, a novel by Voltaire about a Babylonian philosopher, first published in 1747.

2 Rudolf Stulik (?–1938) was the Viennese owner and proprietor of the Eiffel Tower restaurant in Percy Street, the favourite haunt of writers and artists including Augustus John.

for his book on Queen Elizabeth. Afterwards he gave me a fine lunch at the 'Ivy'. At the next table to us sat Ivor Novello & Noel Coward, & two actress-looking hags. I thought Ivor Novello was rather a little rat. But I was distinctly taken with Noel Coward, who looked gloomy & fascinating, with a face that shone like Bronze. I expect he uses a Pink-Brown powder.

I'm very cross (not really because you know I find it almost impossible to be cross) with Horace because he promised to bring his Mavis down to Ham Spray for lunch a week ago on Sunday, & never came, & never wrote to say why he didn't come.

[...] I've done nothing but paint pictures on tiles this last week so feel very stoopid in the head – won't you get Dodo to drive you over to lunch one day? Only warn me early on the telephone when you start. Have you been making any new dresses? When do you go to London to stay with Edie?[1] When you do, you must tell me & I'll come up for a few days and we'll have a fine party!

[. . .] My new studio is a lovely room & one will be able to act some plays in it as it has a fine place for a stage. I think of you very very often my Darling Poppet. Pray do not forget me or love me less.

My love to Queen Dodo
And a great deal to you
xxx your adoring C

To Poppet John

Ham Spray House
[n.d.]
[letter incomplete]

Sad picture of young girl who went mad and thought a 'Forest of Trees' were young men. Two little p [Partridge] birds mourn her sad fate. 'Better love a bird than a wooden tree' they say.

Now I must get up as its very late, and I sit writing to you in bed in my red silk nightdress with Tiber drinking the milk out of my jug on the tea tray. Your midnight bathe and sleeping in the forest sounded very exciting. We still have rasberries. Oh but it takes a forest of raspberries to tempt Miss Poppet over to Ham Spray now. Now I really must get up and leave my love dreaming in her Pine Forest

Farewell Baroness de Foret and remember the 4th of August, not the 5th of November. Cats gone mad and had disappeared under the wardrobe. From your very loving honey sweet C xxxxxxxx

1 Francis Macnamara (1886–1946) was an Irish poet and a keen sailor. His second wife, Edie, was Dorelia John's sister.

Sad picture
of poor girl who
went mad and
thought a "Forest
of trees" were young men

Two little P. Birds mourn her sad fate
"Better Love a Bird than a wooden Tree". they say.

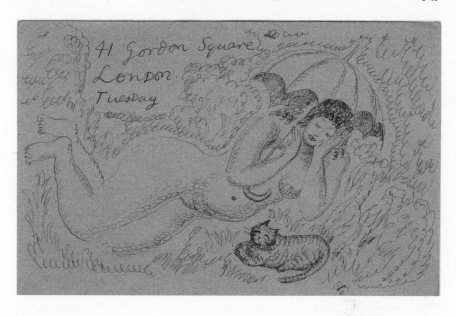

To Poppet John

41 Gordon Square, London
Tuesday, August 1928

My Darling Sweetest Poppet,

I write with a heavy heart for to tell you the truth 'life' & its realities are a very different affaire from the loveliness & gaiety of Fryern. Very different as you will soon find out! When we got back to Ham Spray we found nothing but CONFUSION & CHAOS boilers & pipes everywhere. No hot water, no cold water, no water in the W.C. and two very plain disagreeable men stumping all over the house in dirty boots. So I cooked Ralph some eggs & ate some cold pies & then we went off to London. Ralph in a fine rage at the mess the central heating men are making & trying to pretend it was all my fault – but I soon convinced him it wasn't! London seemed very grey & dreary after our lovely weekend. The elephant [Ralph] fell into a great melancholy & mine was even greater.

I spent a quiet evening with Saxon Turner who is rather like an old grey squirrel. He showed me a great many photographs of Germany where he had been. But that wasn't very exciting, & I longed instead of listening about his holiday in Germany to tell him about our holiday at Fryern!!! I never laughed so much before than at dinner on Sunday evening when you all made those comic faces of grief & boredom. It was a marvellous evening all together in every way.

Today it pelts with rain. I've just bought a new yellow felt hat. But it makes my face look a sort of dingey purple which is rather disappointing! I couldn't think of anyone to have lunch with, so in the end I've not had any, as it's such a bore eating alone. When the rain has stopped I shall go to the Turkish Baths & lie in a hot bath, & have my hair washed & have tea in one of the Turkish beds. I confess it sounds more exciting than it really is – but it's a nice way of passing an afternoon [...]

I hope you still love me as much as I do you. This is a terribly dull letter. But then life seems very dull to tell you the truth, after Fryern. Do write me a letter here. I shall stay here till Friday evening I expect. You are a Darling Poppet you know. [...]

xxxxxxx

To Lytton Strachey

41 Gordon Square, London
en route to Cambridge
Tuesday [7 August 1928]

My darling Lytton,

On Sunday as it was so lovely, we went for the day to Fryern, Ralph Frances and me. We had a superb lunch in the Dean Valley, (East of Salisbury) in a little wood and reached Fryern about half past two. We then went off and swam in their river, the girls, Romilly [John] and the governess. Dorelia sat like a voluminous Sibyl in a flower black dress on the high bank watching us. Ralph looked so lovely and naked, very brown with the sun, swimming like an enormous Neptune amongst these sirens [...]

My studio grows more and more beautiful. You are an angel to give me such a lovely present.

We had a strange party at Fryern on Sunday night, and I had the strangest of strange conversations with old Augustus.

A. 'Do you like Cxxxs [cunts] Carrington?

C. 'Um – yes – I do.'

A. 'So do I. I adore them.'

Then he confided in me all his love affairs. Dear, oh dear! I missed you very much at Ham Spray this weekend. My very fondest love

Your devoted Mopsa

Love to Roger please
[...]

*After a furious row when Carrington, as he saw it, insulted him by sending him
some of Lytton's unwanted clothes and ties, Gerald was at last able to detach himself
from her. He had picked up a girl called Winnie in London and lived with her for
a while.*

To Gerald Brenan

Ham Spray House
Wednesday [30 August 1928]

Dearest Amigo,

It was nice to see you again. You always, you know, charm me rather.
The pleasure of cooking mushrooms and meals with you is unique, if I may
say so. And then you must know my life is conducted on a sort of fugue
basis. I go forwards a few bars and then retreat and pick up the old theme.
No, Ralph tells me little about your life; he was mostly concerned with a
ravishing beauty at the swimming baths! So I heard very little about you,
or Winnie.

[...] I have 60 tiles to paint. And if I leave the house for more than a day,
all the taps will be put in the wrong places. 'So you think.' And so it happens,
I assure you.

Arthur wrote me a fine letter from Wales yesterday with a gloomy
description of the inmates of his asylum. Give Helen my love when you see
her. And do not tear my character to shreds! This morning at 7 o'ck I went
on the Shalbourne Downs and picked mushrooms with Olive. It was an
exquisite pale dewy morning. And I feel very purified inside now. If I come
up again I will ring you up and we'll have a supper party together.

My letters are now written in such a different style that I've lost the old
art of addressing crotchety amigos. Poppet and Vivien are my new correspondents. And the level I assure you is, although infinitely amorous,
infinitely low.

My fondest love
Your C

PS I did not even tell Ralph I had seen you twice! My life is so poor in secrets
I was forced to turn you into one!

To George Rylands

Ham Spray House
20 October 1928

Darling Dadie,

I am not the traitor that you imagine, only one of the leading foremen organizers in/of central heating, bricklaying, wall painting, carpentering, fireplace making, tile designing, apple picking, trade – and as such, there's damn little time for keeping up a correspondence in the style of Swift-and-Stella – you didn't by the way tell me what style, and standard we were to adopt? Are letters to be dated? Is master to correct my spelling? Will they be left lying about? Before I can seriously engage myself with you in this enterprise you must give me more exact information [...]

There were grand goings on at the Beakus Penrose sailor party [...]

Bunny was sick. Alix caught Tommy and me kissing his lady, and went off in a fine huff [...] a great many couples had each other on the analytical couch upstairs to James's dismay – or pleasure? So many revolting patties were crushed into Alix's carpet downstairs that she has had it dyed dark 'claret and ham', in anticipation of the next party.

I got some very passionate kisses out of Beakus [...] but had a much more passionate affaire in Saxon's flat afterwards in a very small camp bed with Poppet John. Oh La! La! As she says [...] Now darling it is teatime so I must put on the kettle for Master.

My fondest love,
Your devoted Carrington
Love from puss

To Lytton Strachey

The Boot, Quainton, Aylesbury
[1 November 1928]

Darling Lytton,

What do you think? You will never guess. I went to a hunt this morning. [...] It was the greatest pleasure imaginable. We watched 'the meet' gather and then pursued them on foot where they found an old fox in a wood. But it was impossible to get the old fox on the run, so the horsemen galloped round and round the wood with the dogs baying inside. Twice we saw the fox quite close, but he always redoubled on his tracks and got back into the wood again. I talked to some strange foot retainers. A farmer, and a perfect

Oiseaux of an old rustic. We stood and listened to the conversation of the huntsmen. I was pointed out 'Tom Gosling, the best steeplechase rider,' a very gay spark, who cracked jokes with the grooms. All the characters of the riders came out so vividly. Hardened old lined nut cracked men who rode without any expression on their faces. Fat Rowlandson ladies with grey buns of hair and veils, bouncing along on their fat horses. Farmers with elbows sticking out on nags not much better than Belle. By the end of the hour I knew every face. Rosamond lives in an absurd little cottage with roses, and arbours. She and Wogan look like that picture of Alice in Wonderland enlarged. They can scarcely move in and out of rooms and their heads touch the ceilings. I shall come back tomorrow early to London. It's very nice here. So hot and the village looks exquisitely beautiful this morning, with shining thatched houses like a broody hen, on the green. Wogan has done two very good pictures down here [...]

Ros, very charming. I had a fascinating long conversation with her last night. Oh, but I long for a hunter; I now see it would be perfect happiness to go galloping across a field with red huntsmen cracking whips and hounds baying. The wily old fox defeated them this morning, to my secret delight [...]

You were so charming yesterday. It was a perfect day. My very dear love to my very dear,

Your loving Mopsa

To Sebastian Sprott

Ham Spray House
20 November [1928]

Darling Sebastian,

What a toad I am to be sure [...]

Yes, I agree my behaviour has no excuse [...] Except that [...] in spite of not writing I think of you perpetually. It is true nearly everyday I say 'I will write to S today.' But then there is the engine to run, the garden to attend to, (for Tom the gardener has left us. Thank God.) Belle is ill & has to have revolting abscesses dressed everyday. I have 60 tiles to paint for Lytton's new fire places, 20 lampshades for the slug Waleys, two carpenters to supervise, who build Lytton a new library. A perpetual correspondence with my darling little John girls to attend to [...] to say nothing of my other arts, & Master's cushions, & footstools to arrange & his spectacles which he loses every few hours ... By the time all these little jobs, (& driving to Hungerford in the gale, & rain) are over, I am so tired I can hardly put pen to paper, & so time passes, & my famous letter to you never gets written [...]

In a whisper Topsy has a new lover. But P[eter] doesn't know, although of course she'll have to tell him soon. But for the moment she's controlling her passion for truth, & enjoying a secret flame!!! So don't you breathe a word. Lytton says he's like a pale chicken with goggling eyes, & yellow hair, and of course only 19. But Dadie told me in a whisper he was 'terribly virile' & had an enormous — but one hardly knows what to believe, people are so inaccurate. Dadie himself is 'in love' with a sweet scotch boy who says 'pardon' every five minutes but nobody yet knows if he is virile or even has a —. Lytton suspects he is lacking. Mary [Hutchinson] comes here next week with Roger Senhouse. My lovely Vicomtesse has deserted her Vicomte, & has come to live in England all for love of a steeple chasing captain who lost all his toes off both feet falling under a train in order to lie with the lovely Vicomtesse, he was in such a hurry. But nothing damps her ardour [...]

My life is a complete blank except for my passionate love affaire with Vivien & Poppet John. They are fascinators. Next time you come here we'll go over to Fryern together. They have the most lovely horses, we go for great rides on the downs, & in the new forest together whenever I stay there ... which is pretty often [...] Lytton sends his very fondest love. Which is a lie, but he is writing & I can't disturb him. But I know he would, so I put it in. Queen E. [*Elizabeth and Essex*] comes out on Friday. Please write & say you still love me, & bear me no malice for being a better thinker, than a writer. But my fondest love darling Sebastian.

Your devoted windswept Carrington xxxxx

To Augustus John

Ham Spray House
23 November 1928

Dodo says you would like a letter so if you do not want one you must blame her. I hope you are enjoying Boston. Your Judge's country house looked to me slightly suburban if I may say so [...]

I stayed at Fryern about three weeks ago and had a lovely time riding on the Downs with your ravishing daughters. We had a fine evening tea party in the New Forest under some Holly trees. Vivien was so particular about choosing a properly romantic spot that it was almost dark when we had our tea and chestnuts. I've hardly been to London this month so I've no gossip to tell you [...]

Please bring back a lovely American beauty for me. But for me remember. Not to be shared. Dodo's little room is exquisite. I must go over soon and finish the cupboards.

I am, dear old chap your loving
Carrington

To Julia Strachey

Ham Spray House
Saturday, late December 1928

Darling Julia,

This is NO Collins but a paean of praise for your lovely Christmas present. It arrived today, and really, saving my face, it looks enchanting! I have, of course, put it on, and will probably upset the ink over it at once, but I couldn't resist wearing it. Ralph and Frances think it very beautiful. But I wish you were here to admire it! [...] I did love my visit to you. I am always only sorry that the time is so short. For some reason there is a strange enchantment about Swallowcliffe for where else could one find laurel groves, and dormitories, castellated ruins and swans? To say nothing of upstanding cockatoos and seagulls? (pardon my humour).

I regret to say I behaved disgracefully after I left you for I was faithless to Dorelia and deserted her after lunch. I pretended I was going back to Ham Spray, but really I went off to – is it possible you can guess? We had a fine evening in Southampton together in the drizzling rain, buying a mattress and stores for the ship. Then in the slushing mud, we tramped through docks and saw great masts silhouetted against the night sky, and lights reflected across the harbour from Southampton, and presently found the *Sans Pareil* with a black cat keeping watch on deck. It's an infinitely romantic ship; with brown varnished cupboards and cut glass handles and a little fire place with a brass mantelpiece. I don't think I've ever enjoyed an evening more in my life, the rain beating down on the deck above, sitting in the cabin lit by lamplight, cooking eggs and sausages over the fire and drinking rum. The Seagull is fascinating on board. He is so in love with his ship that he moons about in a trance opening cupboards and eulogizing over its beauties, in his slow voice. The only disadvantage is, if I may so say, that the bunks aren't built for two sailors alongside. The black puss is a great charmer and sat on the rails on the little balustrade that goes round the bunks peering with green eyes at the midnight feast. The next morning I washed up and cooked an omelette for breakfast and chatted to some sailors who were mending the cabin door.

The Seagull suffered a good deal from my un-nautical language. But was impressed by my lamp trimming. I dashed back to Ham Spray yesterday after lunch, in time to set the house in order, and meet Lytton at the station. I shall tell nobody but you of my romantic evenings because nobody but you discerns the true beauty of varnished woods and silver suns behind lamps. This is a very tiresome letter I expect. As you can't possibly, without having seen the trawler, see how charming it is! [...]

My love,
Your Tante C

1929

To Julia Strachey

Saturday [January 1929]
In haste

Darling Julia,
  [...] Ouff the rain and the wind. The old horse shelters under the oak, but of what avail are oaks in such a blast? The howling of a hundred woolves prowl round the house night and day (which is as much as to say the wind roareth like unto a woolf).
  I had two very striking letters from Poppet and Vivien John yesterday from France. No visitors this weekend, but Ralph and Frances. We seem to live on stewed rabbit day after day, until even the cats turn up their noses. The truth is the keeper caught 4 rabbits in the garden last week. And as 'Economie' is the watch word of our house, we must perforce mange lapin. I've been reading the maxims of La Rochefoucauld, they made such an impression on me that I intend to start a revival of the text habit over the beds ornamented with sprigs of forgetmenots. How do you bear up?
  I heard from Helen that you 'looked so lovely like some mysterious massive tolerant Italian lady of the 16th or 17 century, and she was exquisitely kind to me'. I wish she'd be a little more exact about her centuries! Do write soon and say when you can come. My love dear Poppets xxxx
  Your devoted C

To Poppet John

Ham Spray House
6 February 1929

Darling Poppinjay,
  I am wicked not to have answered your sweet letter before but the truth is I had influenza & was in bed a week & last week went to London, & had so many things to do there was no time to write. How is my Darling Poppet? You cannot think what an aching void your absence creates in my [heart]. I miss you, & Vivien, more than I can say. And when the day is fine I look over towards Fryern across the downs & sigh and SIGH, & Tiber mews & mews & then we fall on each other's necks, & weep because our darlings

are so far away. I haven't any exciting news I'm afraid. Everybody is ill or illish. Frances has been in bed for 2 weeks with her indigestion. Alix Strachey had an operation for Tonsils all the servants have hacking coughs, & colds ... the whole of England resounds with the trumpetings of a million noses. I am sorry the villa was in such an awful country, & that you won't take it. I still can't get over the lovely news that Fryern is yours for ever. And you will never leave it. I went to an exhibition of Dutch pictures in London which I liked very much. Then I saw my lovely Phyllis one morning & went to lunch with a Lord with her, in the Lord's grand house. Two footmen with white gloves to wait on us at lunch & gold coffee spoons. I only had one catastrophe with the black coffee which wouldn't come out of the jug. It was really milk with the skin stuck in the spout. But on the whole I'd rather have our Ham Spray lunches without gold spoons. But I must say the cooking was very fine.

I feel rather dim this morning as for some reason I couldn't sleep last night so feel rather stupid in the head. Fanny has made me some lovely wallpaper for Lytton's new library. The elephant[1] is very well. But rather sad because Frances is so ill. So I haven't seen very much of him lately, as he has to stay I London. Have you had any letters from Romilly & Cathy? Are you studying the geography of France Miss & not the faces of the young men on the Beach. I hope so! Give darling Vivien a thousand kisses & beg her to write to me. She owes me, I would point out, a letter. Very much so.

How is Dodo? Please give her & Augustus my Fondest Love [...]

Belle is much better I shall be able to ride again next week. Now I must get the car to start as I've yet to drive it to the station.

My Fondest Love

My sweet, sweet sweetie and a great many passionate hugs

Your devoted C

PS I loved your postcards please send me some more.

Frances's illness lasted several months and was certainly in part psychosomatic. Her position was not always easy; in November 1928 Lytton had written to Ralph suggesting that she should not come to Ham Spray so often. He maintained that Carrington had not asked him to do so, but his letter surely reflected her feelings as well as his. Ralph was furious, Frances was hurt and they both spent less time at Ham Spray.

---

1 Vivien and Poppet's nickname for Ralph.

To Sebastian Sprott

Ham Spray House
Sunday, 6.30 [early March 1929]

[...] Olive took ill with lumbago 2 weeks ago, so after 10 days of cooking and chamber pots Lytton and I went off to London last Wednesday, (or rather Lytton to Cambridge) and I to London.

I had on Wednesday at the Etoile a lovely, but curious dinner party with Morgan, Boy Joe [Ackerley], Gerald H[eard] and a drunkard called Harold Monro (poet); the latter rather blighted the conversation, and the evening as he was so boringly drunk. But it was in spite of him, a very amusing evening. I liked Gerald quite a lot. Morgan wrote me practically a proposal the next day. Couldn't make head or tail of it, half apologizing for the evening and the rest a bit incoherent. Is he rather unhappy? He seemed as if he was trying to hide his feelings and to be gay in spite of an ache in the heart. But I couldn't see him again, so I never had his confidence which he said he wanted to give me. He said you had influenza. I am sorry dearest. Are you better now? I had it in January and felt very mouldy for quite a long time. Poor Puss was caught in a gin and for two days and a night, at the height of the snow and blizzards, lay in a wood. He is still rather ill, and I fear, will never chase the hare again. This has rather upset me for you know how deeply I love my cat and what a beautiful creature he was.

Since Christmas all our energies have gone to beautifying the house and making the library. At last it is nearly finished. Lytton seems tolerably pleased with it which means – very much so. He has been in very good spirits, in spite of this cruel devastating cold, frozen pipes, broken motor car and no cook. I think he was very set up by the success of Queen Elizabeth and the central heating certainly makes life far less grim in the winter here – sort of pads over the deficiencies of wayward lovers and cold hearted young

men. I've no gossip. Everyone in London seems to be ill. Poor Alix has a
septic eye and has to wear black spectacles. Frances has been ill, but mercifully has now recovered. Bunny's wife is ill. Raymond is poisoned with
American drink, Lionel's wife is with child, Alec Penrose had to pay £500
damages to the wronged husband for his new mistress. Tommy is now an
Honourable. (And Garrow¹ hopes one day to become a Lord.) I have had
lunch twice with Lord Wimborne, in his grand house next to the Ritz with
footmen (very attractive) with white gloves [...]

I go next Tuesday to Cambridge to see *King Lear* and stay 2 nights in the
Pavilion. Lytton said they were both in better spirits. But the restless Peter was
looking for a new mistress; Phyllis unable to stand him any longer. My future
is terribly unsettled. I peer, and peer into the crystal but see nothing but a glass
wall and a plain middle-aged-face. And how are your Nottingham intrigues? [...]

My love

Your devoted C

Carrington had been on a short holiday with the Johns in France.

To Julia Strachey

Ham Spray House
[End of March or early April 1929]

Darling Julia,

I write upside down under the spreading beech tree in the sun. I was
delighted to hear from you. 'Dowager Doris Lady P' if you don't mind my
dear. Tiber is much better. He has taken on a new character and is rather
commanding and since he only has three legs, even Lytton is forced by
Cat-Public-Opinion to get up and open the doors for him. When I was in
France, Lytton stayed at the Old Rectory Hall with sweet Ros, and Wogan
and their little doggies. But I was disappointed that he never once saw her
in the cloud-green-chiffon tea gown writing her novel [...]

I agree with every word you say about the Riviera. In fact I thought it
the most hideous place I'd ever stayed at. Those dingy green pines and the
villas, The Blue Bird, Bella Vista, Rest Dean, Kamjabee, Ma Retreat. But as
Dorelia said it's rather a relief that all the rich odious inhabitants of the
world should collect together in such an ugly place. For they leave the rest
of France empty. I loved Dorelia. She is a most fascinating companion. I've
had some grand pub crawls with old Augustus in the evenings. And went
to some fashionable nightclubs in Monte Carlo with Poppet and Vivien and

¹ Garrow Tomlin, Tommy's brother. Their father, Lord Tomlin (1867–1935), a Judge, had just been made
a peer.

Darling Julia, I write upside down under
the spreading Beech Tree in the sun.
I was delighted to hear from you. —
"Dowager Doris Lady P."
If you don't mind my
dear. — Tiber is
much better. He has
taken on a new character
& is rather comanding
& since he only has three
legs, even Lytton is
forced by Cat-Public-Opinion
to get up & open the Doors for him. When I
was in France Lytton stayed at the old
Rectory Hall with sweet Ros, & Wogan.
But I was dissapointed that he never
once saw her in the cloud-green-
chiffon tea gown writing her novel.
Now we know the explanation of
Dusty answer. Those restful pale mauve
tea gowns.

Kit Dunn. The Dunns are millionaire Canadians who owned the John's Villa.[1] Kit was dimly like Henrietta, very bulky and strong, with school boy high spirits. Sir James D who met our train at Dover with a Pullman was an appalling character 'vigorous at 50' [...]

Augustus had been painting portraits of the Dunn family for 2 months down there. Vivien was fascinating, Poppet slightly enfeebled in the head with falling 'in love' every day with a new young man. For a week it was perfect. Very hot and the most exquisite flowers in the garden [...] I've been rather in despair as Olive is still ill. I really went off for a holiday hoping to find her recovered when I came back, but unfortunately she is still in bed. The doctor says she is 'run down' but I have a sickening feeling it may be something worse so really most of my time lately has been spent cooking and emptying chamber pots. Ralph is bringing down his servant Mabel and her sister for Easter which will be a relief. Then I suppose I shall have to try and get a temporary, or a new girl. It's a frightful bore. I'm not a bit against Tommy's wall-decoration sculpture. It's only sometimes I get into a panic and wonder whether he will ever be able to make it stick on to the wall. (I get these panics when for no reason a great chunk of plaster suddenly falls off on to the lawn.) Don't you think it's rather important to find out some one who has stuck sculpture on to a concrete wall and discover the technique? But I expect Tommy knows about it as much as anybody. Lytton, I think, had a slight feeling that Tommy wasn't very keen on it perhaps. But if he still is, I do hope he will come soon and stay with you and start it here properly. For you must know, darling, that I am such an ardent admirer of everything Tommy does, that I am always in favour of Ham Spray gleaning as many of his works as possible. How is your short story? When I was away in France I told the Slaters to paint the 'back sitting room' cream. On my return I found my favourite blue front sitting room painted out! For they call the 'back' of the house the 'front' and vice versa. So I am rather bored with internal beautifying at the moment!

This weather is enchanting. Lytton and I go long walks and have all our meals in the verandah. He has gone to London today to see the first night of Cochran's Review with Lady Cunard.[2] When will you come here? You must suggest yourselves whenever you like. I've just tidied up my studio and directly this servant crisis is over I shall draw up my 'plan' for your inspection and start on a new era of work and discipline. The spelling seems rather drunk today. I am sorry. I love you so much Julia. I hope Tommy is keeping well and happy.

All my love

Your C

---

1 Sir James Dunn (1874–1956) was a Canadian millionaire industrialist and art collector.
2 Sir Charles Blake Cochran (1872–1951) produced a series of popular musicals and revues.

To Lytton Strachey

Ham Spray House
Wednesday afternoon, 22 May 1929

Darling Lytton,

I send you a budget of letters. I am rather boozed and befuddled with drink so forgive a poorish letter. Dorelia appeared yesterday, very late 8 o'ck with the Earps and Fanny Fletcher.[2] We had a fine dinner with Moselle and burgundy, cold salmon and tartar sauce, followed by gammon and salad, followed by strawberries and kirsch, followed by brandies and coffee. The conversation *seemed* to me very brilliant and amusing, but perhaps it wasn't really. They stayed the night and went this afternoon after lunch. Dorelia sent you her love and Tommy sent his regards. I now lie in a drunken trance with darling Tiber on the sofa. Tiber came in for a tremendous amount of admiration from the cat-lovers. Everyone agreed he was the best cat that they had ever seen. Olive's little sister is better today. There seems a chance that she may recover. A cruel west wind rose up last night and now roars round the house. So basking days seem over. I hope it doesn't travel as far as Cambridge. Chatto have sent you a book on Gibbon. I send their letter. Dorelia loved your library and our botanical Dutch books. I wish she could have stayed but she had Augustus and a tribe of visitors shrieking at Fryern today. In a moment I shall go to sleep but I must first order the wine bottles. I shan't drink another drop now, till you return, and tomorrow I shall start a painting of tulips. Give Dadie my fondest love. I hope you are keeping well and enjoying yourself.

Your devoted loving intoxicated
Mopsa xxx

To Margaret Waley

Ham Spray House
5 June 1929

Dearest Margaret,

[...] I asked John Nash & his wife here for a day yesterday. They are still here. It's rather awful to have a looking glass put up to the past. I used to adore her for some odd reason at the Slade. She is German, & does Folk Dancing, & walks with a Bouncing movement, & has expectant shining eyes

2 T. W. (Tommy) Earp (1895–1958) was an art critic, Fanny Fletcher an art student who designed wallpaper.

& spectacles. But now I see she is just like all other young ladies who teach Eurythmics in the Chilterns. And he is an odd little disappointed man, with an inferiority complex brought about by living under the shadow of Brother Paul, who is now Bloated & Prosperous, whereas they have no servant, & are poor, & struggling, I wondered how at the Slade I spent so much time with them? what we could have talked about? Perhaps everyone is so egotistical at that age one listens to nothing anyone says [...]

Really when Christine Nash said they'd never had a servant since they married, only a girl to wash up once a day, I felt one ought never to complain again in one's life. She is charming. Not in the least embittered. But he is rather sad, & prematurely old, in some way ... Perhaps bad health – They go today, & I shall then start painting, as I've no 'interruptions' till the end of the week & a great deal of work to get done. I'm sad that the tulips are over. There is nothing to my mind that can replace them.

My love dear Margaret

Your C

To Lytton Strachey

Ham Spray House
Saturday, 17 August 1929

Darling Lytton,

Not much news since you left. Ralph came yesterday and was very charming and full of incredible scandals and amazing stories.

Monday, 19 August

Your letter came this morning. I was delighted to hear all your news. I can't write properly, as my head is completely exhausted by an unexpected weekend of endless activity and exhaustion. On Saturday morning little MacCarthys[1] and F[rances] arrived for lunch. Then Saxon for tea and suddenly as Saxon and I were walking in the park we saw a fifth apostle had joined the group in the distance. Even across the park there was no mistaking that fiery red face and short figure, not Norman Douglas, our old friend Beakus.

He had clearly dropped in for a weekend, very vaguely of course. All Saturday evening was spent planning a cinema performance as he had brought his camera. Of course Ralph was very tiresome and destroyed every idea that was suggested until he had to be ignored!

1 Desmond and Molly MacCarthy's children, Rachel and Michael.

On Sunday morning at 7 o'ck I started making 'dummies' and masks and finding properties. Arguments took up most of the morning whilst the sun shone very brightly, almost 12 o'ck when the sun had completely retired, the company got under way. I must say it was great fun. Saxon in the leading role as Dr Turner acted superbly. Rachel was a simple girl called Daisy, the rest of us were lunatics in Dr Turner's mental home. (Of course I forgot that Saxon's father kept a 'Home'!! but I am sure Saxon didn't mind the coincidence.) We didn't have lunch till 2.30 and the whole afternoon was given over to drowning Rachel in the bath by the greenhouse.

This morning I've started before breakfast and at 11 o'ck the film was finished.

The doctor just had time to act his last scene before catching his train!

The mess and confusion left after all the acting is rather devastating and Ralph asked them to stay to lunch, which was rather a bore, as it was a great opportunity to let them go back with Beakus *before* lunch. At least the owl lunatic thought it was – puss played a large part in the film with great success. It is to be performed next Thursday at 41 Gordon Square. I suppose you won't be able to come up? [...]

[...] Please take care of yourself. I love you so much I can't bear you to be unhappy or ill. Now I must go and attend to the lunatics.

My very fondest love

Your loving Mopsa

To Lytton Strachey

Ham Spray House
Monday, 19 August 1929

Darlingest Lytton,

[...] I feel rather in the doldrums this afternoon. Partly because it seems a bit hollow and empty after the wild shrieks and gaiety of the weekend, and then one of those tiresome moods of craving for a little ~~~ came upon me. But I expect it will soon pass, only it's boring to feel so gloomy [...]

You are more to me than anybody else, you know. I don't know what I should do without you.

Your devoted Mopsa

In answer to this letter, Lytton wrote: 'I cannot try to say all you are to me [...] All my fondest love.'

To Lytton Strachey

Coombe Bissett, Salisbury
Tuesday morning, 27 August 1929

Darling Lytton,

[...] On Saturday morning I lay in bed late and recovered from the efforts of entertaining Mr and Mrs Hubert H[enderson]. It was such an exquisite day I wandered about the garden unable to make up my mind to do anything. About 2 o'ck I set off in the car, left the washing and Lord Tiberius at Shalbourne, and reached Salisbury soon after 3. Had my hair washed by a lovely female with a Raphael face. But *not* a very good hair dresser unfortunately. Reached Fryern for tea. After tea we sat in the fields in front of the house and watched Poppet and Vivien jumping gates and hurdles. Practising for the Romsey Horse Show on Wednesday. – I suppose you won't be coming with Mary [Hutchinson]? – They looked so lovely with bare legs and striped jerseys. Kit Dunn was there too. She rides very well. Old Augustus said to me 'Must do a painting of Poppet jumping those hurdles. Only don't you think it would look better it she hadn't those breeches on?' The garden at Fryern is filled with ravishing flowers in spite of droughts. Grapes fell into one's mouth and peaches lie upon the walks [...]

On Sunday morning I looked at Augustus' pictures, and had my usual proposal. He gave me a very romantic poem, not indecent, curiously sad. Then Kit, and Poppet and I went [for] a long ride on the Downs. The horses were very fresh with oats, and we went a terrifying speed. I wish you could walk across that country. At this time of the year with yellow stubble fields, and great dark yew woods it looks very amazing.

After lunch I painted a picture of a thorn apple tree in flower in the garden on a huge canvas. The little Beakus turned up on his way to Southampton at 4 o'ck, followed in 5 mins by Sir James Dunn in a Rolls Royce [...]

But I've left out Col. Lawrence, or Shaw,[1] who appeared in the afternoon on his powerful bicycle. I met him in the garden going off to Augustus' studio to be painted. He looked a measly little man, if I may say so ...

Then we got rid of them and went off in three cars to the New Forest for a picnic. It was dark by the time we got there. The sun just setting. A

---

1 T. E. Lawrence (1888–1935), Lawrence of Arabia, author of *The Seven Pillars of Wisdom*, published in 1927, had adopted the pseudonym T. E. Shaw in 1923 and joined the RAF.

beautiful dinner of cold chicken, and ham, and corton. We stayed there till the stars freckled the sky, and one could hardly see anything but the shapes of the trees. Fanny distinguished herself by singing in a cracked witch voice, songs. Beakus struck up some sea shanties. Old Augustus played hymns on a mouth organ and Edwin [John] sang melancholy French songs. For some reason we had a fight with Edwin and got thrown into gorse bushes. So my legs are now a mass of prickles and thorns [...] Monday morning all the flowers looked very faded. Poor old Augustus as pale as lily [...]

[...] This evening Dodo and I are going to Southampton to see the Macnamaras¹ and visit Beakus' ship! I am enjoying myself very much. Forgive such a straggling long letter.

My very fondest love,
Your devoted Mopsa xxx

To Rosamond Lehmann

Ham Spray House
6 September 1929

Darling,

Did you really write me your first letter? I feel very flattered. It's awful to think what of what you have suffered. I am glad you feel better now.

It must be a queer feeling to have invented a new character with a new shape.² And that in twenty years, when Lytton, and I are both infinitely old, you will come with a ravishing young man to stay at Ham Spray, and it will be the same creature that breaks wind now, & wets napkins [...] But I daresay Wogan won't let his son visit Lytton! He is bound to end up a reactionary if he starts off with cubism [...]

I woke last night and smelt something burning, & looked out of the window, & saw the bonfire that I lit yesterday had fanned itself into a huge blaze. It looked so lovely, flames shooting up under the oak, and the sky quite dark covered with little stars. But I remembered it would probably spread to the marrow bed which is all straw, & was touching the bonfire. So I ran outside, and found it was just catching alight. An owl sat on the stable roof, and hooted at me. I could just see to fill some cans of water, by the conservatory, from the water tub.

1 Francis Macnamara (1886–1946) was an Irish poet and a keen sailor.
2 Rosamond Lehmann had just given birth to her first child, Hugo Philipps.

It was rather fascinating pouring water on the glowing red hot straw. Great clouds of smoke rose up into the dark sky. I saw the vegetable-marrow lying like a huge pale primadonna on her couch, lit up by the footlights. Then the sky grew paler & the owls had a last midnight hunt across the fields, and came hooting back to the farm – one rook after another started to caw, and the owls hooted back angrily. Very far away I heard a cock. Far across the downs.

I went back to my bedroom, but it was so hot that I leant out of the window, & watched the sky grow grey & the stars disappear. Some bats, and moths flew around, & round the house, then all the midnight animals retired. Rooks dominated everything with their cawing, a blackbird started to sing in the laurel hedge, and a pheasant answered him back in the field. Only the horses went on just the same clacking with their hoofs about the field, munching the grass. When it was quite light, a plough boy called the horses 'cum-on, cum-on' and they all very drearily trooped off with funeral tameness [...] you choose a good moment for retiring from the world. For in spite of the pleasures of this tropical heat the disadvantages are serious. Country life is dominated in the day by flies, harvest bugs, & millions of wasps, and at night by Daddy Long legs & cockroaches. And poor Lytton (you can tell this in a whisper to Wogan) has crabs in his bush. He suspects Dadie's guardsmen must leave them behind as mementos at 37 Gordon Square. Everything melts and the telephone is broken, so the Fishmonger will never bring ice again! [...]

I must go to lunch now. You can't think how much I loved your letter, and everything you told me about yourself.

My fondest love darling

Your devoted Carrington

A kiss for Hugo & love to Wogan

Carrington was on another holiday with the Johns.

To Lytton Strachey

Martigues not Ham
Friday, 27 September 1929

Darling Lytton,

We [the Johns] travel so fast that my letters soon get out of date. It is a perfect holiday only I wish you were sitting with us in the car [...]

I think the Rhone valley is fascinating, much better than it looks from the train. They are picking grapes in all the vineyards and one passes continuously great waggons loaded with barrels of glistening berries and as one meanders through villages, buffets of wine come out of the courtyards. I am getting quite brave, imitating Augustus, yelling out 'Monsieur la route pour Nimes?' Typically when we resorted to a map yesterday we almost instantly got lost and spent hours circling round the country in search of Beaucaire!

I have never seen this country look so beautiful as it does now, everywhere these amiable wine activities. Viviers was a perfect town, and quite a good hotel, although very small. We climbed through the town after breakfast and saw the cathedral and peered down on a vast vista stretching up the Rhone valley. Whilst we were watching at some pressing, the owner came out, and begged us to taste his grapes, and with incredibly dirty fingers fished about in huge tub of shining wet grapes, (also covered with wasps, and flies) for a special bunch of muscatels for the Princess Dorelia. At last he found a worthy bunch! I must say they were delicious. He then showed us over his house which was 16 cent covered with curious Renaissance stone carvings. Perhaps I sent you a card. There were old Renaissance frescoes on the walls. But the whole place was incredibly dirty and only used for wine pressing. 'My brother he is cook in England at the Langham Hotel' he told us in French. You would marvel at my long conversations in that language! Dodo is the most perfect companion. I shall never forget the dreamy way she said in Dijon, 'Let's go down to Provence. I am sure it would be very nice down there. I've a hankering to see some olives'. She is longing to buy an old Roman villa in this country, outside Martigues. We passed it yesterday, a divine old ruin, with cypresses, and pines and old columns at the gate way. But infested by mosquitoes, which rather damped Dorelia's enthusiasm. Martigues is an extraordinary place. Filled with fisherman, I have never seen such beauties of both sexes. Paul Cross would look positively plain here. They are enormously strong and brown and, in the evening, flanne up and down under the plane trees, the men walking in threes and fours arm in arm and the girls walking in threes and fours separately. Just laughing and talking and then walking on again. The cafes are filled; Arabs, Spaniards, and fishermen. So far on our whole journey, we haven't heard a single word of English spoken, or seen any English or Americans. Rather a triumph. I drove the car the whole day yesterday till we reached Salon. So I shall come back a very proficient French driver [...]

We drink half a bottle for lunch every day with cheese, and a salad at some small inn. Then another half bottle and a brioche for tea and a whole bottle of very grand wine for dinner. This letter was interrupted by an expedition yesterday to our darling Aix. It was a lovely drive round the edge of the lake and across great red ochre hills with burnt Roman pines on them. When we reached the Negre Coste what do you think? A charming

Negro in buttons rushed out, and piloted our car to the side of the road. 'Tout c'est change ici!' Indeed you would hardly recognize the hotel without our old friend, the waiter. The new waiter is a brisk little Italian, with two under waiters. Lunch served outside under the planes. Old Madame recognized me and was charming and asked after 'Monsieur' and the lunch! Hare pate, grilled red mullet, a marvellous salad and delicious coffee, and Chateau des Papes Telegraphe, a whole bottle; our resolutions for a cheese and salad lunch faded away! [...] We had tea in our old tea shop. Just the same and went to the picture gallery, and saw the Rembrandt, and Ingres. Aix was looking very beautiful. It was an absolutely still day with a hot sun. I drove the car all the way back, and we reached Martigues about 7 o'ck, and had a grand dinner at Pascals, an Italian place where Dorelia is adored, on the edge of the quay. It was pleasant sipping Marsala in a little bamboo hut over hanging the water, listening to the lapping water, and watching the sky grow dark, and dark fishing boats moving across the water with ripples after them [...] I feel slightly depressed at not having heard yet from you. I'll send a wire, if there isn't a letter today [...]

My love trés chère

Votre devoutee Mopsa

To Julia Strachey

Ham Spray House
October 1929

My Dearest Julia,

You have no idea how much I enjoyed staying with you. You are a charmer to be so kind to votre tante. Oh dear I see I am all wrong. I care *far* too much for Ham Spray. I am weak in body, and soul because ever since lunch I have been in ecstasies over the beauty of the fields, the sunlight on the top of the stairs, the beech grove, faded and already tinged with brown, and my family of cats.

They were dreadfully hungry and pleased to see me so I am glad I came back. My lovely Belle recognized me across the field, and came to be patted, so I feel very happy to be back in my animal kingdom. I ran about the garden looking at all the trees and flowers. I found I had forgotten the extraordinary beauty of the Downs, and the garden. Lytton has just sent a wire to say he has been seduced by Dadie and isn't coming back tonight. It makes me a little melancholy to be here alone in this paradise of beauty with no body but the dumb animal kingdom to share it with. Olive is still ill with a cold, so there isn't even her to discuss the beauties of nature with, only my 7 dumb cats and the talking horse. Julia I wish I was a young maid and not a hybrid monster, so that I could please you a little in some way, with my affection. You know you move me strangely. I remember for some reason everything you say and do, you charm me so much. This letter is rather distrait, but I am worn out with going into too many internal ecstasies – and then I was too excited all day to eat anything but some lettuce. I hope you will come on Sunday. Lytton would be delighted to see your beaux I am sure, and I should be to see my Belle.

Forgive me for being one evening, rather ponderous. But you are very long suffering. Now I shall go over all my conversations, the plays, the dances, the proposals, sitting with my cats over the log fire.

My loving darling Julia

Yr most loving Carrington

Around this time Carrington suspected that she was pregnant by Beakus Penrose. She knew she did not love him, nor he her; she had always had a horror of childbirth and shared Lytton's dislike of children ('le petit peuple'). Yet there is no reference to her suspicion, which was correct, in her journal and only hints in her surviving correspondence.

To Lytton Strachey

Ham Spray House
[Monday] 4 November 1929

Darling Lytton,

I feel rather tongue tied always about telling you how much I love you, and incapable of thanking you for all you do for me. But it does you know, make all the difference, in the world. You give me a standard of sensible behaviour which makes it much easier to be reasonable. R[alph] has been so kind also, (I really don't see why such foolishness should be rewarded!). I've been working in my studio all this morning. The rain beats down outside in a most dismal fashion. It's a pity you weren't an actor. I couldn't secretly help watching (split infin.) your ivory hands last night, and thought no movements ever conveyed as much feeling as yours did, on any stage. The rain has washed my brains away I can't write a letter this afternoon! Truly, I am quite happy here. If I feel gloomy I will motor over to Julia, and Tommy for a visit.

I hope you will enjoy London this week. Do ask Dorelia to your Bust Cocktail Party¹. She would like to see the head. I love you so much, and I shall never forget your kindness lately to me.

Your devoted, loving C

1 The party was for the head of Lytton sculpted by Stephen Tomlin.

To Lytton Strachey

Ham Spray House
Wednesday, 6 November 1929

Darling Lytton,

The rain pours down and the Downs are obliterated by clouds. Je pense je suis perdu. I took a very violent ride on Belle all yesterday afternoon along the top of the Downs, mais, sans effect. It is a little difficult to keep one's spirits up, and preserve a sense of humour. Especially with thick grey clouds hanging over one's head and obliterating all the light! I say, I have just been inspecting the cellar and putting away my 1929 slow [*sic*] gin and I see there is *no whiskey*, or *light sherry*, or *brandy* in the spirit department. I thought perhaps you would like to order some.

Puss came clambering in my bedroom window last night mewing piteously in the rain. He has learnt a new trick of climbing up the verandah ironwork. No interesting letters this morning; I send you yours. I sat, listening to the wireless, sewing last night, and felt very middle class and suburban. London was so boring, I was reduced to trying to get foreign stations in the end. I read George Moore in bed last night, the *Celibates*, I found it rather too old fashioned.[1] I think Virginia is fascinating. But I still don't agree that poverty and a room of one's own, is the explanation why women didn't write poetry.[2] If the Brontes could write in their Rectory, with cooking and housework, why not other clergyman's daughters? Have you read it yet? I'll bring the curtains tomorrow with me. Perhaps you'll be in after lunch? Ach. But I am in rather a rage with myself! Better buzz this letter away. Tiber sends his love and so does his mistress dismal-eye erray erray.

To Lytton Strachey

Ham Spray House
3 December 1929

Darling Lytton,
    Thank you for the nicest letter that a Mopsa has ever received [...]
    R was charming all yesterday, we went a walk before lunch along the
terrace and in the afternoon had a great argument for, and against, constancy!
I denied the existence of such a quality. Ralph upheld it, as being the foun-
dation of true love [...]

    No, I really can*not* buy a 'set of books showing God's mission to men
and the circulation of bible in foreign lands' from a sweet faced Christian
female. So after a painful five minutes the grey lady departed with her little
bag of books from the front door [...]
    My fondest love
    Your very loving C

PS Really, I foresee I shall stay here and won't move, out of sheer laziness
this week.

A discreet abortion was arranged and paid for by Ralph. Beakus told him he had
been 'damn decent'. Afterwards, Carrington entertained at Ham Spray as usual.
The sporadic affair with Beakus continued. She appeared to have taken the abortion
in her stride.

1 George Moore (1852–1943), the Irish novelist, published *Celibates* in 1895.
2 Virginia Woolf's landmark essay, *A Room of One's Own*, was published in October 1929.

1930

The Mill Cottage, Swallowcliffe, Wiltshire
Thursday, 23 January 1930

Darling Lytton,

No time for a letter, as life is so rushed and whirling – as you rightly guessed we dash about the country to Fryern, and Coombe Bissett and drink and talk like magpies without a pause. I painted a picture for the Lambs, in a panel in their passage, which seemed to please them. Julia and Tommy are in very good spirits and we have had a lovely time together. I paid two visits to my rustic dressmaker in her little thatched farm. My new dress is very grand. I loved your letter, thank you so much for writing to me. I will see you tomorrow at 6.20 at Hungerford. I go back early tomorrow morning. Tommy and Julia send their fondest love. And so does your very loving
[C]

To Sebastian Sprott

Ham Spray House
23 April 1930

Darling Sebastian,

I am sorry to have been such a long time answering your letter but what with one thing & another – time flies – & no letters are ever written. You can't think how much I loved seeing you again ... I tell you more than I tell anybody else which proves in a way how much I care [...]

It was rather a grim time last Christmas but Lytton & Ralph were so kind, it wasn't nearly as bad as it might have been. I rather enjoy my love affaire. We have great fun boozing in Southampton pubs & playing the gramophone in his trawler-cabin & eating sailor's 'hashes' (?) cooked by a sort of Caliban old salt who lives on Board with him. The only terror is if it wasn't for that particular sword of Damocles that hangs over my head every month, life would have no thorns, or the thorn would have no prick or the prick(le) have no sting. I can't for the moment hit on the exact quotation [...]

Do come here again. It would be nice if you came alone, or at any rate in the middle of the week when there weren't visitors. I shall have 2 servants soon & hope to have more time for painting. Lytton comes back tomorrow from Rome. I've missed him rather a lot. I had a lovely ride on Belle yesterday along the Lanes. It was a miraculous beautiful day. Do tell me how you are, & about your intrigues?

My very fondest love
Your loving C

To Julia Strachey

Ham Spray House
Monday evening, 10 o'ck [n.d.]
[This letter was never posted]

Darling Julia,

[...] There was so much I wanted to talk to you about the other day that I feel breathless to see you soon again! I painted 150 tiles. The weight of them in a box nearly kills me. But they are now all packed up ready to start off tomorrow. I feel rather lonely this evening. There is so much beauty strewn about, hay fields, birds singing and the warm evening breeze stirring in the oak tree and nobody but a mad cuckoo to talk to, except the cat, who has gone off chasing moles.

'To have a craving
for a bird
Is but raving
I'm afear'd.'

And now I must go to bed. I only felt I didn't tell you, darling, properly this afternoon how much I'd like to see you again.

Your loving
Tante C xxxx

It was into her journal, not her letters, that Carrington put her increasingly melancholy feelings about her life and her unsatisfactory lover. She was often lonely, had alarming dreams and was tending to drink too much. She dreaded approaching the age of 40.

A long entry in June 1930 describes what happened one evening after dinner at Ham Spray.

There was a wireless. I hoped he would sit alone with me or go for a walk, but he insisted on listening. I couldn't listen. I watched him half asleep in his chair, and thought he was probably after all a figure head. I remembered how all day I'd been looking forward to him coming and now how bored and flat it seemed. And I felt not the slightest interest in me. After the wireless, I suggested going to bed and left the room. F[rances] with what I call the 'frustration of lover's movement,' at once put on the wireless. I told R[alph] that Lytton was longing to go to bed and begged him to put off the wireless. He was cross, in the engine house. I saw Lytton wandering disconsolately in the sitting-room; it was half past ten. I saw F was determined to play the wireless dance music. Then Roger [Senhouse] and B[eakus] started ping pong. I suddenly saw the similarity between Lytton and my position. Both unable to do anything because we longed for our bed companions who were equally indifferent, to put it bluntly, about coming to bed. I couldn't bear to see Lytton unhappy, so I went out and sat in the moonlight on a stump under the Ilex with Tiber who was prowling about on our lawn [...] I thought B has never once wondered where I have gone to [...] Lying in the cold grass I suddenly realized that he was completely indifferent to my sensations, incapable of any love. Only quite ready to go to bed if there was anyone ready to go to bed. Probably thought it was expected of him by me.

To Julia Strachey

Ham Spray House
Wednesday morning [about 10 June 1930]

Darling Julia,
    Thank you for your very charming letter [...] It's difficult to describe my feelings because they are so illogical. It's partly the effect of having laid two years in the coffin untouched, so as to speak, that these last months of animal affection rather ruined my moral. It's difficult to go back to coffin life again and with my numerous complexes not very easy even if one wanted to, to get a transfer ticket onto someone else. Fortunately it's mostly a matter of bodily lusts I have to deal with in other respects.

> 'You are always first, in spite
> of strange birds of flight
> One, whilst flying o'er the sea
> dropt a "something" on to me
> "something" can be wiped away,
> But FRIENDSHIP lasts till crack of day.'

[...] To tell you the truth when the Gull said ages ago 'I wish you'd wear black silk stockings, or dark brown, they show off a leg, so much better than

those awful white ones you always wear' I realized our PATHS lay differently. I shall mourn in secret this week, painting my tiles and then go back to my coffin and enjoy the company of my friends again. Actually I gave up a good deal of my time which I might have spent at Swallowcliffe and Fryern, washing up dishes on board for this unworthy Gull!! So now I'll wash dishes, and bake pies for my darling Julia, who *doesn't* crab my white stockings.
[...]

To Julia Strachey

Ham Spray House
Friday morning [June 1930]

Darling Julia,

I wish a hundred times you were here today. Just to weep tears on your shoulders? No but to drive away the melancholy of the drizzling Scotch mists that envelope the downs and the bitter west wind that batters against the window panes. It's all very well aiming at being a stoic, but a different matter carrying out one's philosophy. I woke up in an ecstasy of love this morning very early to find my mouth full of sheets which I was biting passionately. Tomorrow 'company' as the servants say, will arrive and I'll get over my despairs. I feel it dreadfully ignominious to mind living alone. But the difficulty is not to let one's mind wander off into abysses of gloom that lead but to munching sheets by moonlight in bed.
Your very loving
Tante C

Carrington also suspected Beakus was carrying on with someone else. She wrote several lovelorn poems around this time. One ended:

He to another mistress flies
I listen to the owls' sad cry
And wish tomorrow would not rise
And I in my grave might lie.

Even so, the affair went on.

To Sebastian Sprott

Ham Spray House
Sunday [July 1930]

Darling Sebastian,

[...] I've never been so happy in my life as on our voyage. The Seagull was particularly charming and I may say that I am so badly gone on that boy that one 'night' sets me up for days afterwards. We had a lovely time in London last Friday evening: a cinema and sipping sherry in the little bed room at Gordon Square out of a tooth glass. Madame Penrose has had a stroke and is very ill so that Alec has become head of the family and is in a terrible state of fuss and agitation. Consequently wants to dominate Seagull and has been very tiresome. So there's a very complicated family feud brewing up. Rather tedious. However it means the Seagull will be in London more often, which suits my interests [...]

This weekend we have Dadie, Dorothy and Janie [Bussy]. Dadie in his highest high brow mood. 'I don't think I can agree. You find in Shakespeare's sonnets ...' comes through the window, from Dadie on the verandah. 'It is essential that the poet, as indeed all writers, should use words etc. etc.' However the ladies are delighted and very impressed. Only one pussy cat on the sofa writes to another pussy cat and miaows!

'There is a great deal of very serious moral idea in the poem as a whole etc.'

Please write me a letter with all your adventures. *Nothing* to be left out. I wish I wasn't so mashed on this sea captain. I can hardly think of anything else and I can't bear to make any plans in case I might see him [...]

Falmouth was a fascinating town. But I don't think quite your style. I have a notion the Devonshire and Cornwall inhabitants are not au fait with that taste. Is it possible? I didn't see a single queerie. ('Listen to this: "The expedition of my careless love outran the etc." Then there is a very good commodity passage in *King John*. Listen to this ...' etc.)

All this at 11 o'ck in the morning and it's been going on for 2 hours!

I loved your post card to Lytton. Now really I must dash off and compose a lunch. I love you so much, for being so sweet and listening to my tedious confidences but I love you also for better reasons for – but perhaps you will never know.

Your loving C xxx

To Julia Strachey

Ham Spray House
Wednesday [1930]

Darling Julia,

Do tell me how your chart progresses? and your general state of health? Dorelia told me that they paid you a visit last week and were very upset to find you away. They took several hours circling round the swallows nest like vultures, so were sad after going some 100 miles up and down narrow lanes, to find no prey. Do ask them to dinner, or tea, one day. Augustus would be delighted and Dorelia longs to taste your Wiltshire-renowned-pasties. We had Seagull with us last weekend so I feel rather flattened at the moment. High jinks may be alright for girls in their teens but old Harridans ought to be pushed by old sea salts in Bath-chairs on the sea front instead of being pushed – fill up at your pleasure. Lettice [Ramsey] has measles so will not come here this week. Secretly I am slightly relieved. Tiber is looking very lovely today and sits in pensive vein, staring into eternity. – puzzling out some obstruse problem by Whitehead [...]

My love to T and very much to you
Your devoted Tante C

Lytton and Ralph are up in London so tomorrow I am going to do a day's painting as my record is deplorable this year so far.

To Lytton Strachey

Back at Ham Spray House
Saturday, 2 o'ck, 9 August 1930

Darling Lytton,

I hope you had a peaceful journey. Now you are in the thick of horse shows, and Irish intrigues. I give you a month! Really there is nothing to tell you, as I've hardly done anything since you left. I painted 18 tiles. But will have to go back next week and do another 20 in order to finish [...] I saw Gull on and off, fairly often. When I'm not with him I am quite immune but face to face I become like treacle! Ralph came and had tea with me over my tiles yesterday. He was very sweet. He thought letting Ham Spray to Penroses quite a good idea. I gathered Alec was very keen to have it. What do you think he had better pay? Last night I spent with James

[Strachey], we saw a lovely film together and at last I've seen a Mickey Mouse. I thought it was almost a work of genius! We laughed tremendously (aloud!) over it [...]

Puss is in very high spirits, delighted to see me again. Dodo has just rung up and asked me to Fryern, so after seeing my mother I shall go over there. My adorable oiseau Edwin is there! Ham Spray looks so peaceful and beautiful, with our white pigeons dancing a quadrille on the lawn.

The sky of course is grey with rain, so there's really nothing to do but sit in doors, and admire the view. Now it's crashing down. I hope Ireland doesn't suffer from the same depression. Ralph has a secret: that Gerald is engaged to be married!! To an American lady authoress [Gamel Woolsey] that he met in the Powys world. But [it] is a deadly secret so you're not to tell anyone! She sounds a little too 'Lolly Willowes'[1] but nobody has been allowed to see her yet!

Now I must go and wash my hair and start off again on my travels. It's very sad to be here without you. To see so many lovely dahlias blooming unseen.

My fondest love
Your most loving Mopsa xxx
[...]

To Lytton Strachey

Ham Spray House
End of the year, December 31st, 1930

Darling Lytton,
I am ensconced in your snug library, as it's so much warmer than downstairs. I hope you don't mind. I am doing nothing but write letters. No chapatties on the floor! Oh, what a day to end a year. What a finale! The wind and rain lash the window panes, and it's as cold as the north pole. I've had tremendous talks with Julia. Rather agitating, and very melancholy. But I suppose it's impossible to alter the situation now. Yesterday we drove down to Southampton, and met the Seagull and old Macnamara and Witch Edie. We had tea and went to some lovely pubs. I had one amazing conversation with the Queen of the Horse and Groom. I wish I could draw her for you. [...]

---

1 *Lolly Willowes*, a novel about a witch by Sylvia Townsend Warner, was published in 1926.

It's a marvellous pub, with stuffed bears, canaries and a band that plays old fashioned tunes and gay barmaids who run about singing as they serve the sailors and Sebastians.

We went to another, a very different style, Edwardian, with a little old lady behind the bar and 1880 photographs of the war and ferns and flowers hanging from the ceiling. After dinner we went to the Musical Hall and saw George Robey and Marie Lloyd's sister, Rosie Lloyd.[3] She had some of Marie's old tricks and songs. It was lovely sitting in a box and examining them very closely. I do love Music Halls.

As the lights of the car weren't working very well, for some reason Julia and I stayed on Beakus's ship. It was very romantic waking up in the shiny mahogany cabin this morning [...]

I wish I wasn't such a mass of mixed feelings. I feel absolutely exhausted now just by having felt so much, so intensely, these last 12 hours. Gull was rather gloomy and preoccupied, worrying over something I suppose, so was rather unapproachable. Although I know it's absurd, I mind so much, (partly because I see him so little) if when I do see him, he isn't happy. And yet really of course the whole thing is a chimera, a mirage of my own making. He is quite incapable of understanding my odd cravings and feelings about him.

Yet in spite of my miseries I would not have had anything different. Would you? For, one perfect evening seems to me, even in memory, to make days of gloom worth putting up with. But this letter is getting as involved as a mooncalf's labyrinth. So I will stop. Olive, and Phyllis have gone out for the evenings, so I shall be able to eat chapatties on the floor. (Downstairs, *not* in your library) to my heart's content tonight, with Tiber – 'Lady into Cat.' [...]

My love to Pippa and you darling
Yr very fondest C

3 George Robey (1869–1954) was a leading music-hall actor and singer, as were Marie and Rosie Lloyd.

1931

Lytton's health had always been delicate. During 1931, it began to get worse. Carrington was full of forebodings. In March, while helping Lytton organise his library, she wrote in her journal:

I thought of Sothebys and the book plates in some books I had looked at, when Lytton was bidding for a book and I thought: These books will one day be looked at by those gloomy faced booksellers and buyers. And suddenly a premonition of a day when these labels will no longer be in this library came over me. I longed to ask Lytton not to stick in any more.

Meanwhile she was making Gerald and Gamel a patchwork quilt as a wedding present.

To Gerald Brenan

Ham Spray House
29 March, 1931

Dearest amigo,

I fear I shall not be able to join in your nuptial celebrations (G: good heavens, but we forgot to invite her!) Yes, you forgot to ask me but unlike the fairy Gruffenough I will <u>not</u> blight your happy life with horrid spells. I will only stick two pins into your waxen effigy – can you guess where? – and quickly murmer a few mystic words over your (nearly finished now) patch quilt which will give you on certain nights when the moon is full strange dreams. Talking of which I had a <u>very</u> strange dream of you last night. Do you know although I suppose I think of you quite often – I dream very seldom – I sat on your knee because there was no room owing to the little branches of trees & people moving about at a sort of party out of doors, & you put your arm so tightly round my waist that I could hardly breathe & it was difficult to find breath to answer your questions. I woke up almost suffocated, & found my own arm pressing my lungs. So you would stifle me would you? [...]

When will you come back to England? I'm afraid I've not heard of an hotel yet in Rome for you. I asked in vain. They all sounded so expensive. It is still terribly cold here. East winds, & gales. Did you reach Sicily? I hope you saw the corpses of dead aristocrats in the caves of Palermo.

I spent last week in London. Rather pleasant for a change from this wind swept wilderness. One evening Dodo took me to see Vivien dance at her

dancing school. It was a marvellous world of jeune filles, exquisitely beautiful, half naked, dancing, & learning somersaults. I hope Gamel is keeping
well. Please give her my love & accept some for yourself. Barbara & Nick
arrived this weekend in their Baby Austin. But I will not say one word against
them, such useful members of society ... I will leave that to Ralph. I feel I
have learnt a few golden rules of conduct all the same from Barbara. – God,
strike me dead, if ever I discuss 'Milky Puddings' or 'rheumatism & old age'.

I hope you are enjoying yourself in Italy. I must now go for a walk with Little
Barbara although writing to you is so much more to my taste this afternoon.

My love

Yr loving amiga Cirod

To Lytton Strachey

Sans Pareil, Falmouth
12 May 1931

Darling Lytton,

[...] Falmouth looks so sympathetic in spite of the rain and mist. We sit
in the harbour not very far from the Green Bank Hotel. George is cooking
dinner in the galley and I sit over a little fire with a grey tabby cat. I hope
it will be fine tomorrow. The old salt 'William' says it is going to be hot.
Please tell Olive I shan't be back on Thursday, and tell her you'll let her
know about the weekend if you haven't decided before you go to London.
I will go back Monday to Ham Spray to tell her. Could you possibly send
me from the bottom drawer in my wardrobe a red silk dress, with a red belt
and a black and green check silk blouse and from the bathroom cupboard
a pair of pyjamas either blue or blue checked? It would be *extremely* kind of
you if you could, as thinking we would only be away 3 or 4 days, I didn't
put in any clothes. Olive would pack them for you. I hope you'll be very
happy with puss and your fire. You've no idea how much I loved last weekend
alone with you and our excursion to the forest of Savernake. I feel I've been
rather dull lately darling but truth is ma Coeur etait craque – comme le dos,
you told me about and I've been trying to rivet it together again, which was
rather painful and I felt made me often self absorbed and tiresome. Your
friendliness means more than I can ever express. Coming in the train (it was
too shaky to read Proust all the way) I thought of you and how happy you
made me by living at Ham Spray. I wish you were here to prowl up the little
streets with although I confess tonight it's hardly an evening for flanning.

Proust is fascinating, but the end of Charlus is almost too terrible. It
has the appalling horror of Lear, in quite a different way. I wish I could

write properly. The emotions and curious visions that come back to one sitting in this little cabin and seeing Falmouth again. It seems rather a waste often to have so much material and to be able to make nothing of it. Now I must go and show George how to make our fried bread and sugar sweet [...] I hope you'll have lovely weather for next weekend and enjoy yourself very much.

My very fondest love,

Yr most loving Mopsa

PS Don't leave this for the abigails to read please!

To Rosamond Lehmann

Ham Spray House
Thursday [early June 1931]

Darling,

How very kind of you to write. It was a beautiful surprise this morning after a terrible night of thunderstorms, nightmares, and glooms. You couldn't have been as disappointed as I was. I was really so savage, Wogan will tell you, I started cutting off the innocent heads of the verbena on the verandah with a kitchen knife.

Beakus is better this morning.[1] So I feel it was probably worth while giving up London and staying here.

I suppose you wonder sometimes why I am so fond of him. It's really very little to do with him actually, but because he is so like my brother who was killed. I couldn't say this to anyone. Please don't show my letter to Wogan, as I am awfully self conscious of being a romantic, and rather stupid. My brother was very silent and removed. I hardly ever was allowed to be intimate with him and I always put it off, thinking one day I'd be able to show him how much I cared and then it was too late. And partly because he wasn't reported killed, it took me ages to ever believe consciously he was dead. I don't know why I shouldn't say this to you. Only you were so nice to write about your feelings and glooms. I don't agree about your being 'stuck'. I think Wogan puts almost too much emphasis on 'movement' and 'adventure'. Well that's not quite what I mean to say, really I think it's NO good being anything but what you are and the great thing is never to do anything one doesn't feel genuinely inside oneself. (This is Lytton's creed, not *my* invention!) And actually one can be very tame inside in spite of all

---

1 When Beakus fell ill with jaundice, Carrington nursed him at Ham Spray.

one's dashing about. People like Sandy and Bryan[1] aren't truly progressive characters I am sure. James Strachey is more advanced, although he hardly ever budges from his gas fire. I think your writing is what is really important and if you found the house and domestic things hampered *that*, I would agree with you about it being bad for you. I always see Rebecca West when literary women are mentioned! I am sure really everyone has to find their adventure in different ways. Wogan clearly finds stimulation in parties and excitable people, but I don't see why you shouldn't get, in other directions, quite as intensely. I am sure you do. I pass over your cauliflower moan. It's just the result of all your horrors and lying in bed. I am eight years older than you are darling, so if one's going to start talking in the cabbage vein, you must condole with my later winter broccoli. Ralph is always blowing *me* up for not settling down to a purple sprouting old age and hates me going off to parties and boozing! – and holds up Beryl de Zoete as a warning! I will try and get hold of Brett. Perhaps she will be in England this year. She could, if she would, tell you far more about Katherine M[ansfield] than I could. Another person who could is Koteliansky and Gertler, but you'd have a job sifting the evidence.

I am so glad you liked the tulips. Yesterday Paul Cross[2] and an aunt (?) (a dreadful old lady with a white nose – truly like a cauliflower and clothes that gave one the creeps. She was quite friendly, but so lacking in some quality of charm that is rather essential to spidery ladies of 56, if you understand) and Angus Wilson and another young man, came over after tea. Ham Spray was looking beautiful, untidy and dusty. I am afraid they were rather appalled. And then the old aunt said: 'And you live here all alone Mrs Partridge, *how* romantic, and after we go you'll go on weeding the garden? and you don't mind the loneliness, No? of course not, not with this view.' I was half longing when I was showing them the mosaic that Beakus would appear in his pyjamas wandering to the W.C. Now I must go and see about lunch. I read *Dr Moreau's Island* to Beakus all yesterday afternoon. Have you read Vita's book? Very *unoriginal* I thought.[3] James said Alix was getting on much better now and will soon be well. Lytton has asked T[ommy] and Julia for the weekend. I do hope they'll be able to come. Your reproaches towards yourself for not writing more, make my cheeks *burn* with shame. For really I used every excuse not to do any proper painting. It's partly I have such high standards that I can't bear going on with pictures when I can see they are amateurish and dull. This is a tediously long letter darling and it was meant to be a bright ray of sunshine to cheer your invalid cell instead

1 Brian Howard (1905–58) was fashionable and flamboyant. Sandy was his current boyfriend.
2 Paul Cross and Angus Wilson (not the writer) lived nearby and were known as the Tidcombe Boys.
3 Vita Sackville-West's latest book *Sissinghurst*, about her new family home, had just been published.

of which it's as heavy as suet pudding. I am sorry. I'll ring Wogan up tomorrow. All my love darling.

Yr very fondest loving C

Although Julia and Tommy's marriage was in trouble, Carrington stayed close to them both. She hoped she and Tommy might work together on a ballet.

To Stephen Tomlin

Ham Spray House
Monday, July 1931

Dearest Tommy,

This is a *very* private letter and I shall MURDER you if you show anyone my scenario, or pictures. You must read *Goblin Market* to understand, I expect, the gist of my ballet –

Do you think

(a)   There is anything in it?
(b)   If there was would you combine with me over the dresses and masks, and scenery?
(c)   If there isn't any of (a) will you say so and say no more.

I am too impatient to draw it out nicely, also I've a terrible cold and a temperature so can't concentrate. The dairymaids would be dressed in my favourite rustic china-figure-1840-style. You would have to make my masks and help with the inventions, please. I then thought, supposing you thought it possible, we might draw it out neatly, with colours, and ask Lydia [Lopokova] and Constant Lambert to give us a £100 and put it on stage. Or shall we ask Mr Cochran and get £100 and sink art and ambition?

But all this depends on your cooperation. (Excuse me Dr Jones, for hesitating over that word.) When shall I see you again? Derek and Poppet[1] have just left us, a *strange* pair of turtle doves.

My fondest love
Your devoted C

PS I am going to suggest to Derek that he has a head done of Poppet, by you. Don't you think it would be a good idea??

PS the moral I confess of this ballet seems a little obscure. The triumph of Lesbianism?

1 Poppet was engaged to Derek Jackson (1906–1982), a millionaire scientist and amateur jockey.

In July, Carrington, under the name Mopsa, went in for a competition in the Weekend Observer *to write an obituary of a writer in his own style. She wrote one of Lytton. To his delight, and hers, she won with the following entry:*

Crouching under the ilex tree in his chaise longue, remote, aloof, self occupied, and mysteriously contented, lay the venerable biographer. Muffled in a sealskin coat (for although it was July he felt the cold) he knitted with elongated fingers a coatee for his favourite cat, Tiberius. He was in his 99th year. He did not know it was his last day on earth.

A constable called for a subscription for the local sports. 'Trop tard, trop tard; mes jeux sont finis.' He gazed at the distant downs: he did not mind, – not mind in the very least the thought that this was probably his last summer; after all, summers were now infinitely cold and dismal. One might as well be a mole. He did not particularly care that he was no longer thought the greatest biographer, or that the Countess no longer – or did he? Had he been a woman he would not have shone as a writer, but as a dissipated mistress of infinite intrigues.

But – lying on the grass lay a loose button, a peculiarly revolting specimen; it was an intolerable, an unspeakable catastrophe. He stooped from his chaise longue to pick it up, murmuring to his cat 'Mais quelle horreur!' For once stooped too far – and passed away for ever.

To Lytton Strachey

Ham Spray House
Saturday, 18 July 1931

Darling Lytton,

My most venerable Biographer, knitter of coatees, most dissipated of masters, do you know your wire gave me more pleasure than anything in the world? You were kind to think of sending it to me. Terrible to think I nearly lost my two guineas through cruelty! Ralph is really more delighted than I am, I believe! But of course they will all say you wrote it for me. In fact I am terrified when I send my address the editor will refuse my prize [...]

A mad hatter's tea party this weekend. I wonder how it will go off! I rather dread the lady poetess, Madame Gamel Brenan. Tommy Earp sends very enthusiastic wires 'Looking forward very much to weekend.

Arriving 4.10 with happy anticipation.' I hope he won't be furious to find you not here.

The cats all send you their loves and pussykisses. Tiber is very proud to at last be immortalized in print. What about our chaise-longue now?

Did you hear that Bunny was sent for by Sir Philip Sassoon and has been asked to Lympne for a weekend, to fly in an aeroplane!

I send on all your letters, which seem pretty dreary. I shall miss you very much. I rather favour the curly mirror. But have not quite made up my mind yet. Again it is the expense, which is rather serious.

I hope you'll have a lovely time at Cambridge, and enjoy yourself very much darling.

I shall stay here, and paint next week, and try and improve the house a little, and the garden, before your return.

Dodo's garden was looking very beautiful. She gave me some rare cactuses for my greenhouse.

Poppet, and Derek, are coming to dinner tomorrow to complete the congress of mad hatters!

I love you so much, and think of you very often. Please write to me, as I shall miss you very much.

All my love

Your devoted and most loving Mopsa xxx

To Lytton Strachey

Ham Spray House
Sunday, 19 July 1931

Darling Lytton,

I had a lovely ride with Bryan [Guinness] on Friday evening, and a nice chat with Diana [Mitford] over the fire after dinner alone.' She told me a great deal about [her brother] Tom's character. Rather interesting. I stayed too late – but it is the disease of my old age I foresee, lingering on till everyone falls unconscious with sleep. But what do you think! On the way home I met a badger on the road. And what did the badger say to Mopsa? You will never know. But really it was rather exciting. I could see it very clearly as it ran along in front of the headlights of the car and finally climbed up a bank and went through the hedge. A quiet weekend here. Julia has gone to sleep most of the time. Tommy, Eddie [Gathorne-

---

1 Bryan Guinness, 2nd Baron (1905–1992) had a large fortune from the brewing dynasty. A poet novelist and patron of the arts, he married Diana Mitford, the third of the notorious sisters, in 1929.

Hardy] and I sat up till about 2 o'ck arguing and boozing last night. Today Woggies [Rosamond and Wogan Philipps] come to lunch and we tea at Fryern. Julia wants to stay on with me next weekend for some days. Will that be alright?

All the covers have been washed in the sitting room. It looks quite smart. 20 bottles of gooseberries for the winter and some pots of red-currant jelly for you and your mutton pies. Pansy [Lamb] has sent me her essay for you to read. I hope you are happy darling.

All my love and love from the cats

Your fondest Mopsa

Olive made some really *delicious bread* for us, this weekend.

Along with Fryern, Biddesden House, where Diana and Bryan Guinness lived, had become one of Carrington's favourite places. Both she and Lytton admired Diana's 'moon goddess' beauty and were amused by her Mitford mannerisms. Bryan commissioned Carrington to paint a trompe l'œil *fresco of a maid and a cat on an outside wall as a surprise for Diana.*

To Lytton Strachey

Ham Spray House
Tuesday, 28 July 1931

Darling Lytton,

[...] I went with Julia to lunch with Diana today. There we found 3 sisters and Mama Redesdale. The little sisters were ravishingly beautiful, and another of 16 very marvellous, and Grecian. I thought the mother was rather remarkable, very sensible and no upper classes graces.

We were half an hour late having spent nearly an hour wandering about the byways and footpaths of Glanville. Julia as you might guess wasn't much good with the map! Mercifully lunch was late as they had only just come back from Stonehenge.

The little sister was a great botanist, and completely won me by her high spirits and charm.

Now I must send this to the post.

I talk with Julia all day, on rather painful topics and get rather gloomy. I do not know what to advise, for I have very little faith in there being any happiness for human beings on this earth.

I shall not come to London, as there will be preparations to make for the weekend and I think Julia stays with me till Friday probably. I miss you more than I can say.

The *Sans Pareil* has just reached Lisbon. I had a post card yesterday [...]

All my love to you darling,

Your fondest Mopsa

In September, Lytton went for a short trip by himself to Nancy, in central France. He, Ralph and Carrington were planning to spend part of the winter in Spain. The social life in and around Ham Spray continued.

To Lytton Strachey

Ham Spray House

29 October 1931

Darling Lytton,

Oh dear! Inanimate objects are very animated down here! I can pay no attention to elections and tariffs when motorcars refuse to start, scissors disappear and gloves walk off and hide themselves. I got up at half past 7 this morning in order to start my picture at Biddesden early. Bryan had asked me to breakfast. The car refuses to operate and it was 10 o'ck before I got to Biddesden. Then, typically as you would say, the moment I started to paint it came on to rain. So all my paints got mixed with water. My hair dripped into my eyes and my feet became icy cold. Diana was delighted. Bryan kept it a complete surprise from her till 3 o'ck. May joined in the joke, and kept my presence dark all this morning and pretended I had walked over from Ham Spray as my car had to be hidden. Diana, of course, thought nothing of my walking over in the rain and merely said 'But Carrington you *ought* to have let me send the car for you.' I had tea there and then came back. Diana is sweet. She was looking very lovely today, in a curious dark bottle green jersey with a white frill round her neck. Bryan ate 2 huge slices of his birthday cake for lunch! It was his birthday yesterday. Diana gave a very amusing account of an excursion to see Miss Mona Wilson and Mr Young at Oare. 'Oh Carrington I cannot *tell* you how *dreadful* they were.'

Bryan – 'Carrington you musn't believe it. It was *fascinating* afternoon.'

'Ough, she smoked a pipe and Mr Young talked about the middle classes and had a blob at the end of his nose.' etc. etc. etc.

Diana says 'Will you tell *Mr* oh indeed to remember the christening on Monday' [...]

Don't come back too exhausted; remember our literary weekend! *You* are responsible for the dazzling conversations. I shall just put opium in the pies to mitigate Aldous's brilliance. Puss sends you his love and a kiss. I must go to bed now as I am half asleep. I take the car into Newbury tomorrow. Really it is too much to BEAR. Biddesden was looking ravishing today. The afternoon was beautiful and hot. It's rather a relief to know nothing of elections.[1] Ham was quiet as a dead mouse.

My love darling *Mr* Oh indeed!

Yr loving C

Ralph's mother died in November. Bloomsbury disliked and avoided all religious ceremonies, but Carrington dutifully attended the senior Mrs Partridge's funeral. From the beginning of that month, Lytton's health had taken a sudden turn for the worse.

To Gerald Brenan

Ham Spray House
24 November 1931

Dearest Amigo

I've been bad at writing. But then I am not a writer ... and lately I've been very much of a painter, & haven't had an atom of time to write any letters. Is it true that you & Gamel will be in London soon?

I feel completely exhausted today as all yesterday for 8 hours I attended the funeral ceremony of La Grande Perdrix. At last she is no more, & the clotted red clay of Devonshire corrupts her flesh. But I am completely exhausted, & almost dead myself. Never again will I attend a funeral. I think it is appalling that to ¾ of the English nation a funeral is what a Fair (at Salisbury) is to us. They gloat over those menacing services, they adore the damp sordid scenes over the grave, & the Beef, & Yorkshire pudding luncheon with black crows afterwards.

How are you both? Is your cottage windproof & snug?

I write Gamel a separate letter to tell her my favourite poems, & give her secret female messages.

I have been gallivanting in London lately & riding madly over the Downs down here. In fact, I've been enjoying myself very much in my way.

---

1 At the General Election held on October 27, the National Government led by Ramsay MacDonald won a landslide victory.

This funeral was rather a full stop in my happiness. I had forgotten that side of life existed. Black cotton stockings. Bunches of white chrysanthemums. Do write to me. My love

Your amiga C

To Julia Strachey

Ham Spray House
Thursday, 6 o'ck [n.d.]

Darling Julia,

Virginia, and Leonard have just been down here for the day. They are a fascinating couple. I found Virginia's conversation irresistible. She is *very* enthusiastic about your story, and so was Leonard. They gave you a tremendous high praise, your old Tante was delighted. She has been struggling with a cover, but how not to look like Mr Whistler (Rex). That is the problem. How to cram in the socks, penknives, ferns, inkpots, wedding cakes and jellies. All very difficult. I suggested to Virginia that she should get *you* to illustrate your own masterpiece (C. 'her drawings, only of course she never lets anyone see them and always crosses them out, are equal to her writing'), I regret to say Virginia refused to be lured away from her horrid intentions. But seriously my dear why don't you do them? Then, ah then, no fault could be found by the author with the illustrator.[1]

I am mad about my grove and spend all my time weeding, and carrying nettles on to bonfires. When the heavenly grove is finished poor Tante C will, I fear, be so bent double she won't be able to look about her and appreciate the darker shades. It's been very pleasant here this week, such lovely quiet weather. No winds. Olive is ill, so a nice person call[ed] Mrs Walters from the lodge waits on me. She is a sweet character. How are you? You never write now, Piggie. What am I to imagine? Your doggie picture is at 16 Great James's Street so go and see it if you want it. It is literally 16 years old. Almost as old as Vivien. Is the 'cook and the pussy cat' an improvement? If you'd tell me that, I should then know whether to go on with my painting or take to poker-work. My love to Tommy and you darling.

Yr fondest old Tante C

---

1 The Hogarth Press was going to publish Julia Strachey's first novel, *Cheerful Weather for the Wedding*, and had asked Carrington to design the cover.

Lytton's condition was deteriorating fast, and trained nurses as well as his sister Pippa moved in to help Carrington and Ralph look after him. His symptoms – fever and diarrhoea – suggested typhoid. In fact he was suffering from stomach cancer.

To Rosamond Lehmann

Ham Spray House
Thursday, November 1931

Darling,

I'll write tonight because tomorrow may be rather a busy day. Lytton is really a little better today, temperature lower, and no haemorrhages, but he feels worse, I suppose because of the low temperature and exhaustion. I feel so relieved when each day is over, as I gathered from a specialist that if there is a turn for the worse it will be in the next few days probably. I sat all this afternoon with Lytton, sponging his face, and hands with scent and water. There is practically nothing one can do. The nurses are very kind and let Pippa and me go in and out of his room when we like. Lytton is so good. He lies without moving day after day and never complains. They still can't find the germ in any of the blood cultures, but apparently it is undoubtedly typhoid from temperatures and other symptoms. Pippa is such a remarkable character, she adores Lytton and yet never betrays her grief, or thinks of herself. Oliver came down yesterday and stays at the Bear and comes up for meals and spends the day with us. James is coming this weekend I think. Lytton is too weak to talk much, so one sits in his room by the fire without talking. He sends you and Wogan his love. He was so touched by your enquiries and letters.

I feel dreadfully upset about Garrow.[1] I felt I'd been so stingy not caring for him, when probably quite a little affection might have made him happier. Julia said Tommy was terribly upset in her letter to me yesterday.

I met Mrs Hammersley[2] at the Guinnesses' last Saturday evening and was fascinated by her. She talked a *great* deal about you. She is so beautiful in a romantic Russian style. I couldn't take my eyes of her. Bryan longs to visit Wales. 'Do you thing they would mind if we all made an expedition and visited them? and Diana we could look at *all* the cathedrals on the way!'

'Oh Bryan, *must* we, I do hate cathedrals ...'

Mrs Hammersley said she'd join the party so about the 6th Jan. you must expect the invasion! Ralph went up to London today but he will be back

---

1 Garrow Tomlin had been killed in a flying accident.
2 Mrs Violet Hammersley (1877–1962) was an old friend of the Mitford family.

tomorrow. The owls have come out of their hiding, and hoot round the house tonight and the lawn is white with frost. I'll write when there is more news. I gather the climb down hill for Lytton will be very slow. You are dear to write such cheering letters. I've been feeling in a black dungeon all this week. Nightmarish day and night.

Your most fond Doric

By Christmas, there was still no clear diagnosis and Carrington swung between hope and despair.

To Diana and Bryan Guinness

Ham Spray House
Christmas Day, 1931

Darling Diana and Bryan,

You can't think how I loved all your presents. You are geniuses to know the colour of my stockings, my socks and my favourite necklace. Please don't be cross if your surprise isn't quite ready by the time you get back. I hope it will be, but there never seems any time now [...]

I can't write today as I feel rather crushed and flattened by horrors. I gather now the worst is over, at least they hope it is. Yesterday was a terrible day. You can't think how I look forward to seeing you both again.

Lytton asked for you today and sent you his love. Your letters were very supporting. Your fondest, with a great deal of love,

Carrington

10 o'ck
PS The nurse has just told me that the temperature is lower tonight.

To Sebastian Sprott

Ham Spray House
Tuesday evening [December 1931]

Darling Sebastian,

Lytton was pleased this morning when I told him of your present. He said: 'How sweet of Sebastian. Do send him my love. I knew Du Maurier was a traitor' and gave me a long account of him. It always astonishes the grand doctors how clear his brain is and how good his spirits. We had Dudgeon the grandest pathologist in the world here on Sunday. He confirmed Cassidy's opinion about the ulcerated colitis, but gave a new treatment, more drastic washing outs and pills. So far there is no visible result but I suppose it's too soon to expect it yet. The temperatures are still high, they go up to 102 and 103, but pulse is better which is the important thing. The local doctor seems pleased at the way Lytton is holding his own and hopes the bugs and abscesses are being held in check. Your love means so much. I'll write when there is any change and when it's possible to have you here darling. I hope you are a little happier now. And next year will be better. Did you see 'an elderly respectable stockbroker' got pinched, in yesterday's paper, for buying female underclothes in D.L. draper's shop. It is a scandal.

My fondest love,
Your loving C

To Gerald Brenan

Ham Spray House
26 December 1931

Dearest Gamel & Gerald,

Thank you <u>very</u> much for a most beautiful present of a rare & exquisite Ham. Lately everything has been so unreal that I can't believe there is another life – a life I can't believe of Christmas parties, Conversations, foxes (?), & appetites. This summer which was suspended, & defeated, seems a prologue to this December of tragedies & melancholies. I feel now that all my feelings 'that nothing this year "counted"' was a cynical preparation for these all too poignant packed days. But I like to think of you, & Gamel gay over your snug fire, cracking jokes. I do hope very much you are happy. – This is to wish you <u>everything</u> you both most want next year.

Lytton is much the same. But I am almost insensible now. I feel incapable of hoping, or despairing. Everyone has been very kind. Dodo came over, & saw me, & Tommy came for two days. Thank you so much for your comforting letter Gerald. Forgive my gloom but I oughtn't to write. Yet I had to, because of your letter, & the ham.

Your very loving Carrington

1932

As doctors and visitors came and went, Carrington worked in the garden or made glass pictures in her studio. She wrote a stream of daily reports on Lytton's condition to their friends.

To Roger Senhouse

Ham Spray House
Sunday, January 1932

Darling Roger,
Dr Cassidy has just been down this evening. He was very hopeful. He said he thought Lytton was in a better state than 2 weeks ago, & was bearing up marvellously. He thought he had a very good chance of recovering. He is a blunt man, & extremly honest, so I felt one could believe what he said.

Lytton asked me to send you his Love. I gather the improvement will have to be very slow for weeks, because there is so much poison in the colon. He suffers from boredom dreadfully.

It is so frightfully monotonous lying in a dark room, & nothing to do but eat broths & tea.

I hope you had a lovely Christmas, & enjoyed yourself. If you see Raymond tell him the specialist was hopeful, & thought everything was as good as could be expected. I think of you so often.

All my Love & Best Wishes for a Beautiful New Year.
Your loving Carrington

To Roger Senhouse

Ham Spray House
Thursday, January 1932

Darling Roger,
Lytton loved your flowers. He asked to hold them in his hands & for a long time buried his face in them, & said 'How lovely'. He sends you his fondest Love. I am planting cuttings of the sweet Herb.

The Doctor said Lytton's state was much the same this morning. He couldn't say there was any improvement. The Diet is to be altered today. Perhaps it will have a good effect on the digestion.

Leonard, & Virginia dropt in today. It was nice to see them. Your freezias look so beautiful against the dull green-yellow wall in a pewter mug.

I will write tomorrow.

All my Love

Your fondest C

Carrington and Pippa would sit with Lytton and sponge his face. Friends and relations gathered nearby: the Stracheys stayed en masse at the Bear Hotel in Hungerford, as did Gerald and Tommy. Ralph, himself acutely anxious, wrote desperate letters to Frances (they thought it best for her to stay mostly in London) about his conviction that Carrington was planning to commit suicide if Lytton died.

On the afternoon of 20 January, while she was bathing his face, the semi-conscious Lytton suddenly whispered: 'Darling Carrington. I love her. I always wanted to marry Carrington and I never did.' True or not, it was what she had always longed to hear. When he fell asleep, she was suddenly terrified, writing in her journal: 'I thought of the Goya painting of a dead man with the highlight on the cheekbones.'

That night, around 3 a.m., the nurse told her Lytton was unlikely to survive the night. She went in to see him. 'I gave him a kiss on his cold forehead, it was damp and cold. I gave Ralph a kiss and asked him not to come and wake me. I saw him sit by the fire, and sip some tea in Lytton's room. James went downstairs. I walked very quietly down the passage and down the back stairs. It was half past three. The house was quiet and outside the moon shone in the yard, through the elms across the barns. The garage door was stuck open. I could hardly move it.'

Fearing that the sound of the engine would wake the household, she waited till dawn, going back inside once to drink some whisky before getting back into the car and turning the engine on.

'I turned out the light again and lay down. Gradually I felt rather sleepy, and the buzzing noise grew fainter and fainter [...] I thought of Lytton, and was glad to think I shouldn't know any more.' At around six, with Lytton on the point of death, Ralph realised Carrington was missing and then heard the sound of the car. He found her unconscious, and pulled her out. 'Ralph held me in his arms and kissed me, and said: How could you do it? [...]'

James came and talked to her. 'I felt no remorse. I must confess I felt defrauded and angry that fate had cheated me in such a way and brought me back again.'

She went back to Lytton. 'I sat there thinking of all the other mornings in Lytton's room and there was Pride and Prejudice, *that I had been reading the evening before still on the table [...] Suddenly I felt very sick, and ran out to my bedroom and was violently sick into the chamber pot. I remember watching the yellow water pour out of my mouth and thought it is the same as what is in the chamber pot.'*

She went back to Lytton's room and stood waiting, her arm round Pippa's waist. James and Ralph joined them. When the nurse suggested 'you ladies' should leave the room 'I was furious and hated her'.

Lytton's breathing grew shorter. 'I could not cry, I felt if he woke up we must be there not depressing or melancholy [...] Ralph brought me some glasses of brandy and some sal volatile to drink. A blackbird sung outside in the sun on the aspen. We stood there. I do not know for how long [...] Suddenly he breathed no more. Nurse McCabe put her hand on his heart under the bedclothes and felt it.

'I looked at his face. It was pale as ivory. I stepped forward and kissed his eyes, and his forehead. They were cold.'

Later, she went back with Ralph and kissed him again. The next day, 'Ralph brought me some bay leaves, and I made a wreath. I tried it on my head, it was a little large. I went in and put it round Lytton's head. He looked so beautiful. The olive green leaves against his ivory skin. I kissed his eyes, and his ice cold lips.'

The next day Ralph took her for a drive to Savernake Forest. 'I knew while we were away men would come and take him away.'

Back at the house she went to bed. Tommy came up and read her some poetry. Ralph told her Lytton could never have recovered.

'It is ironical,' she later wrote 'that Lytton by that early attack at six o'clock saved my life. When I gave my life for his, he should give it back.'

In the days after his death, she wrote endless answers to letters of condolence from their friends.

To Roger Senhouse

Ham Spray House
Saturday, January 1932

Darling Roger,

Thank you so much for your letter. I think of you very often – I have known you for so many years intimately through Lytton, & have loved you because of his love for you, more than anyone. I am so grateful for you for giving Lytton all you did. You made these last years so complete for him. And this autumn he was so happy to have got over the slight emotional troubles that sometimes used to assail him, & to have reached a plain of tranquillity, & contentment. I shall never forget Lytton's pale ivory hands clasping the pewter mug, & his face buried in your freesias. Ham Spray is my only consolation at the moment. I cannot quite let myself realize everything. You will come here later? His hankerchiefs, & tie pin, are in London but I will send you them later. Would you like a photograph, or did he give you one? It wouldn't have been any good Roger if you had come. I asked him once, whether he would like to see you. But he was too weak, & so anxious to conserve all his strength that he said he would rather not. That was just before Christmas. Your love helps me more than you can think.

Darling Roger never forget how much happiness you gave Lytton, & how much he loved you.
Your very loving
Carrington

To Stephen Tomlin

Ham Spray House
Saturday evening

Darling,
I miss you very much. I wish you had not gone. This afternoon I made a bonfire and laid some grass under the yews. I hope you had a lovely ride with Diana on the downs. Julia seems better. I can't write a letter you see, so I had better stop. You made this last week bearable which nobody else could have done. Those endless conversations were not quite pointless. Today has been a great improvement in one direction. Ralph seems much calmer and more natural. I think of what you said to me very often. Forgive me for going to bed yesterday, but you had no idea how bad my headache was. It really was cracking my skull. I didn't want to complain and fuss. Now you are gone I can! But I had had it all the morning. I hope you had a lovely evening with sweet H.[1]
All my love darling supporter
Your very loving C x

I am sending you some ties, and handkerchiefs belonging to Lytton just to keep. Later if there's anything else you would like, you must tell me. He loved you so much that I'd like to give you some of his books for you to keep always but you must choose.

To Mary Hutchinson

Ham Spray House
24 January 1932

Darling Mary,
You know a little of what I feel. He talked so much of you to me. For we shared each other's excursions into other worlds. I grew to love you knowing you secretly through Lytton. I know he talked of me to you

1 Tomlin, who was bisexual, had taken up with a youth always known simply as H.

sometimes. You gave him so much happiness, and helped him so often through dreary moments. Will you try & help Roger if it's possible? I know Lytton would have wanted that. Last night some lovely flowers came. They stand on my bedroom mantelpiece against the pale blue walls. So beautiful. I thought of you, although they said there was no name in the box.

For a little I think I'll stay here. Ralph & Tommy are here with me. & Julia comes next week. Later it would be happiness to see you. Darling Mary, nothing can ever make life what it was before. Your love meant so much to him all through these endless days. If there is anything of Lytton's you loved, tell me.

Your very loving
Carrington

To Vanessa Bell

Ham Spray House
Thursday, January 1932

Dearest Vanessa,

You & Duncan both wrote me very perfect letters. I would like to thank you. – He loved you both almost more than anybody. And it is of the friends who he loved most I think of now. Later I would love to come & see you.

I shall never forget your kindness coming here.

All my fondest love,
Your Carrington

To Ottoline Morrell

Ham Spray House
[n.d.]

Dearest Ottoline,

Thank you so much for all your love for Lytton. I thought you would like to know that nothing anybody could have done could have saved his life, they found afterwards. It is a consolation to know he wasn't defeated, & we weren't, by anything, that could have been combated. He died in his sleep without any pain. It is to you I owe the happiness probably of my life with Lytton. I thank you for those days at Garsington where I grew to love him.

My love
Your Carrington

To Virginia Woolf

Fryern Court, Fordingbridge
Thursday, February 1932

Darling Virginia,

Thank you so much for your letter. There are only a few letters that have
been any use. Yours most of all because you understand. I've just been
reading a diary Lytton kept in Nancy this September, again. It is a comfort
because he was so happy. Sometime James will give it you to read. His
emotional troubles were over and it was a perfect holiday by himself, enjoying
all the accumulated pleasures of his lifetime.

Do ask Ralph to see you some time. He is so lonely and I think it would
make him happier to talk about Lytton with you. I can't quite bear to face
things, or people. But you are the first person I'd like to see when I come
to London.

Please give my love to Leonard.

All my love darling Virginia.

Your very fond Carrington

*Tommy had made Carrington promise not to kill herself for four weeks, because
after such a shock no one should make an irrevocable decision. The trouble was that
without Lytton she did not see the point in living.*

From Carrington's Journal

12 February

I can think of nothing but the past, everything reminds me of Lytton. There
is no one to tell one's thoughts to now and the loneliness is unbearable. No
one can be what Lytton was. He had the power of altering me. So that I
was never unhappy as long as he was with me [...]

Oh darling did you now how I adored you, I feared so often to tell you
because I thought you might be encumbered by your 'incubus'. I knew you
didn't want to feel me dependent on you. I pretended so often I didn't mind
staying alone. When I was utterly miserable as the train went out and your
face vanished [...] What does anything mean to me now without you. I see
my paints and think it is no use, for Lytton will never see my pictures now
and I cry ...

While James began to sort out Lytton's books and papers, Carrington dealt with his
personal possessions.She burned underclothes and his spectacles on a bonfire. 'In a
few years what will be left of him? A few books on some shelves, but the intimate
things I loved, all gone.'

From Carrington's Journal

In the Library
17 February

I dreamt of you again last night. And when I woke up it was as if you had
died afresh. Every day I find it harder to bear. For what point is there in life
now [...]

It is impossible to think that I shall never sit with you again and hear your
laugh. That every day for the rest of my life you will be away. No one to
talk to about my pleasures. No one to call me for walks to go 'to the terrace'.
I write in an empty book, I cry in an empty room. And there can never be
any comfort again.

To Sebastian Sprott

Ham Spray House
Sunday

Darling Sebastian,

I wanted to give you these ties and the belt to keep. Later you must tell
James if there is anything of Lytton's you want. Something you remembered
here. You understand more than anyone what it means. I long to be here
alone. But everyone seems to be my enemy and insists on treating me like
an imbecile invalid. They want me to go to Dorelia for a week but I hope
I shall persuade her to let me return if I can't bear it. Forgive this letter and
don't write back. Later come here and stay with me alone and talk to me
of Lytton and yourself.

Your very loving Carrington

To Rosamond Lehmann

Ham Spray House
Tuesday

Darling Rosamond,

I am so sorry you are still ill in bed. This is just to send you all my love and thank Wogan for writing to me. Next week perhaps I'll be able to face London, if I do, I will come and see you. Ralph says he will go and see you for me. I am alone at last, it is for some reason a relief. I feel a happiness in just wandering in the garden and being able to sit by myself in the library. I find Ralph's grief almost too much to bear. He has been so kind to me, but I feel we only make it harder for each other in some ways. Please give Wogan my love. Do take great care of yourself and don't get up too soon. I've been planting daffodils and snowdrops under the yew trees, making a little grove. It begins to look rather beautiful. James and Alix come next weekend and Ralph and Frances.

My love darling
Your fondest D

Carrington was finding Ralph's unhappiness, his watchfulness and insistence that she not be alone oppressive. She arranged for him to go away for a few days with Frances.

To Rosamond Lehmann

Ham Spray House
Sunday

Darling Rosamond,

Will you do the greatest thing I can ask of anyone, help me to bear something that is a little too much? Ralph's grief? I think he would be happy with you, and Wogan. It was the only place he thought of going to. I thought if he had the car he could go off with Frances sometimes if you had people to lunch, or if you had to go out. For a little I shall stay here. I can't bear going away. Tommy and Julia will be with me. Nothing Rosamond will ever be the same again. He was more completely all my life than it is possible for any person to be. By being kind to Ralph you will be helping me more than I can say. Your love for Lytton and me meant so much these last two months. I will write soon to you darling. My love to Wogan and you.

Yr D

To Rosamond Lehmann

Ham Spray House
Saturday evening

Darling,

Thank you so much for being so kind to Ralph. He came back looking so much better and so did Frances. I long to see you. But I don't think I can face London for some time. Will you come here later on? I really want to stay here alone for a bit, but Ralph seems rather opposed to the idea, and insists on my going to stay with Dorelia next week. So I suppose I shall have to. I expect I shall be there for some days after next Tuesday, a week perhaps. I am not facing things. I can't for a bit. The impossibility of it happening, a possibility I never believed in my worse moments of despair, still makes it seem a nightmare. I find it difficult to go on with ordinary life and I almost hate anybody else who can, although I know it's unreasonable to expect the world to stand still. I dread leaving here. Forgive me if I can't write, but you know I love you. Later you must tell James or Ralph if there is anything of Lytton's you would like as a keepsake. Anything here that you loved particularly. Ralph told me you weren't looking well. Please take care of yourself in London, and DO darling, go to a specialist about the glands. I am so glad the book is finished. My love to Wogan and very much to you.

Your loving D

To Gerald Brenan

Ham Spray House
18 February 1932

Dearest Amigo,

I've just heard from Ralph that Gamel is ill with her heart. I am so sorry. I hope it will soon be better. It must be a great worry for you [...] I felt somehow I hadn't written a very grateful letter for your nice one, but there's no denying the fact I am against the world, and all good advice, at the moment [...] But hearing you were in trouble I at once felt fond of you, & wished to send you <u>both</u> my love. I am alone, & a little calmer. I find it very difficult to behave [illegible], it is so difficult when I see my glooms depressing R & have to stifle them.

I am reading Hogg's life of Shelley & Keats' letters. In fact I've moved completely into that world, & go on to table talk with Rogers[1] over my

---

1 Samuel Rogers (1763–1855), poet and friend of more famous poets. He recorded their conversations, and *Recollections of the Table-Talk of Samuel Rogers* was published in 1903.

meals. – When you next come to Ham Spray you'll see a very romantic grove with snowdrops under the Laurels, & Yews. If ever you see on your expeditions any mourning figures, or urns in the worst Victorian style suitable for my grove you might let me know [...] Give Gamel my very fondest love. Please see Ralph if you can. He is still so unhappy. & I am no use – for I've become an embittered morbid old amiga.

To Vanessa Bell

Ham Spray House
Friday [March 1932]

Dearest Vanessa,

I thought you might like a photograph of Lytton which was taken last year – I will look out some snapshots one day, and have some copies done for you, and Virginia. Will you ask Ralph and Frances round one evening. Ralph feels terribly upset, and only cares I think to see people who loved Lytton also. It would be very kind if you would please give my love to Duncan.

My love
Yr very
loving C

To Sebastian Sprott

Ham Spray House
March 1932

[...] You see I'm not a modern cynical character really, I mind terribly the changes. And nothing seems to me worth anything in comparison with that perfection of jokes and intelligence. It breaks my heart every night I sit in the library to think of all the hours Lytton spent arranging his books and putting in book plates and cleaning them, all to see them within a few months dispersed and probably sold. I know these things are bound to happen and are always happening. But if one person really flavours all life for one it is difficult to see how to set about starting a new one. Yes, that is what I should ask you this evening. Alix says one's object must be to maintain and live up to, those standards of good and intelligence that he believed in. But for whom? You see my weakness is that I only led, or tried to lead, a 'good' life to please Lytton, left to myself I lapse (secretly) into superstition, drink and mooning about. Come, write me on your typewriter a discourse on 'the object of life.' You must know the preliminary lecture by now. Can you refute Mr Hume? But unless you write before Thursday afternoon Ralph will be back and will read your letter. So perhaps you had better leave me alone to my mooning meditations.

To Gerald Brenan

Ham Spray House
6 March 1932

Dearest Amigo,

A & J [Alix and James] arrived down here on Friday morning for lunch [...] I felt very tired, and the unhappiness of remembering everything came back as usual when I entered Ham Spray. A little girl in the kitchen told us that Olive was ill with influenza so there was no lunch. Despondently we looked at dull letters & old newspapers – suddenly your Box appeared from a bundle of papers!!! It was an inspiration!!! We ate it for lunch with exquisite Brown toast, and lemon juice, and the miseries of life were instantly lightened.

'Only Gerald, the poorest of our friends thinks of such presents,' said Ralph. Thank you, & Gamel very much. I hope you are both keeping well. Most people in the country seem to have influenza or colds and we spend this weekend at Biddesden with Bryan Guinness as he was alone there, and we had no servant here, with R & F & Bunny. We have just come in. It's such a lovely house and we had a beautiful ride across the Downs [...] and afterwards a picnic in some woods with a blazing bonfire, & omelettes, & sausages. It is rather a pleasant trait in Bryan's character that his greatest happiness should be fried sausages, and sitting in damp winter woods, or eating chicken in the kitchen – which we did last night – Perhaps it proves that there isn't as much point in having £20,000 a year after all as we thought!!

I find everything rather difficult. But as everyone tells me it will get better I resign myself ... actually I find it hard to believe. I hope you are both writing. Do go up to London, and stay with Ralph sometimes, if you feel like it. I know he would love it if you both would.

I stayed 3 days in London last week. But it was rather more difficult than living here. So I don't think I'll go up again for a bit. I send you all my love amigo. I wish I could write you a letter to tell you how much I loved your present, but I feel unable to express anything tonight intelligently.

All my love to Gamel.
Your fondest amiga
C

This was Carrington's last letter to Gerald. On the back of the envelope he wrote: 'How can I think of anything but you?'

At Biddesden, Carrington was heard to ask Bryan if she could borrow a shotgun to shoot rabbits, as she had done before. She did not take a gun away with her, but went back after a few days to collect it.

On 10 March, Virginia and Leonard Woolf went to Ham Spray and found Carrington alone. She had insisted to Ralph that she would be all right, as she was leaving within two days for France with the Johns.

With Virginia, she wept and said, 'There is nothing left for me to do. I did everything for Lytton.' Virginia could not console her. 'I did not want to lie to her. – I could not pretend there was not truth in what she said. I said life seemed to me sometimes hopeless, useless when I woke in the night and thought of Lytton's death.'

Early the next morning Carrington put on Lytton's yellow silk dressing gown, stood in front of a long mirror with her back to one of the windows at the front of the house, placed the barrel of the gun against her heart, and pulled the trigger.

POSTSCRIPT

Carrington did not die at once, alone in an empty house. Ralph and Frances were woken early on 11 March by a phone call from the gardener, who had discovered her on her bedroom floor fatally wounded in the side. She had aimed for her heart but missed. He called a doctor but there was little to be done. They drove down to Ham Spray, David Garnett at the wheel, and picked up a nurse on the way.

Ralph and Frances found Carrington still conscious, lying where she had fallen as the doctor feared moving her. According to Frances, when Carrington saw Ralph break down in anguish on seeing her she told him she would try to live after all. She maintained that she had shot herself by accident while aiming at a rabbit on the lawn, as she had indeed done many times in the past. She died later that afternoon and accidental death was the verdict at the inquest held two days later. The stigma of suicide was thus avoided.

When David Garnett saw her body, he thought she looked triumphant. Gerald arrived soon afterwards, as did Alix and James Strachey. Yet emotions were mixed for Gerald – he felt anger as well as pity: she had killed herself, he thought, to prove the importance of Lytton's death. 'Or perhaps', he later wrote, 'it is merely that I am obliged to go on reproaching her – for the last act as for so many other acts of her life.'

Bloomsbury was godless, and on principle did not hold funerals, or observe any of the social rituals around death; there had been no ceremony for Lytton, and a strange vagueness persists as to what happened to Carrington's remains. She was cremated, and had left Ralph a letter suggesting that her ashes be scattered in the grove at Ham Spray where she had planted snow-drops. She also asked that Stephen Tomlin might make a statue to be placed there. Her requests were ignored; the idea of a shrine in the garden was anathema to Ralph. Much later he told a friend that Carrington's ashes had eventually been placed under the yew trees as she had wished.

It was Tomlin who took the news to the Woolfs in London. Virginia, too, found herself angry, not with Carrington but with Lytton. 'Lytton's affected by this act', she wrote in her diary. 'I sometimes dislike him for it. He absorbed her, made her kill herself.' A week later, on a fine spring day, she added, 'I am glad to be alive and sorry for the dead. Can't think why Carrington killed herself and put an end to all this.' Nine years later Virginia walked into the River Ouse with stones in her pockets and drowned herself.

Mark Gertler was told what had happened by Brett. Neither of them had seen anything much of Carrington for years. Mark's life was difficult: always short of money, he had become a society portrait painter, his marriage was troubled and his health was poor. He killed himself in 1939.

Inevitably, there were some in their circle who blamed Ralph for leaving Carrington alone and for supplanting her with Frances, even though he had done all he could to prevent her killing herself and they had made it plain that Ham Spray was her home as well as theirs. Others assumed that after such tragedy they would move elsewhere. But there was never any doubt in their minds that they would live together at Ham Spray. In one of several ominous conversations, Carrington had told Ralph she hoped they always would and that they would one day have a child. They married in 1933, and Burgo Lytton Partridge was born in 1935. Carrington's studio became his nursery. Apart from that, very little changed from the days when the trio had colonised it; lampshades and Christmas decorations she made were still in use decades later, and the same relations and friends continued to gather at Ham Spray until 1960, when Frances sold the house after Ralph's death.

Carrington's correspondence with Gerald is held in the Ransom Centre library in Austin, Texas, where I have spent weeks on end over the years working in their rich collection of British literary manuscripts.

When I came to the end of the over 400 letters Carrington wrote to Gerald Brenan between 1920 and 1932, I found something that astonished me. A snowdrop, brittle and faded, was pressed between the pages of the final letter she wrote to him, on 6 March 1932, five days before she died. My head was full of images from her last days and weeks, when in the chill of winter, deep in the misery of Lytton's death and her own suicidal despair she planted snowdrop bulbs around the yew trees and planned her own memorial. Snowdrops flower in February; perhaps, I thought for a moment, she had picked one for Gerald. Before the romance between them died she had been in the habit of bringing him flowers to London from the Ham Spray garden.

Coming to my senses I realised that it was impossible that a snowdrop picked in March 1932 could possibly be intact and folded into a letter in a library in Texas eighty years later. Her letters had been sorted, packed, typed up, filed and refiled, and read by many researchers both before and after they arrived in Texas. They had passed through many hands, including the scrupulous ones of David Garnett, who first edited the letters in 1970 and Gretchen Gerzina, who published her biography in 1989. The librarian and archivists were as surprised as I was when I showed them the letter and the snowdrop. They removed it – leaving a faint outline on the paper – and put it in a plastic pouch. Future researchers will not find it as I did. The sensible explanation must be that someone working on Carrington's life and death quietly left it there as a tribute. Little about Carrington was ever sensible; she was always a mystery to those who knew and loved her and, as her letters show, often mysterious to herself. The ghostly snowdrop seemed somehow appropriate.

NOTE ON SOURCES

After Carrington's death all her letters, papers and copyrights became the property of her husband Ralph Partridge. On his death, these passed to his widow, Frances Partridge, who died in 2004, and formed part of her estate. For permission to publish them I am indebted to her literary executor, Gill Coleridge.

The following archives and libraries have major holdings of Carrington's letters, and I am grateful to them all for allowing me access and permission to take copies.

The British Library (letters to Alix Strachey and Lytton Strachey)
The Harry Ransom Center Library, University of Texas (letters to Gerald Brenan, Noel Carrington, Mark Gertler, Augustus John and Poppet John)
King's College, Cambridge, Archive Centre (letters to Frances Partridge, John Maynard Keynes, Peter Lucas, Rosamund Lehmann, George Rylands and Sebastian Sprott)
University College, London (letters to Julia Strachey)
Tate Gallery Archive (letters to John and Christine Nash, and Arthur and Margaret Waley)

Minor letter collections consulted include those to David Garnett (North Western University), Diana Guinness (Chatsworth Archive), Roger Senhouse (Berg Collection, New York Public Library) and Virginia Woolf (Sussex University).

Carrington kept two journals, not as a chronological record of her life but an occasional outlet for her thoughts and feelings. Both volumes were in the possession of Frances Partridge, until the first, from the early 1920s, went missing and cannot be traced. I have quoted from the extracts included in David Garnett's edition of the letters. The second, from 1928 until her death in 1932, entitled *D.C. Partride (sic) Her Book* is now in the British Library.

SELECT BIBLIOGRAPHY

Bell, Anne Olivier (editor): *The Diary of Virginia Woolf*, vols 1–4 (Penguin, London, 1985)

Bingham, Emily: *Irrepressible: The Jazz Age Life of Emily Bingham* (Farrar, Strauss and Giroux, New York, 2015)

Blythe, Ronald: *First Friends* (The Fleece Press, Huddersfield, 1997)

Boyd Haycock, David: *A Crisis of Brilliance* (Old Street, London, 2009)

Gathorne-Hardy, Jonathan: *Interior Castle: A Life of Gerald Brenan* (Sinclair Stevenson, London, 1992)

Gerzina, Gretchen: *Carrington* (John Murray, London, 1989)

Hill, Jane: *The Art of Dora Carrington* (Thames and Hudson, London, 1994)

Holroyd, Michael: *Lytton Strachey: The New Biography* (Chatto and Windus, London, 1994)

Holroyd, Michael: *Augustus John: The New Biography* (Chatto and Windus, London, 1974)

Knights, Sarah: *Bloomsbury's Outsider: A Life of David Garnett* (Bloomsbury, London, 2015)

Levy, Paul (editor): *The Letters of Lytton Strachey* (Penguin, London, 2005)

Partridge, Frances: *Julia* (Penguin, London, 1984)

Partridge, Frances: *Memories* (Chatto and Windus, London, 1981)

INDEX

DC = Dora Carrington; FM = Frances Marshall; LS = Lytton Strachey;
RP = Ralph Partridge

work xvi, xvii, 164, 167, 172n; lectures 221, 222, 234; at Mill House 222, 223
Fryern House, Hampshire 327 *and n*, 336, 339, 345–6, 350, 354, 362, 384

Garnett, David ('Bunny'): meets DC 17; and LS 33; works as fruit farmer with Grant 41n; and Charleston 54; and Alix Sargant-Florence 64, 80, 129; compared with Geoffrey Nelson 100; visits DC at Mill House 107—8, 167; sets up bookshop with Birrell 162n, 237, 280n; marriage 165n; his *Lady into Fox* a success 218–19 *and n*, 222, 251; sends books to Brenan 236; his American girl friends view Mill House 236–7; gives birthday party 248; forms Cranium Club 289 *and n*; sick at Penrose's party 348; invited by Sir Philip Sassoon to Lympne 384; and DC's death 404; edits her letters (1970) xiii, xvi, 406; *DC's letters to* 51, 93–4, 218–19
Garnett, Rachel (Ray) (*née* Marshall) 143n, 165 *and n*, 167, 190, 232, 356; wood-cuts 218–19
Garsington Manor, Oxfordshire 15 *and n*; a refuge for pacifists 38; DC sleeps on roof 44; naked bathing 43 *and n*; 'like Clapham Junction' 49, 50, 51, 52; weekend guests 65–6 (1917) 122–3 (1919); the garden 85–6
Gathorne-Hardy, Hon. Edward ('Eddie') 318, 384–5
Gaudier-Brzeska, Henri 86 *and n*
General Strike (1926) 305–6
George V 306
Gertler, Mark: at the Slade xvii, 5; exempted from military service 10, 84; befriended by Lady Ottoline Morrell 17; relationship with DC xiv, 5, 16, 17, 18–20, 21, 23, 24, 29, 33, 34, 36–7, 38, 42, 43, 47, 48; and LS 18, 21, 46 *and n*; picture rejected by New English Club 24, 26; portrayed in

Cannan's novel 27n; and Monty Shearman 40; and Loulou Harcourt 40–41; swims with DC and the Hutchinsons 44; at Cholesbury 45; professionally photographed 53; finally goes to bed with DC 54–5, 57; unhappy about her relationship with LS 64–5, 70; their affair continues 65, 70, 75; attacks LS 81, 82; on Armistice Day 102; entertains DC 103; his paintings liked by DC and Fry 103, 107, 108, 135; kept in the dark by DC 126; with her at Garsington 130; and Valentine Dobrée 170n, 209, 213–14; 'white and worn' 156; paintings too expensive 196; ill with TB 300; with Lady Morrell 309; and Katherine Mansfield 381; suicide 405; *DC's letters to xiii, 5, 17–21, 24, 26–9, 36–7, 45–6, 48, 51–3, 54–5, 56, 57, 73–4, 77–8, 82–4, 106–8, 112–14, 116–17, 126–7, 300–1*
Gerzina, Gretchen: *Carrington: A Life* xvi, 406
Gilbert (W. S.) and Sullivan (A.): *HMS Pinafore* 199
Gimson, Ernest 130
Glover, Mr 161
Gogol, Nikolai: *The Nose* 315
'Goldie' *see* Dickinson, Goldsworthy
Gosling, Tom 349
Gosse, Edmund 161n
Gosse, Sylvia 161 *and n*
Gower Street, London: No. 3 49, 50, 51, 52, 55, 57, 58, 63, 64, 65, 233; *see also* Slade, the
Goya, Francisco 13, 116, 117, 118
Grant, Duncan 25n; and Vanessa Bell xv; former lovers 25n, 160n; and DC's painting xvi, xvii, 33, 150; with DC at Asheham House 25, 26; rents Wissett Lodge with David Garnett 41n; and Omega Workshop 74n; critique of his painting 142–3; his picture interests DC 161; and Philippa Strachey 163; holds a studio

Olivier, Noel 124 *and n*, 173
Omega Workshop 60, 74 *and n*, 75
Oxford University 10, 14*n*, 34, 67, 87, 90,
    116, 121*n*, 124, 142, 274*n*; balls 125, 126;
    Boat 144 *and n*, 147

Partridge, Dorothy 135, 175, 221, 252
Partridge, Frances *see* Marshall, Frances
Partridge, Jessie 135
Partridge, Dorothy 116, 117, 139
Partridge, Mrs 133, 135, 173, 175, 221, 235,
    249, 252, 262; death
and funeral 387, 388
Partridge, Reginald Sherring ('Rex';
    'Ralph') (RP) xiii, 87*n*
    1918–22 brought to Mill House by
        Noel Carrington 34, 87; in Scotland
        with Noel and DC 87–9; DC's
        judgement on 91–2; and LS 91–2, 94;
        begins to fall for DC 92; takes her
        to ballet 94; writes to her from Italy
        100, 102; intolerant and conventional
        113; in Spain with DC, Noel and his
        sister 116, 139; gardens at Mill House
        119; influenced by DC and LS 34–5,
        120; portrayed by her 121, 124, 126,
        127, 138; swims with Noel 122; at
        Garsington 122, 123; a perfect dancer
        125; in training for Henley 125; in
        Cornwall with DC and Noel 127–8;
        LS infatuated by 126, 128; with DC
        and Brenan in the Cotswolds 129–31;
        leaves for Spain 130 *and n*; weekends
        at Mill House 132; out with DC in
        London 133, 134; helps Barbara
        Bagenal paint 135; has closer rela-
        tionship with DC 136, and LS 135,
        137, 138; reads DC's letters to Brenan
        138; and LS's four-poster 141–2;
        dances with DC at Oxford 142; loves
        Cambridge 143; turns down place in
        Oxford boat 144 *and n*; visits Brenan
        in Spain with DC and LS 145, 147,
        153; in Madrid 145–6; in triangular
        relationship with DC and LS 146,

147, 148; with DC at the MacIvers
149, 150, 151; employed at Hogarth
Press 152, 153, 160, 162, 166; pressures
DC to live with him 152–3, 156;
weekends at Mill House 154, 155;
and Forster 161 *and n*; and Augustus
John 162; drawn by DC and Brett
165; at Gordon Square party 165;
busy with Hogarth Press books 166,
167; and Ray Garnett 167; has break-
down over DC 168–9; DC agrees to
marry 169–70, 172, 174; and Mill
House chickens 171, 193; marriage
and honeymoon 35, 175, 176; visits
the Woolfs 177; his future with
Hogarth Press discussed 177, 178;
works hard 178; with DC and
Brenan in the Lake District 179, 183,
184–5; suspicious of DC 186, 187, 198;
picks apples at Mill House 189;
works in London 189, 191; DC's
Christmas presents to him 192;
cured of wanting children 194; goes
to Vienna with DC 196; with her at
the Dobrées 200; his affair with
Valentine Dobrée 200, 204*n*, 210, 213,
214, 217; and the 'Great Row' 205,
206, 208, 209, 213, 214, 220; happier
214, 216; has further affairs 35, 217,
226; argues with Alix Strachey 217;
employment at Hogarth Press ends
200, 217, 218, 219, 222, 223, 224, 234,
244
    1922–35 meets FM 219; importance of
        DC/LS triangle to 219–20; meets
        DC back from Normandy 221; goes
        to Fry's lecture and Grant's party
        221–2; and Garnett's *Lady into Fox*
        222; relationship with DC improves
        225; and Brenan 226 *and n*, 236, 237;
        'completely altered' 227; dines with
        Anrep 229; in London with DC 229,
        230; no longer jealous 231; falls in
        love with FM 231, 232, 244, 250, 252,
        253; plans to set up Tidmarsh Press